THE ART OF JOHN CANEMAKER

AN ANIMATOR'S GARDEN

Foreword by Josh Siegel,
Curator of Film, The Museum of Modern Art

Interior design and layout by Nancy Levey-Bossert

Cover Design: Beach Design

Edited by Victor Wartman
Copy Edited by Diane Hodges

Set in Futura PT, Banshee Std used courtesy of Adobe Typekit, all chapter titles by John Canemaker,
New Press Eroded by Galdino Otten

Printed in Korea

First Edition: 2025

ISBN: 979-8992564549

Library of Congress Control Number: 2025943158

please visit theoldmillpress.com

FOR JOE

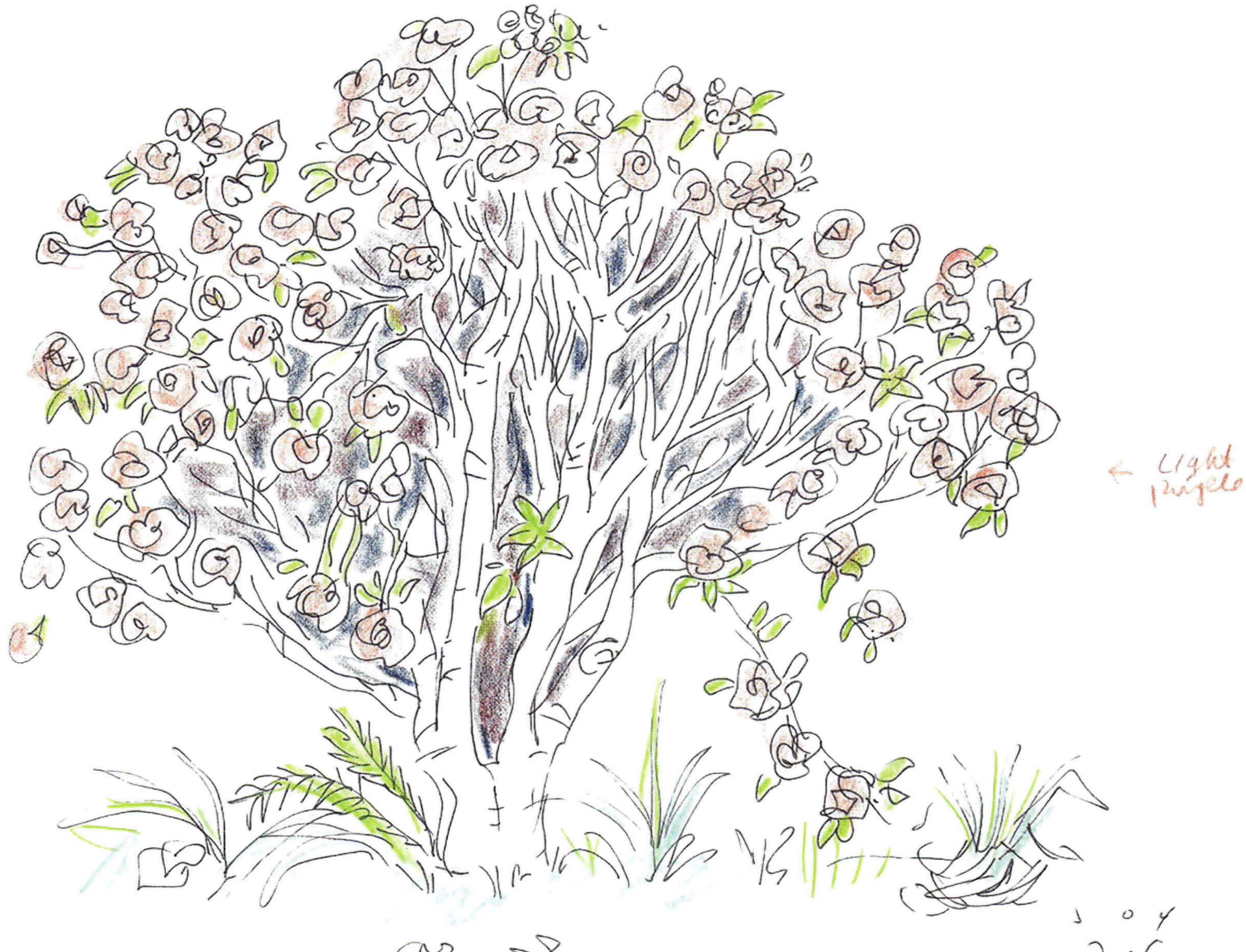

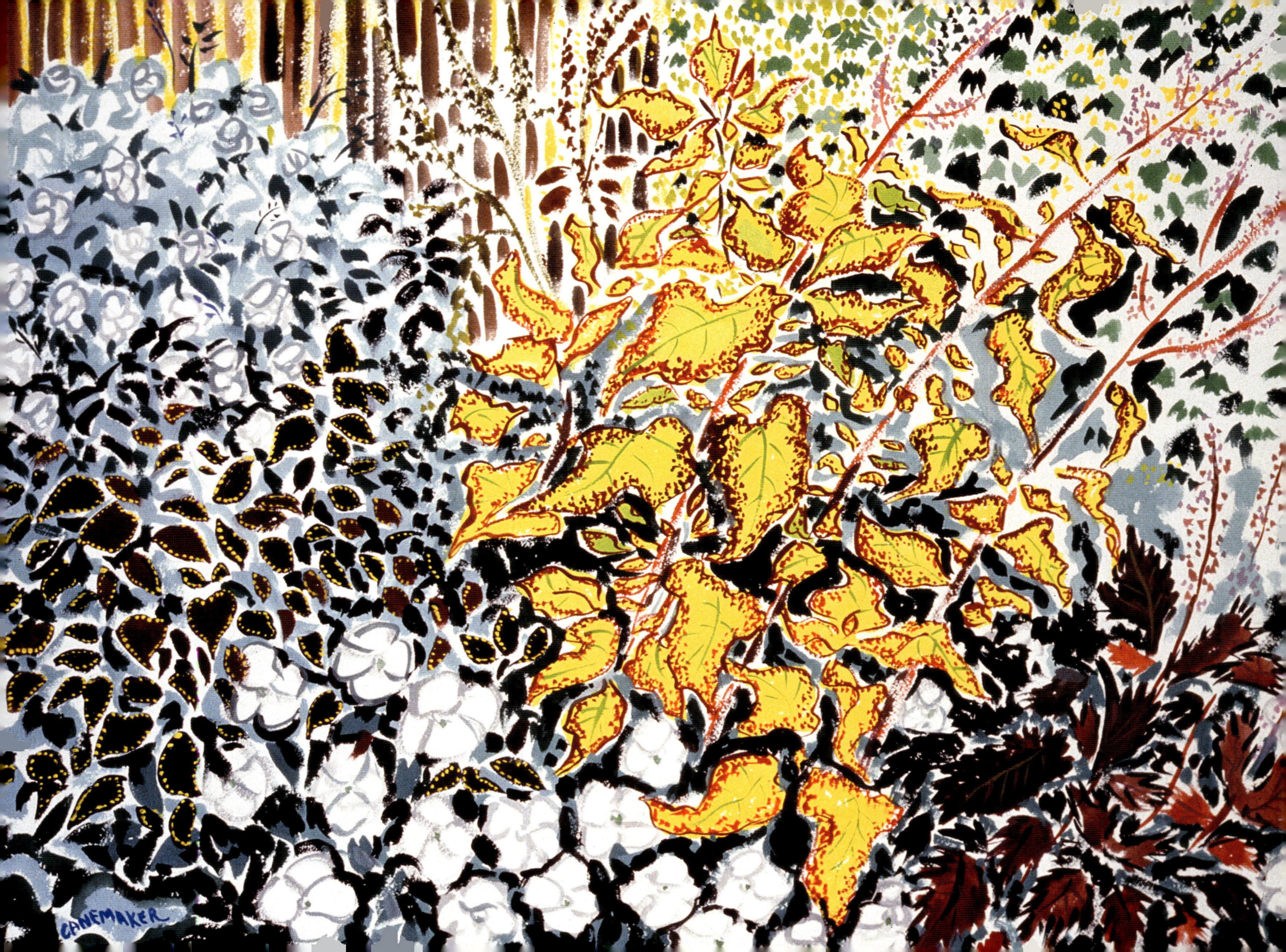
CANEMAKER

TABLE OF CONTENTS

Left: SHADE GARDEN 18x24" gouache 1998

FOREWORD

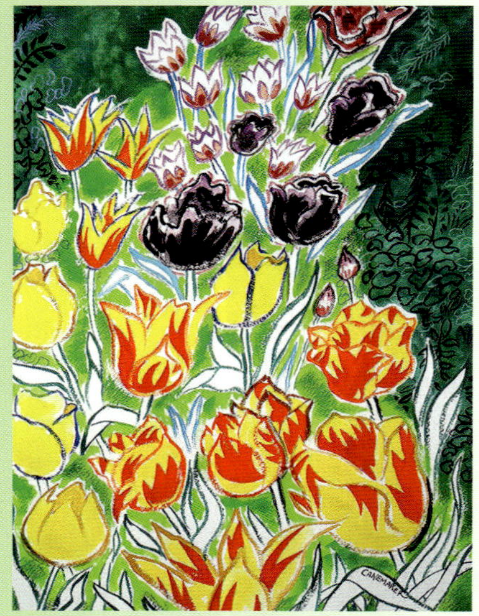

How is it that a gentleman of quiet demeanor and sly smile, a man who when he goes out in public almost invariably dresses in a navy blazer with gold buttons, smartly pressed slacks and polished loafers, who pairs his pale blue Oxford button down with a pale yellow, Windsor-knotted tie and a polka-dotted pocket square peeking out just so—how is it that this paragon of prep and dignified reserve should be capable of producing such exuberantly joyous symphonies of color and movement in painting and animated film: riotous blooms of gladiola and canna on which a dragonfly has just alighted or a katydid basks in the sun; as well as creatures who wear their emotions on their sleeve, the shyly elegant borzoi, the devilish satyr, the otherworldly dead-leaf mantis?

Vincent Van Gogh, in his heartbreakingly evocative letters to his brother Theo, often describes the garden as a "living, breathing world": a haven of serenity, to be sure, but also a ground for radical experimentation, for exploring shape and color, texture and light, with wild abandon.

He wrote, "Yesterday I drew a very large, rather rare night moth there which is called the death's head, its coloration astonishingly distinguished: black, grey, white, shaded, and with glints of carmine or vaguely tending towards olive green; it's very big. To paint it I would have had to kill it, and that would have been a shame since the animal was so beautiful."

"To paint it I would have had to kill it." What a strange notion, that the image Van Gogh created in his mind's eye of this night moth, with its exsanguinous colorings, would have necessitated insecticide had he committed it to canvas. John Berger said of Matisse that "he clashed his colors together like cymbals and the effect was like a lullaby," as if Matisse, in his own art, was always and only aiming for seduction and peaceful contentment, for "luxe, calme, et volupté." What Matisse said of himself, though, was that "if people knew what Matisse, supposedly the painter of happiness, had gone through, the anguish and tragedy he had to overcome to manage to capture that light which has never left him, if people knew all that, they would also realize that this happiness, this light, this dispassionate wisdom which seems to be mine, are sometimes well-deserved, given the severity of my trials."

John Canemaker is also a painter of happiness, offering in beautiful films like *Bridgehampton* (1998) his painterly impressions of seasonal change. But he too is no stranger to life's trials. He has taken on difficult and painful subjects throughout his career, themes of child abuse, cancer, bigotry, and the threat of nuclear destruction, and in his most deeply felt yet emotionally conflicted work, *The Moon and The Son: An Imagined Conversation* (2006), his unresolved relationship with an Italian immigrant father who, after serving five years in Attica for arson, returned home to inflict his anguish on his wife and two sons.

Do not believe, then, that the clean-cut kid who tried his hand at drawing in the benevolent shadow of his first art teacher, Sister M. Jeanne; the soldier who sketched stage sets for army revues while sitting stiff backed in a starched military uniform at his easel; the diligent scholar, aging gracefully with impeccably trimmed and parted salt-and-pepper hair, who has dedicated his career to preserving the history of animation through his books and his teaching and has furthered it through his own artistry—do not be lulled or seduced into believing that he effortlessly came to the arcadian images you see in this book. Van Gogh, borrowing an expression from horticulture, described painting as "hard graft": "I long so much to make beautiful things," he observed. "But beautiful things require effort and disappointment and perseverance."

Van Gogh committed himself to the struggle, right up to the end, knowing its inestimable reward: "Try to walk as much as you can, and keep your love for nature, for that is the true way to learn to understand art more and more. Painters understand nature and love her and teach us to see her. If one really loves nature, one can find beauty everywhere."

John Canemaker paid heed.

-Josh Siegel, Curator of Film, The Museum of Modern Art

INTRODUCTION

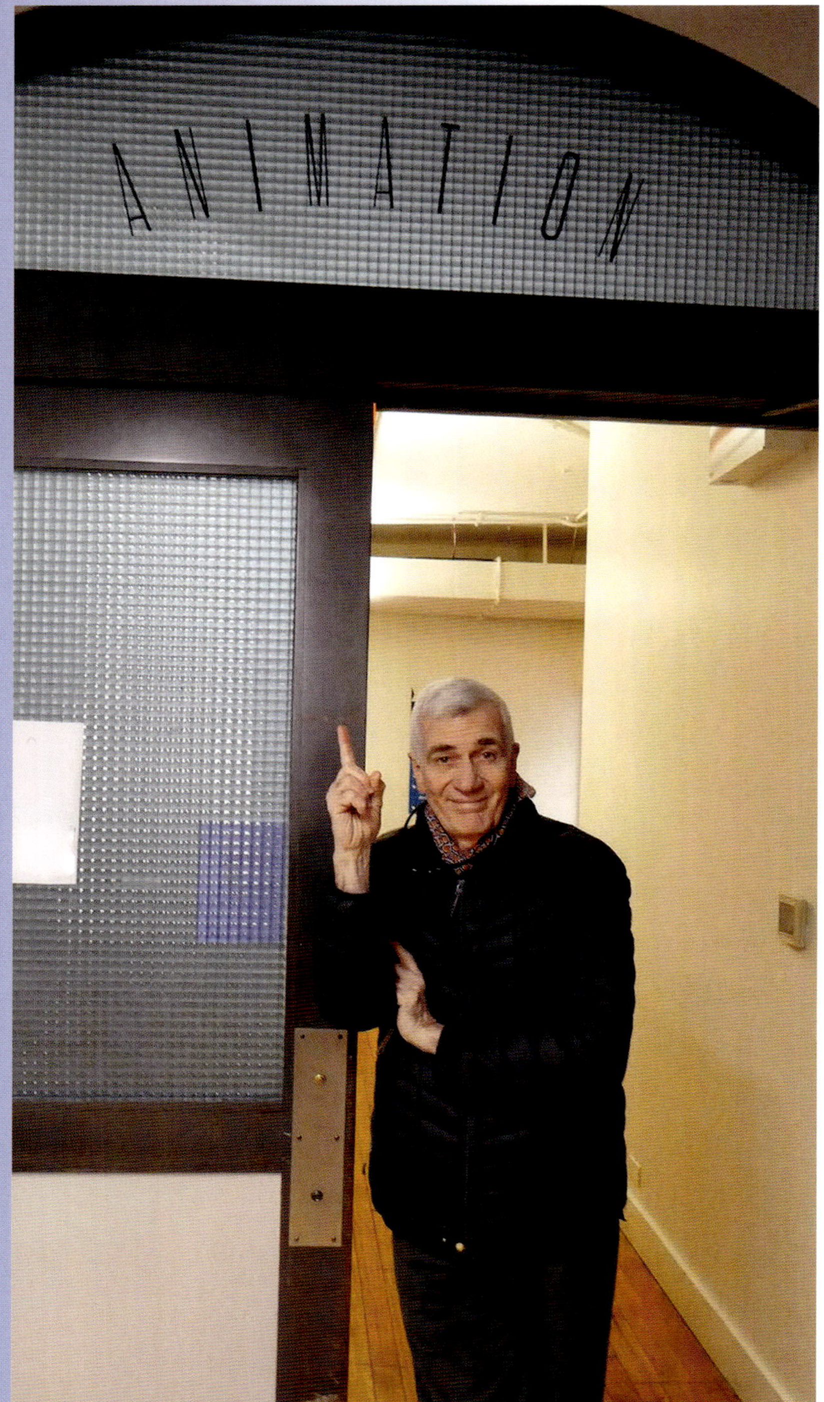

The best introductory description of myself is, I think, "octogenarian polymath." For in my long creative life, I have played many parts: actor, film historian, author, NYU professor, animator, producer/director of an Academy Award and Emmy Award winning film, and, as showcased in this book, a painter of motion and color.

Left: Professor John Canemaker at the entrance to NYU Tisch School of the Arts Animation Area, where he headed the program from 1988 - 2022. Photo by Russell Merritt.

Page 9, left: Six-year old John Cannizzaro (later a.k.a. John Canemaker) in his hometown Waverly N.Y. circa -1949.

Page 9, right: At Notre Dame High School in Elmira, N.Y. in 1957- 61, John drew posters for school events and a weekly cartoon for a local town newspaper.

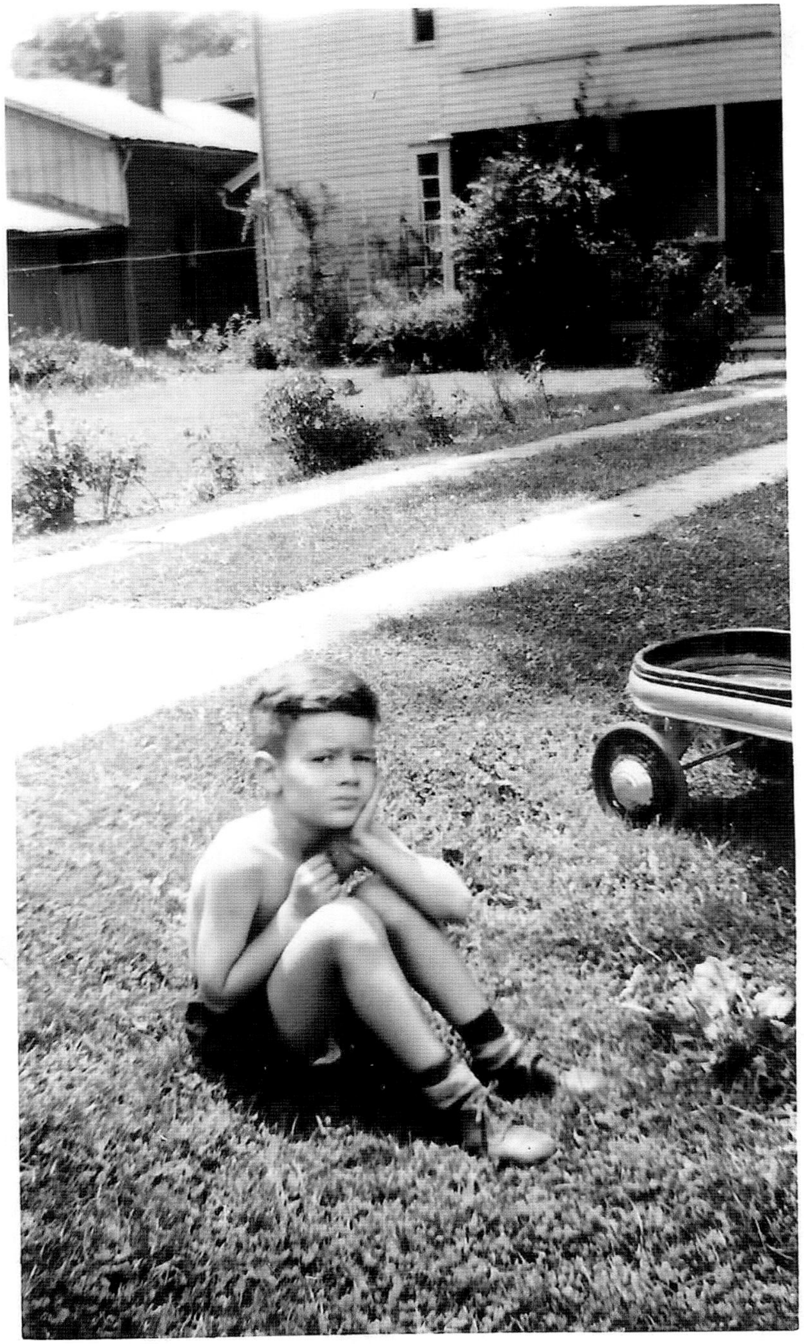

I was born John Cannizzaro in 1943 in Waverly, New York and raised in nearby Elmira. I drew constantly during a tumultuous childhood. My volatile father's run-ins with the law and subsequent incarceration for five years left my mother to become the sole support of me and my younger brother, Tony.

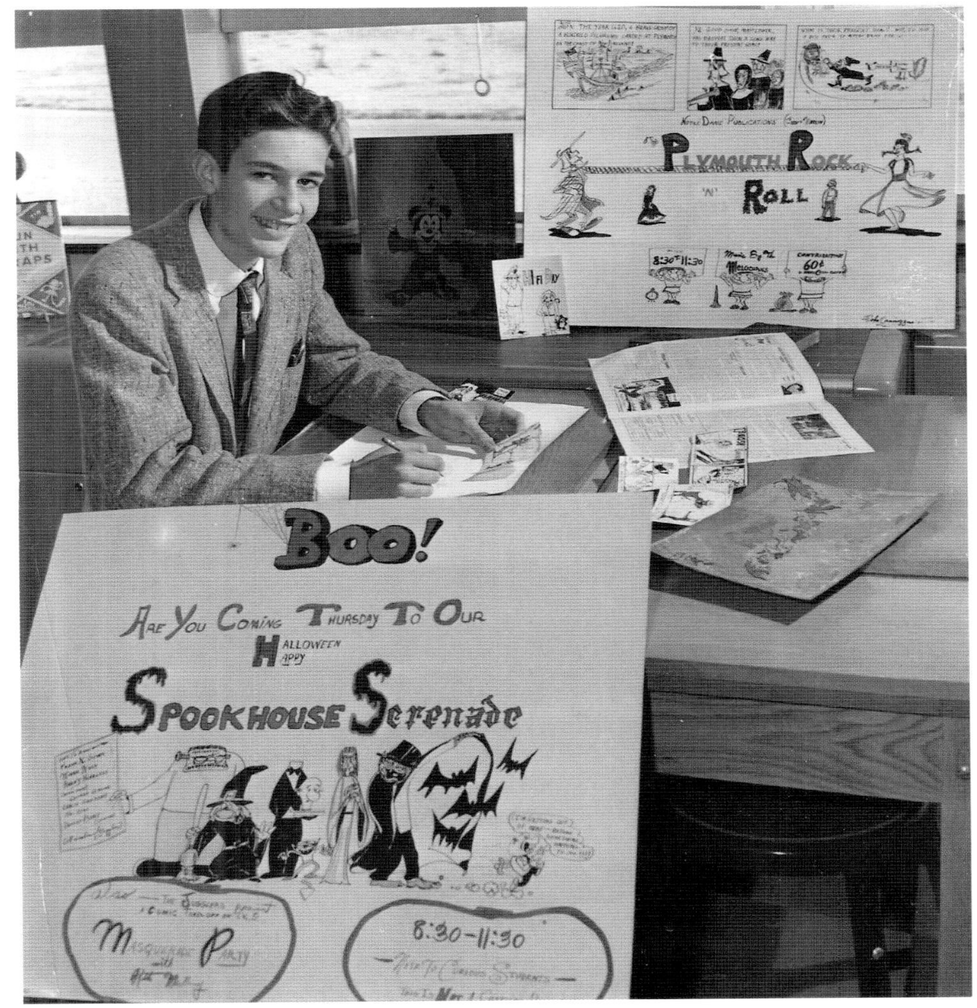

MARYLEAF - 1957

MARYLEAF

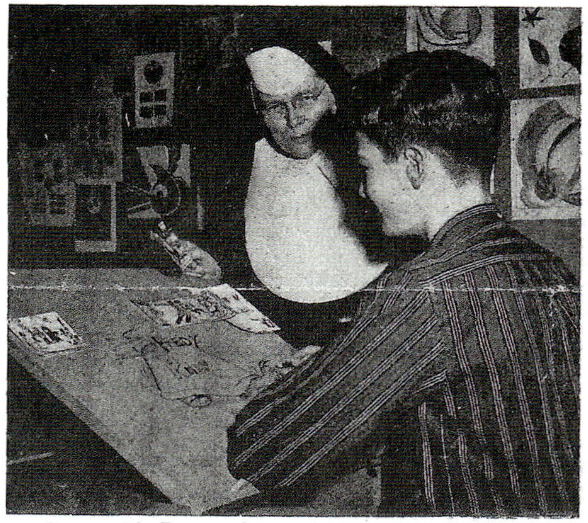

CARTOONIST

Sister M. Jeanne inspects Maryleaf cartoons.

JOHN PROVES HOBBIES PROFITABLE

John Cannizaro, talented freshman from 110, is this year's Maryleaf cartoonist. Very soon after he enrolled in art class, Sister Mary Jeanne discovered he was no ordinary student. Although none of his family is specifically engaged in art work, John has been doodling and drawing since he was small.

John estimates that he spends eight hours a week on his hobby, with at least three hours of work every Saturday on the animated cartoon he is in the process of making.

He modestly credits his progress to two friends—Joseph Marino, who taught him the art of poster making; and Art Abrams, who taught him the rudiments of animation. While his art supplies are rather expensive, John can usually make his allowance cover the cost.

With Walt Disney as his inspiration, John plans to be an animator for television commercials or for cartoons. His greatest need now is a 16 mm. camera; to this end he is saving his pennies.

Already John, generous and alert, has contributed his talent in school activities. Besides drawing cartoons for the Maryleaf he has made posters, and is now working on a handbill for Mission Day. "Let John do it" may become N. D.'s byword.

At Notre Dame High School in Elmira, N.Y. in 1957-61, I was the geeky kid who drew posters for school events and a weekly cartoon for a local town newspaper. I developed an intense interest in visual storytelling by watching animated films, thanks primarily to the 1954 anthology television series *Disneyland*, created and hosted by Walt Disney. The weekly series introduced many a youngster to both the history and techniques of animated films. Also, a 1956 reissue of Disney's *Fantasia* (1940) at a local theater inspired this 13-year-old to create his first animated film.

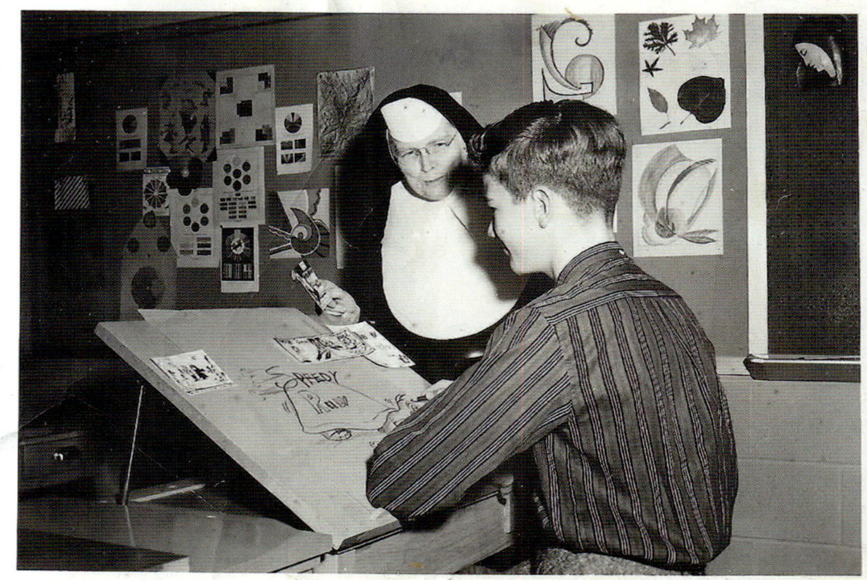

Left: Sr. M. Jeanne, Notre Dame High School art supervisor, and John Cannizzaro (later a.k.a. John Canemaker), school cartoonist. Maryleaf school newspaper, 1957.

Above: The original photo used in the "MARYLEAF" article.

Elmirans, Age 15, Prepare Animated Cartoon for Film

2-B ELMIRA TELEGRAM Sunday, August 24, 1958

Horace Horsefly Local Answer to Mickey Mouse

By ED VAN DYKE

Coming up soon—at least its very young producers so hope—is the premiere for the Elmira-produced animated film melodrama "To Kill the Fly."

Starred will be the film's two characters, "Boris the Fly Hater" and "Horace the Horsefly."

The producers, ladies and gentlemen, will be Mr. John Cannizzaro Jr. and Mr. Michael Rybak Jr.

Mr. Cannizzaro and Mr. Ryback, it should be explained, are each 15 years old. John, of 1050 Magee St., is the artist-cartoonist and Michael, best known to Elmirans and the film industry alike as plain Mike, living at 1071 College Ave., is the photographer—beg pardon—cameraman.

Both boys, school friends for many years, will be sophomores at Notre Dame High School this fall.

Over 3,000 Drawings

Both Boris the Fly Hater and Horace the Horsefly, the buzzing hero of the animated film to come, are brainchildren of young Cannizzaro, who already has drawn them over 3,000 times.

John, a slender, studious and imaginative lad, long has been interested in art and his drawings have gained much attention in school circles.

"I started drawing things when I was about 3," John admits.

It wasn't, however, until John saw Walt Disney's highly popular "Fantasia" that the idea of animated cartoons really took root.

So interested was he that he obtained advertising brochures from local theaters and even wrote the famed Disney for ideas and advice. Others who helped John in his search for knowledge on the subject were Art Abrams of the Elmira Art Club and Joseph Moreno, Elmira sign painter. Abrams, especially, was helpful on phases of film animation.

Next Step, Film

After conception of Horace and Boris, John joined with his friend Mike in furthering the project.

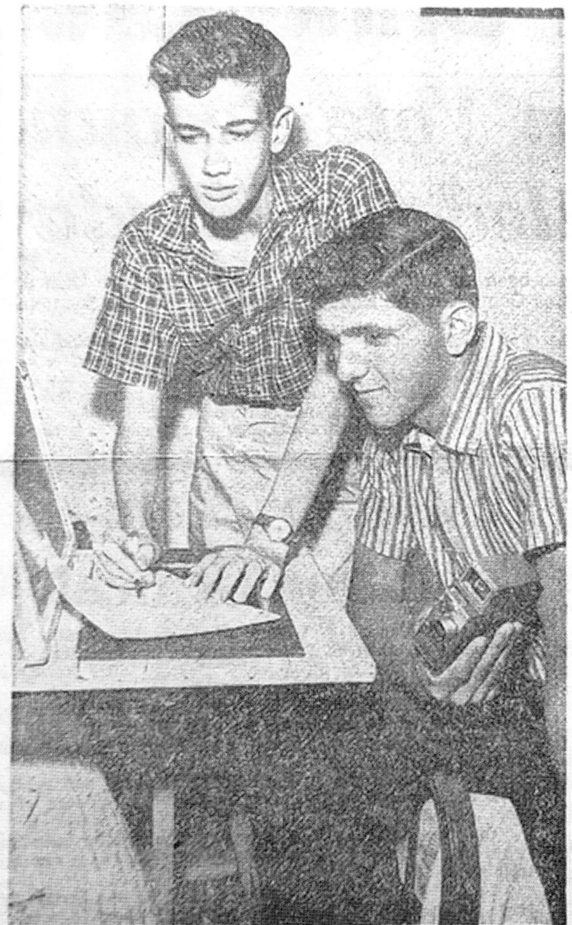

John Canunizzaro, standing, the artist; and Mike Rybak, cameraman.

Mike's talent contribution was essential—he possesses an 8-millimeter movie camera.

In addition to John's drawing board, other equipment was devised for use of Mike's camera. John went to work in drawing sequence cartoons of boris and Horace and then enlisted a highly necessary technical staff of inkers and painters, made up largely of staff members of the Notre Dame High School Art Club.

As fast as Mike produced cartoons, they would be turned over to his inkers, to ink a reproduction of the cartoon on used X-ray material from hospitals.

Painters would take up the next step, painting the reverse side of the cartoon green. Then, with a suitable background for the cartoon, the product would be placed in a special case, and young Rybak would make his photographs on movie film.

The Organization

Cannizzaro and Rybak call their organization the Can-Ry Cartoon, with these staff aides:

Inkers, Joan Flynn, a Notre Dame graduate and Mary Lou Morse, an ND student. Painters are Cassie Kosloski and Sharon Short.

There will be sound effects, of course, reproduced by tape recording. The sound effects "staff" is young Dick Wereley of 1555 Lincoln St.

"This sound-effects business is going to take considerable time and study," confesses artist and co-producer Cannizzaro. "We'll have to round up gadgets for proper crash and other noise effects and work out the right timing routine."

The voice of Boris the Fly Hater will be that of the versatile Wereley. It will be up to him, too, to produce the proper buzzing sounds of Horace the Horsefly.

Plot Sounds Simple

The cartoon plot is based on the annoying presence and mischievious behavior of Horace the Horsefly on the much irritated Boris. Boris does his best to eradicate Horace, but never quite succeeds.

The Can-Ry operation faces one big obstacle. The 8-millimeter camera isn't of required size—a 16-millimeter Graflex or Polaroid movie camera is imperative. So, Can-Ray is appealing for loan of the 16-millimeter.

"If someone helps us out with a camera, we'll name him a technical assistant on our staff," young John promises.

Serious Aims

There's a serious side to this Boris-Horace production, for it is an initial step in the boyish ambitions of both John and Mike—particularly John.

He dreams of making animated cartoons for a career and plans all necessary study of art and allied subjects to make his dream come true.

"The Sisters of the staff of Notre Dame High School have been most helpful and encouraging—and so have the pastors and sisters of my church, St. Anthony's," he adds.

Encouragement helps a lot, John admits.

When the Boris-Horace film is completed, John will have drawn at least 3,000 cartoons—and camerman Mike will have shot a lot of film.

The first showing, says John, will be at Notre Dame High.

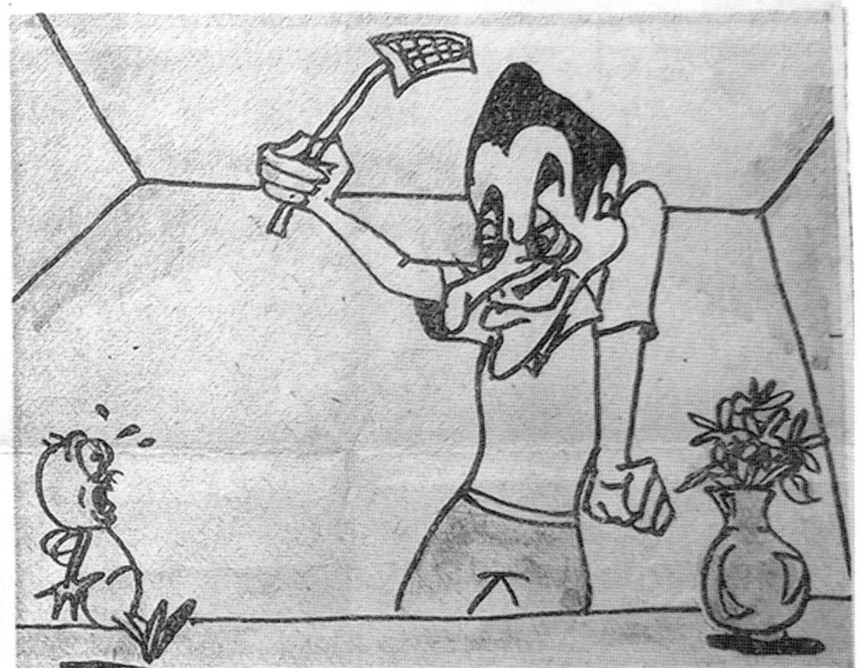

The subject and the predicament: These are Johnny's cartoon characters: Horace the Horsefly and Boris the Fly Hater.

A 15-year old high schooler, working on his first animated film, garnered local newspaper coverage in the Elmira (N.Y.) Telegram newspaper, Aug. 24, 1958. Pictured are John and classmate/cameraman Mike Rybak.

At age 15, I began work on that first animated film, apparently a happening so unusual that a newspaper wrote a "Local Boy Makes Toon" article. A year later, the *Elmira Star-Gazette* newspaper did a follow-up story.

In that year, my film subject had changed. It now focused on a history of the art and techniques of animation (which, ironically,

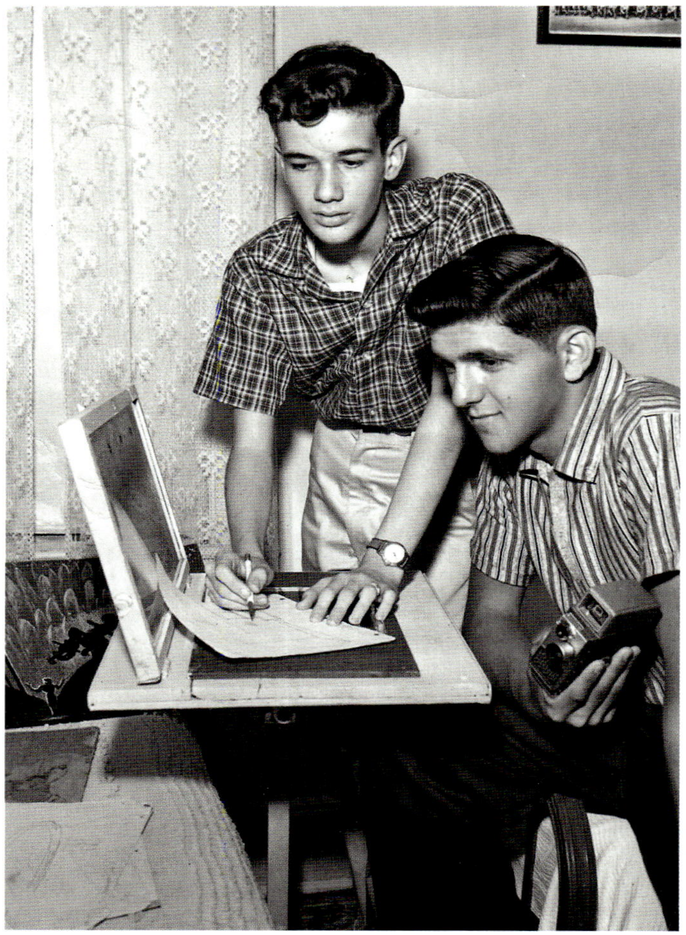

This page, left: Original photo used for the article "Horace Horsefly Local Answert to Mickey Mouse" in the Elmira newspaper, August 24, 1958.

This page, right: A year later, The Elmira Star-Gazette did a follow-up the story about the teenager's first animated film.

Page 13: A print ad based on one of the 15 TV musical commercials John appeared in for the American Dairy Association.

Young Elmiran Makes Movie

Producer Cannizzaro, 16, Unveils 15-Minute Film

In Dallas there's a boy who blasted off a three-stage rocket; in Indianapolis there's a high school halfback with 47 college offers; in Philadelphia a singer, age 16, has turned down a Hollywood contract. In Elmira there's John Cannizzaro. He draws cartoons.

A half dozen witnesses watched at Notre Dame High School a week ago as John unveiled "Animation," a 15-minute cartoon movie. It was done by John, a Notre Dame junior, with some student help and a smattering of adult advice.

If this were a critic's piece it would have to be noted that in the 15 minutes there are some rough spots and some weak moments when what the artist is attempting to convey doesn't come completely across. John Cannizzaro is no Disney—not yet. But where was Disney at age 16?

* * *

"ANIMATION" is the cartoon story of, says the prologue, "the art of bringing life and action to drawings."

It begins with the drawings on the caveman's wall and "King Toot's" pyramid where stiff Egyptians suddenly break into a jitter-bug.

The movie brings us up to the first U. S. animated cartoon—"Gertie the Dinosaur," used by Winsor MacKay in a 1909 vaudeville act; and to "Steamboat Willie" that launched Mickey Mouse for Disney in 1928.

It delves into the entertainment, commercial and scientific uses of cartoons today with a look at the inevitably complicated drop of water under a microscope.

* * *

THE STEP-BY-STEP drawing of a cartoon is explained and here we meet the only "live" people in the film—models Alice Prechtl plus brother Anthony Cannizzaro with dog "Tiny." Here also it's explained why supplying the animation for a 15-minute film is difficult: It takes 24 drawings for the 18 inches of film that supply one second of watching time.

The conclusion is a cartoon description of the words to "I Believe" as sung by a non-Notre Damer named Como.

* * *

AS IT STANDS the film has a weakness. It has a narration prepared but no sound. This is because the producer also has a weakness—lack of funds. It will cost about $100 to add the sound.

As it stands the film also has strength. The style is modern. Basically it employs moving things against a motionless background. Same thing happens every day to Huckleberry Hound and Quick Draw McGraw.

Some 30 years ago this would have been professional fare in movie houses; today it's at least a fantastic accomplishment of a young artist.

Like the teen-age rocketeer, the football sensation and the boy with the voice, John Cannizzaro has a talent on which he almost has to cash in—someday soon.

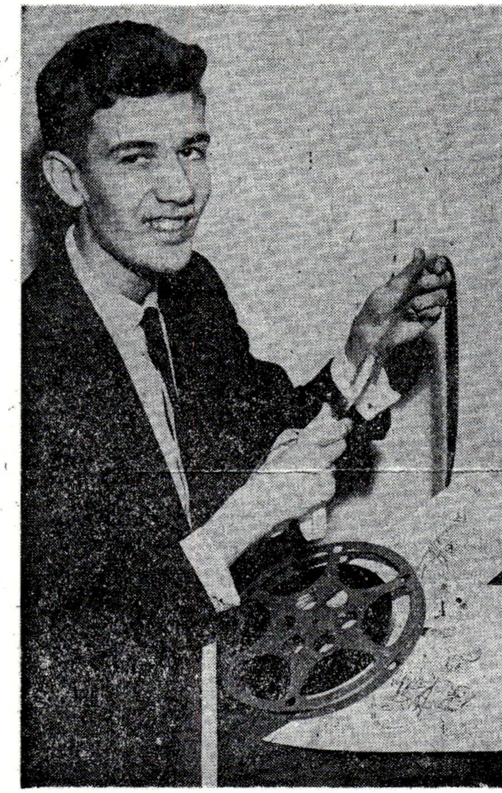

TALENTED 16—John Cannizzaro sits with his animated cartoon film and some of the art work he's done in the past for The Telegram's School News Page.

years later became a major part of my adult career). I was heavily influenced by a particular *Disneyland* episode, "The Story of the Animated Drawing," which was broadcast in November 1955. The program was the first time I learned about film animation pioneers, including Winsor McCay, who, three decades later, would be the subject of my McCay biography.

Other early life experiences included performing in amateur theatrical productions in Elmira and a summer stock company in New Hampshire. At age 18, I left home for New York City. My family had no money to send me to college so, I figured I would become an actor. At first, I supported myself as a doorman at Radio City Music Hall and a singing waiter in Greenwich Village while studying acting techniques at the American Academy of Dramatic Arts and the Herbert Berghof (HB) Studio (where 16-year-old Liza Minnelli was a classmate).

Soon, I began using the professional pseudonym "John Canemaker" (an alleged translation of "Cannizzaro") in Off-Broadway plays and summer and winter stock companies, performing in everything from Gertrude Stein's *The Making of Americans* to *Hello, Dolly!*. My numerous appearances in national TV commercials, promoting such products as Foster Grant Sunglasses, Armour Hot Dogs, Benson & Hedges cigarettes and the American Dairy Association, among others, proved lucrative. (You earned residual money from each showing on television.)

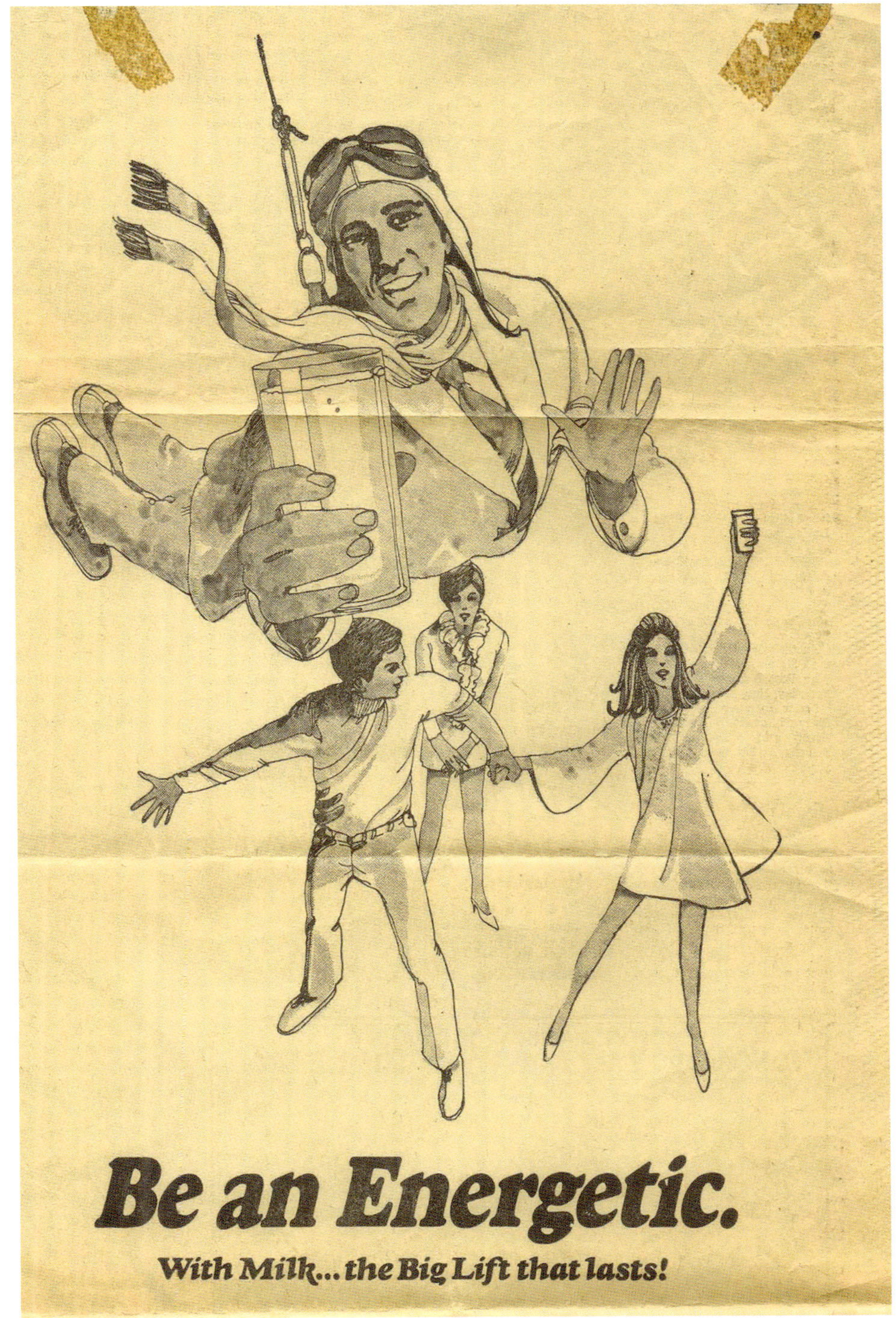

Below: Moving to New York in 1961, John became an actor in summer and winter stock companies, off-Broadway shows, and over 20 national TV commercials for numerous products, including Armour Hot Dogs.

Right: In 1971, John performed in a Clio Award-winning TV commercial for Foster Grant Sunglasses.

★ **BEST: PERSONAL ARTICLES**

Foster Grant Sunglasses
"Blind Date"
Agency: Geer, DuBois, NY
Production: Zieff, NY
Details: Film, 60 Seconds, Color
First Telecast: December 30, 1970
Client Superv: Mauri Edwards
Acct Superv: Colin Smith
Copy: Mike Drazen
Art Dir: Carol Nelson
Agency Prodr: Magi Durham, Telpac
Film Prodr: Dick Clark
Film Dir: Howard Zieff
Cameraman: Ted Pahle
Editor: Stan Siegel
Actors: John Pleshette, Candy Azzara, John Canemaker, Heather MacRae
Voice Over: Jerry Orbach

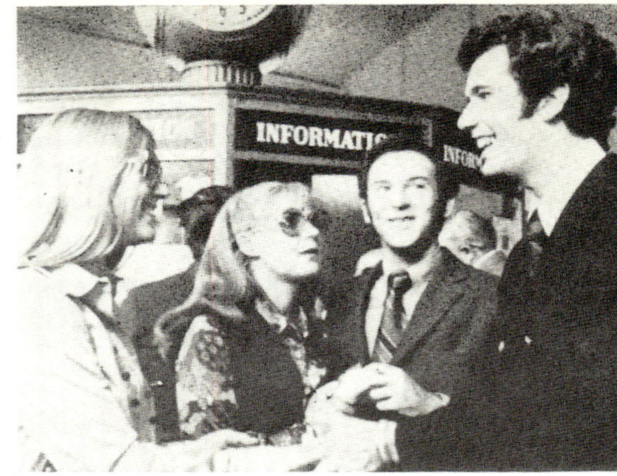

Foster Grant

★ **BEST: PERSONAL ARTICLES**

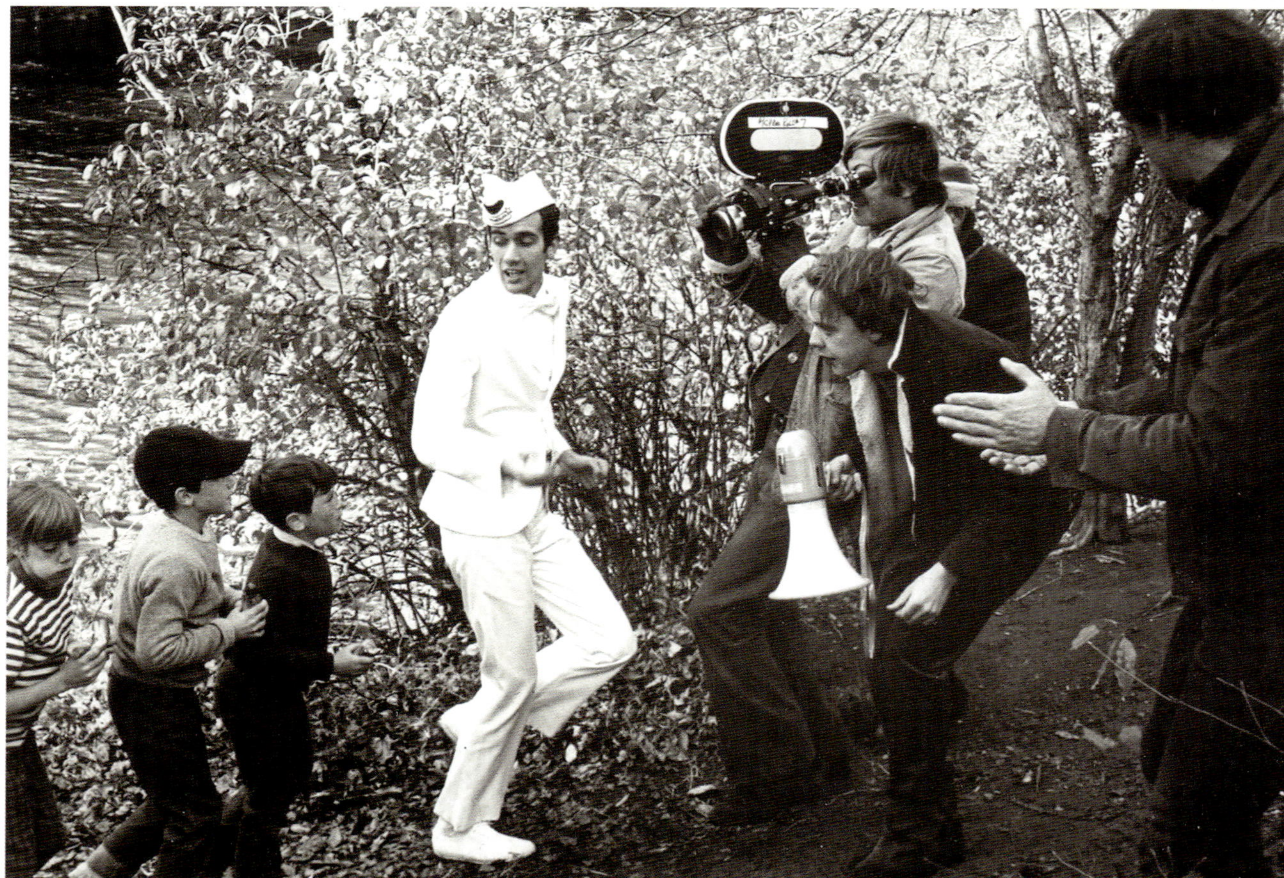

ovator"
Y
Color
970
g
en
d Pahle
tural"
NY
ers, NY
Color
1970
der
schmidt
er
nettes"
NY
Color
971
lecki
earns

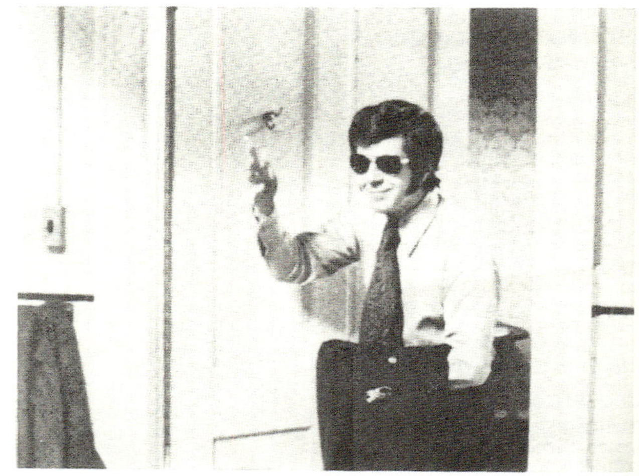

Remington

Timex Electric Watches
"Commuter"
Agency: Warwick & Legler, NY
Production: Jerry Shore, NY
Details: Film, 90 Seconds, Color
First Telecast: February 16, 1970
Client Superv: Robert E. Mohr
Acct Superv: James M. Ellers
Copy: Kenneth Teason
Art Dir: Jerry Prestomburgo
Agency Prodr: Roger Harvey
Film Prodr: Len Lipson
Film Dir/Camera: Jerry Shore
Editor: Eddie Friedman
Voice Over: Mike Wager

Timex Electric Watches
"Mindreader"
Agency: Warwick & Legler, NY
Production: Stan Lang, NY
Details: Film, 90 Seconds, Color
First Telecast: November 16, 1970
Client Superv: Robert E. Mohr
Acct Superv: James M. Ellers
Copy: Kenneth Teason
Art Dir: Jerry Prestomburgo
Agency Prodr: Herbert Miller
Film Prodr: Sanford Cohn
Film Dir: Mike Cuesta
Editor: Steve Schrieber
Voice Over: Bob Landers

32 AWARDS JOURNAL/CLIO, June 1971

In 1965, I was drafted into the U.S. Army, and served for two years at Fort Dix as part of the Special Services team. I staged and designed sets for plays, organized concerts (featuring Duke Ellington, Dave Brubeck, the Shirelles and Stan Getz among others), and provided recreational bivouac entertainment for military trainees.

Returning to civilian life, thanks to the G.I. Bill and residual payments from TV commercials, plus continuing work as an actor, I put myself through college starting at age 28, . Within five years I completed a BFA degree at Marymount Manhattan College and an MFA degree in Film from New York University.

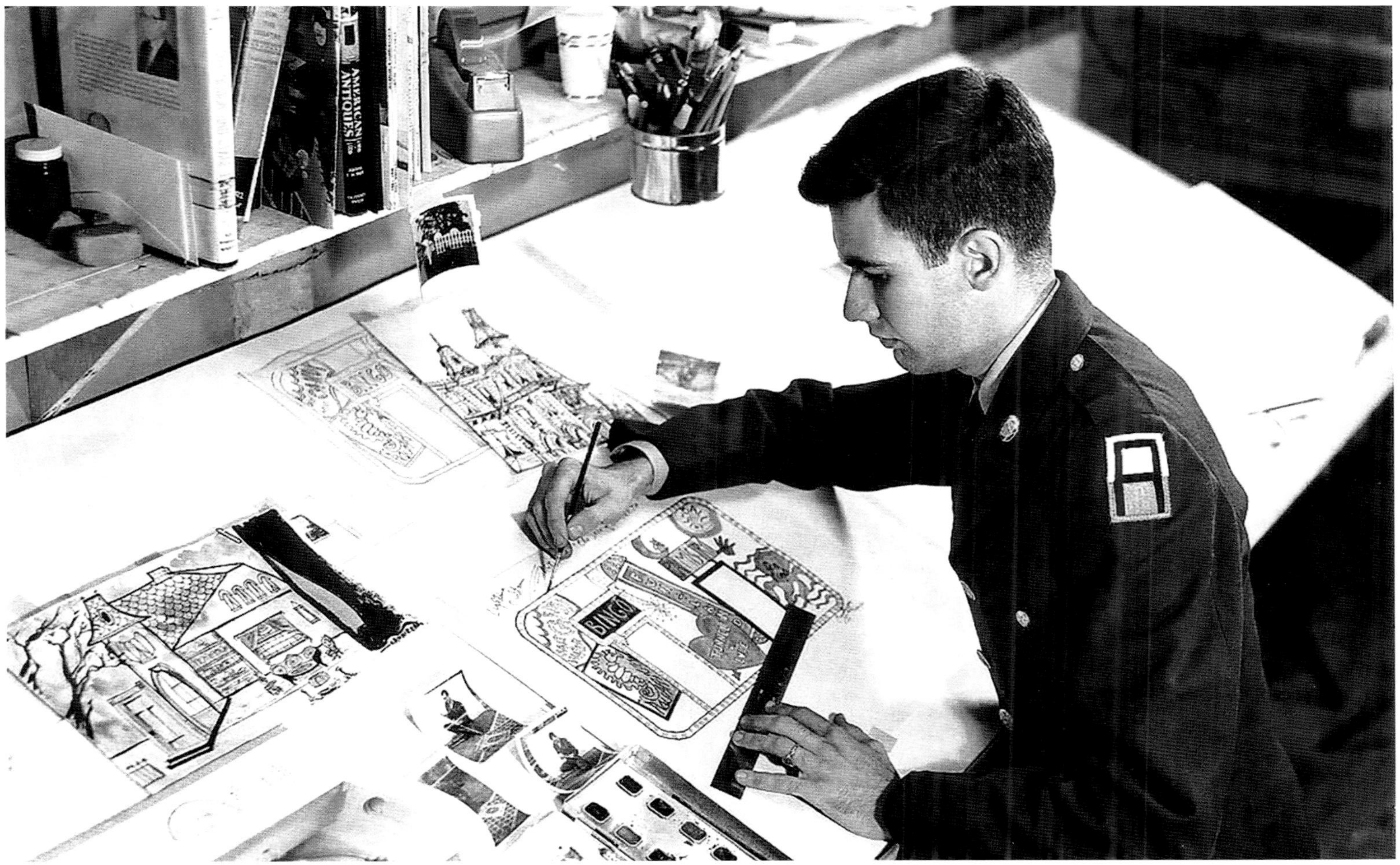

Drafted into the US Army in 1965, John served two years in the Special Services team, producing plays, designing sets and costumes, and booking concerts (Duke Ellington, Dave Brubeck) and entertainment for military trainees.

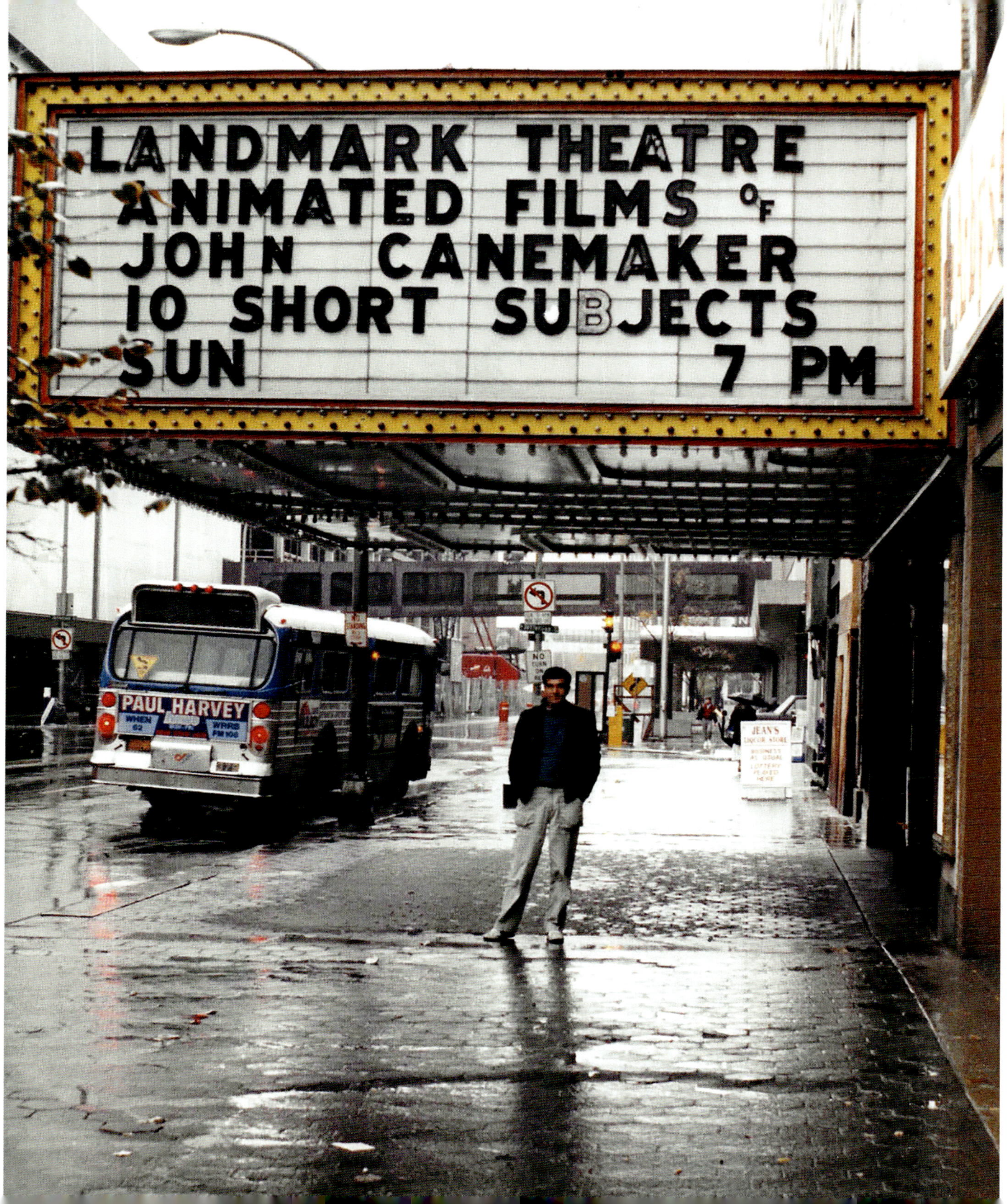

John Canemaker Productions Inc. founded in 1981, produced 40 years of prize-winning animated films. A 1986 program of Canemaker shorts in Syracuse, N.Y. Photo: George Konder.

Right: John Canemaker's ***The Moon and the Son: An Imagined Conversation*** *won a 2005 Academy Award and a 2006 Emmy Award.*

Far right: John Canemaker and producer Peggy Stern holding their Oscars for ***The Moon and the Son*** *at the Hollywood ceremony in 2006. Photo: Joseph Kennedy.*

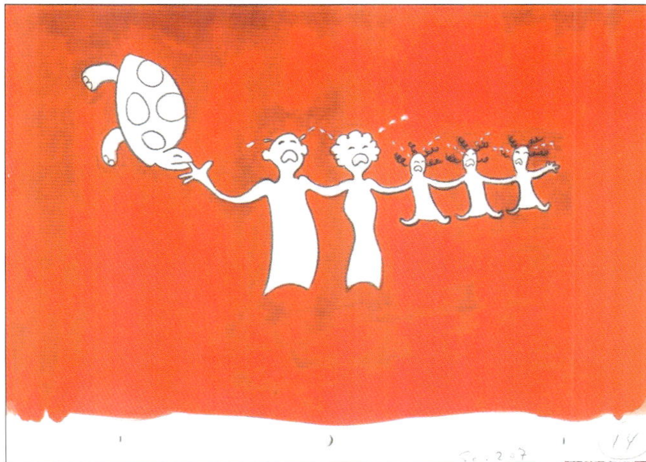

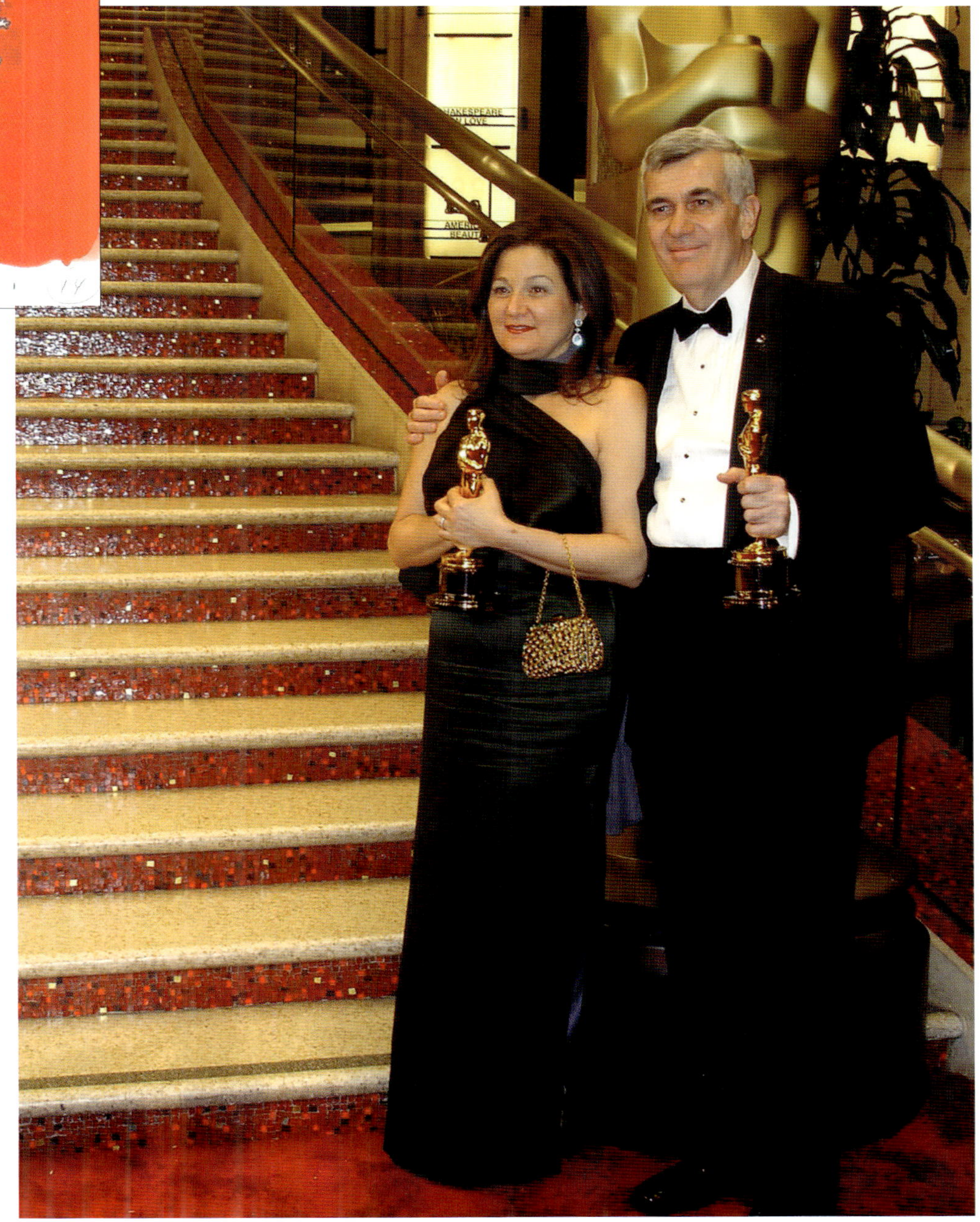

During this period, my early interest in animation reawakened and a new career direction began to quickly snowball. Joining ASIFA East, the New York chapter of an international animation collective, introduced me to local animation filmmakers. While attending college full time, I also enrolled in an evening animation production class at the New York's School of Visual Arts. A short film I made at SVA led to subsequent hirings as a journeyman animator for independent short film producers at Children's Television Workshop's *Sesame Street* (such as Derek Lamb, Michael Sporn and Bruce Cayard), and CTW's *The Electric Company, Pee-wee's Playhouse, Captain Kangaroo*, and the Broadway musical *Woman of the Year*.

I continued animating both personal shorts and sponsored works-for-hire for nearly forty years, forming my own production corporation when I created an animation sequence in Warner Bros.' *The World According to Garp* (1982). My films, including the autobiographical Oscar-and Emmy Award winning *The Moon and the Son: An Imagined Conversation* (2004), are in archival collections at MoMA and the Academy of Motion Picture Arts and Sciences.

In summer 1973, it was a Marymount teacher who arranged for me to earn credits toward a BA degree by researching Disney animation history at the newly opened Walt Disney Archives in Burbank, and to writing a paper on what I learned. My visit to the Disney Studio was the first of many times I would interview several of the master animators I'd seen years before on the Disneyland TV program, and to view films and examine original artworks from *Fantasia, Snow White,* and *Pinocchio*, among other classics. Two of the animators (Frank Thomas and Ollie Johnston) became my close friends and mentors, inspiring my filmmaking with tough love.

A version of my college report was published in a film industry magazine, which encouraged me to research and publish more periodical articles on the lives of early animation pioneers, such as producer J.R. Bray, John Fitzsimmons (Winsor McCay's film assistant), distributor Margaret Winkler and Felix the Cat animator/director Otto Messmer, among others). Soon I gained a reputation as an animation historian, and became animation editor of *Millimeter Magazine*. My report on the making of Richard Williams' feature *Raggedy Ann & Andy* (1977) led to the first of my twelve books on film animation history. The books' subjects range from the silent era (Winsor McCay, Felix the Cat), the Hollywood Cartoon (Tex Avery, Chuck Jones, UPA), numerous Disney and Pixar animators, storyboard and concept artists. My essays and film and book reviews have appeared in many periodicals, including *The New York Times, The Wall Street Journal, Print Magazine, Esopus,* and *Film Comment.*

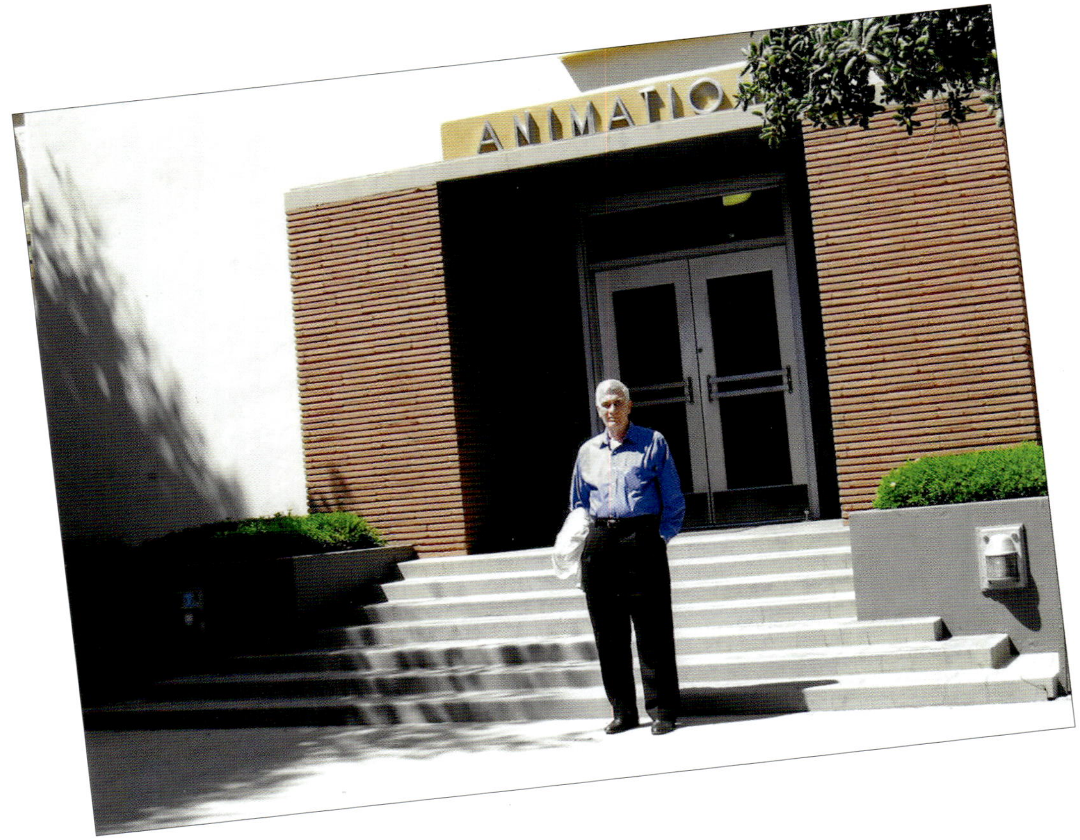

Above: A 1973 visit to the Disney Studio Archives sparked John's simultaneous career as an animation historian; subsequently, he has published over 100 articles and reviews in numerous periodicals, including The New York Times and The Wall Street Journal.

Right: Since 1977, John Canemaker has written twelve acclaimed books on the history of the art of animation and its artists.

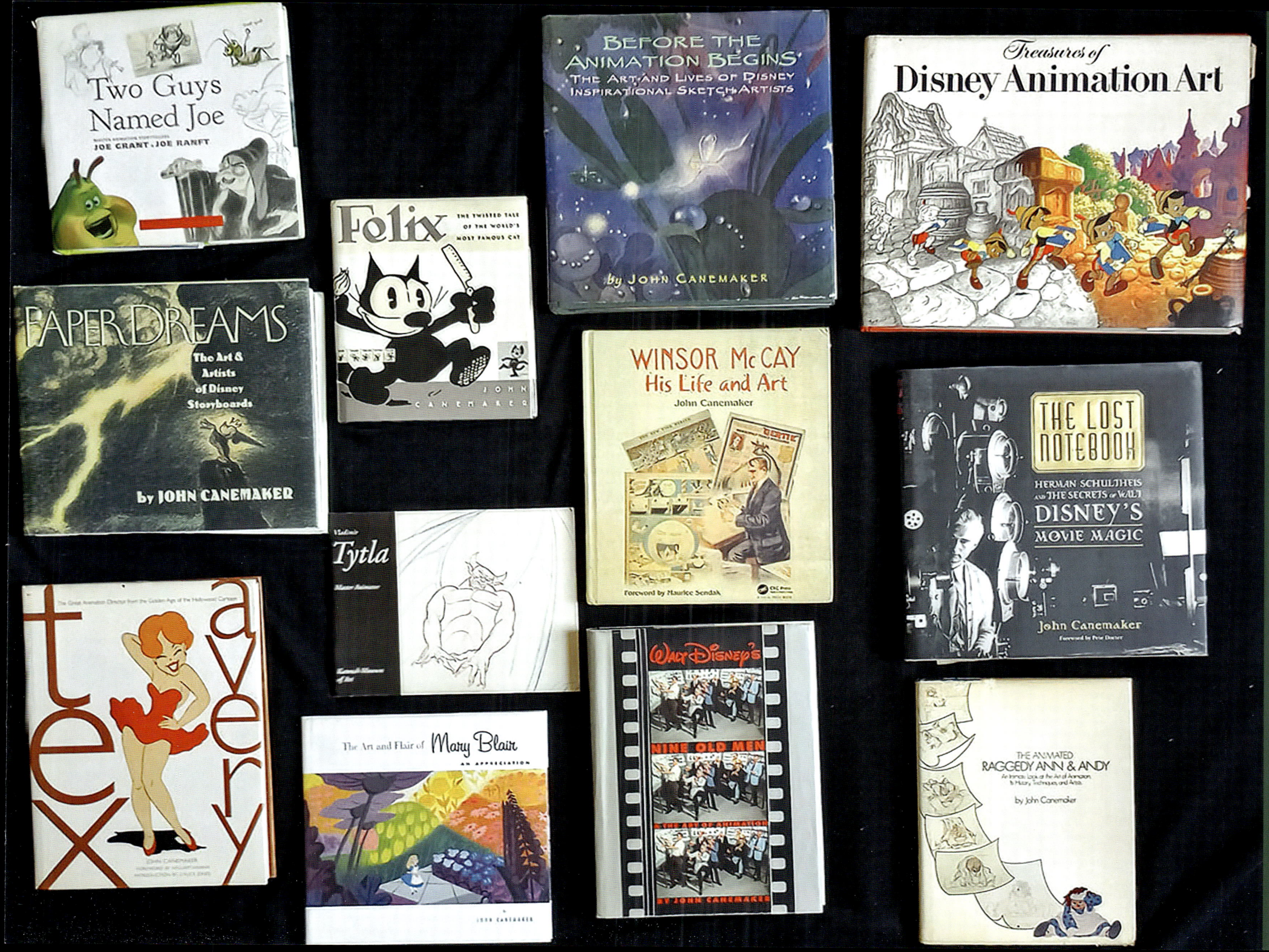
Two Guys Named Joe
JOE GRANT & JOE RANFT
Felix
THE TWISTED TALE OF THE WORLD'S MOST FAMOUS CAT
JOHN CANEMAKER
BEFORE THE ANIMATION BEGINS
THE ART AND LIVES OF DISNEY INSPIRATIONAL SKETCH ARTISTS
by JOHN CANEMAKER
Treasures of Disney Animation Art
PAPER DREAMS
The Art & Artists of Disney Storyboards
by JOHN CANEMAKER
WINSOR McCAY His Life and Art
John Canemaker
Foreword by Maurice Sendak
THE LOST NOTEBOOK
HERMAN SCHULTHEIS AND THE SECRETS OF WALT DISNEY'S MOVIE MAGIC
John Canemaker
Tytla
tex avery
The Art and Flair of Mary Blair
AN APPRECIATION
JOHN CANEMAKER
WALT DISNEY'S
NINE OLD MEN
& THE ART OF ANIMATION
BY JOHN CANEMAKER
THE ANIMATED RAGGEDY ANN & ANDY
by John Canemaker

In 1980, New York University Tisch School of the Arts invited me to teach while developing their fledgling animation department. Eight years later I accepted a full-time position as director of the program, rising from adjunct teacher to tenured full professor until my retirement in 2022.

Teaching is a joy that has given a rich quality to my life. I've had the great pleasure to share my love of animation with many young people who found their own joy, personally and professionally, in the art form. In 2009, I received NYU's Distinguished Teaching Award for "exceptional teaching, inside and outside the classroom." In 2025, the Animation Educators' Forum selected me for its Hall of Fame "dedicated to the artists and scholars whose teaching influenced the history of animation."

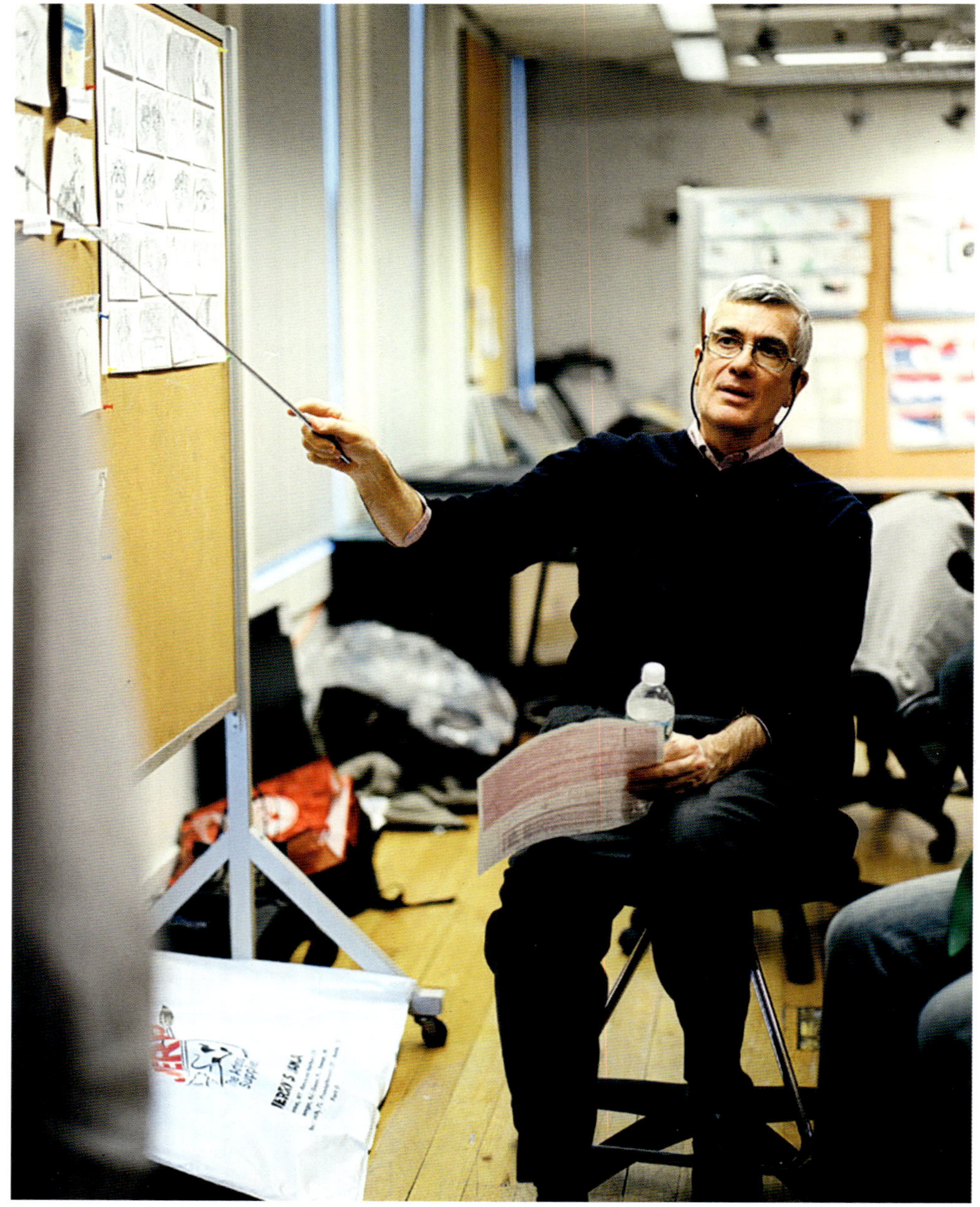

This page: John Canemaker teaching a Storyboarding class at New York University, where he taught from 1980 through 2022, and headed the animation department for over 30 years..

Page 21: Canemaker has lectured around the world on animation history. For example, in 2009 he was the first Visiting Fellow at Ireland's National Film School at IADT; and, in 2018, (pictured) he gave master classes at the Nemo Academy of Digital Arts in Florence, Italy. Photo: Ruth Miriam Carmeli.

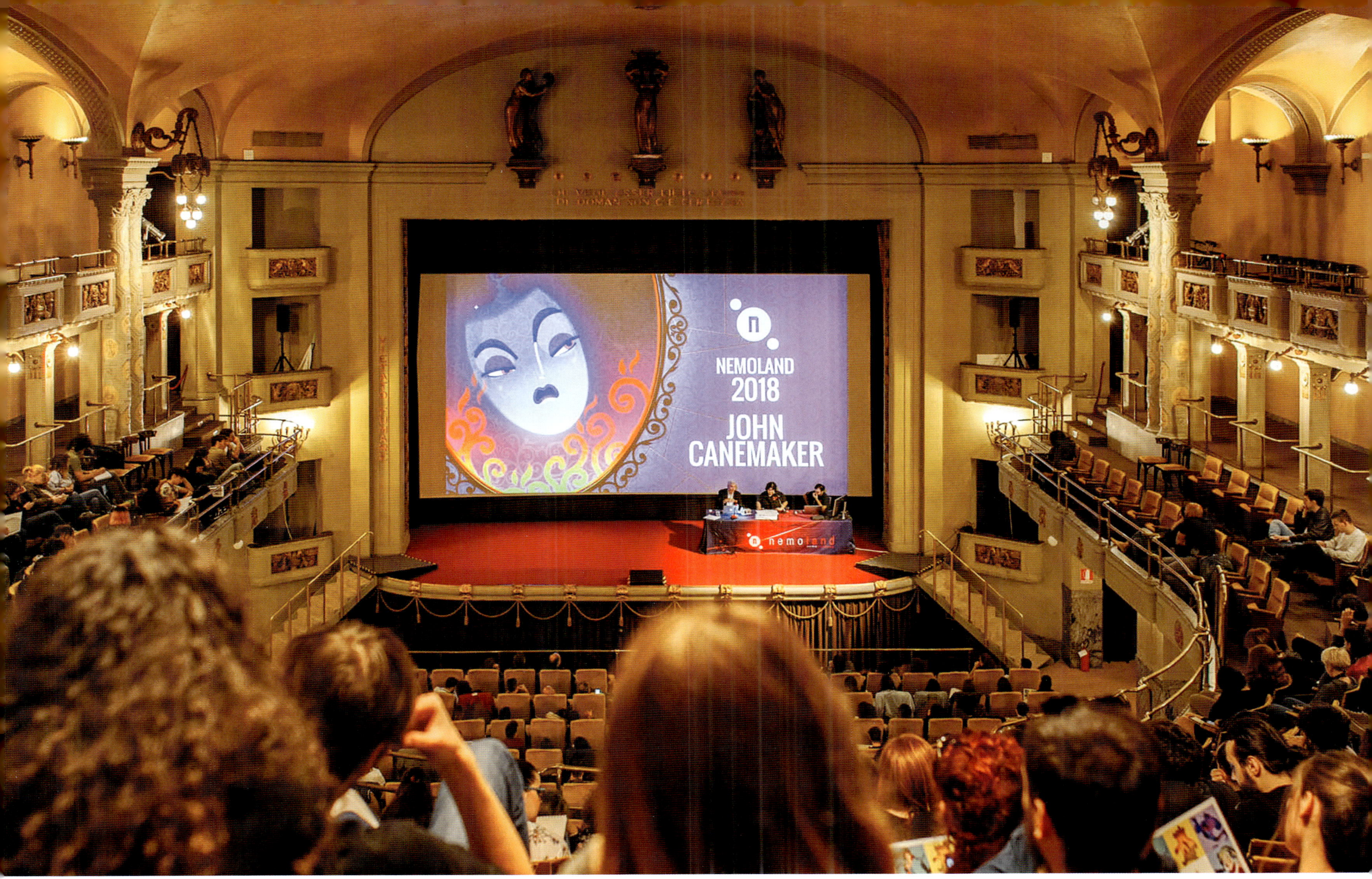
NEMOLAND
2018
JOHN
CANEMAKER
nemoland

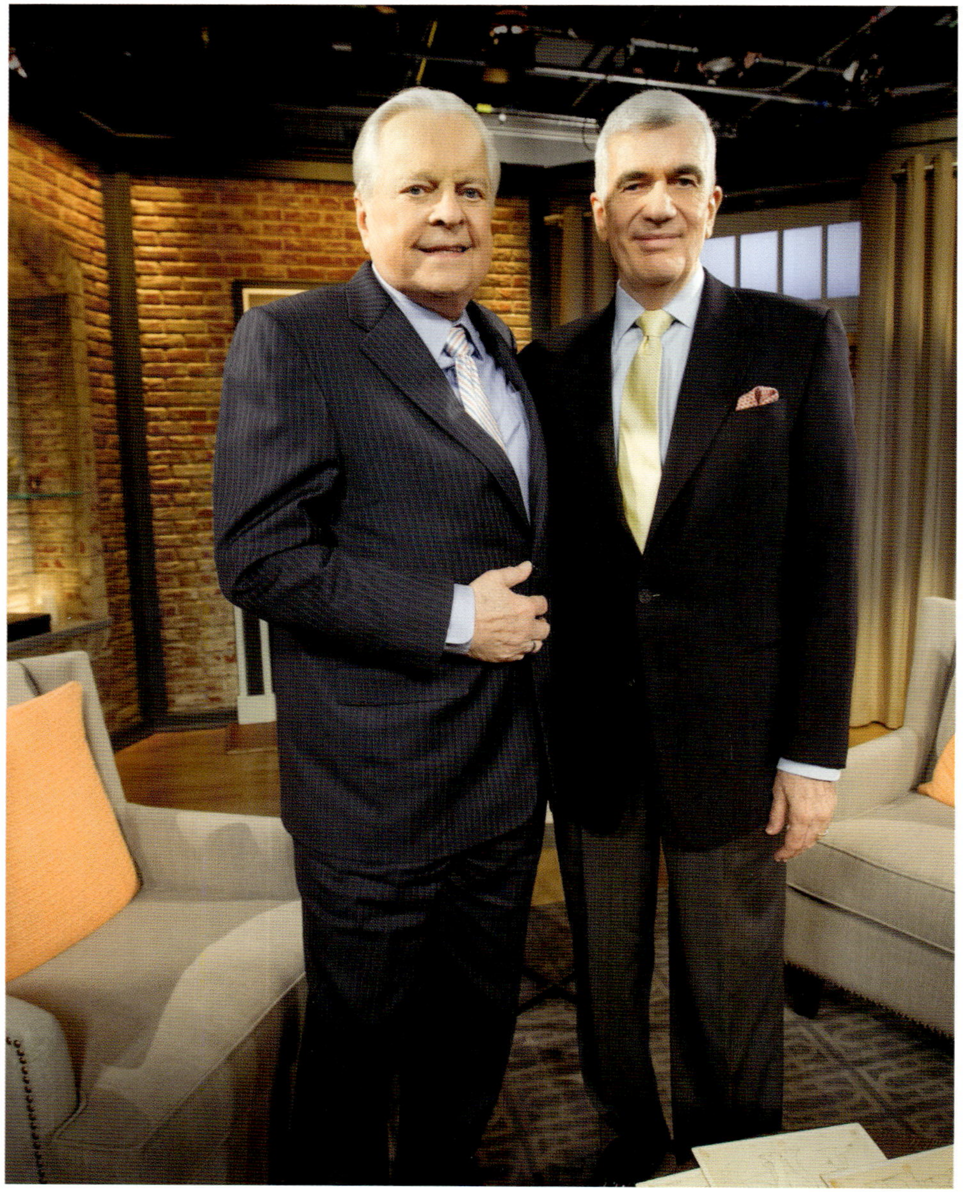

In 2014, on Turner Classic Movies, John Canemaker co-hosted with Robert Osborne a program of films by pioneer animator Winsor McCay. Photo: Joseph Kennedy.

Through the years, I've conducted master classes at Ireland's National Film School/Institute of Art, Design & Technology; Italy's Nemo Academy of Digital Arts; Germany's Filmakademie Baden-Württemberg; UCLA, Kansas City Art Institute, Savannah College of Art & Design; and Yale University.

More than fifty years of my animation history research is available to scholars, students and the general public in the John Canemaker Animation Collection at Fales Special Collections in NYU Bobst Library; Canemaker paper research documents are also at MoMA Film Study Center; AMPAS Margaret Herrick Library; and Billy Ireland Cartoon Library & Museum, Ohio State University.

I have lectured throughout the United States and in Brazil, Canada, England, France, Germany, Ireland, Italy, Japan, Slovakia, Spain, Switzerland, and Wales. In 2007 I was the first animation historian to receive the prestigious Jean Mitry Award from Italy's Le Giornate Del Cinema Muto for my "reclamation and appreciation of silent cinema . . . We are aware you are a true pioneer making claims for the importance of Winsor McCay and Otto Messmer even when silent film historians were ignoring them."

Also, in 2007 ASIFA-Hollywood honored me with the Winsor McCay Award "for distinguished lifetime contributions to the art of animation." That same year, the Tribeca Film Festival celebrated "The Animated World of John Canemaker," and Marymount Manhattan College awarded me an honorary Doctor of Fine Arts degree. In 2013,

I was a guest lecturer at the San Francisco Silent Film Festival as "The Pied Piper of Animation." In 1999 and 2009 I was awarded residency grants from the Rockefeller Foundation's Bellagio Center in Italy.

In 1988 for The Katonah Museum of Art in Katonah, N.Y., I was curator of *Dreams in Motion: The Art of Winsor McCay*, and, in 1994, *Vladimir Tytla – Master Animator*. As guest curator for the Walt Disney Family Museum in San Francisco, I produced *Magic, Color, Flair – The Art of Mary Blair* in 2014; *The Lost Notebook: Secrets of Disney's Movie Magic* (2014); and *Wish Upon a Star - The Art of Pinocchio* (2016). For television's Turner Classic Movies (TCM) in 2014, I co-hosted with Robert Osborne a special hour on the animated films of Winsor McCay.

In 1988, my husband Joseph Kennedy and I bought a small house in the village of Bridgehampton, N.Y., on eastern Long Island. Sitting on three eighths of an acre, the house was bookended by a plain front lawn and a backyard of overgrown crabgrass and weeds, and a few tired rose bushes left behind by the previous owner.

"Let's make a garden," Joe said.

Nothing formal, we decided. More on the order of a charming English country garden: asymmetrical, natural and surprising.

So, we dug in, as it were, with all the excitement and naivete of true amateurs.

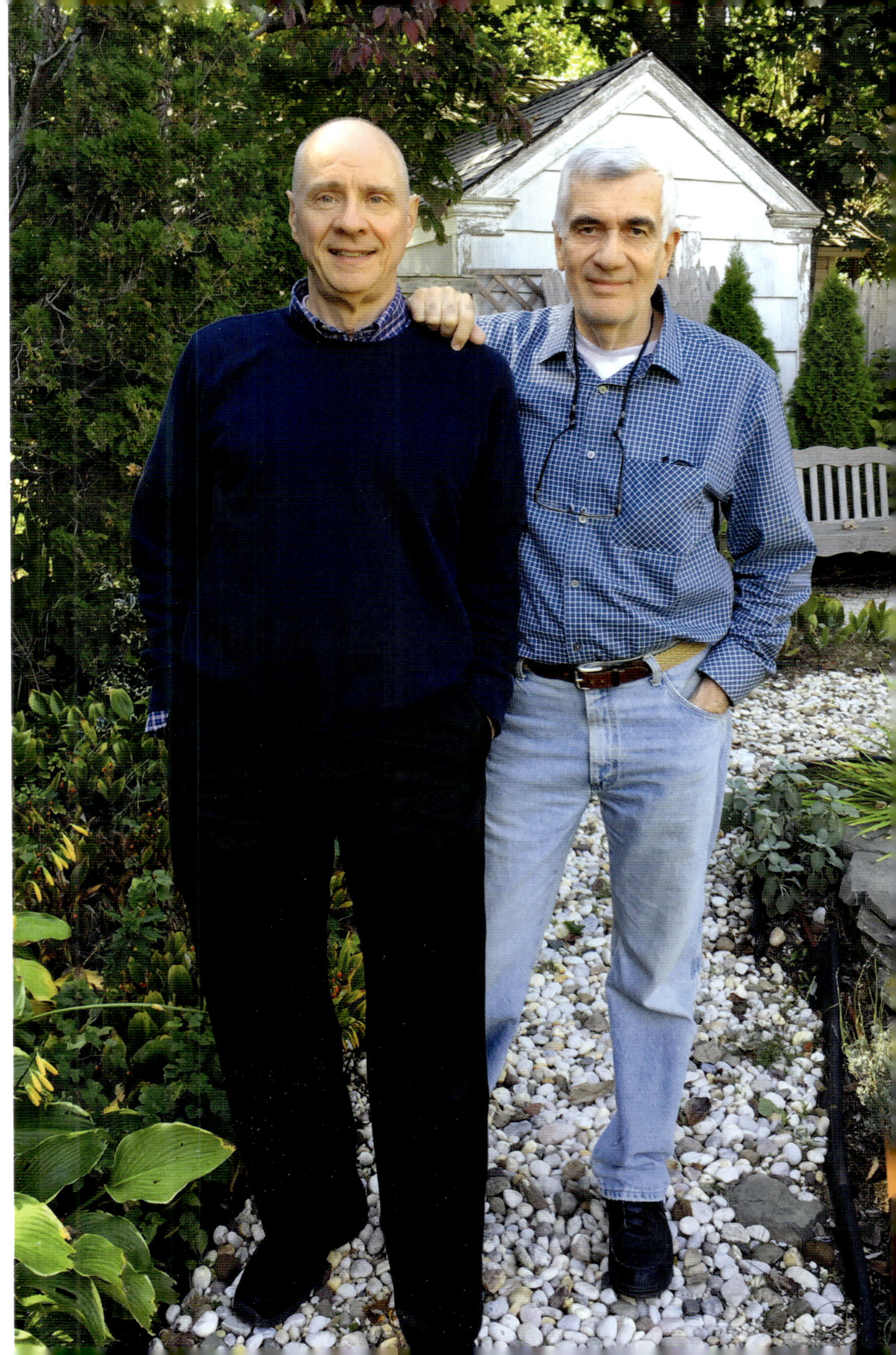

This book of paintings started in 1988 when John and Joe Kennedy purchased a house in Bridgehampton in Eastern Long Island. Photo: Zoya Baker.

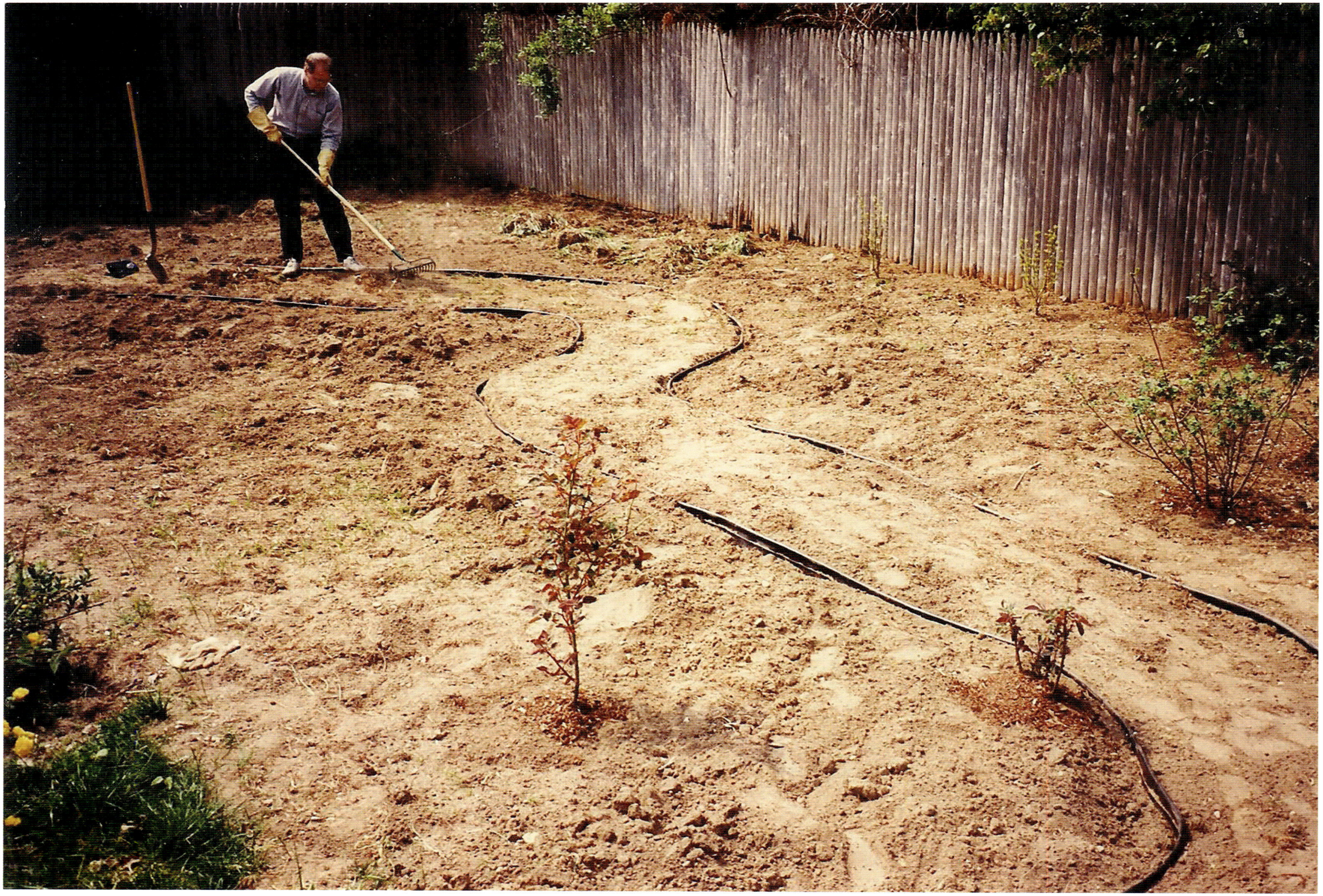

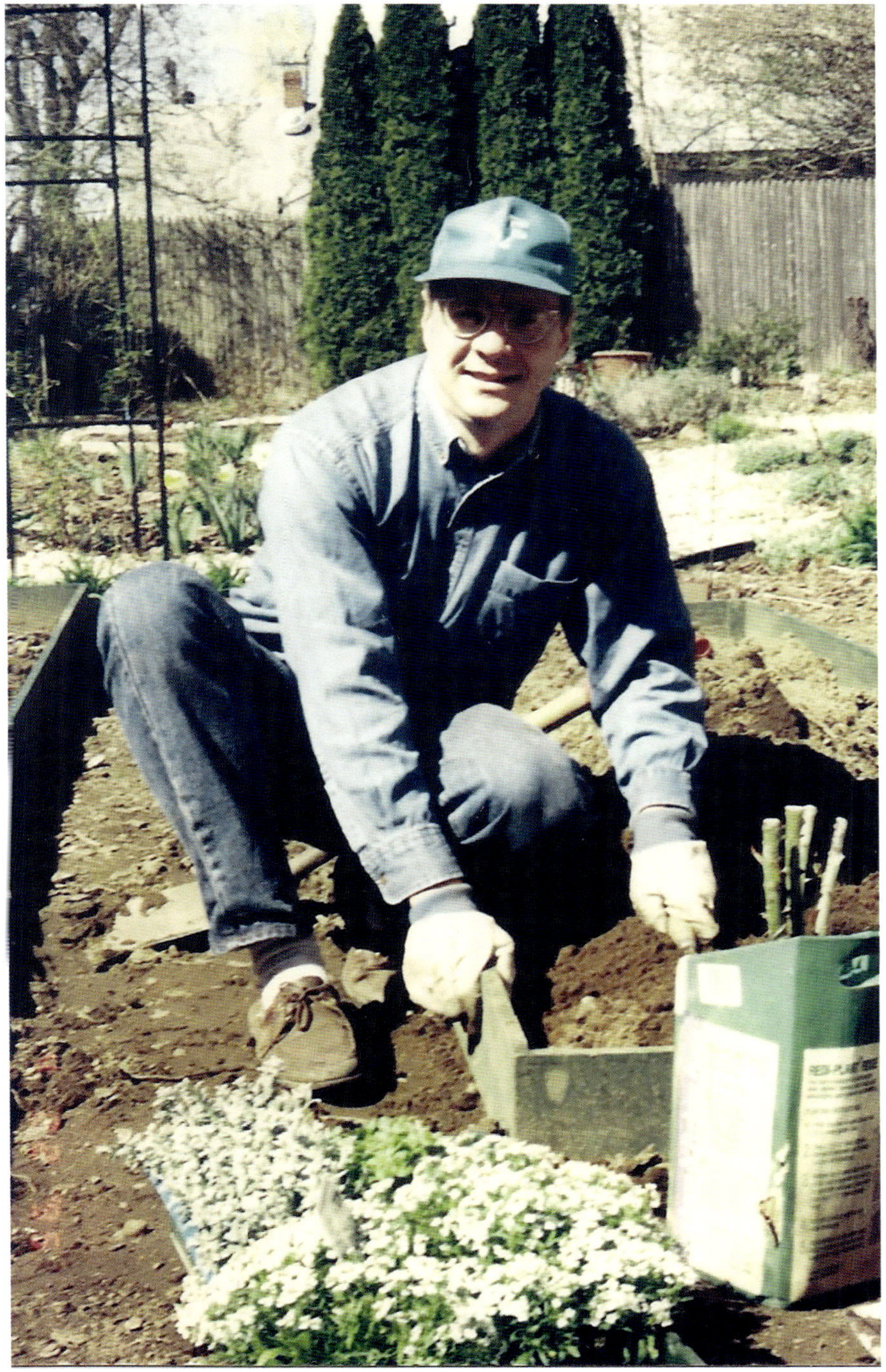

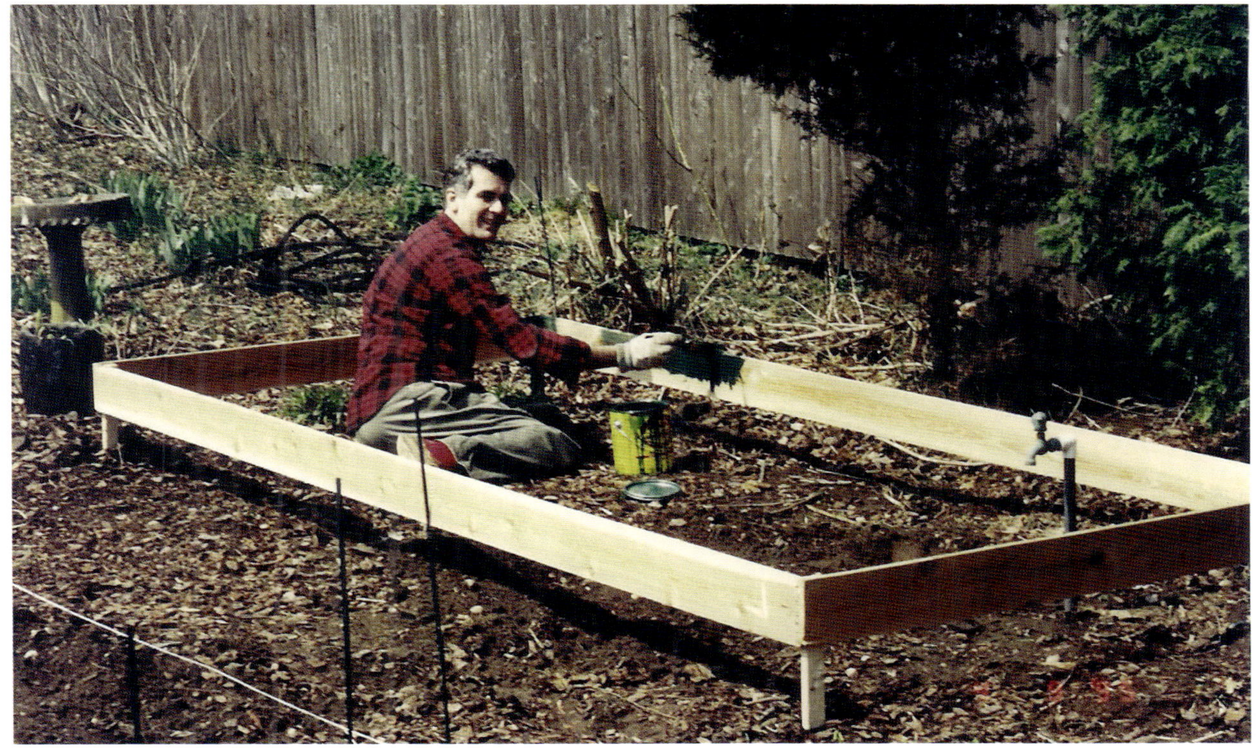

Page 24: The nearness of nature inspired the idea of creating a personal garden in the backyard. First, came the labor of mowing weeds, tilling the soil, and setting down a future pathway for varied plantings.

Left: Joe set down the first roses within wooden flower bed containers..

Above: John, already painting.

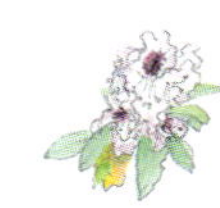

After roughly eyeballing a possible layout in the yard's northwest corner, we rented a rototiller and cleared a considerable amount of brush and weeds. Then we prepared a rambling curved pathway, filled it with small stones and, untutored, began planting a dense variety of whatever flora struck our fancy: perennial and annual flowers, vegetables, shrubs, vines and trees.

Year after year, we nurtured, replaced, moved, divided and added to our ever-growing domain: roses, foxgloves, hosta, sunflowers, hollyhocks, daylilies, hydrangea, peonies, poppies, iris and ferns, including vegetables, tomatoes, lettuce and squash.

Through many errors, we learned what and what didn't work in this small patch of earthy paradise. All the while, enjoying the wonderful seasonal changes reflected in the plantings' life cycles, which we shared with many fascinating critters, including insects, feral cats, rabbits, squirrels, moles, voles, birds, and the occasional garter snake.

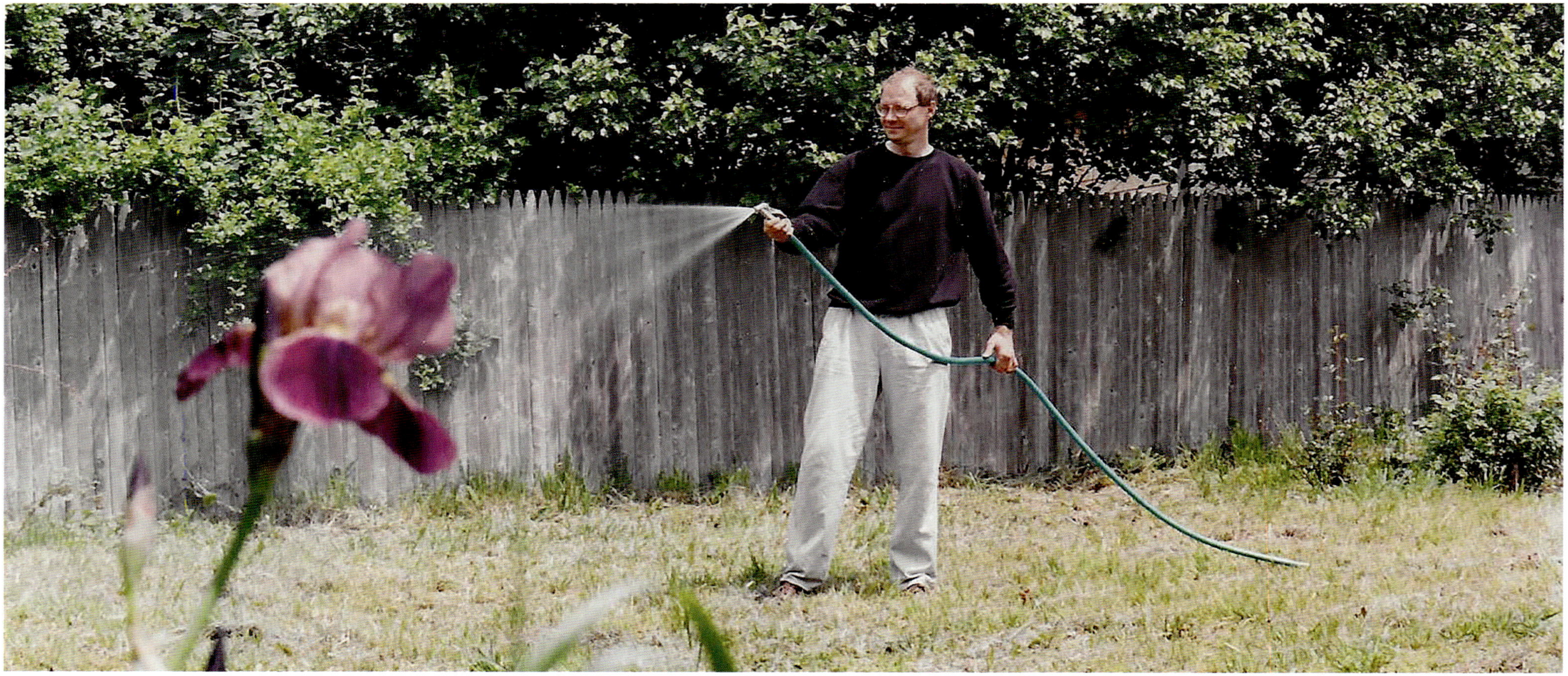

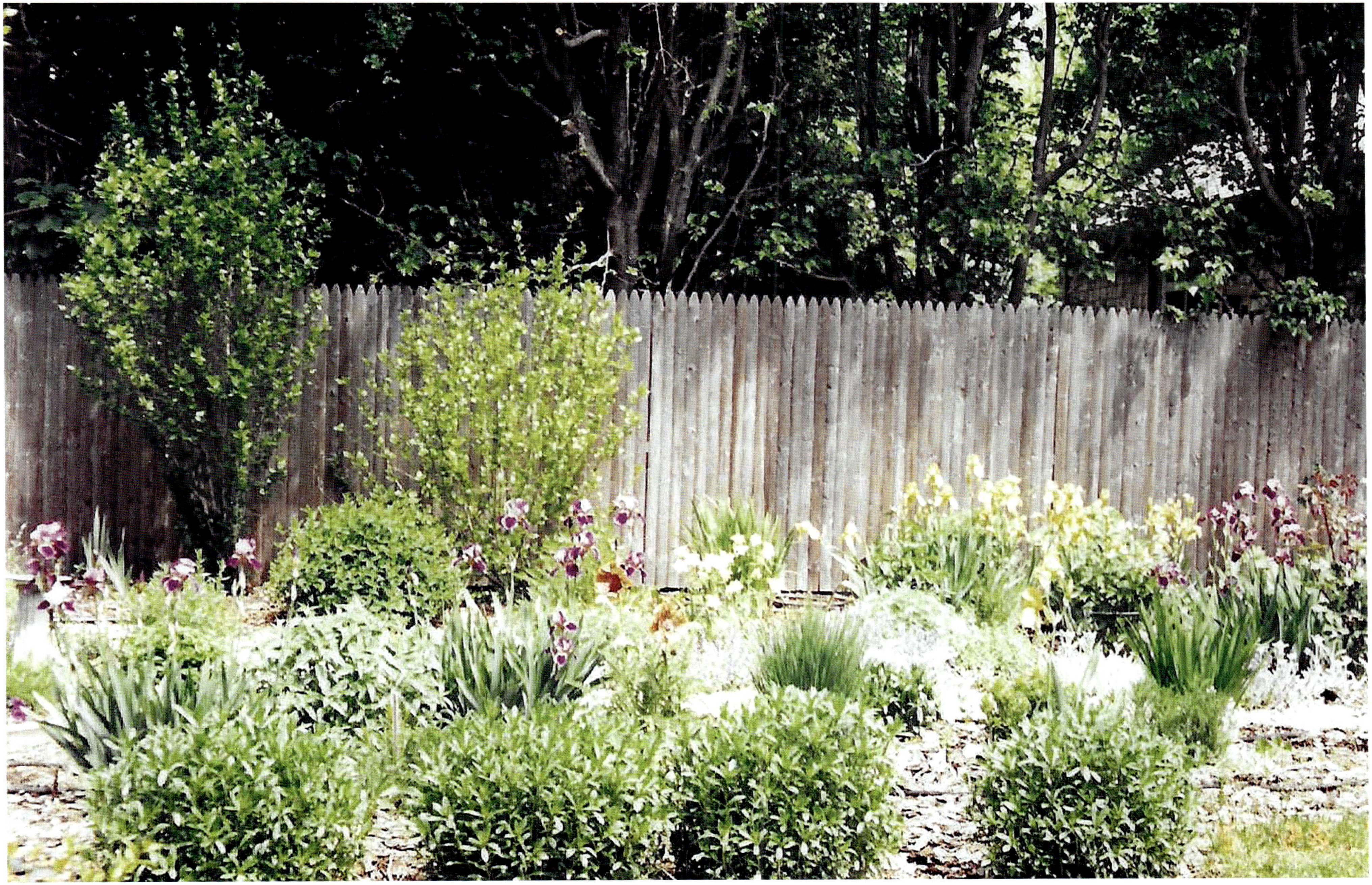

Left, page 26: Joe waters a first (apparently giant) iris.

Above: Early spring plantings begin to flower by June.

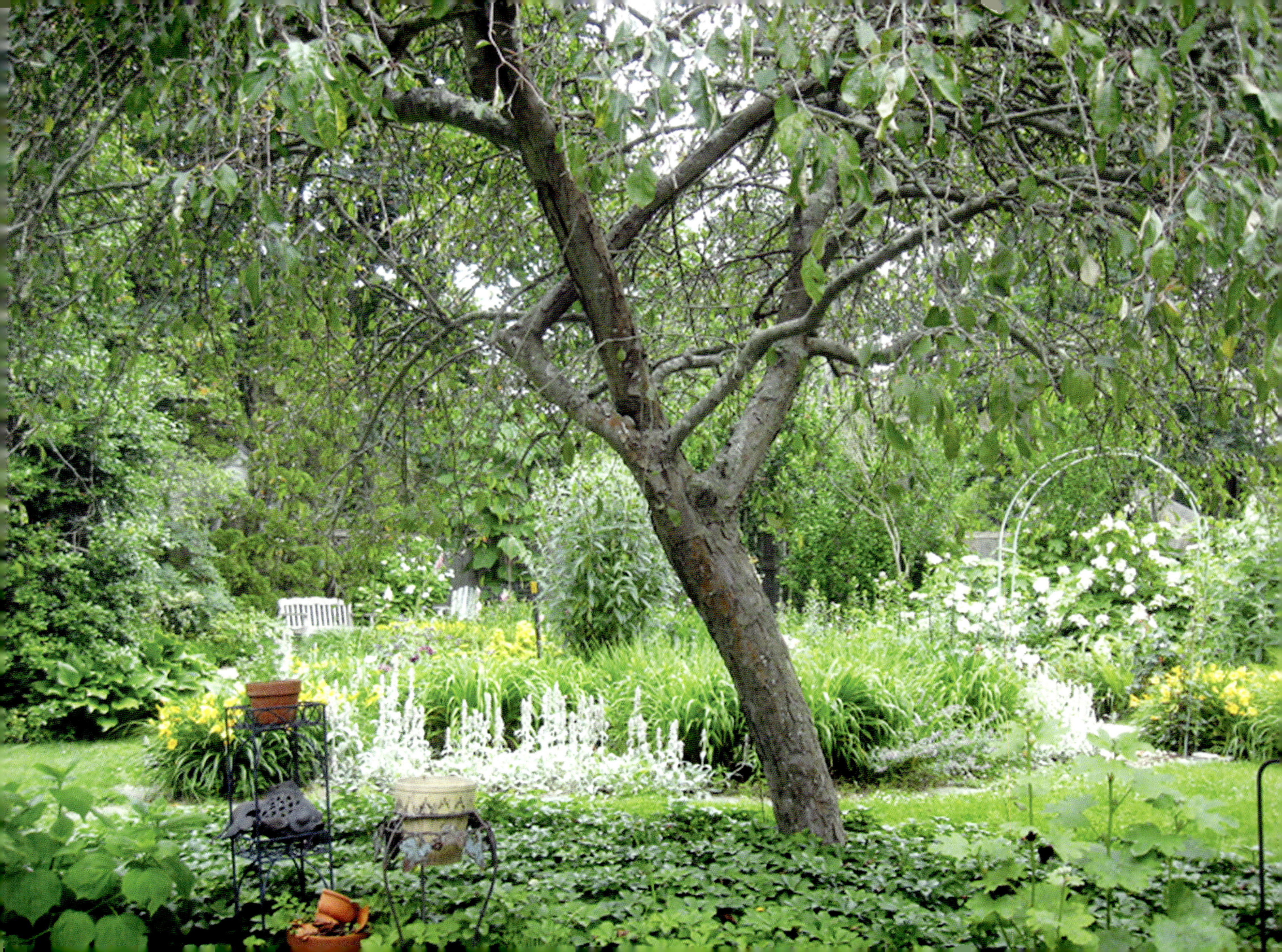

Gardening is fascinating, exhausting work. "In the spring," according to Margaret Atwood, "at the end of the day, you should smell like dirt." But it is worth it for the intimacy gained from participating in nature's life cycles. Luther Burbank claimed flowers improve lives: "They are sunshine, food and medicine for the soul."

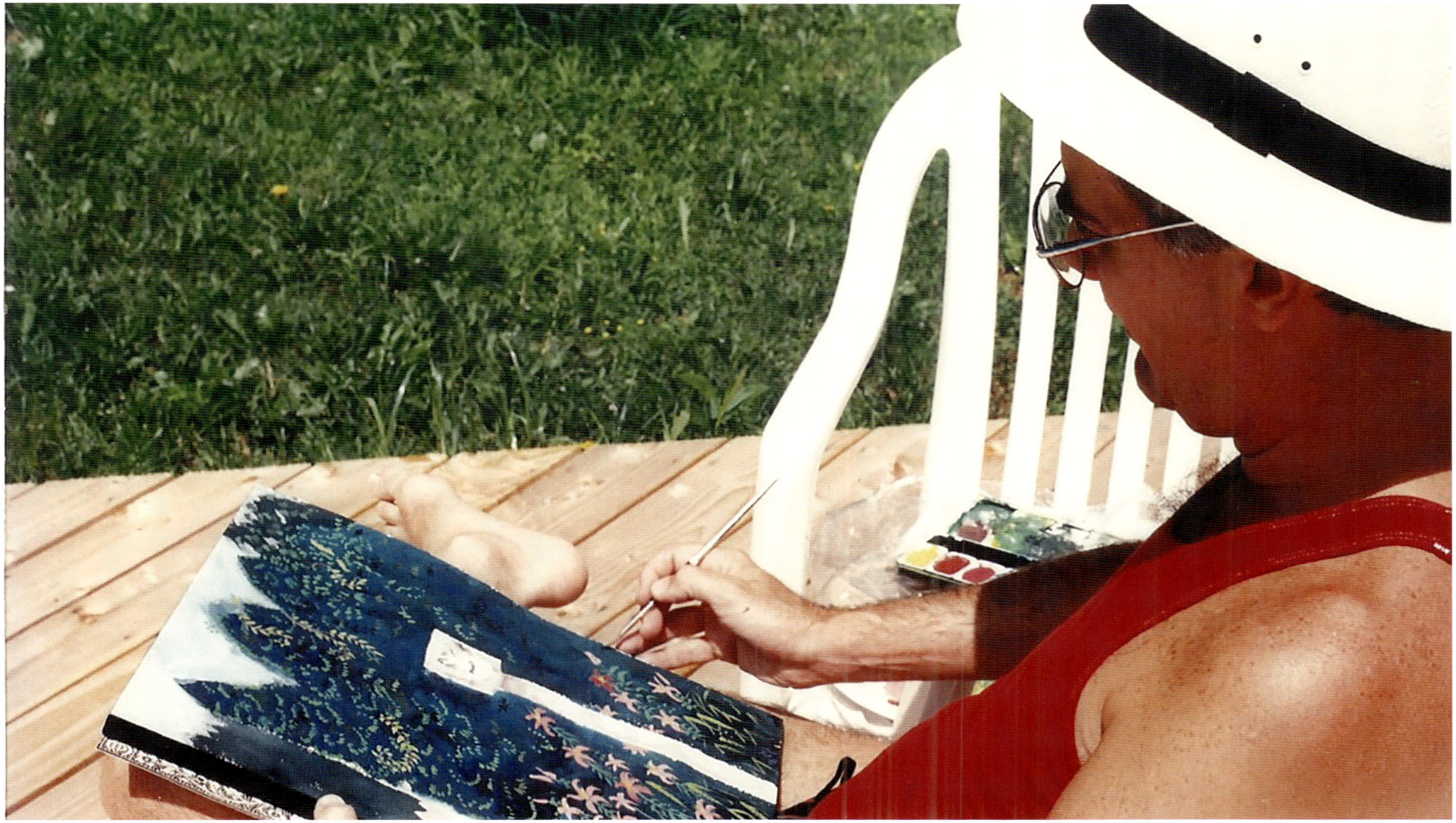

Left: Fast forward several decades to John and Joe's lush, serene garden. Photo: Michael Sporn.

Above: The garden inspired John's many en plein air paintings.

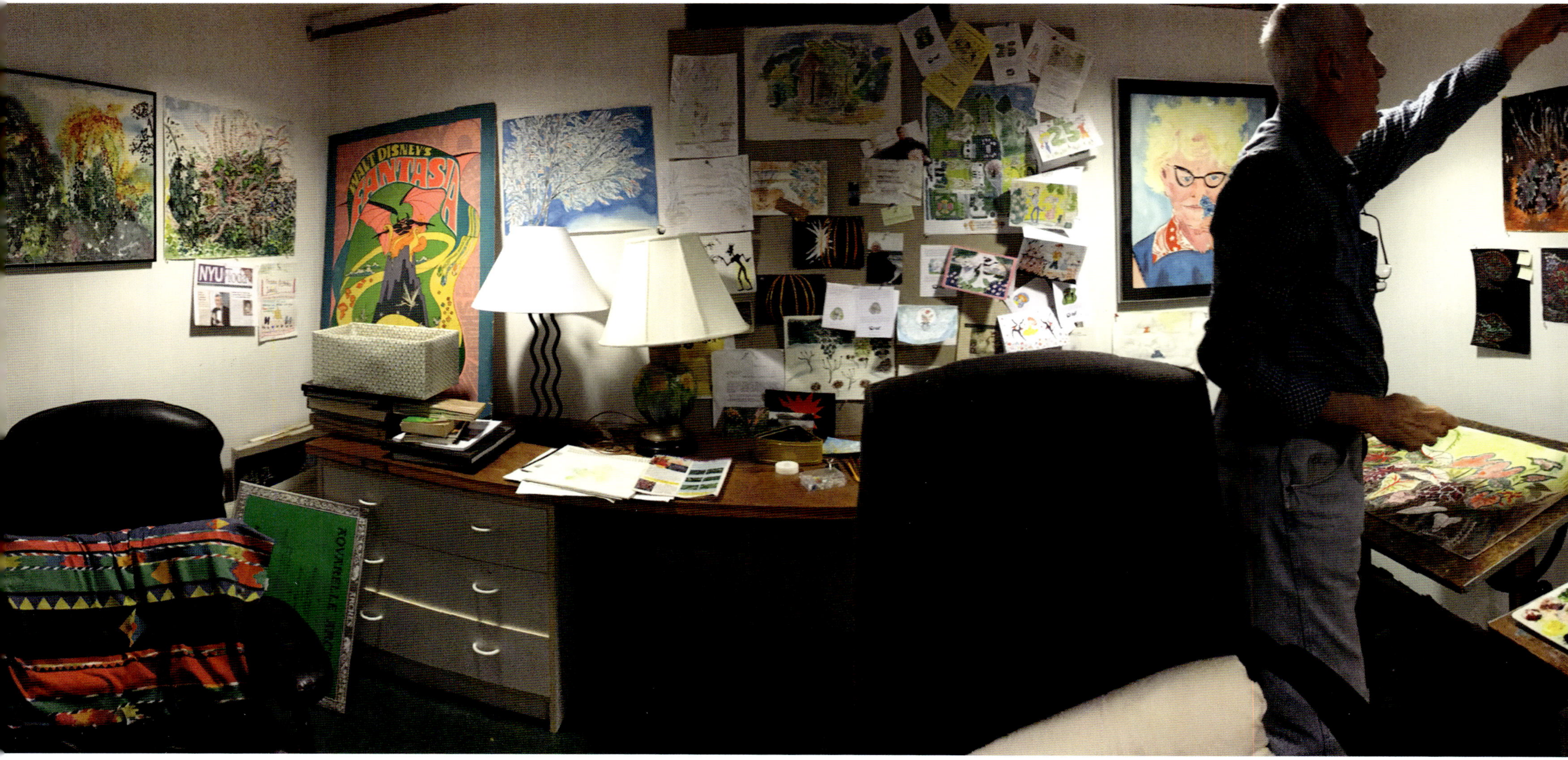

For more than three decades, our garden enthralled and delighted us. It literally inspired me to create watercolor and gouache paintings of its increasingly lush growth and the surrounding landscapes and forests in all their seasonal phases. Eventually, as an animator I wanted to bring my paintings to life, which resulted in a six-minute animated short released in 1998, titled *Bridgehampton*, with an original music score by the virtuoso jazz pianist/composer Fred Hersch.

In the current book, you'll see the garden in colorful, vibrant gouache and pencil on paper, works that, in turn, inspired my animated film, *Bridgehampton*. The film is available on a compilation dvd of my

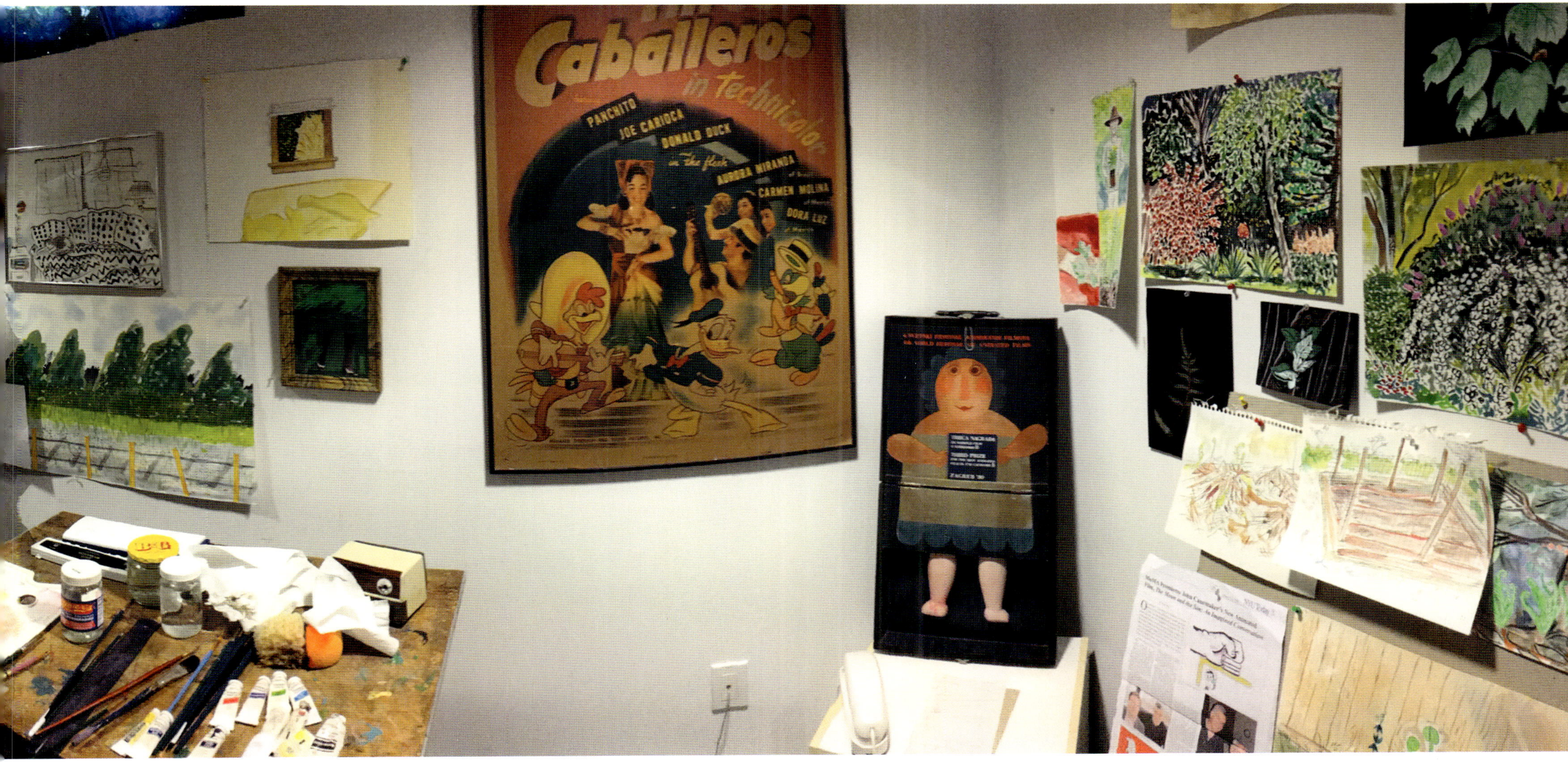

John's basement studio in Bridgehamton. Photo: Zoya Baker

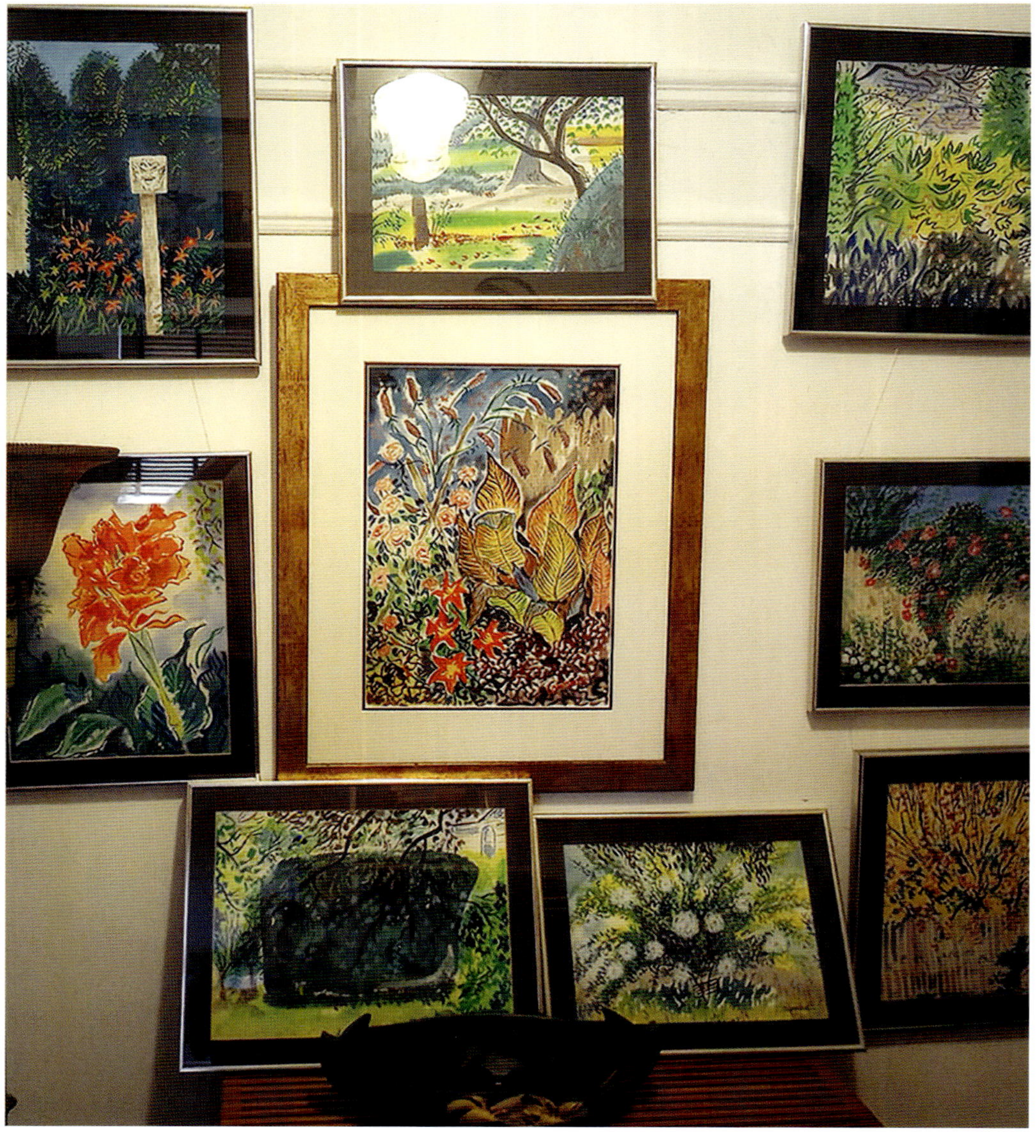

films distributed by Milestone Film & Video: *https://milestonefilms.com/collections/the-animation-magic-of-john-canemaker/products/john-canemaker-marching-to-a-different-toon.*

International festivals embraced the film. The Tribeca Film Festival in 2007 featured *Bridgehampton* in a program showcasing my films. The director of the Ottawa International Animation Festival, Chris Robinson, described *Bridgehampton* as a "beautiful, subdued lyrical work." The Museum of Modern Art's 2008 exhibition, *Jazz Score*, continuously screened it alongside an installation of original drawings from the film, and added it to their permanent collection of my short films, as did the Academy of Motion Picture Arts and Sciences.

In *The Art of John Canemaker – An Animator's Garden*, I happily share with you my joy in painting, and a look at the making of the film, *Bridgehampton*. Each involved a creative process that on many levels I found profoundly nourishing and life-giving.

—John Canemaker

Left: The garden, framed and hung.

Page 33: Paintings led to conceptual art for an animated film that brought the garden to life. See the final chapter on the making of the film, "Bridgehampton."

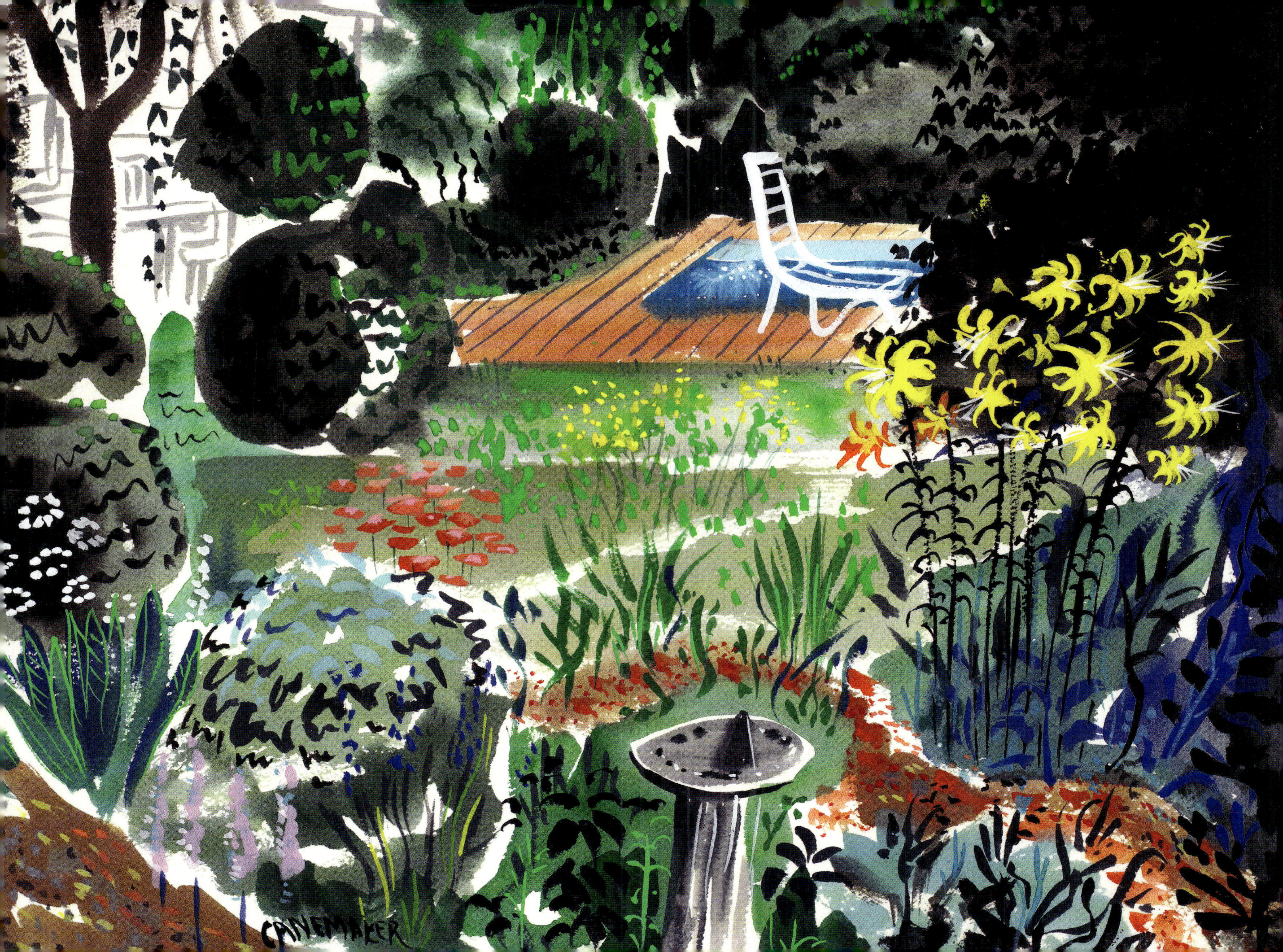
CANEMAKER

SUMMER

"All gardening is landscape painting."

- Gertrude Jekyll

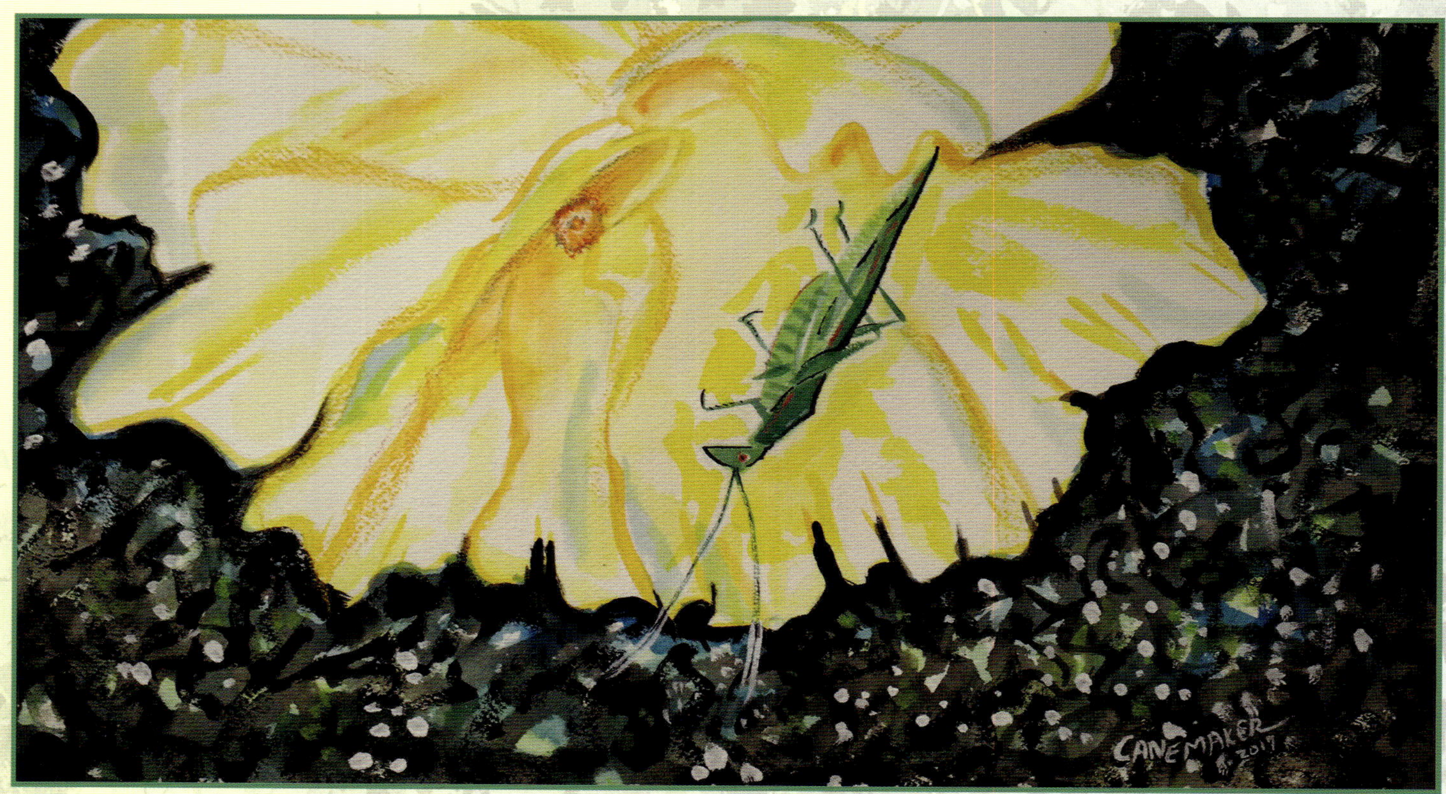

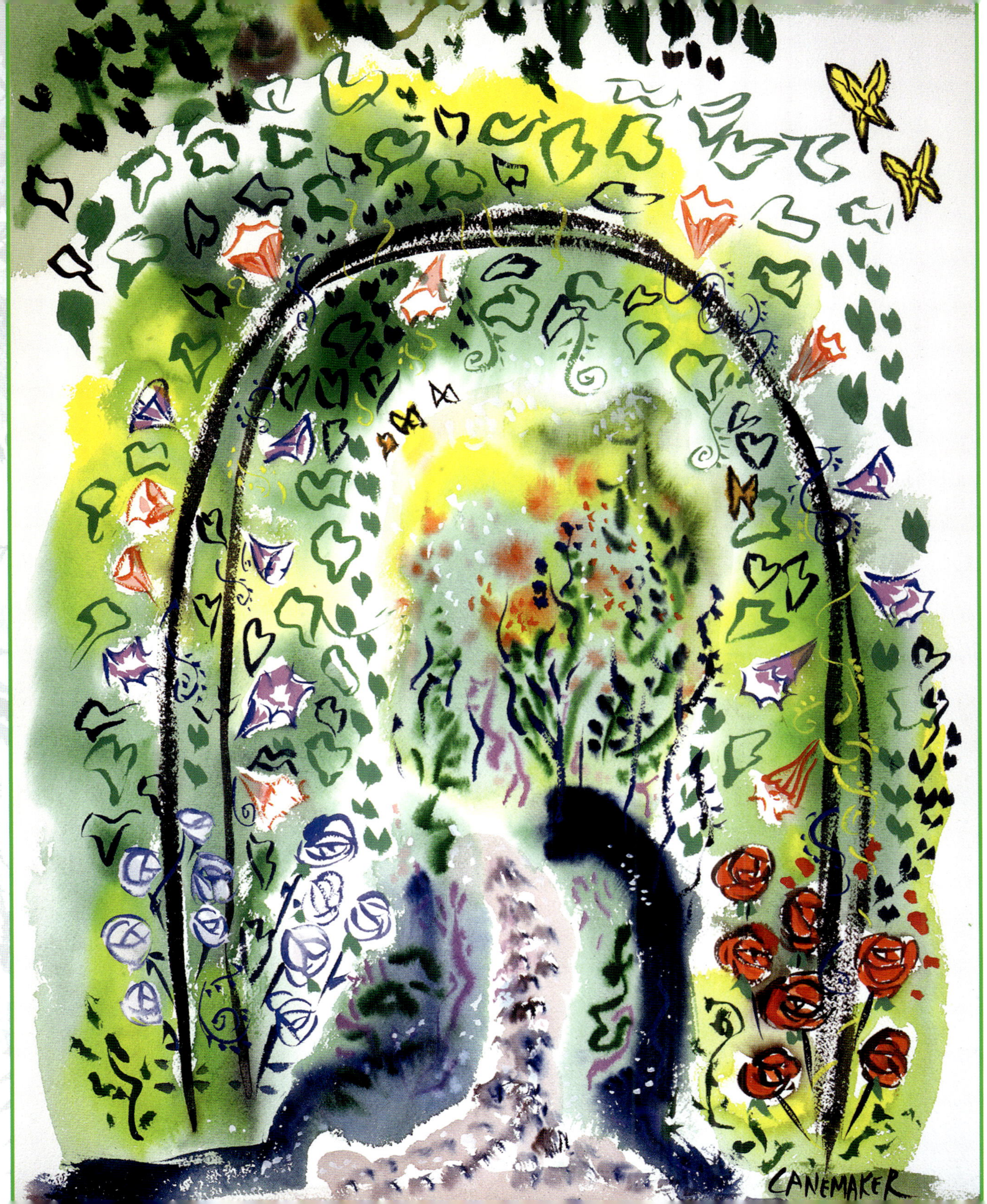

Far Left: KAYDID UPSIDE DOWN
18x12″ gouache 2017

Left: ARBOR 18x24″
gouache 1993

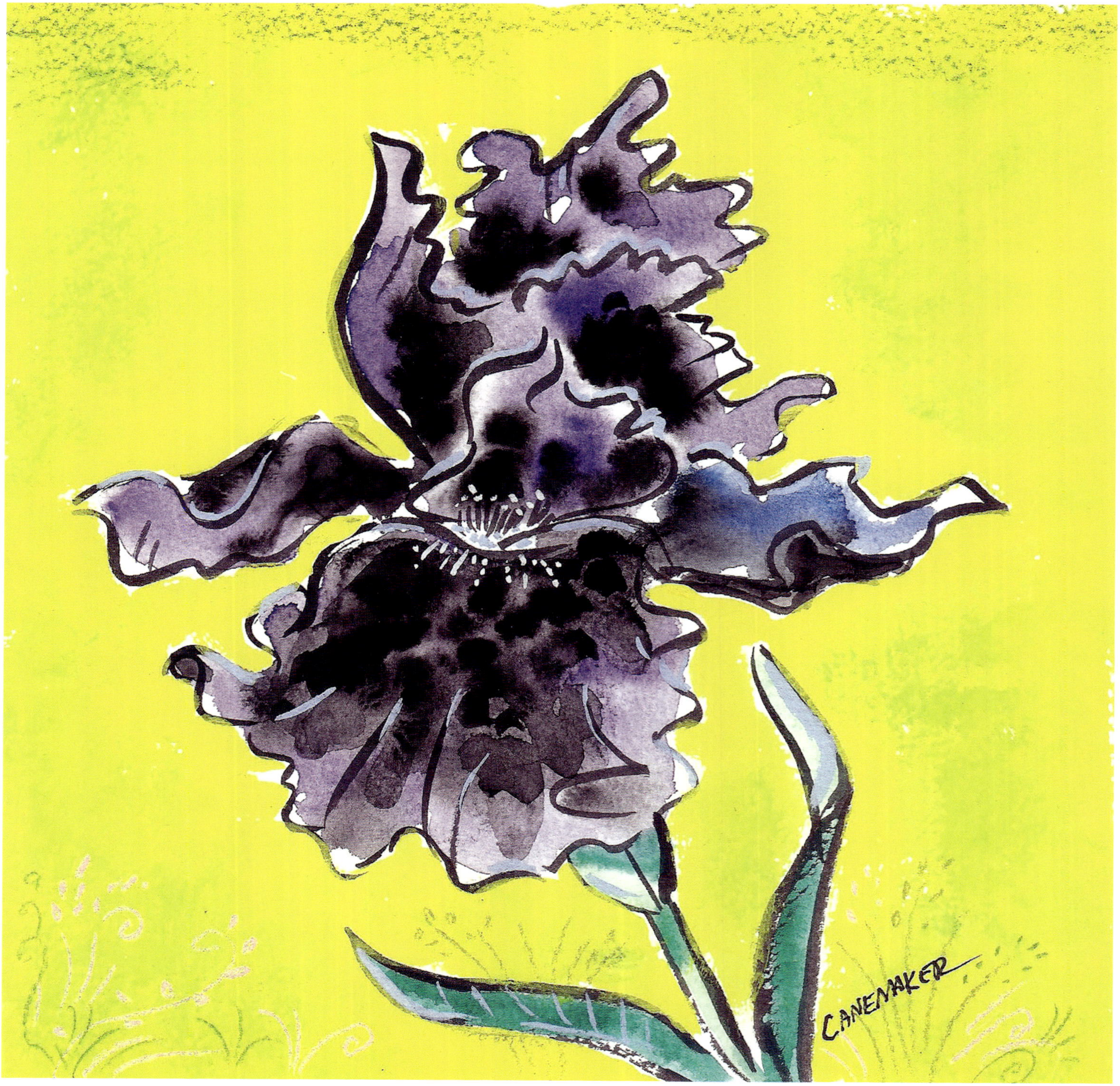

Left: BLACK IRIS 8X8" gouache 2021

Right: CANNA & GLAD 15x11 1/2" gouache 1991

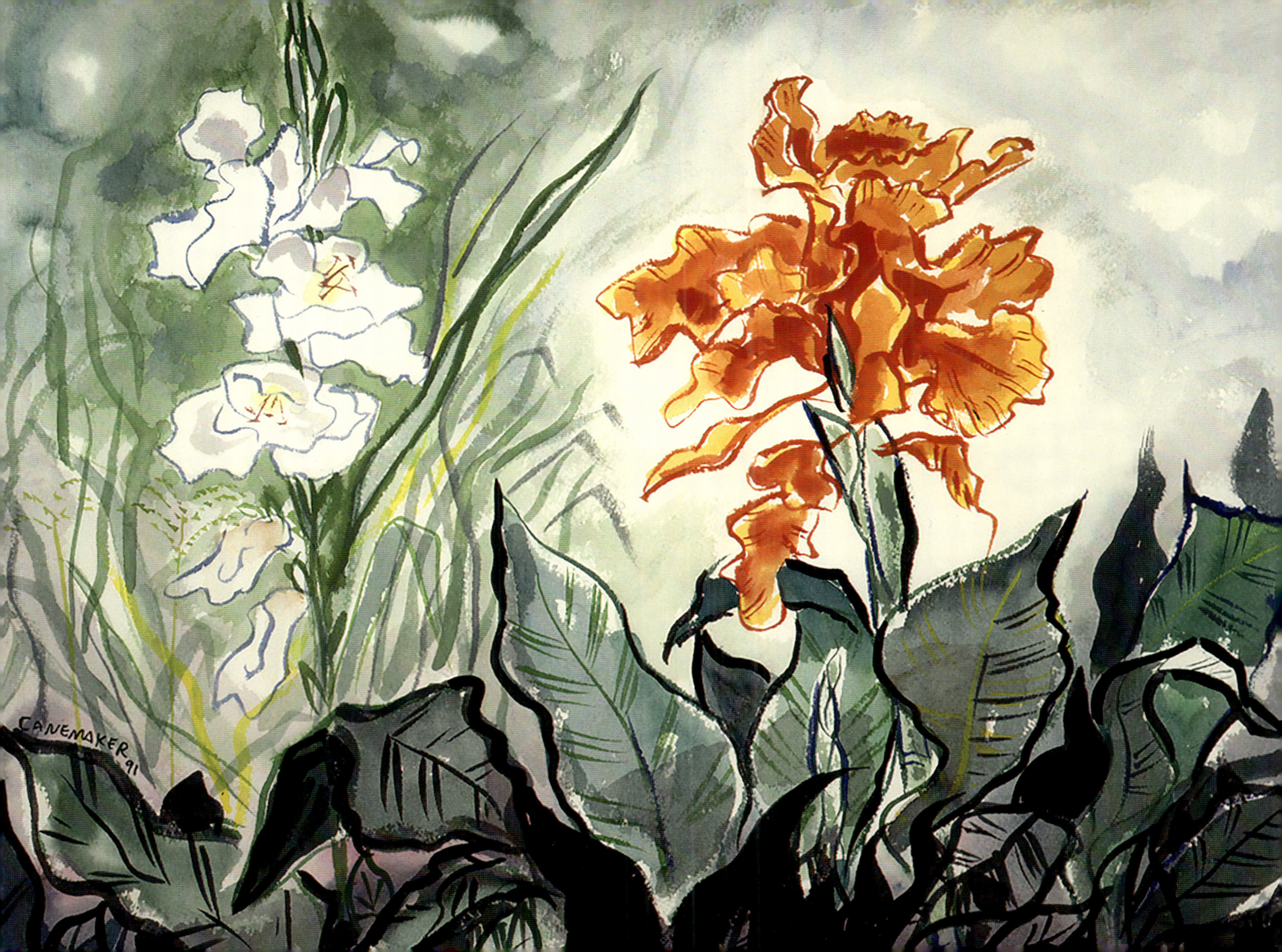
CANEMAKER '91

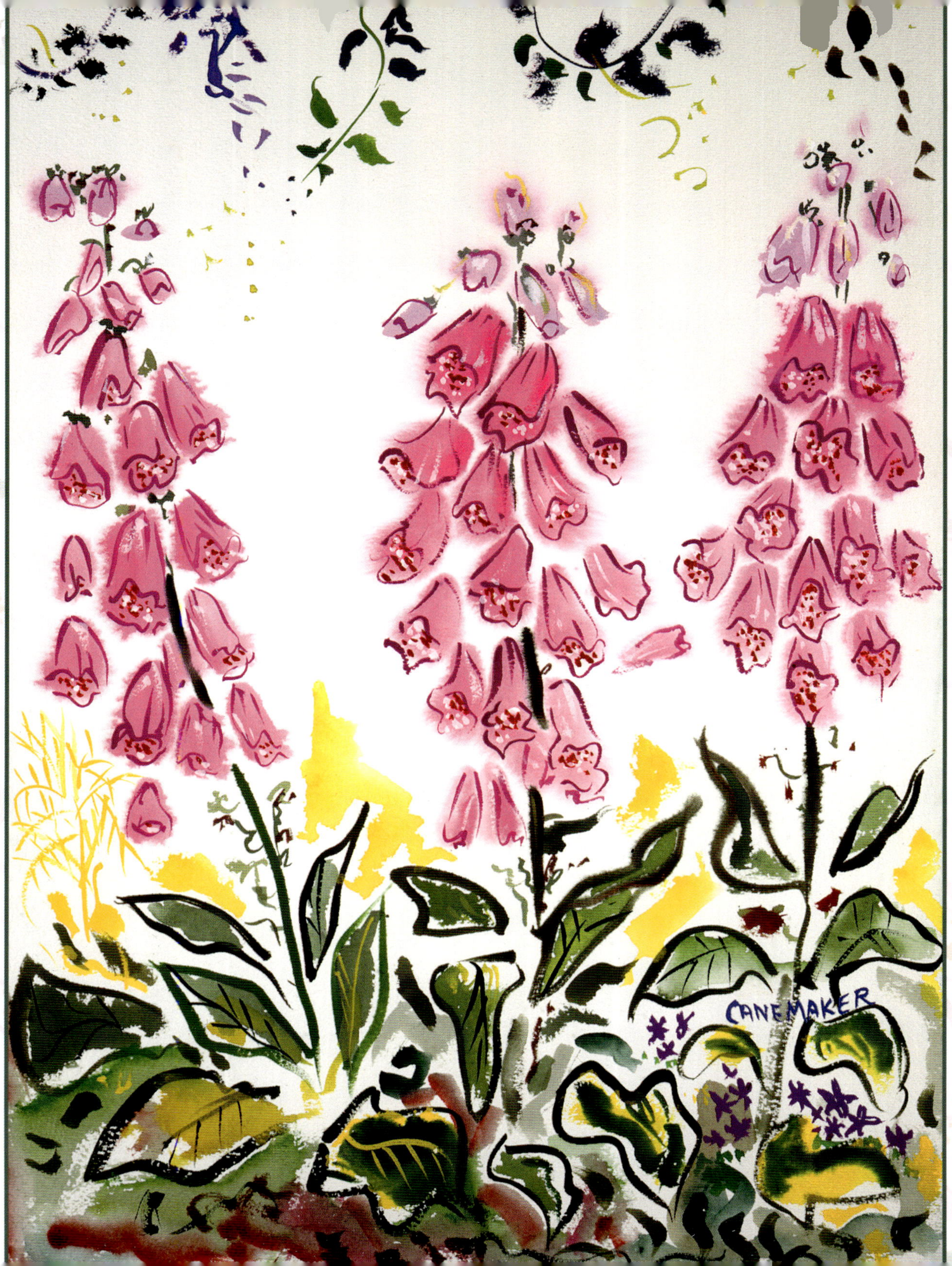

Left: DIGITALIS 19x13 1/2″ gouache 1994

Right: DRAGONTAIL BUTTERFLIES 12x16″ gouache 2024

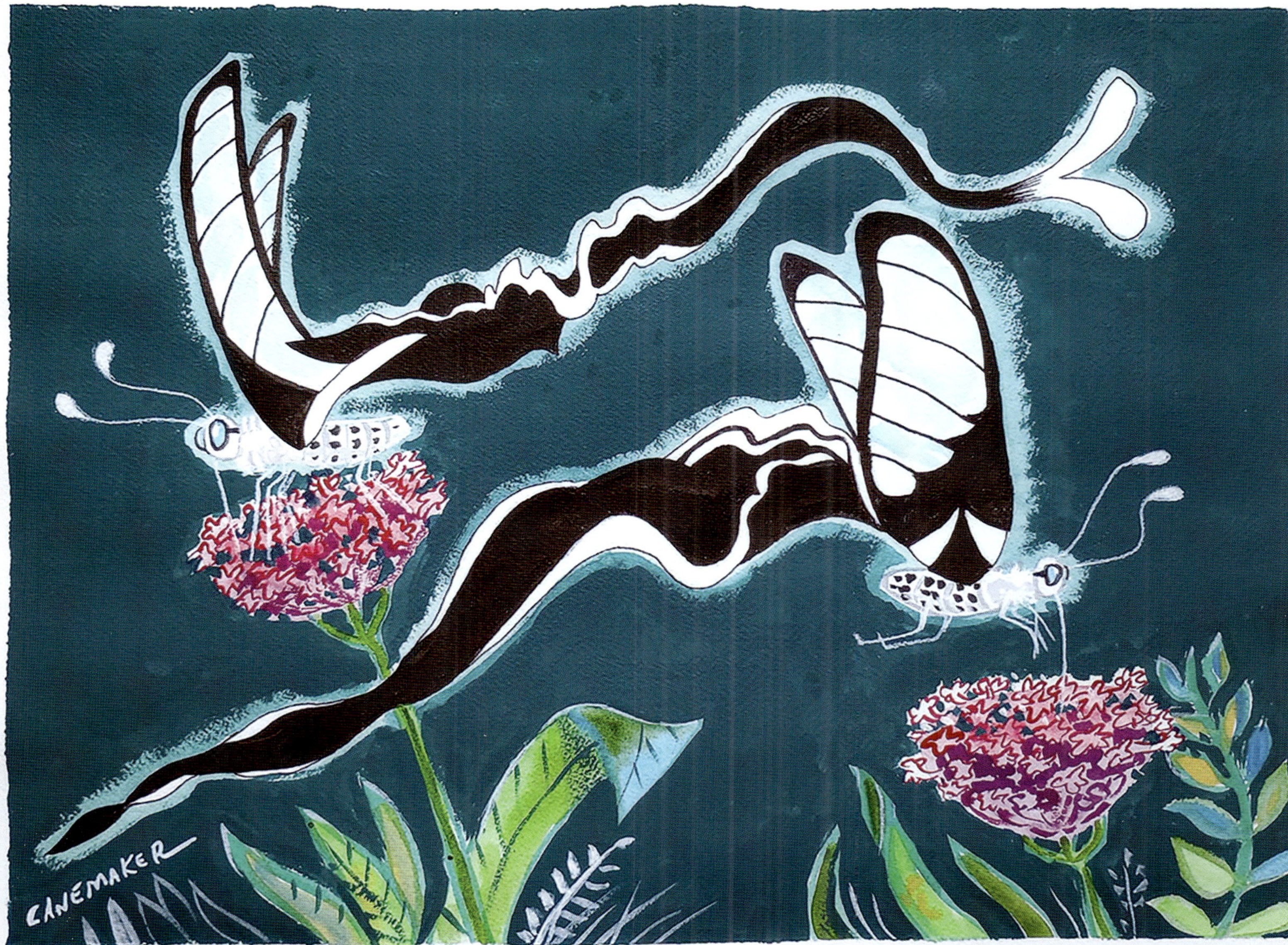
CANEMAKER

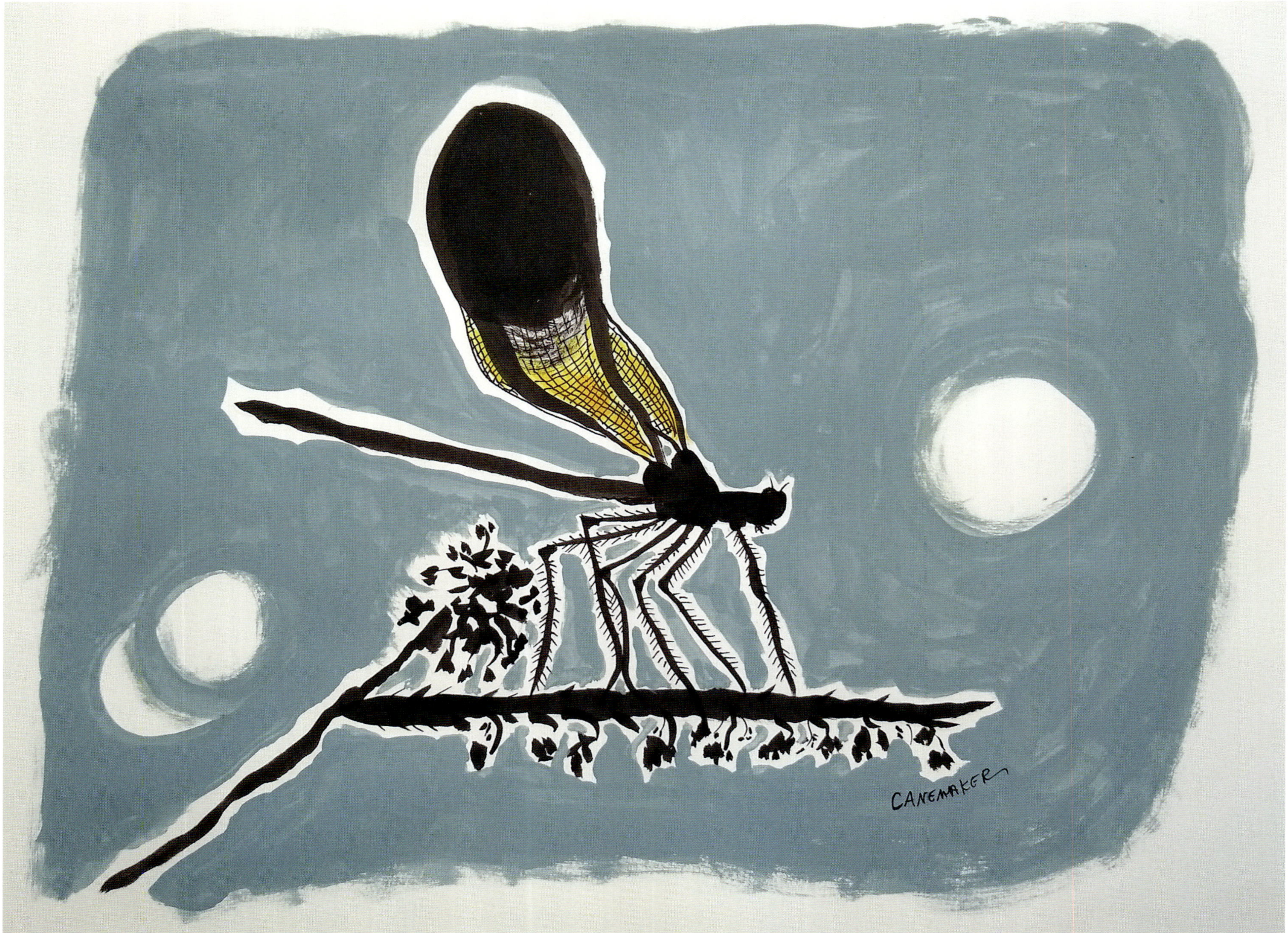
CANEMAKER

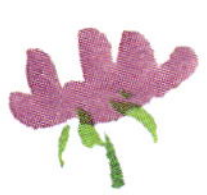

Left: *MIDSUMMER NIGHT DRAGONFLY 12x16"*
gouache 2022

Right: COSMOS 15 1/4x11 1/2" gouache 1991

Following pages
Page 42: HYDRANGIA 15x11 1/2" gouache 1991

Page 43: IN THE SECRET GARDEN 10X14"
gouache 2023

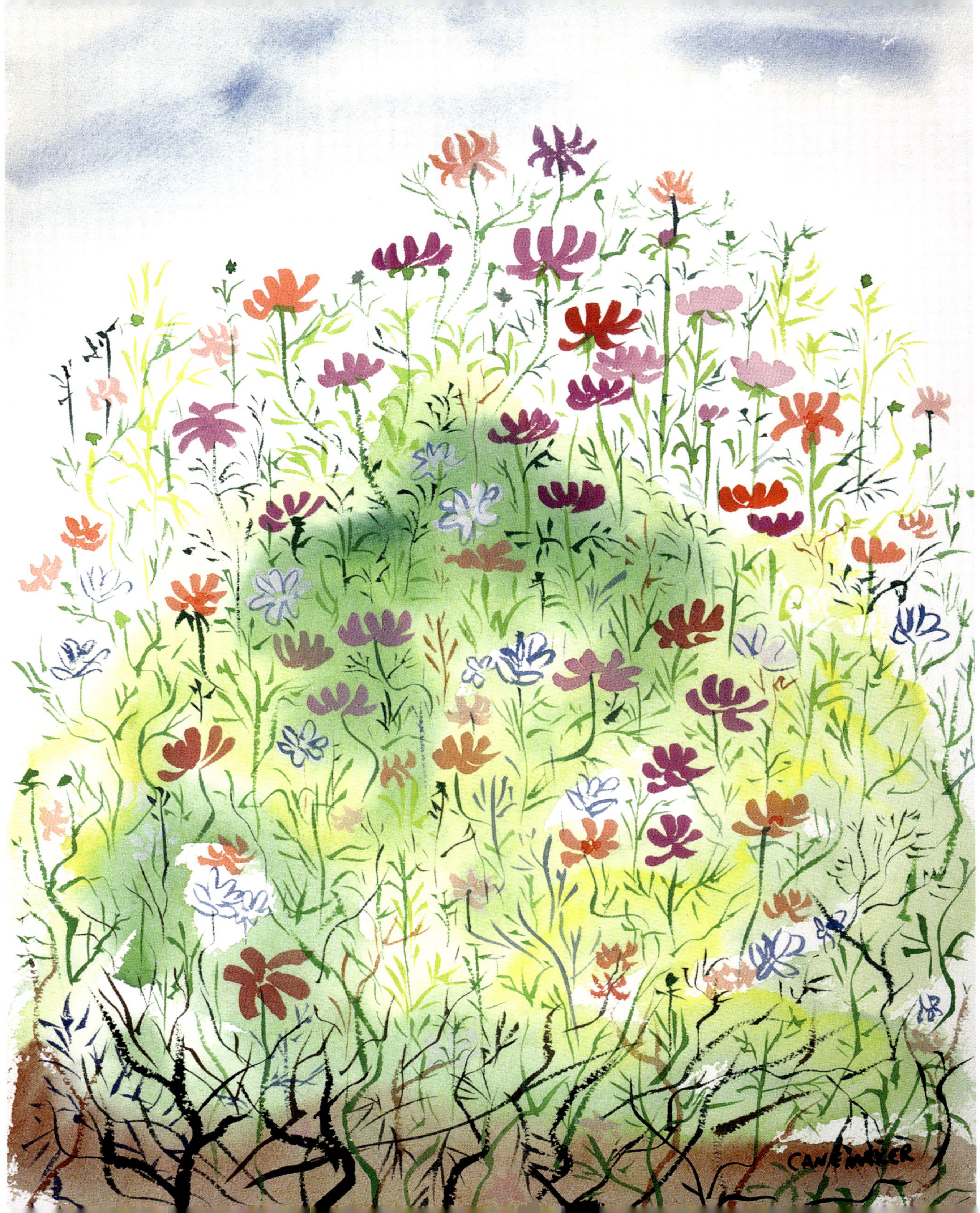

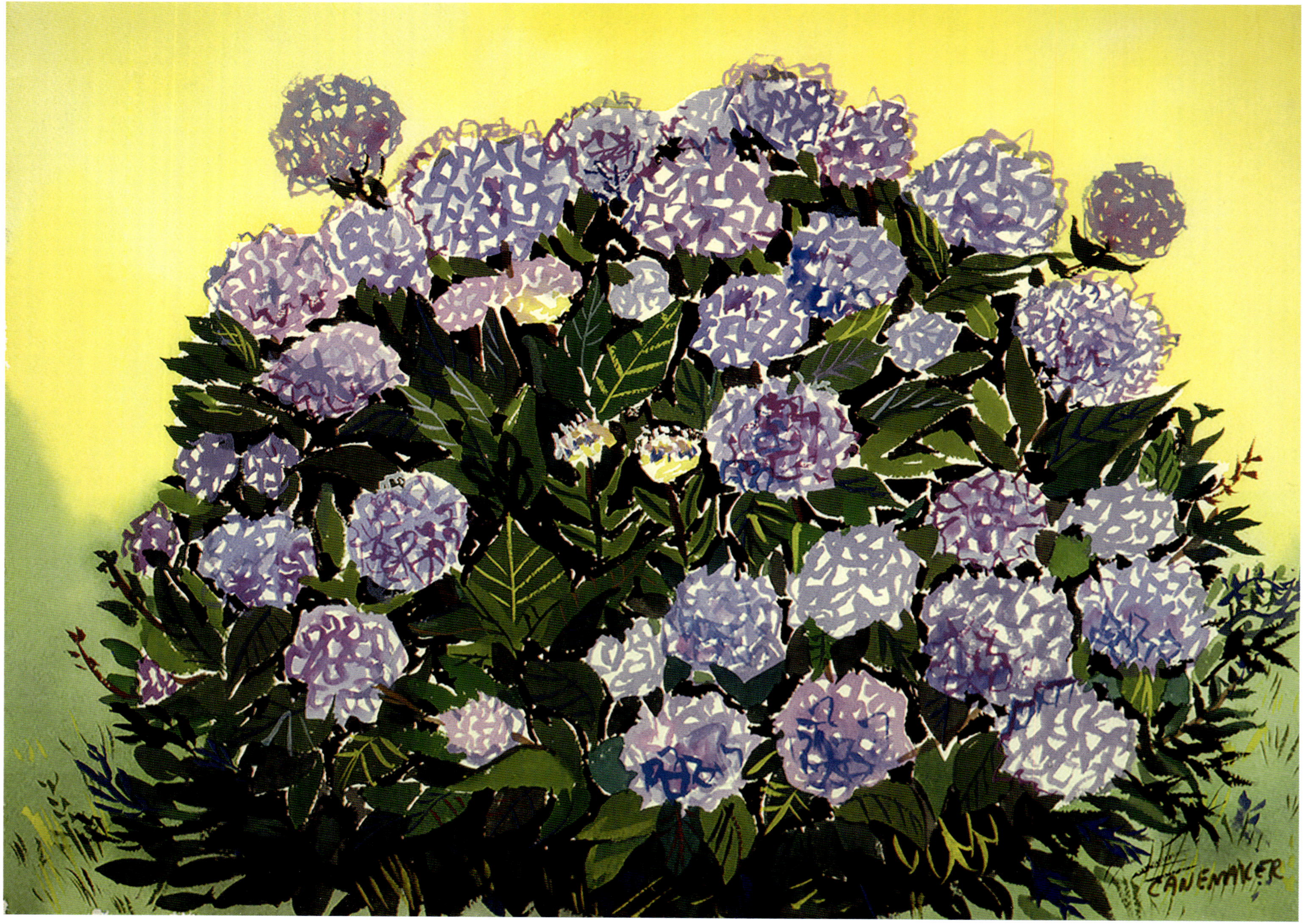
CANEMAKER

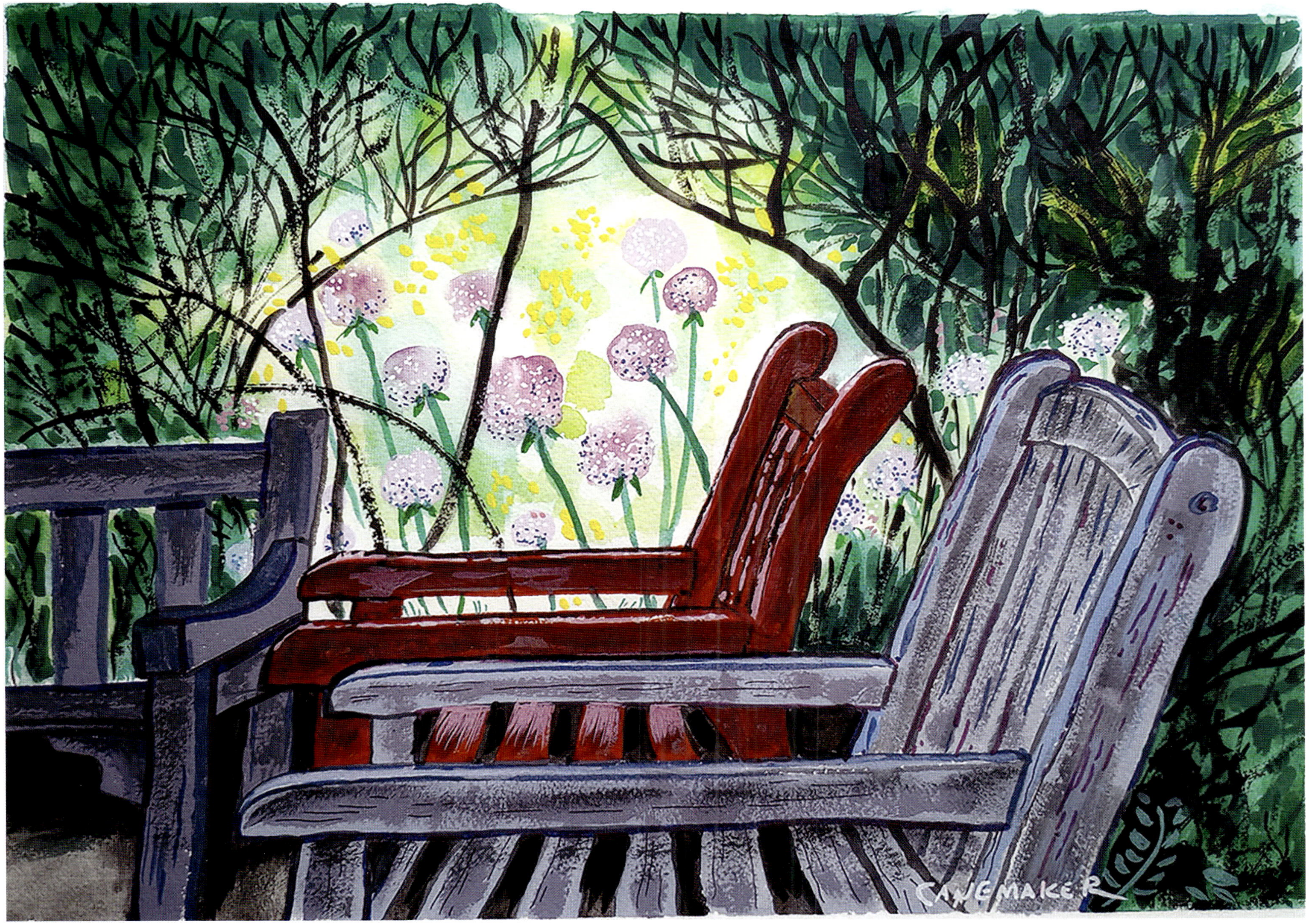
CANEMAKER

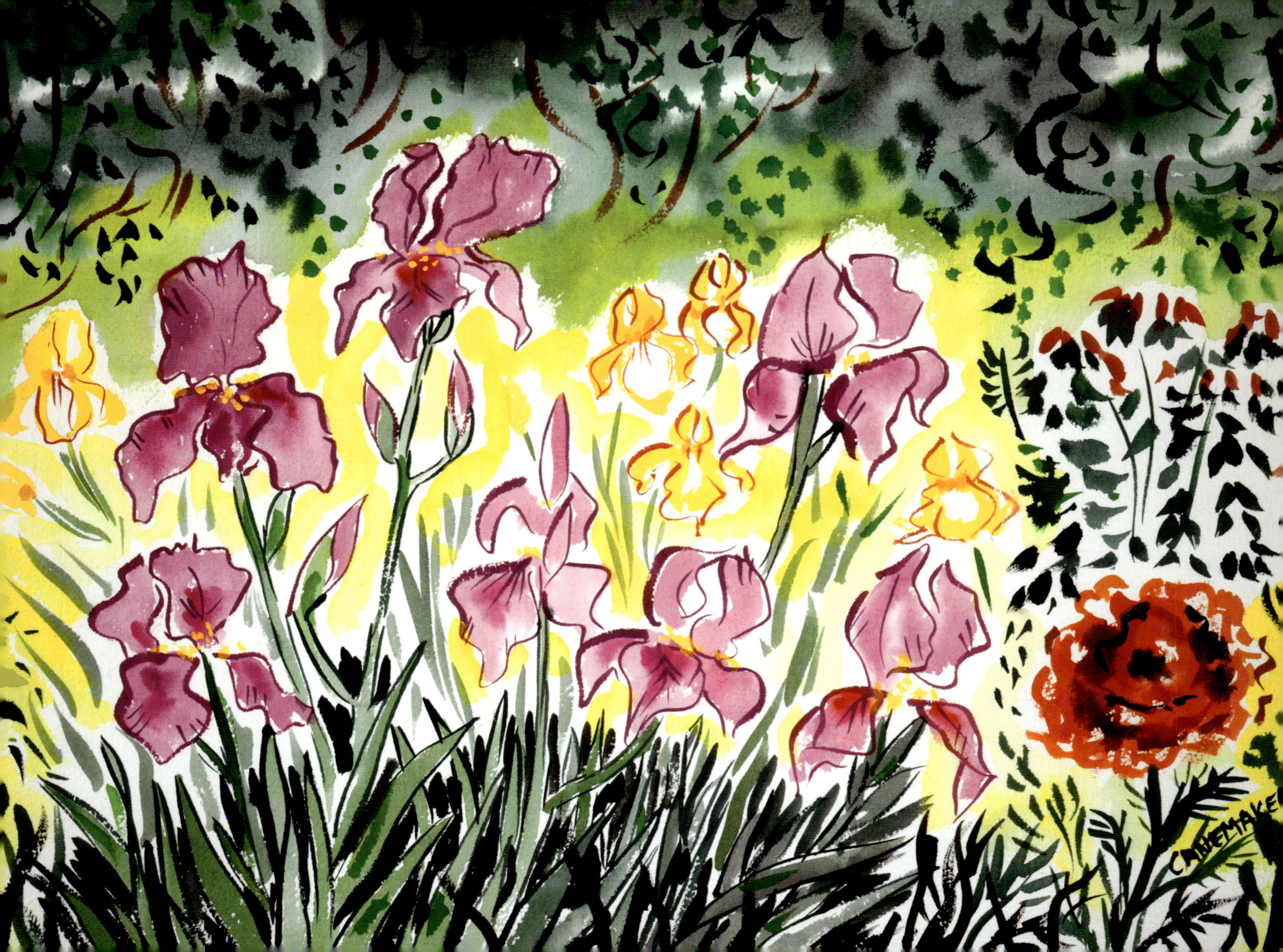

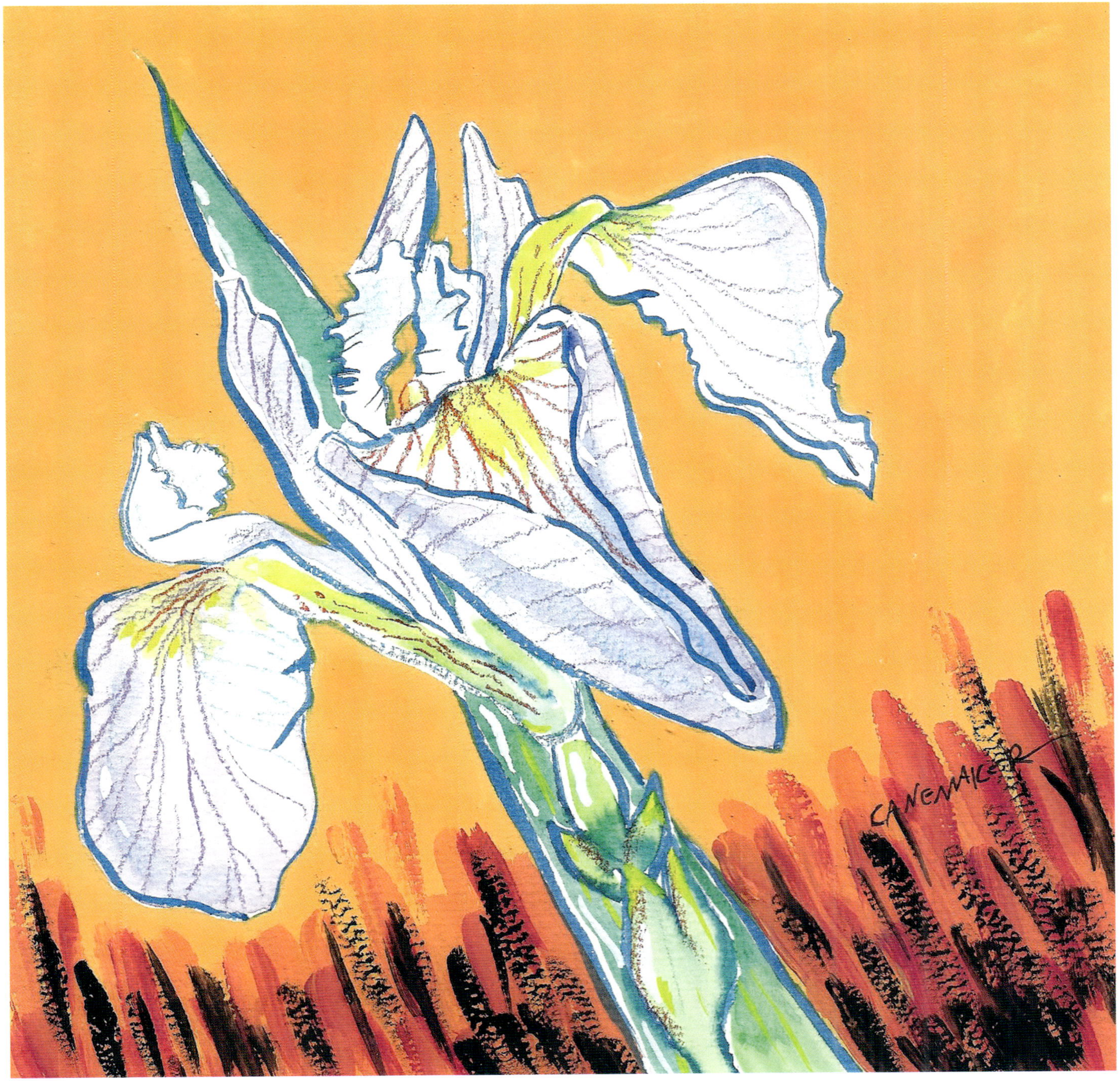

Far Left: IRIS 10x14" gouache n.d.

Left: INSATA IRIS 8X8" gouache 2021

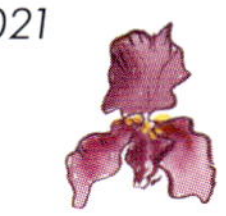

GREEN & YELLOW CATALPA 20x14 1/2" gouache 2004

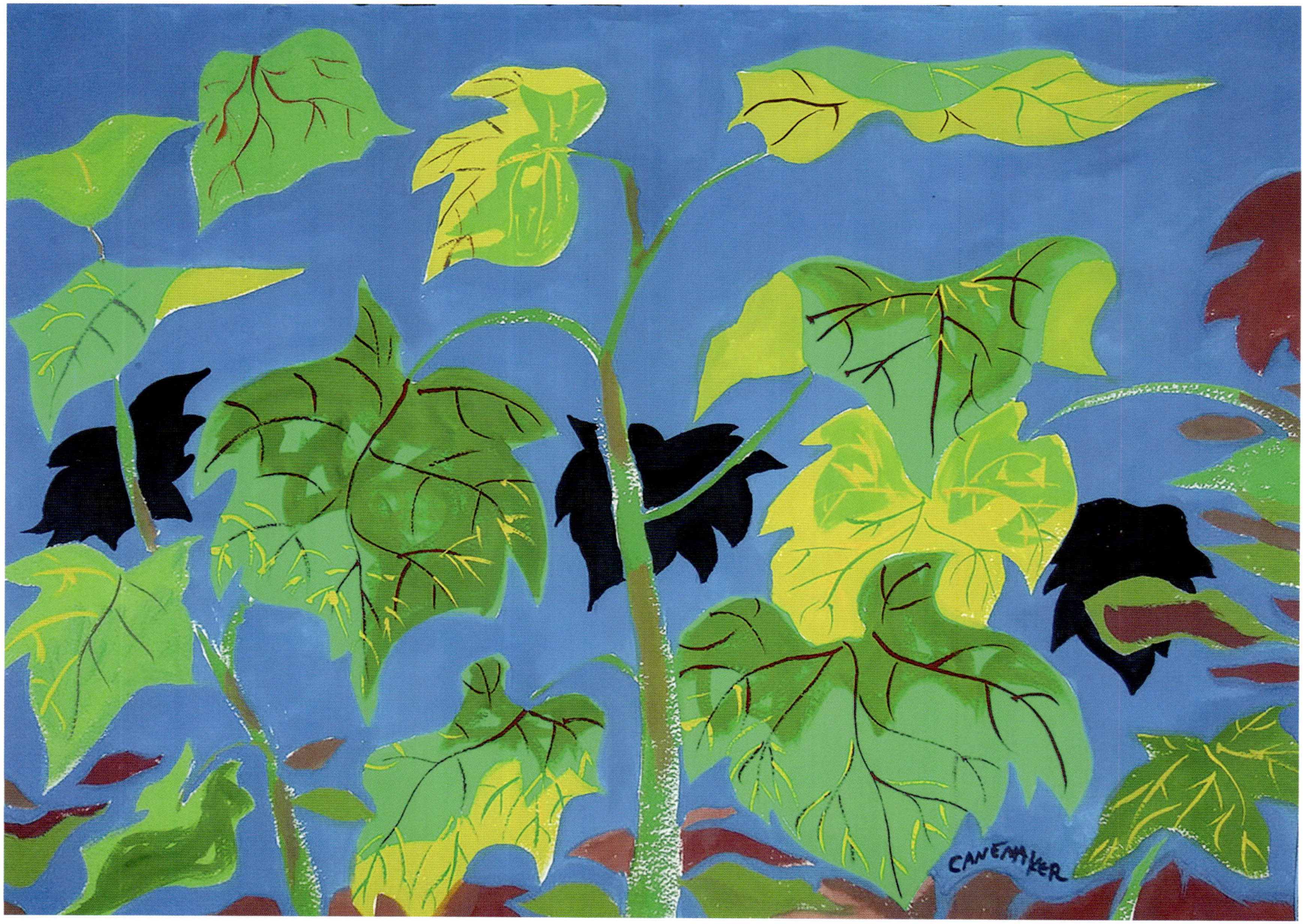

POLYPHEMOUS MOTH ASCENDING 14x20" gouache 2021

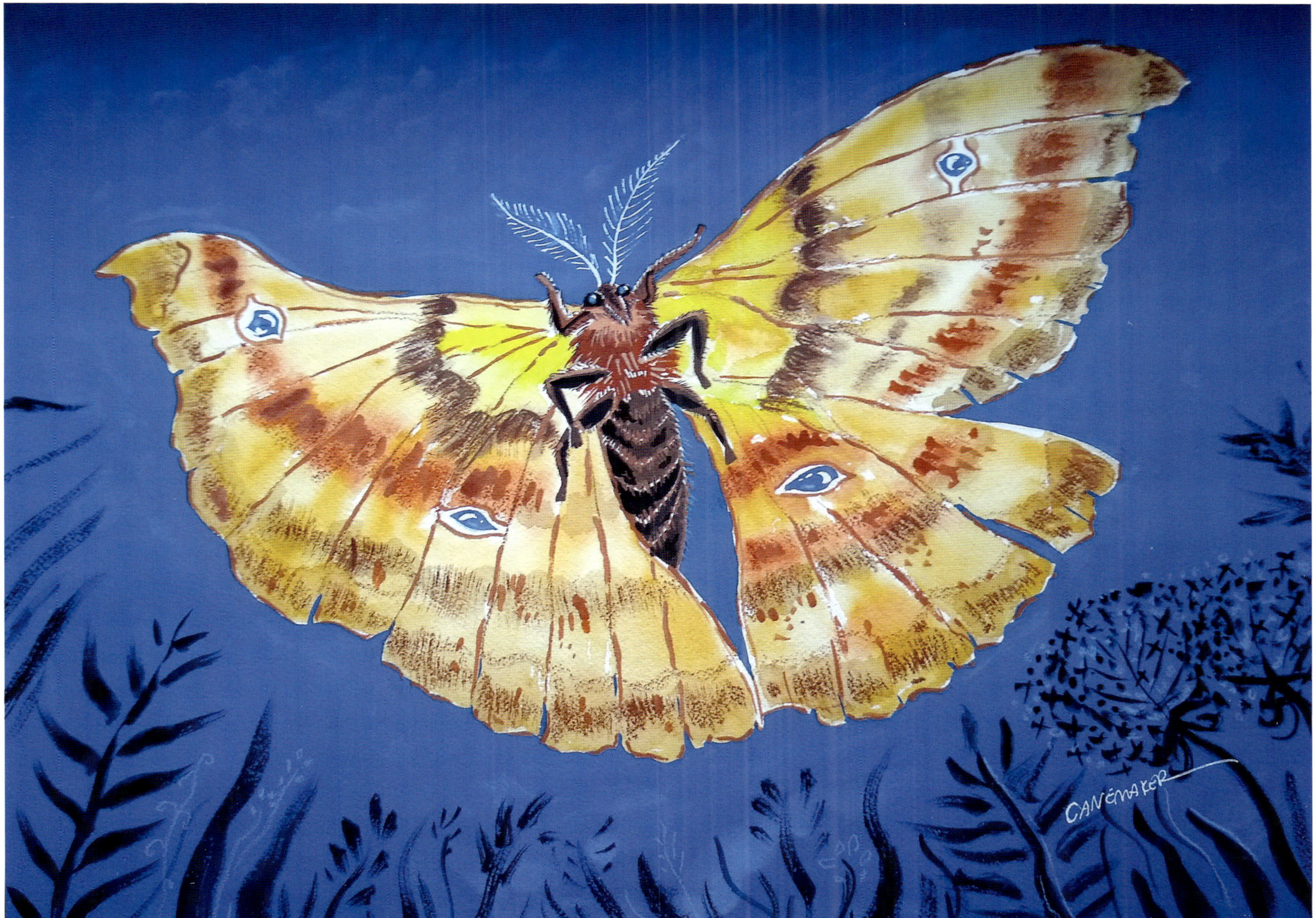

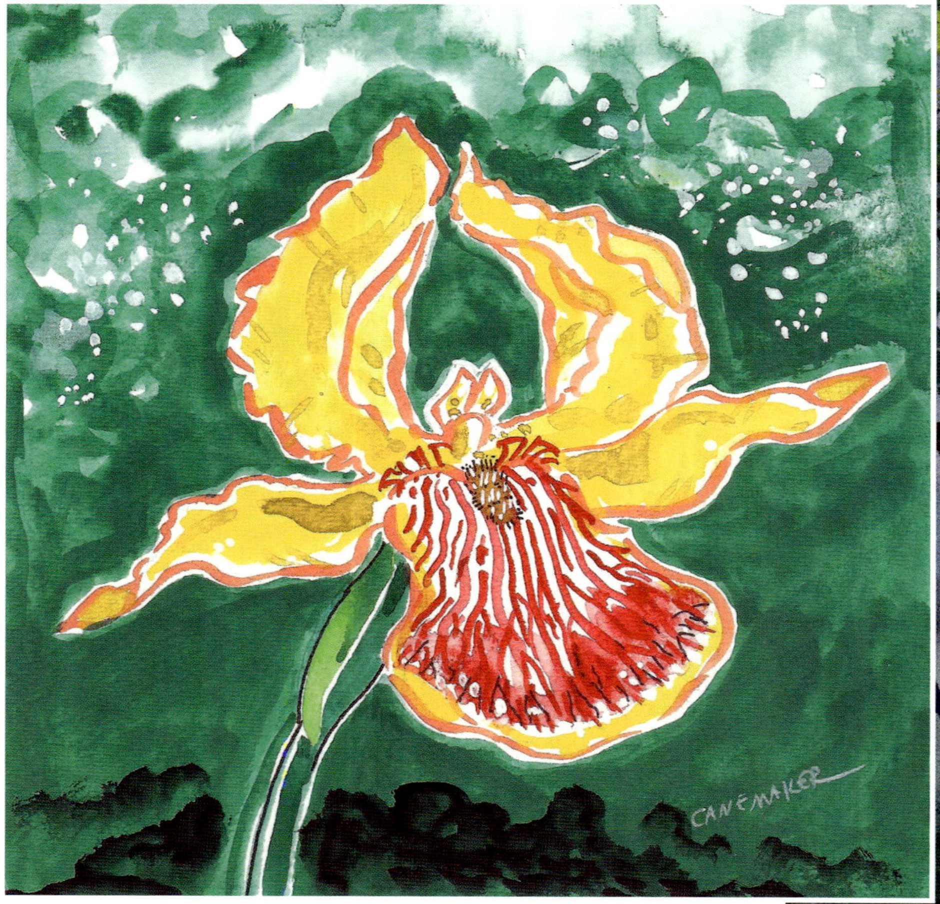
CANEMAKER

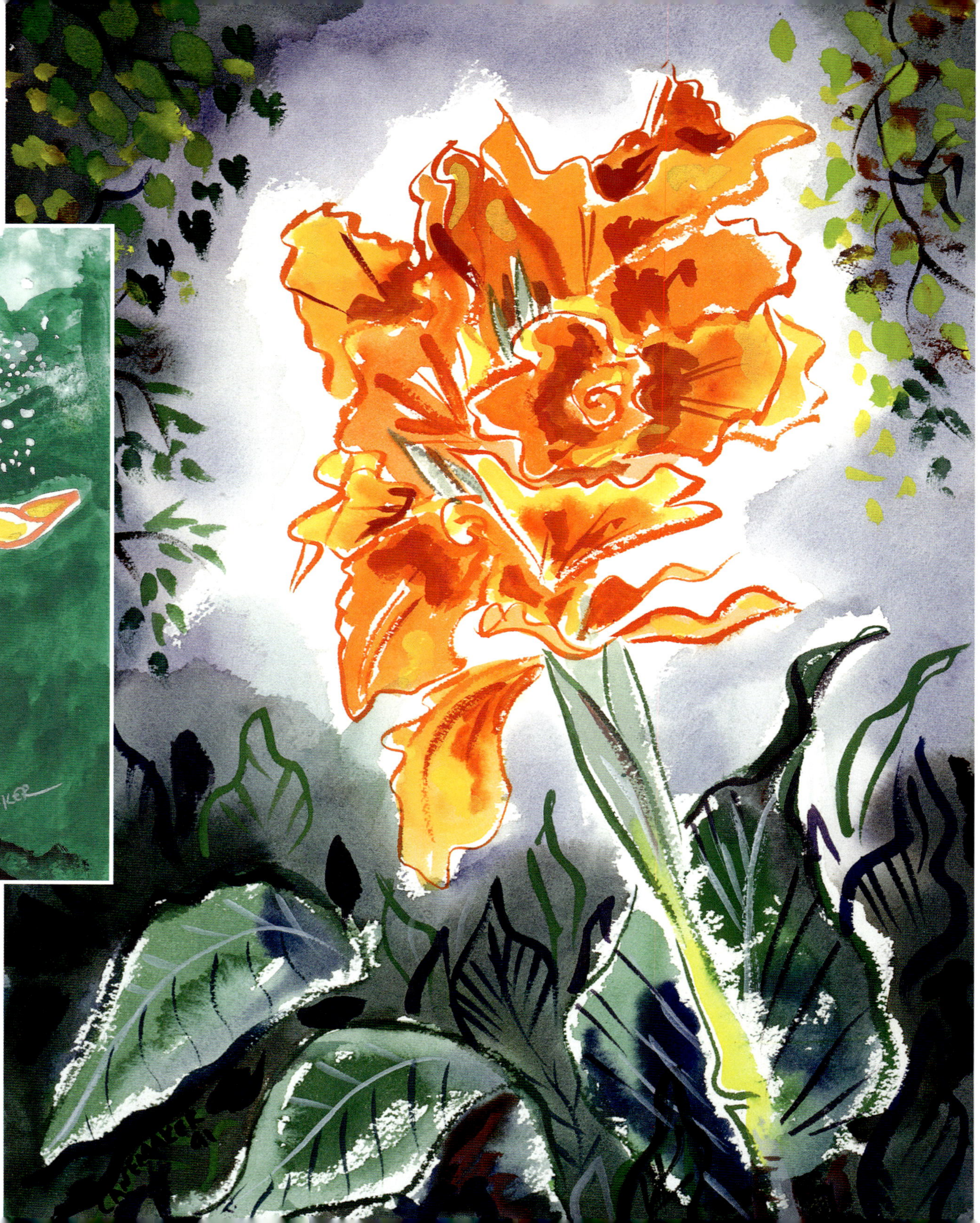

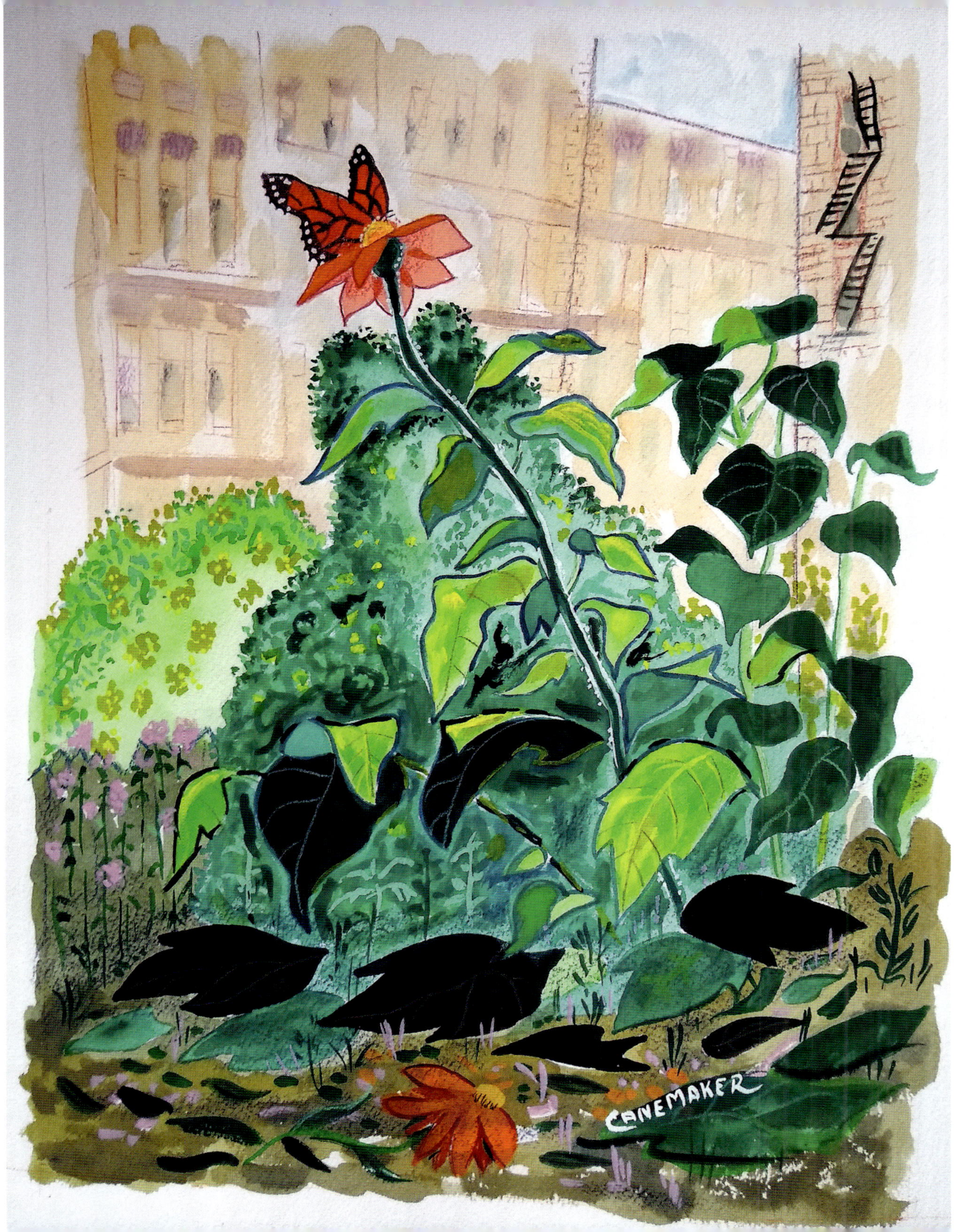

Far left, page 48: STRIPED iris 8X8" gouache 2021

Left, page 48: RED CANNA 15X12" gouache 1991

This page: THE MONARCH OF BRIDGEHAMPTON 16x12" gouache 2020

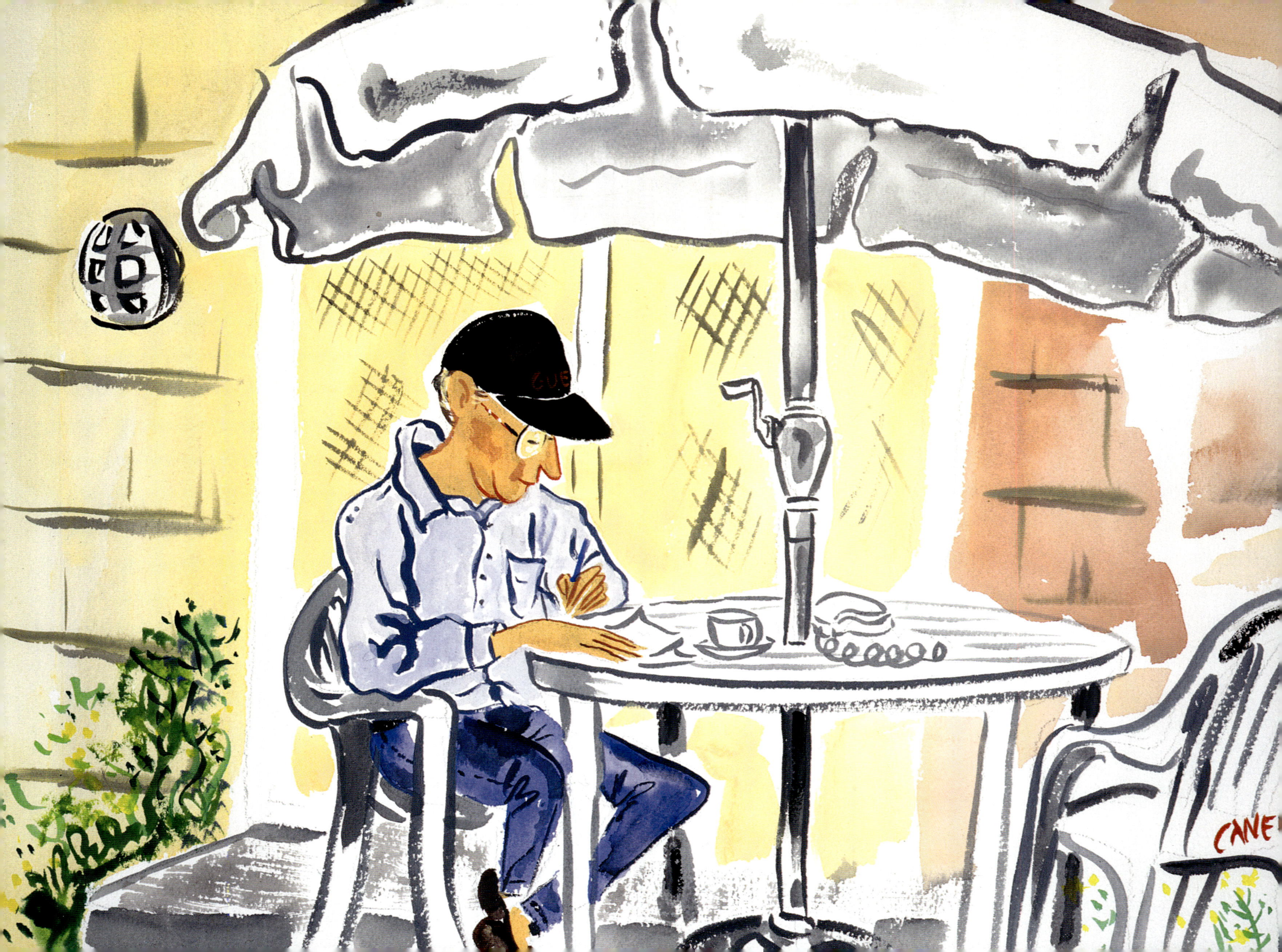
CANE

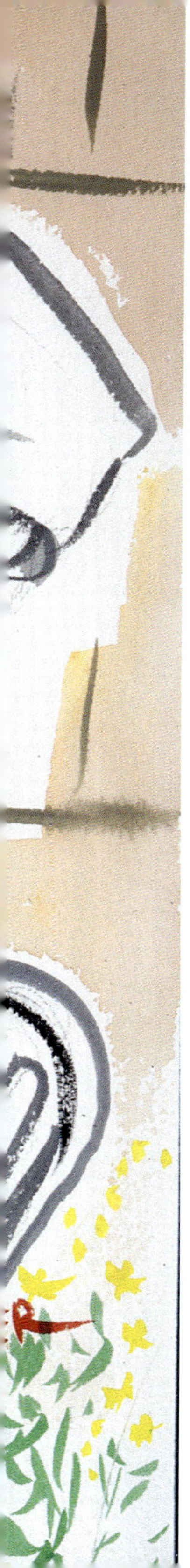

Left: JOE AT WORK 4x20" gouache 1994

Right: SELF-PORTRAIT John Canemaker 14x20" 1994

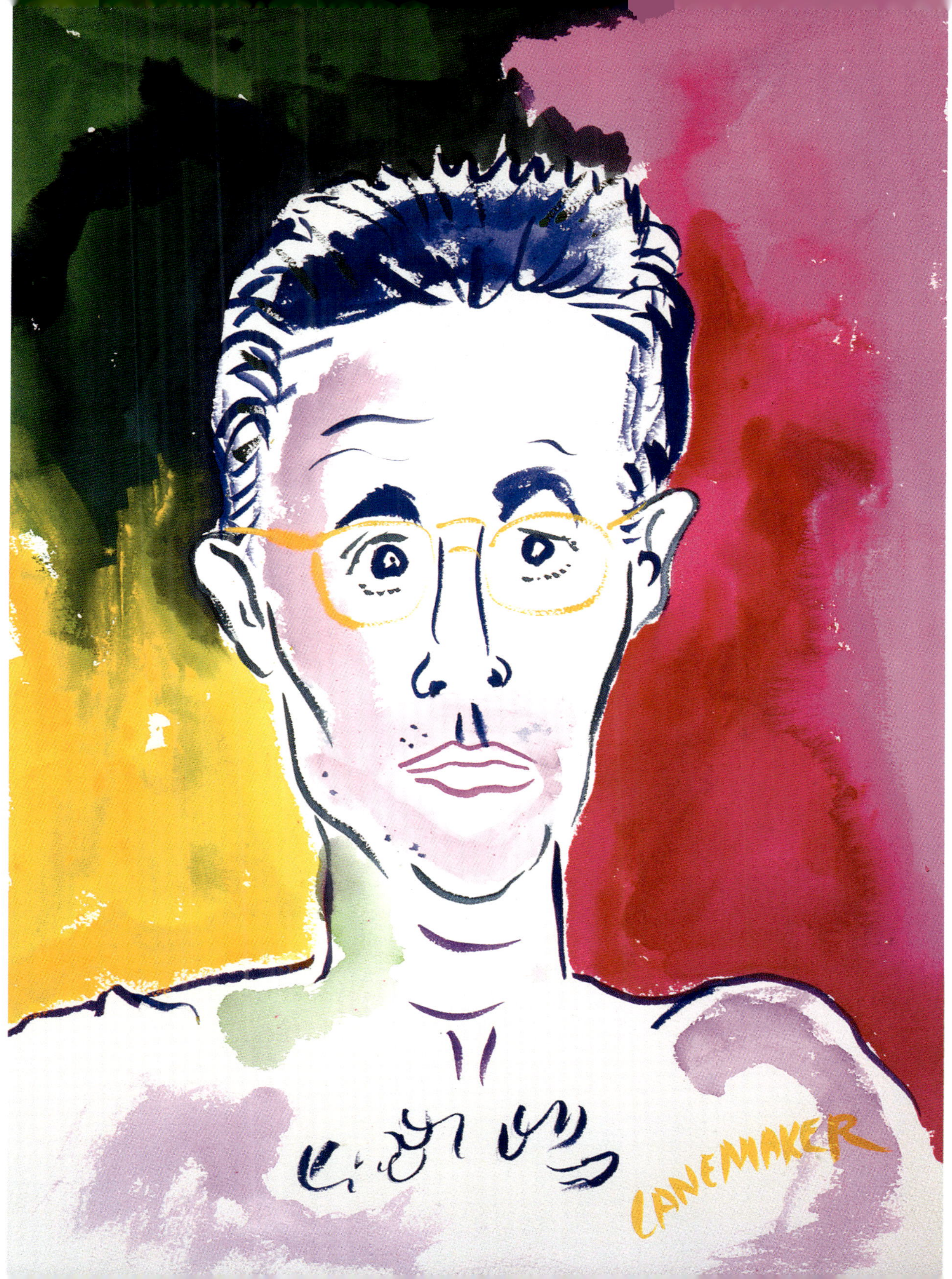

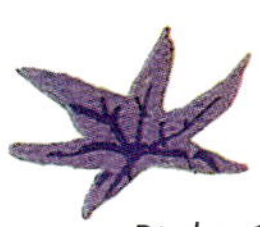

Right: O FRABJOUS DAY! 12x16" gouache 2020

Far Right: ROSE MALLOW 10x14" gouache 1991

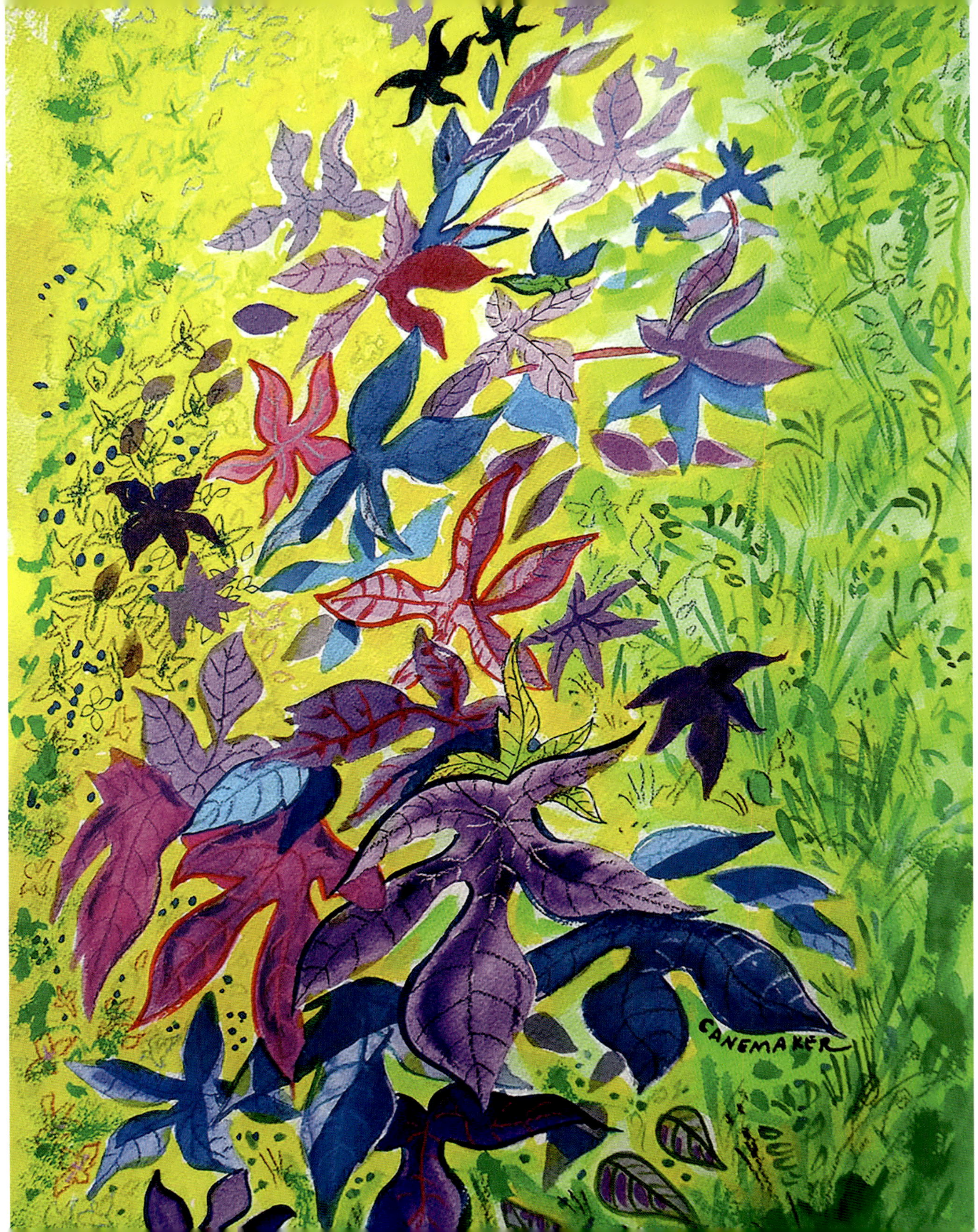

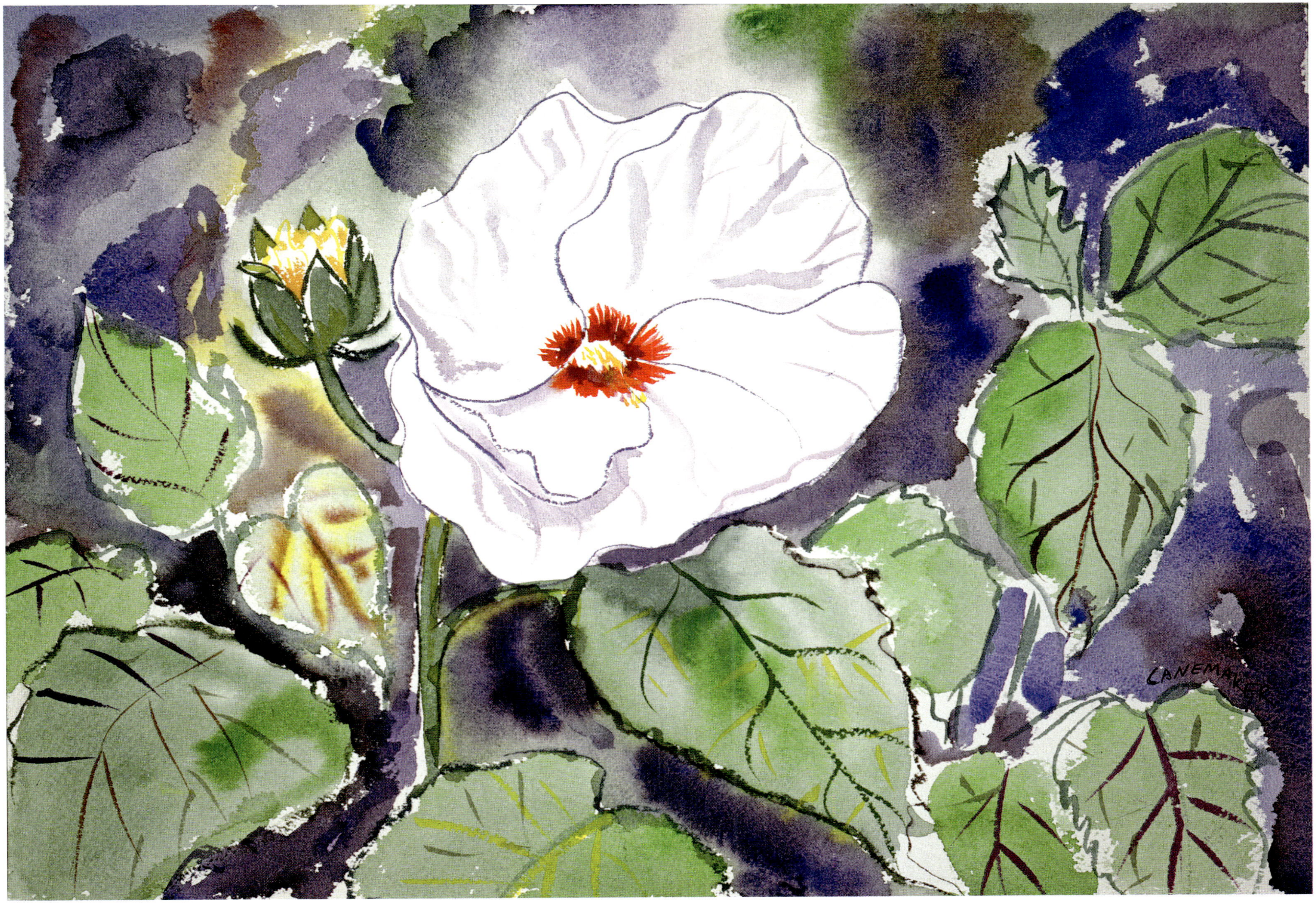
CANEMAKER

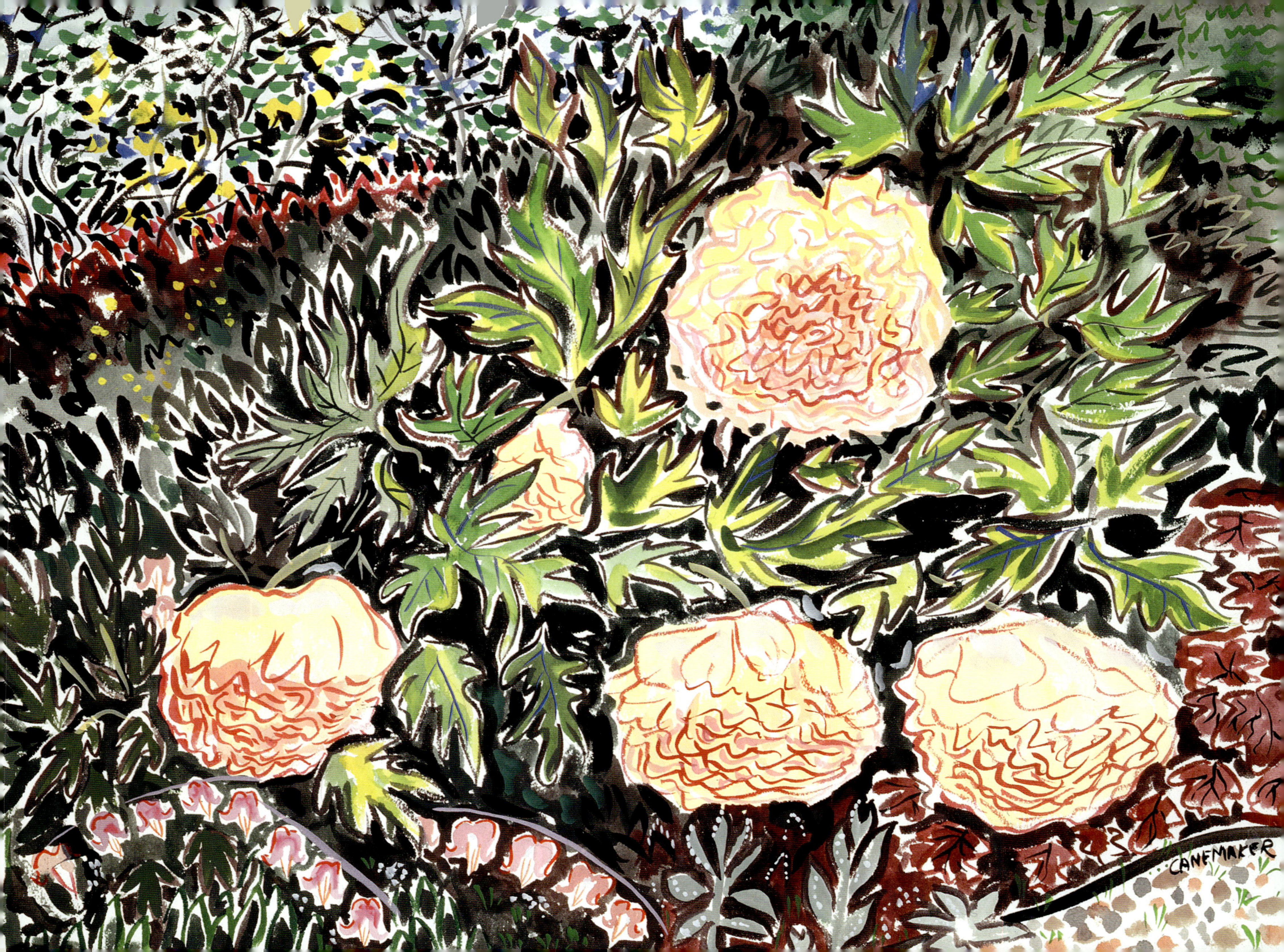
CANEMAKER

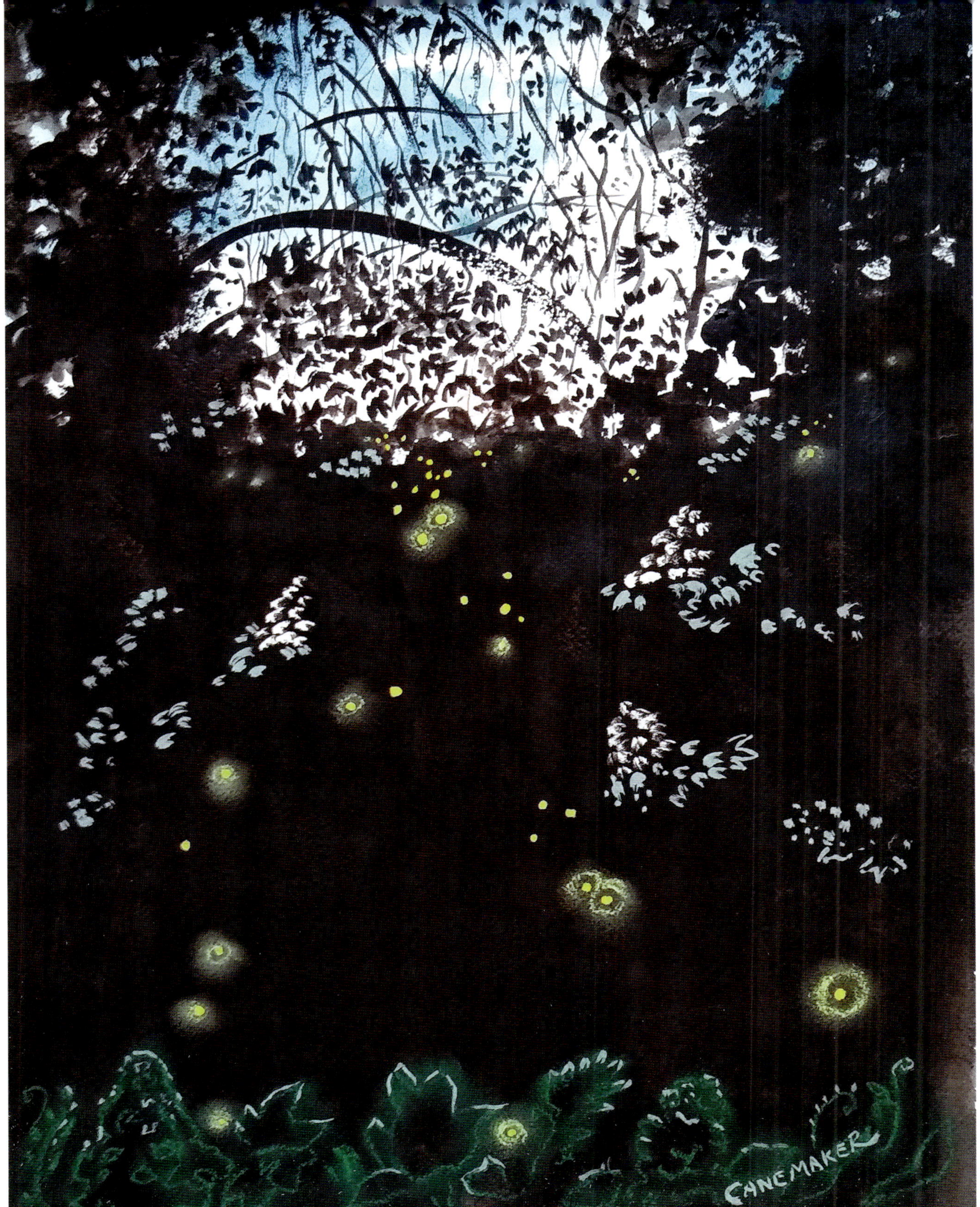

Far Left: TREE PEONIE & BLEEDING HEARTS 24x18″ gouache 2000

Left: MIDSUMMER 12x16″ gouache 2021

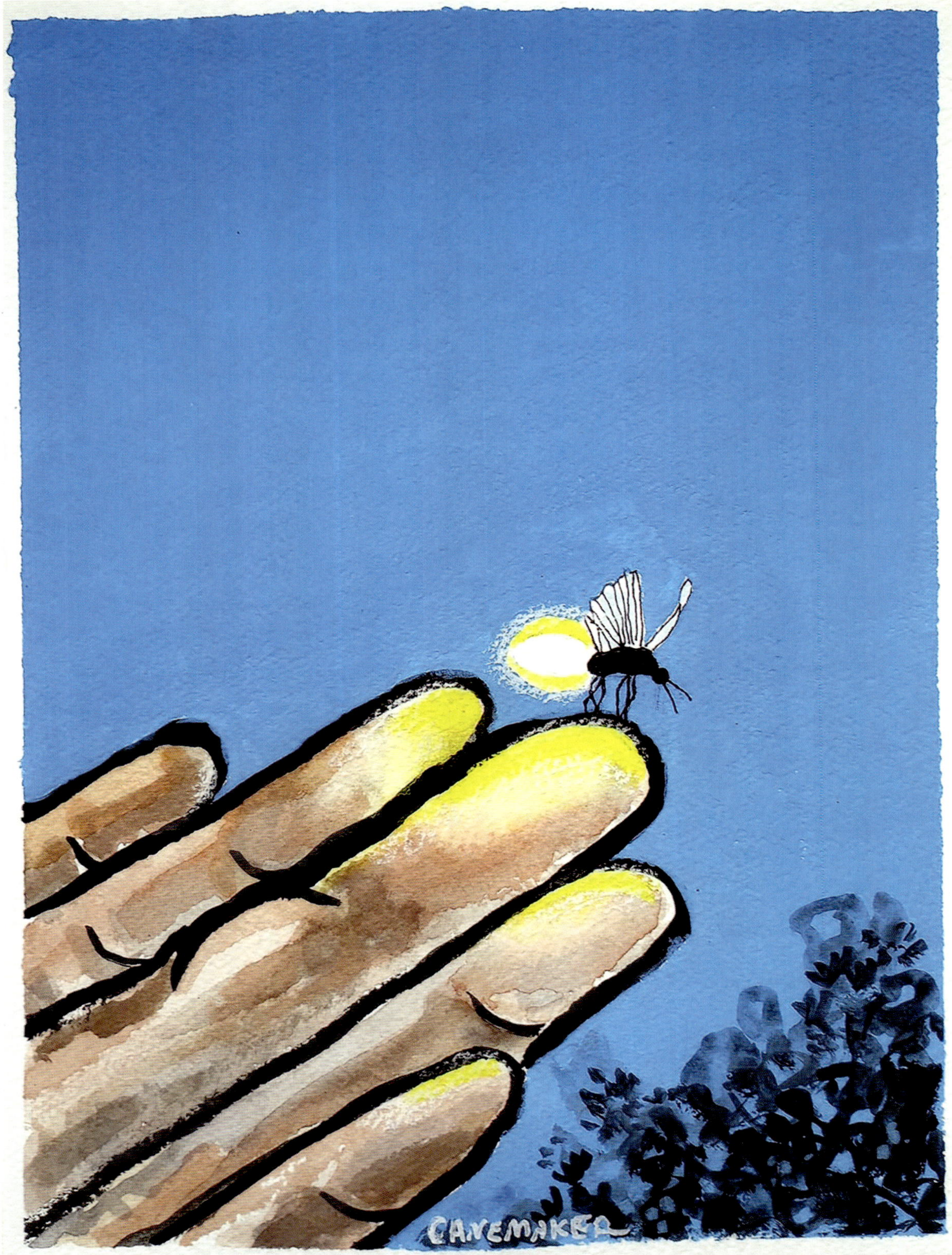

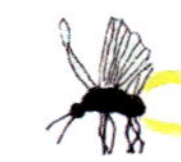

Left: NIGHT LIGHT 9x12″
gouache 2023

Right: SUMMER NIGHTIME 10x14″
gouache 1991

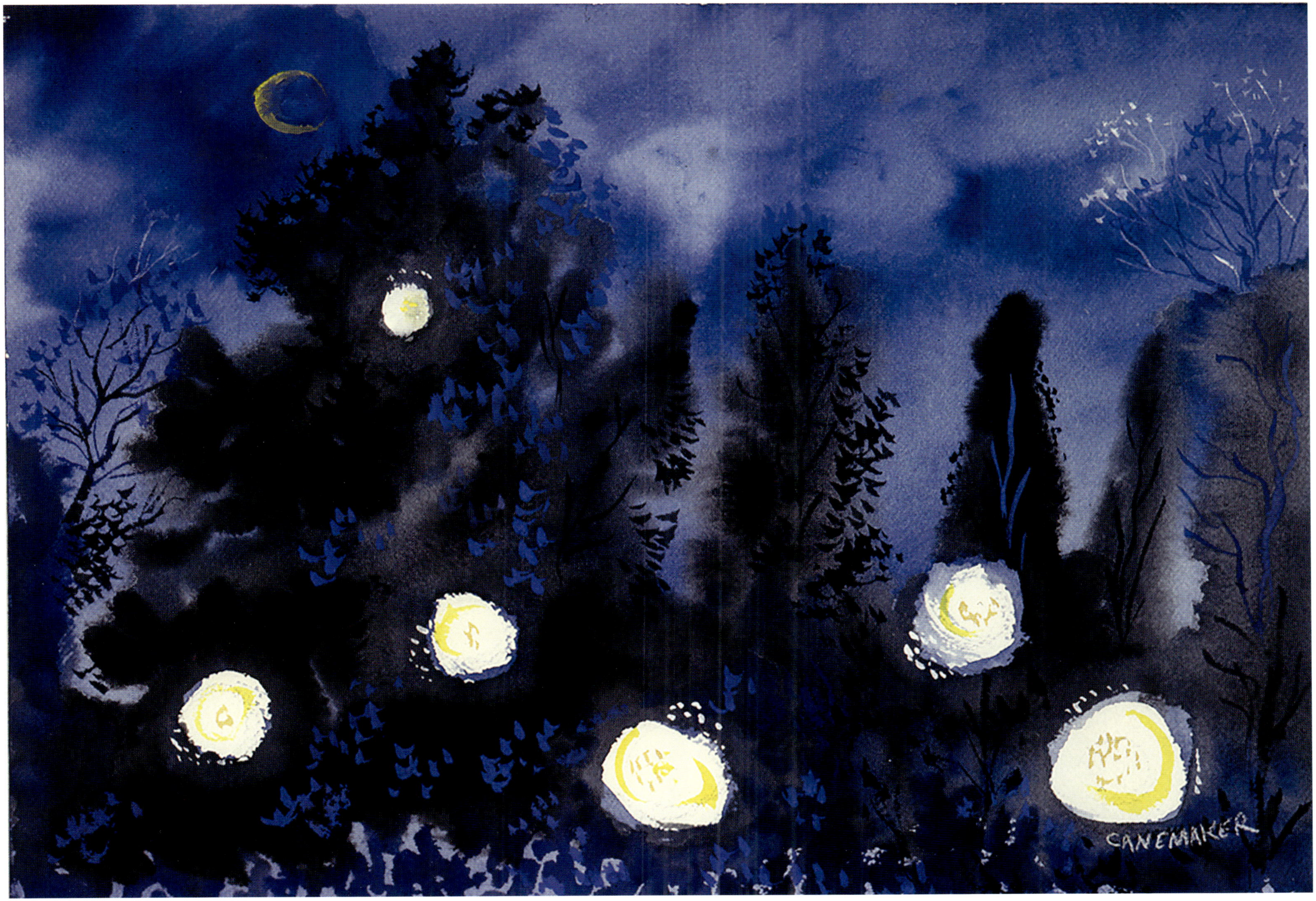
CANEMAKER

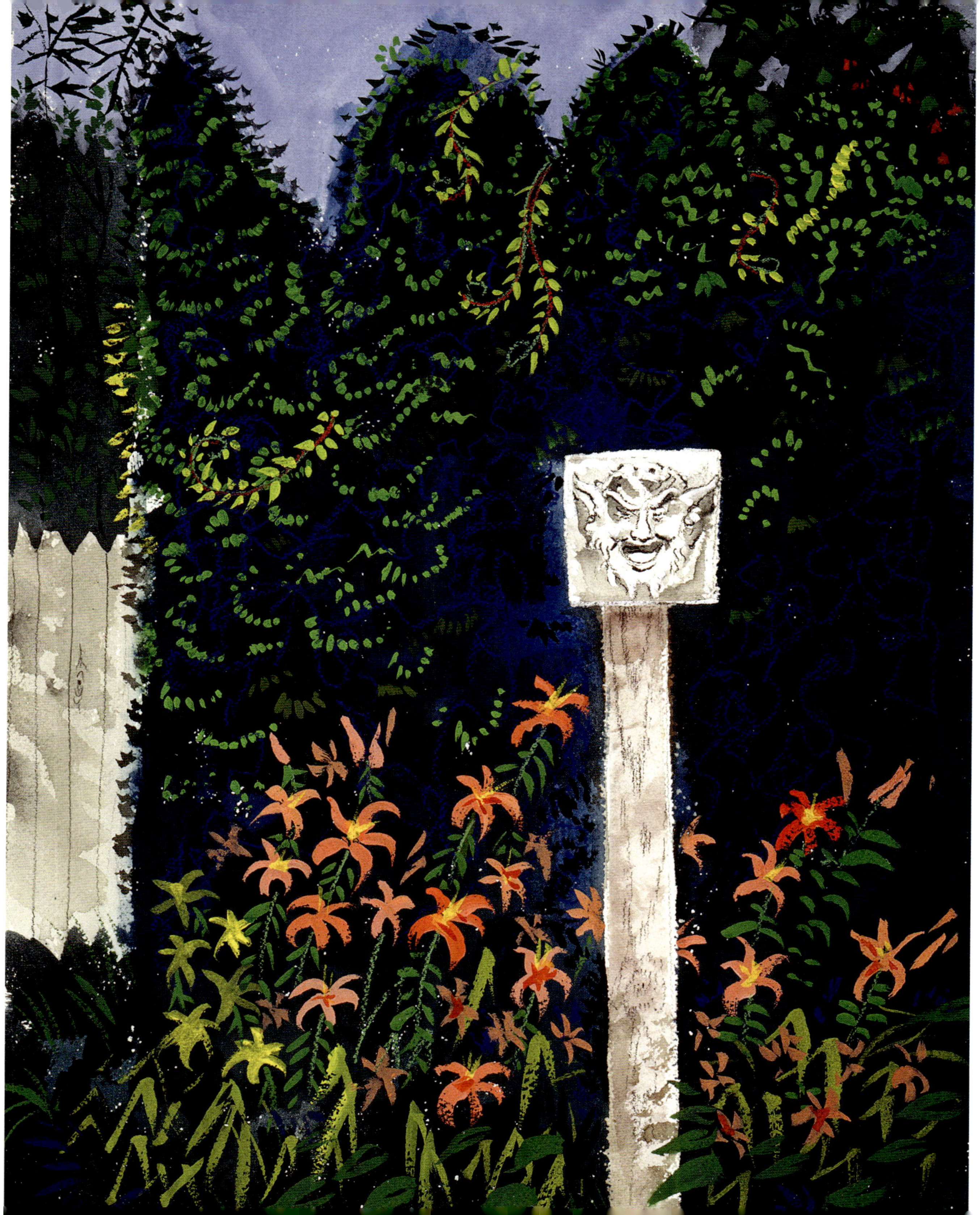

Left: SATYR 15 1/2x11 1/2
gouache 1990

Right: OVER THE FENCE 16x12"
gouache 1991

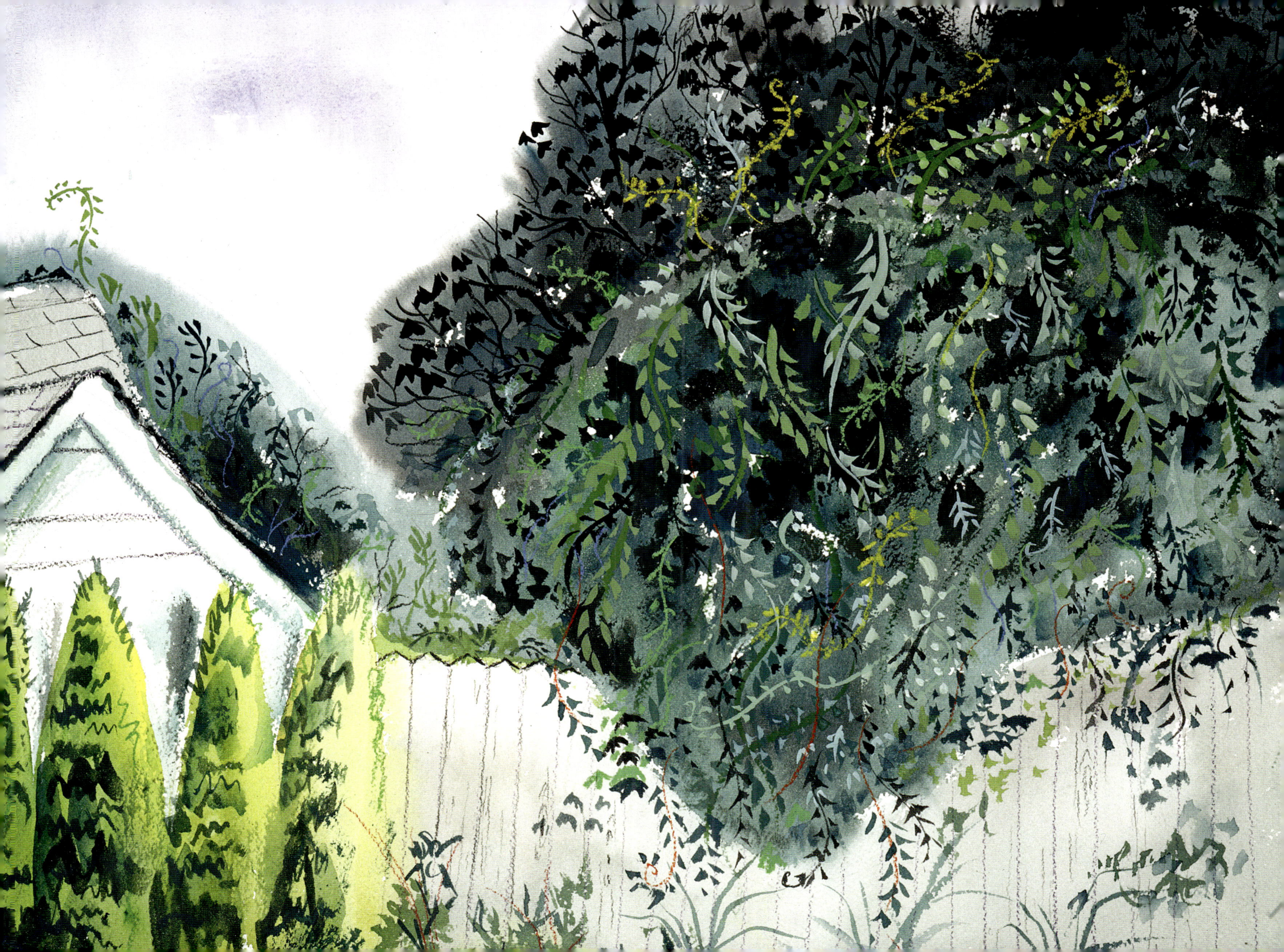

Autumn

"I am no pantheist or sentimentalist in my love of Nature but simply an idolater of leaf, hill, stream and stone."

- V. S. Pritchett, *The Turn of the Years*

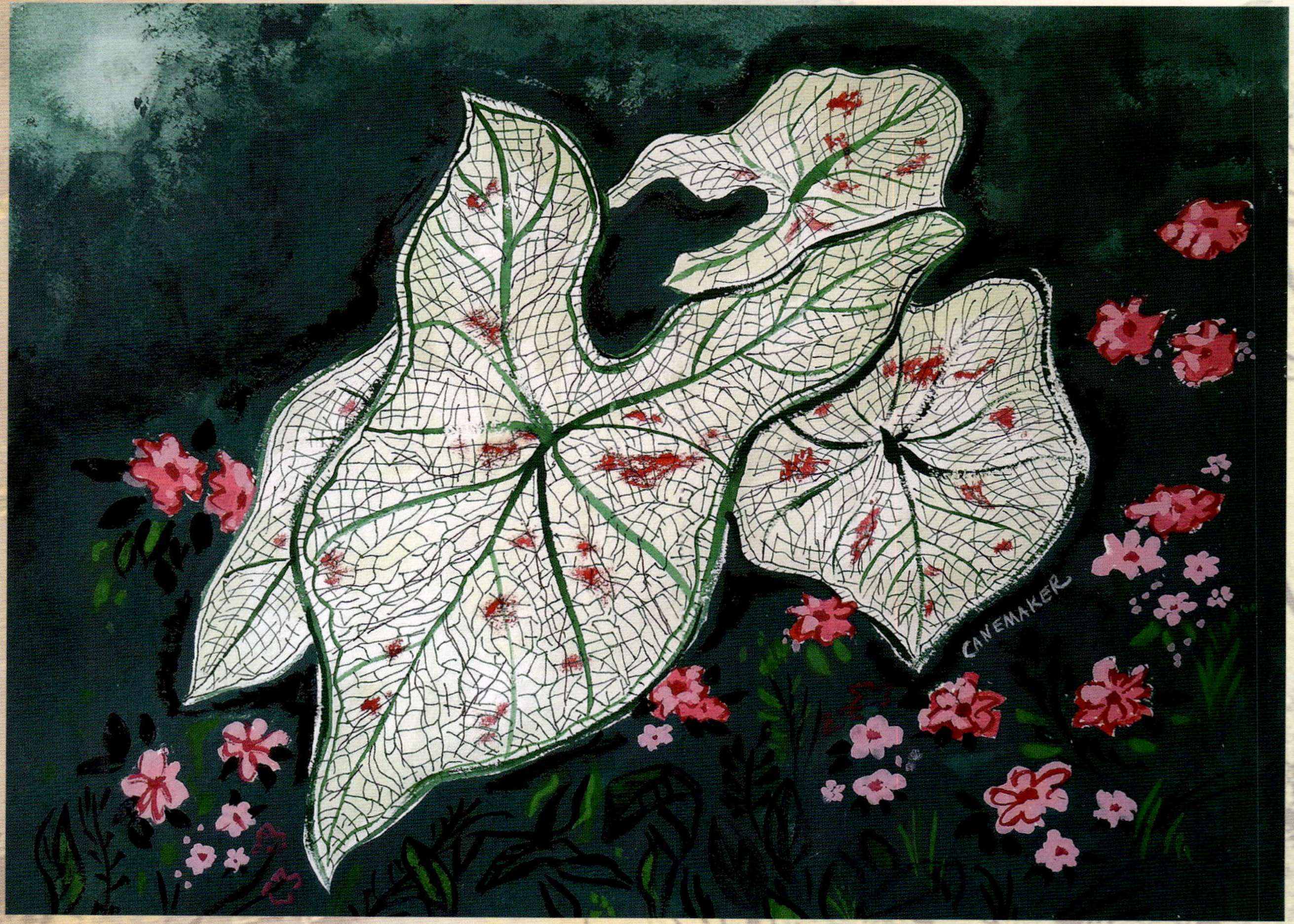

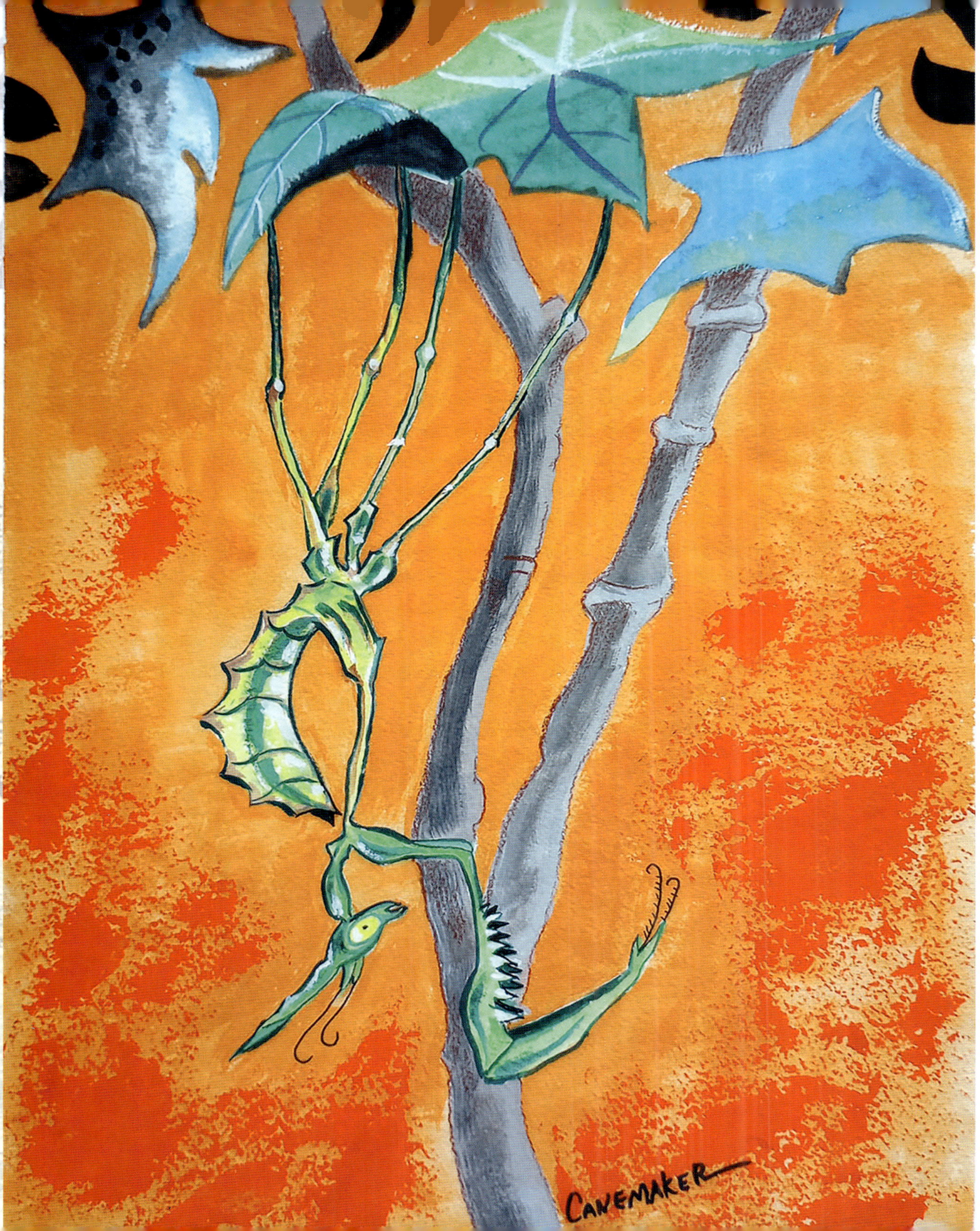

Far Left: CALADIUM BICOLOR - QUEEN OF LEAFY PLANTS 12x16" gouache 2020

Left: WANDERING VIOLIN MANTIS 12x16" gouache 2023

QUEEN ANNE'S LACE 10x14" gouache 1991

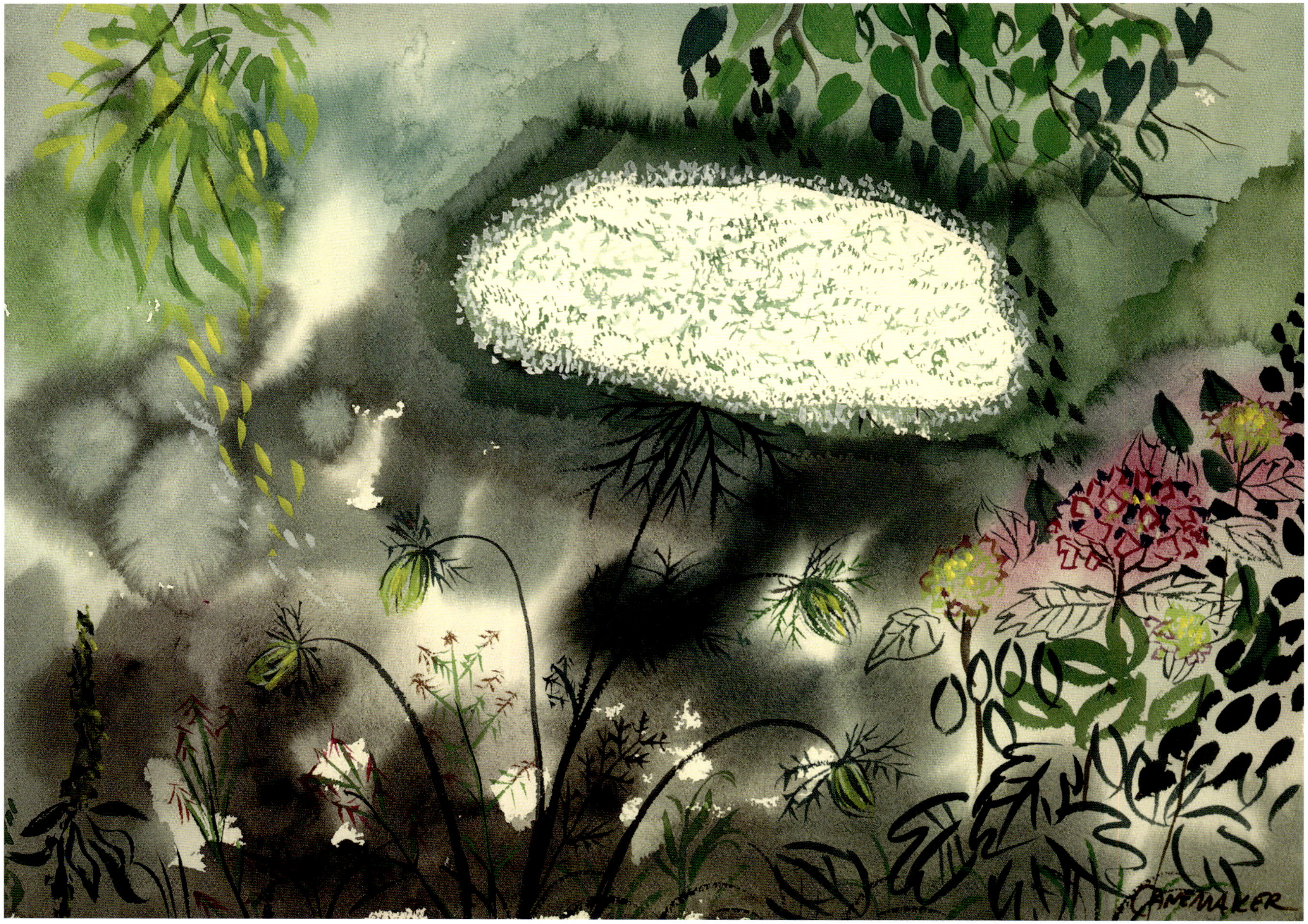

QUEEN ANNE'S LACE 14x10 1/4" gouache 2019

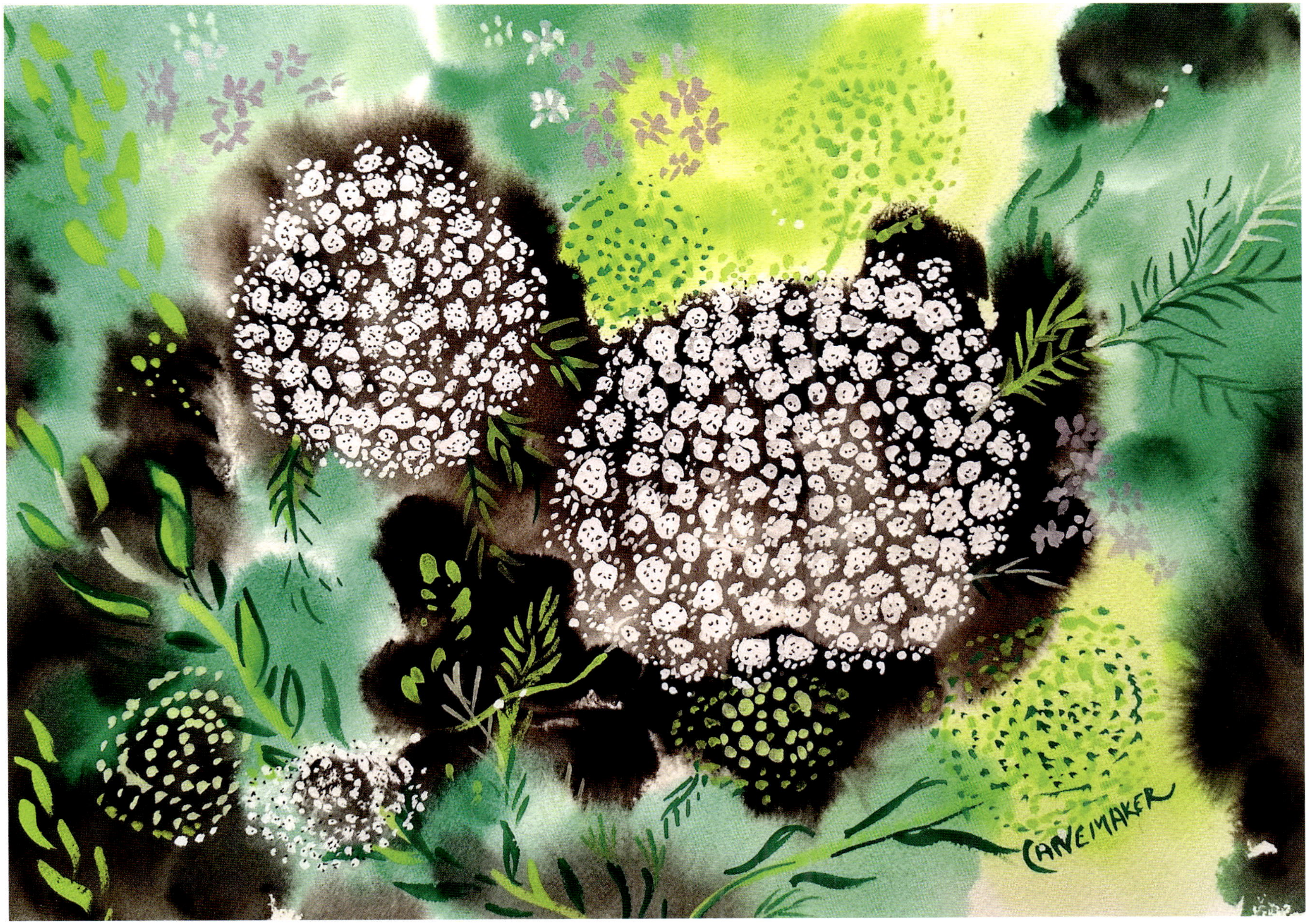

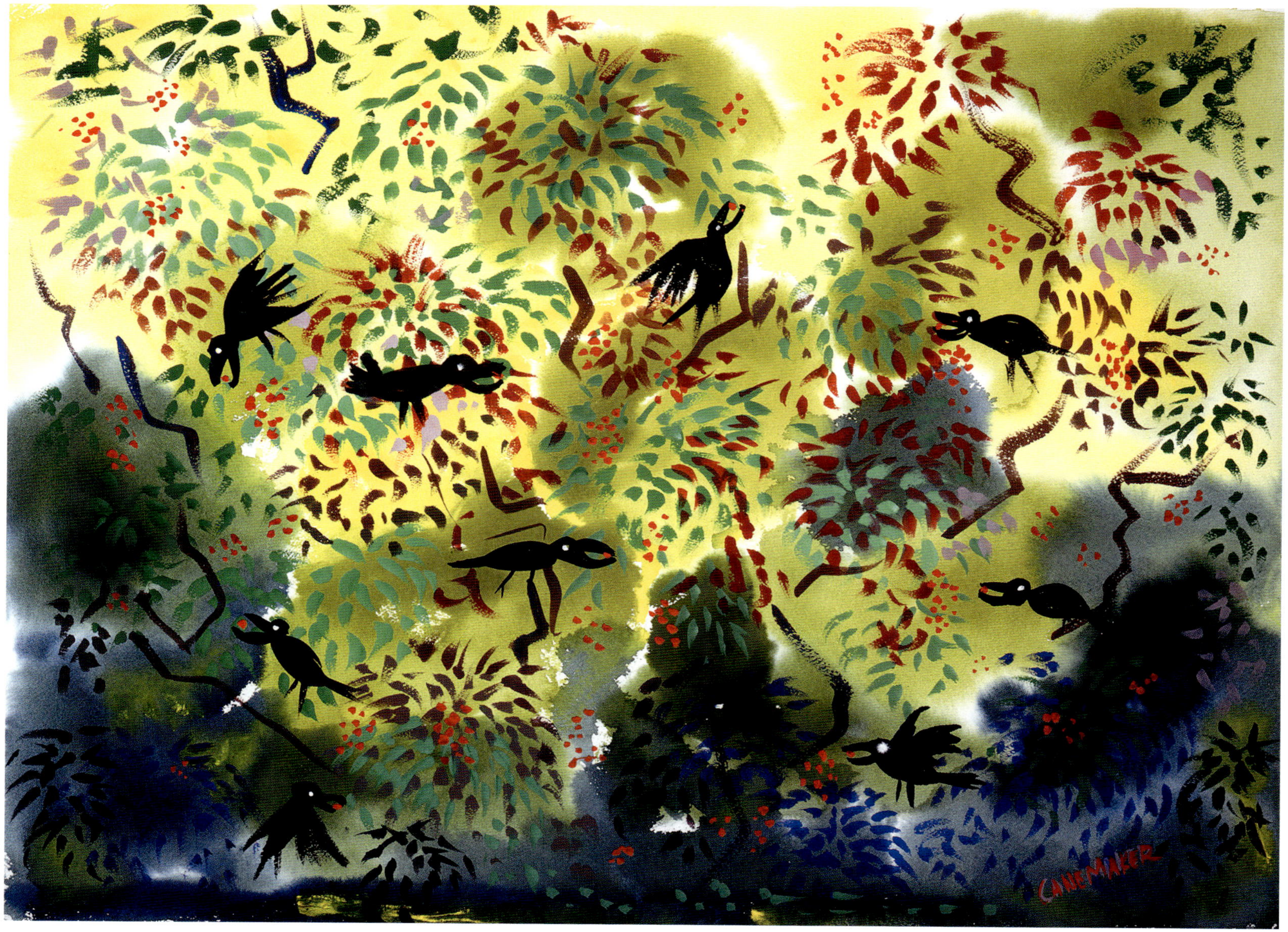

Left: RAVENOUS RAVENS 24x18″
gouache 1993

Right: GARDEN RHYTHM 19x13″
gouache 1994

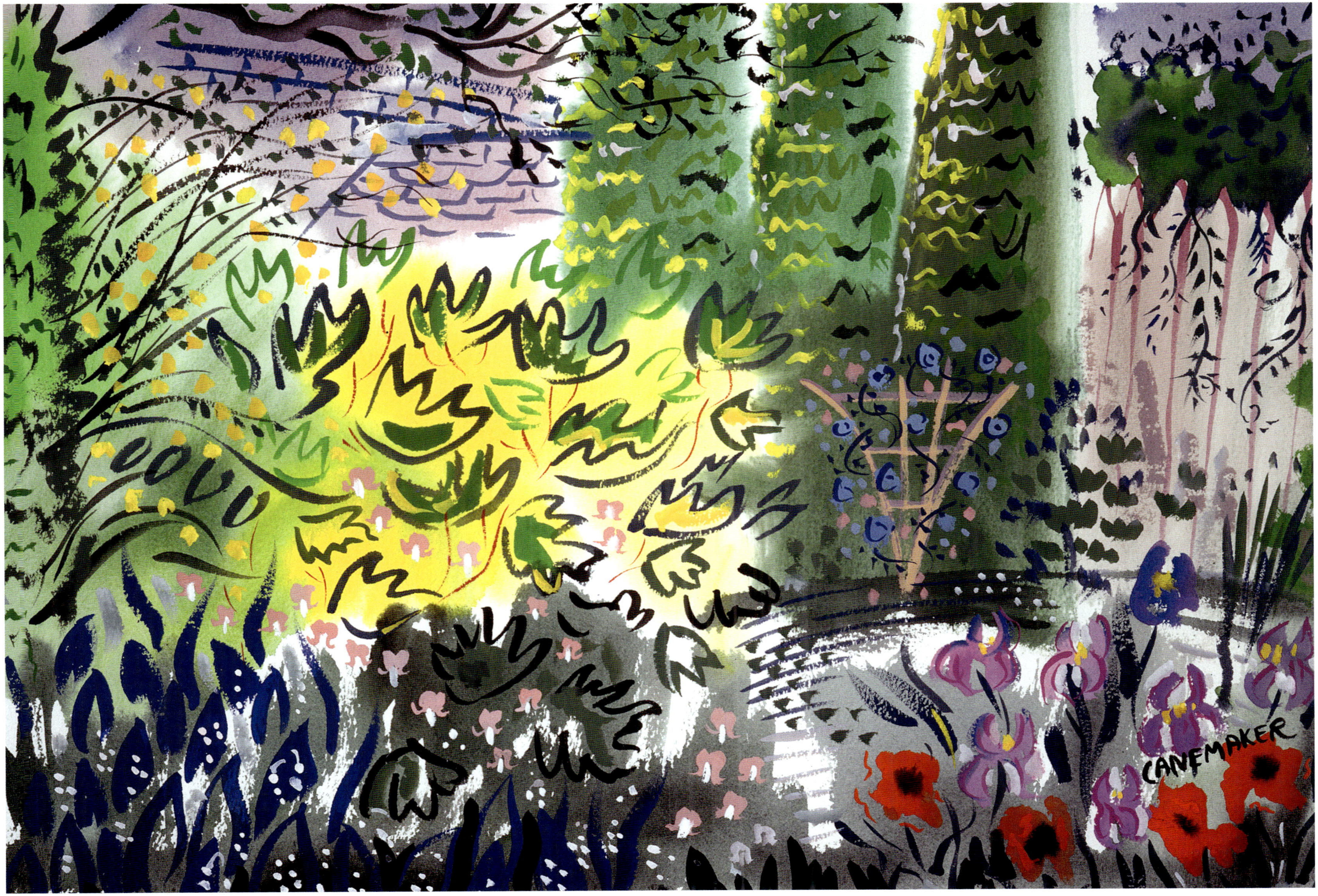
CANEMAKER

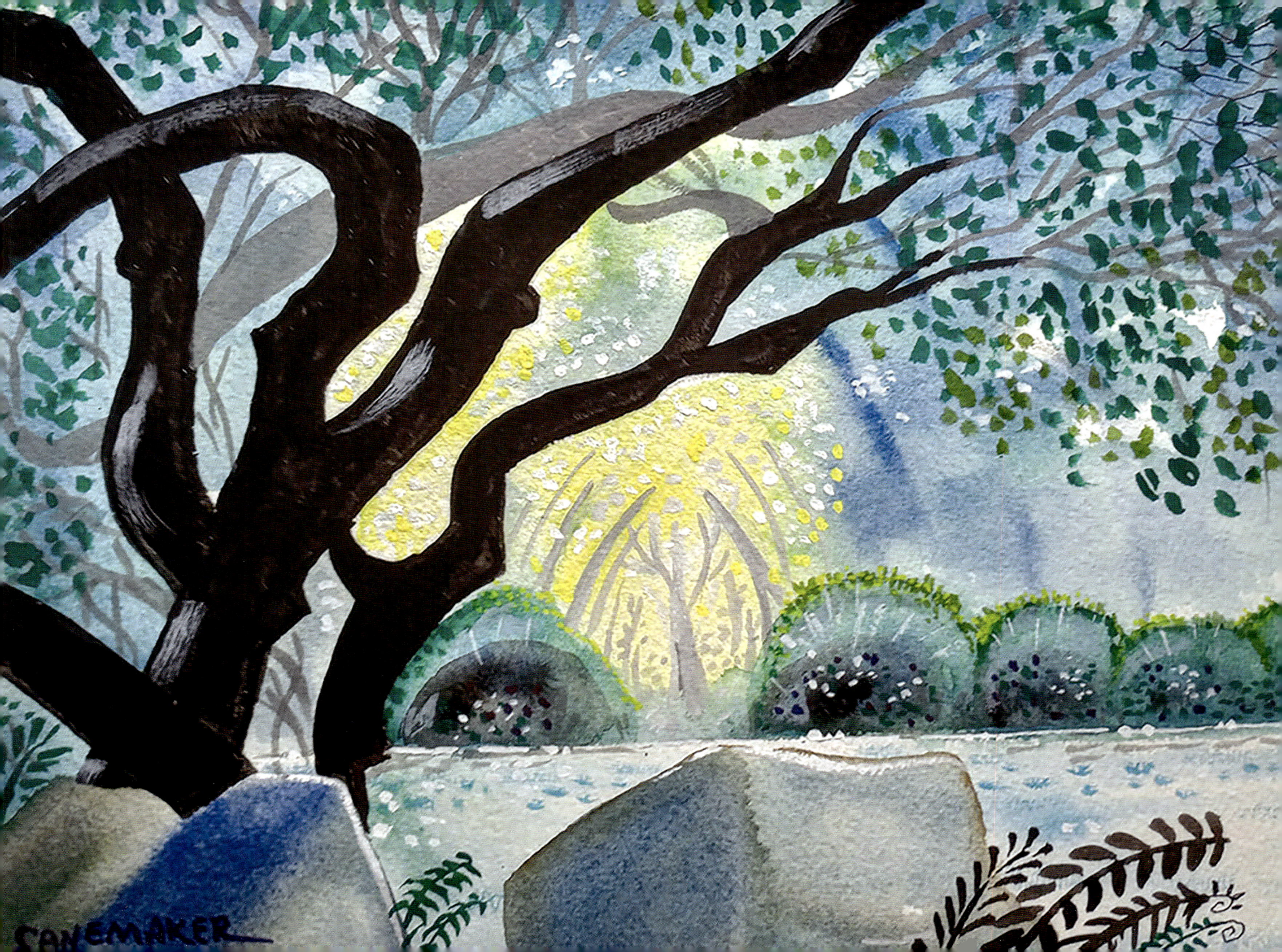
CANEMAKER

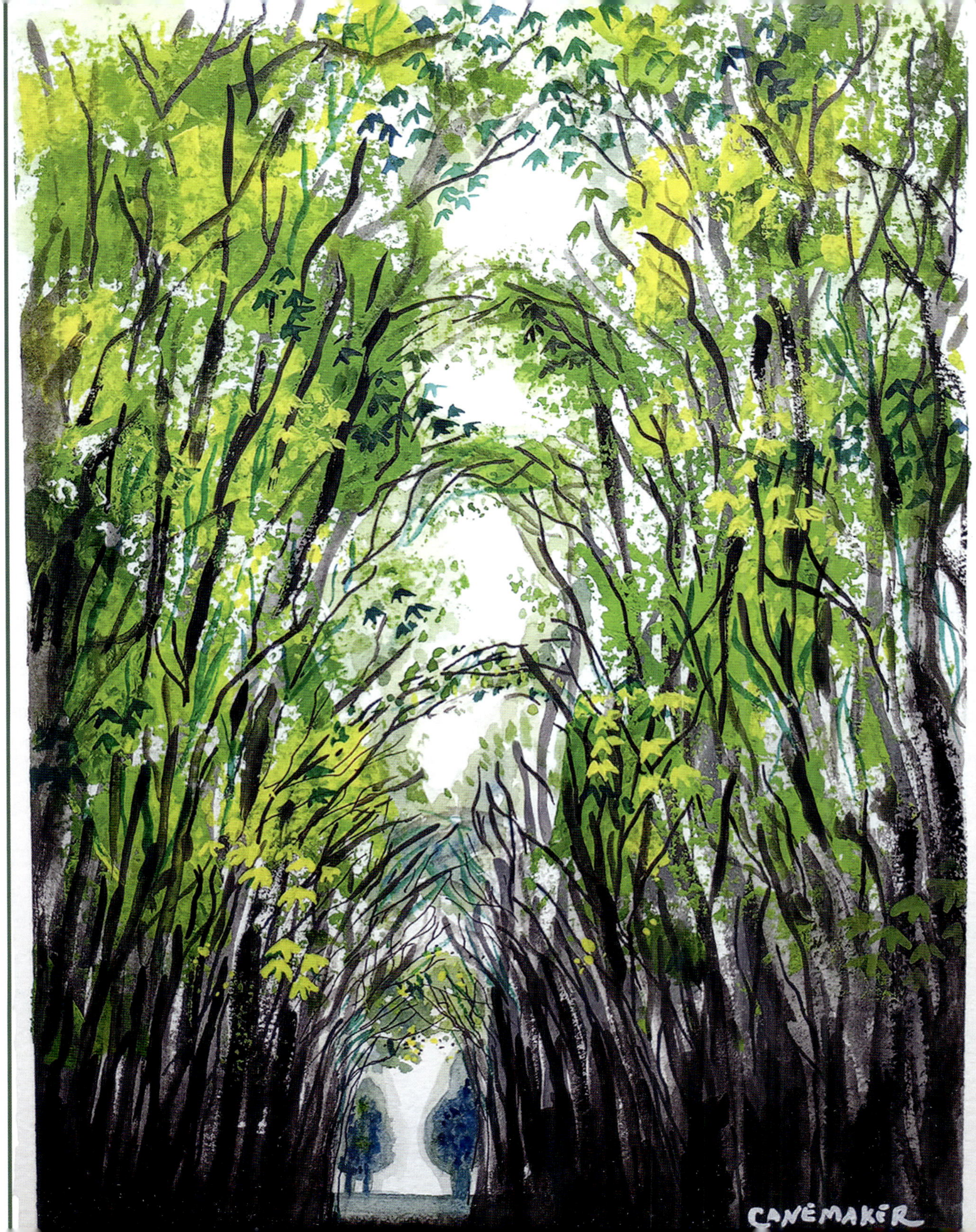

Far Left: STILL LIGHT 9x12" gouache 2023

Left: ALLEE OF CHESTNUT TREES 9x12 1/4" gouache 2023

WILD RASPBERRY 15 1/2x12" gouache 1990

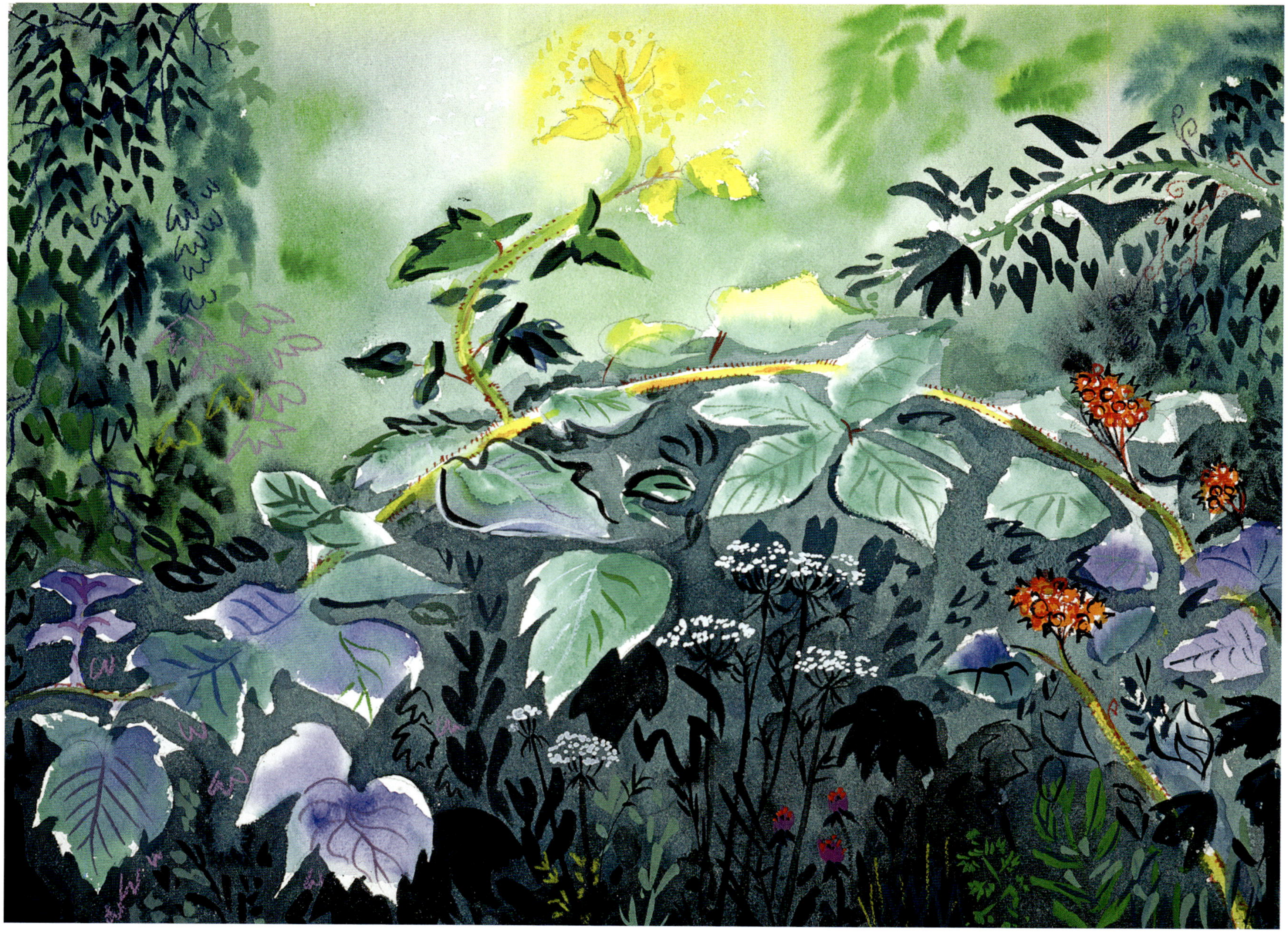

AUTUMN DAWN 13 1/2x 19" gouache 1994

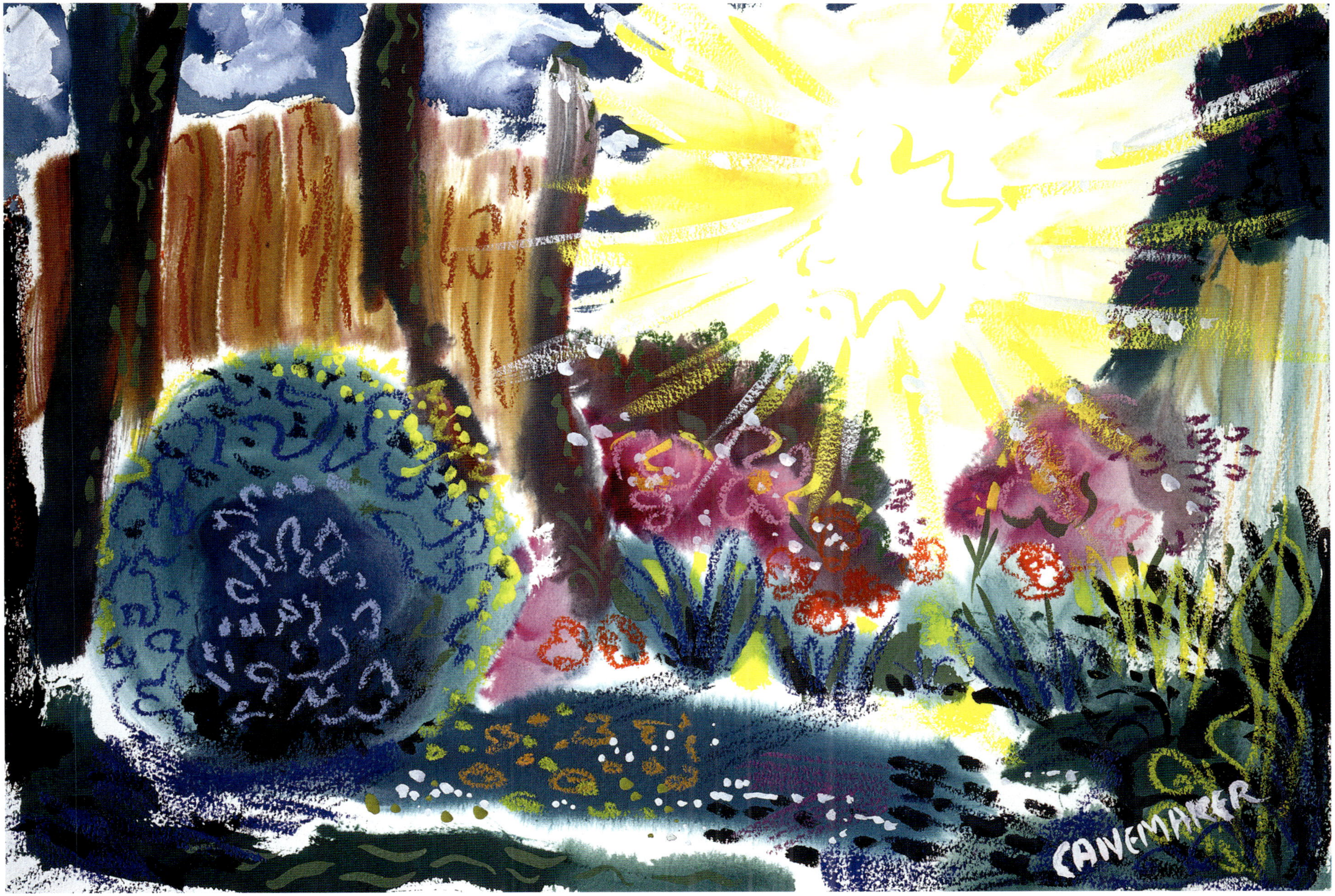

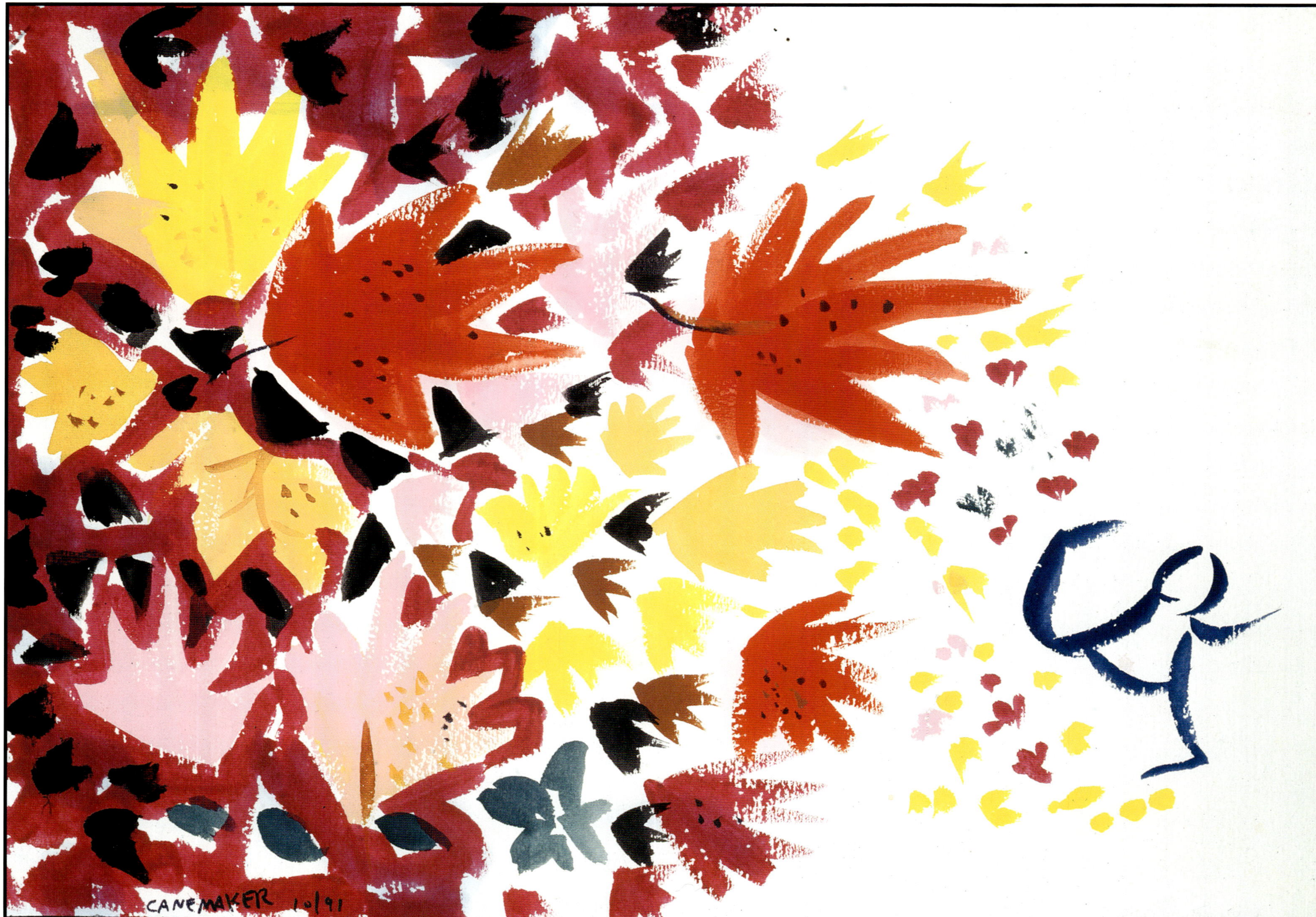
CANEMAKER 10/91

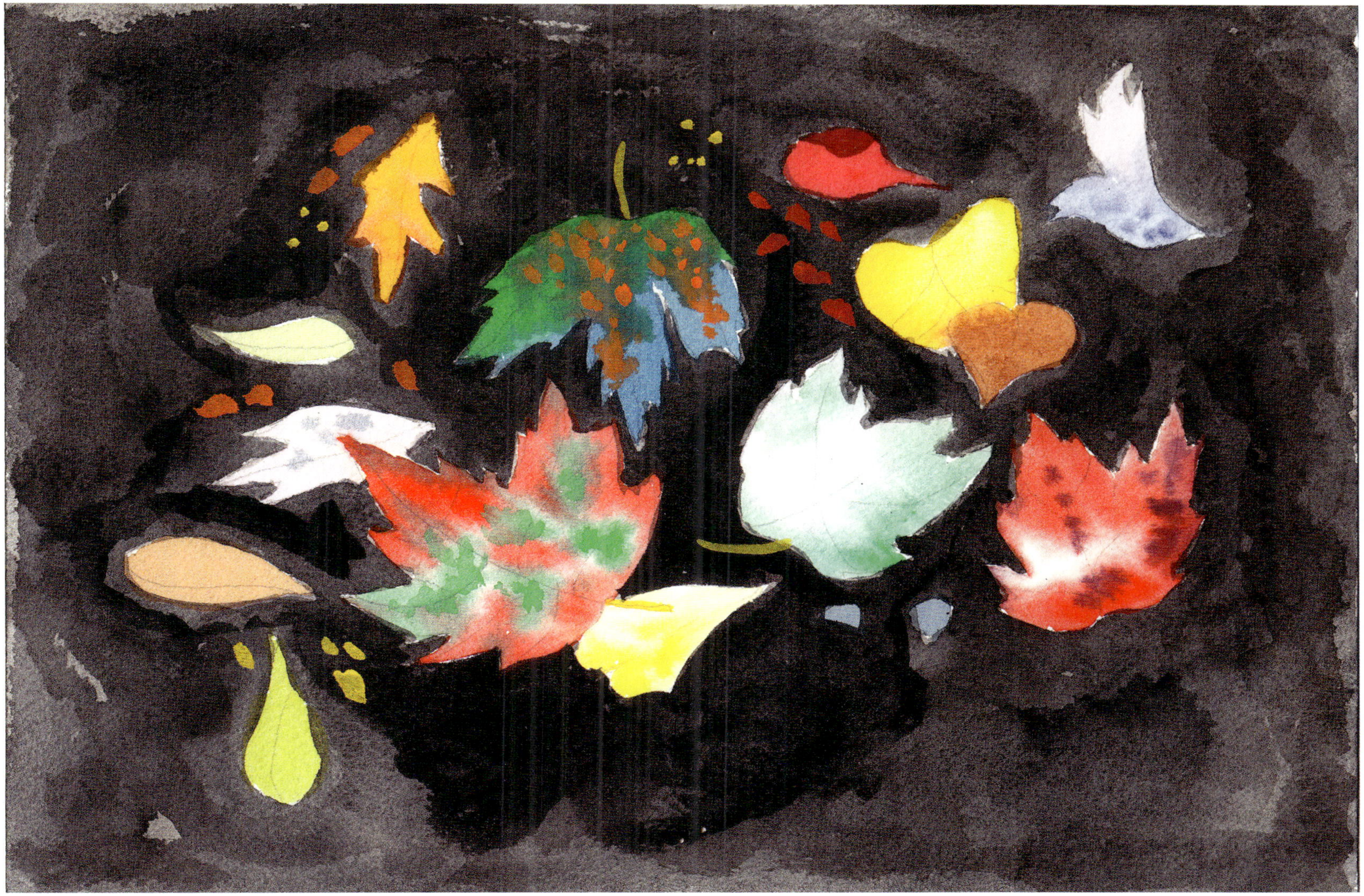

Left: AUTUMN KICK 14x10″ gouache 1993

Above: AUTUMN DANCE 9X12″ gouache 1998

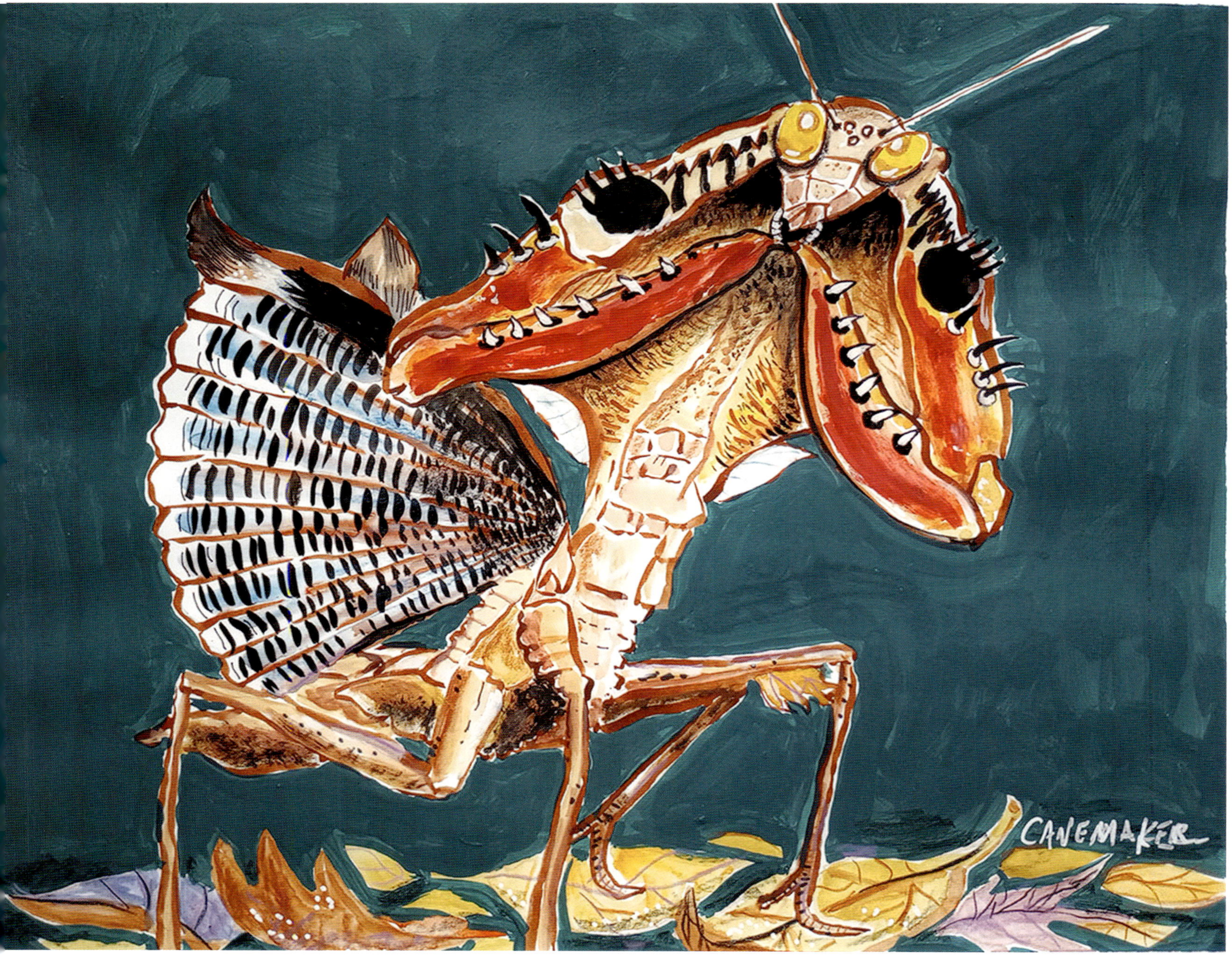

Left: DEAD LEAF MANTIS 11x14"
gouache 2023

Right: MILKWEED EXPLOSION 10 1/4x7"
gouache 2020

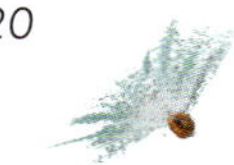

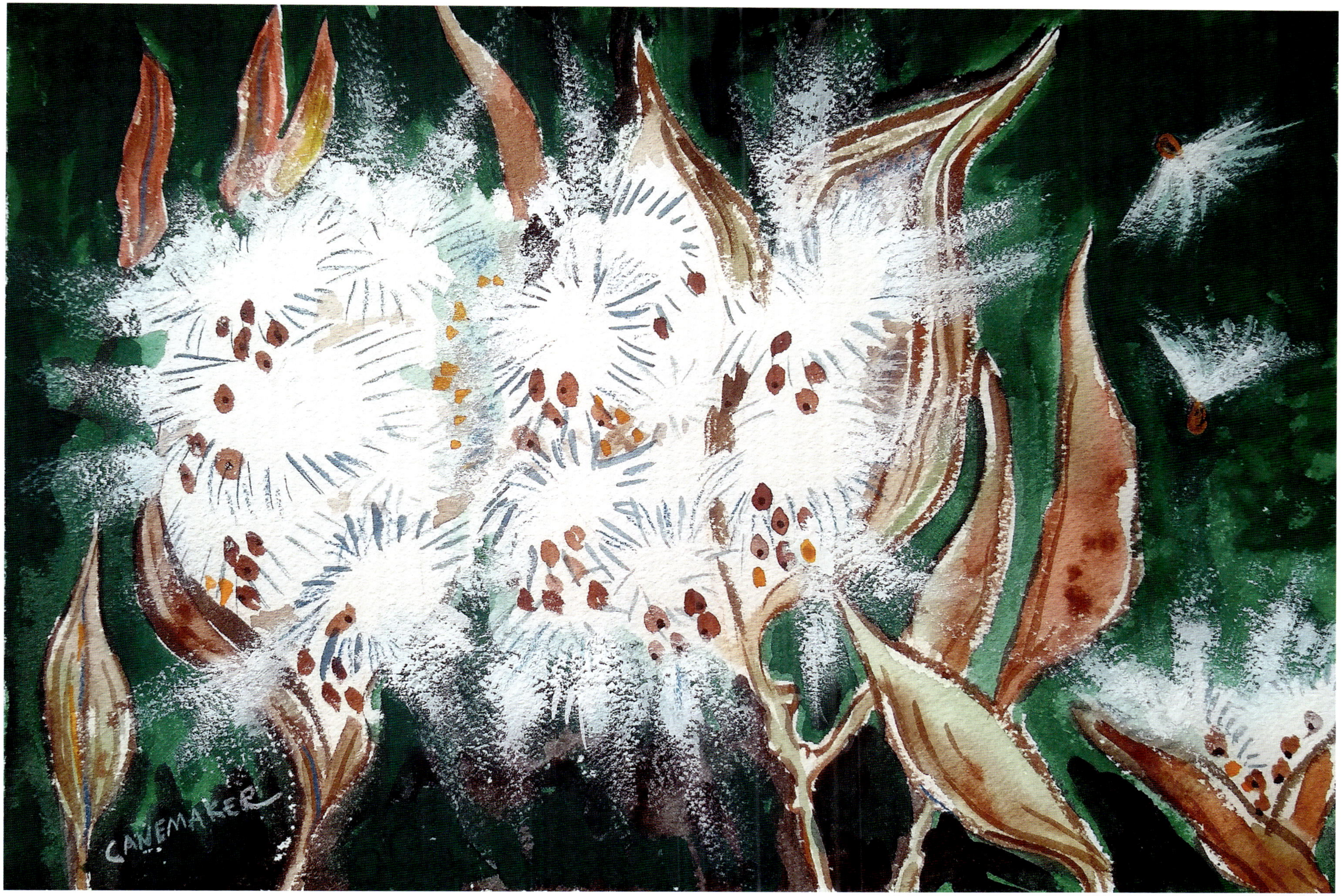
CANEMAKER

Right: SMOKE BUSH 12x16" gouache 2021

Far Right: HYDRANGEA 16x12" gouache 1991

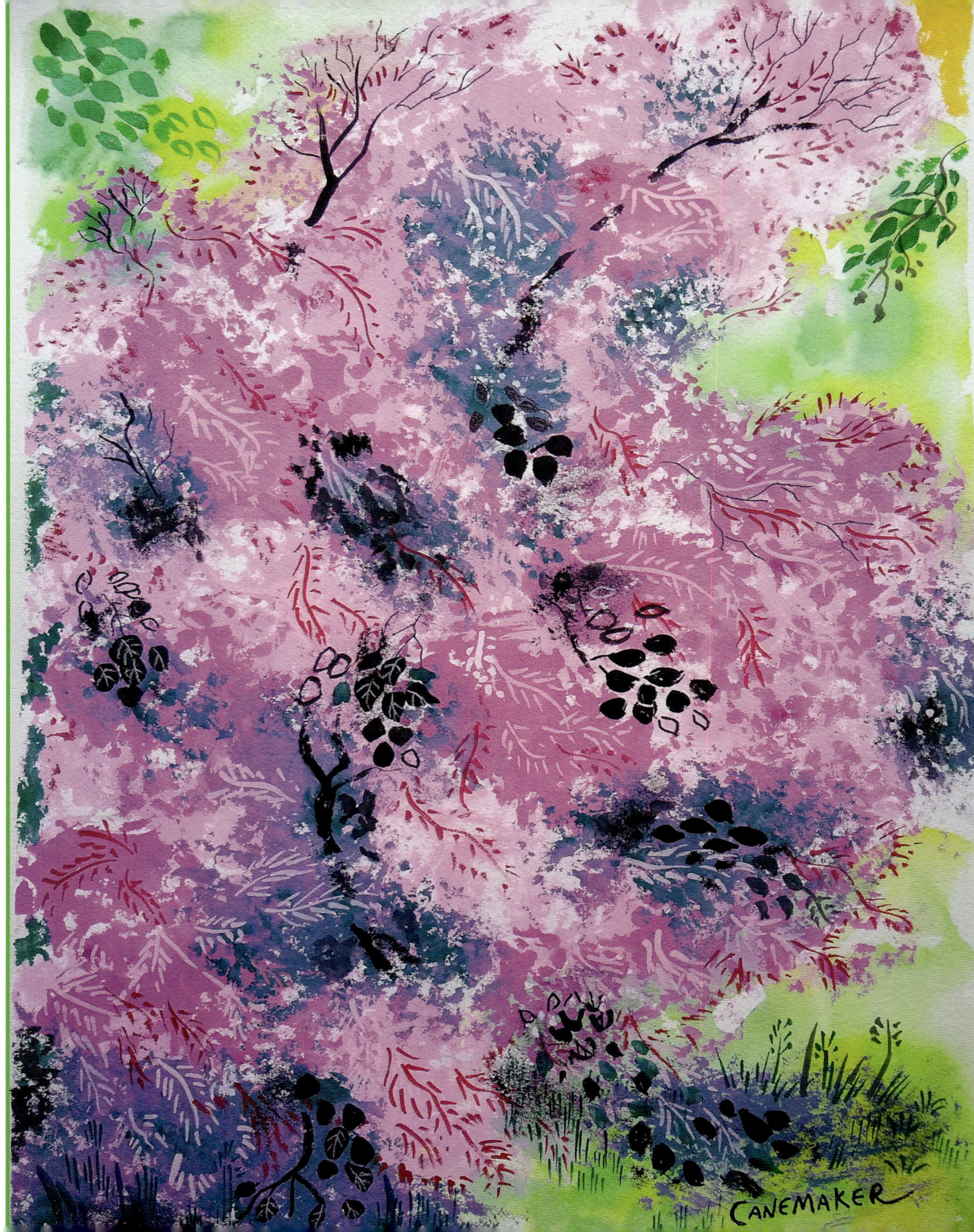

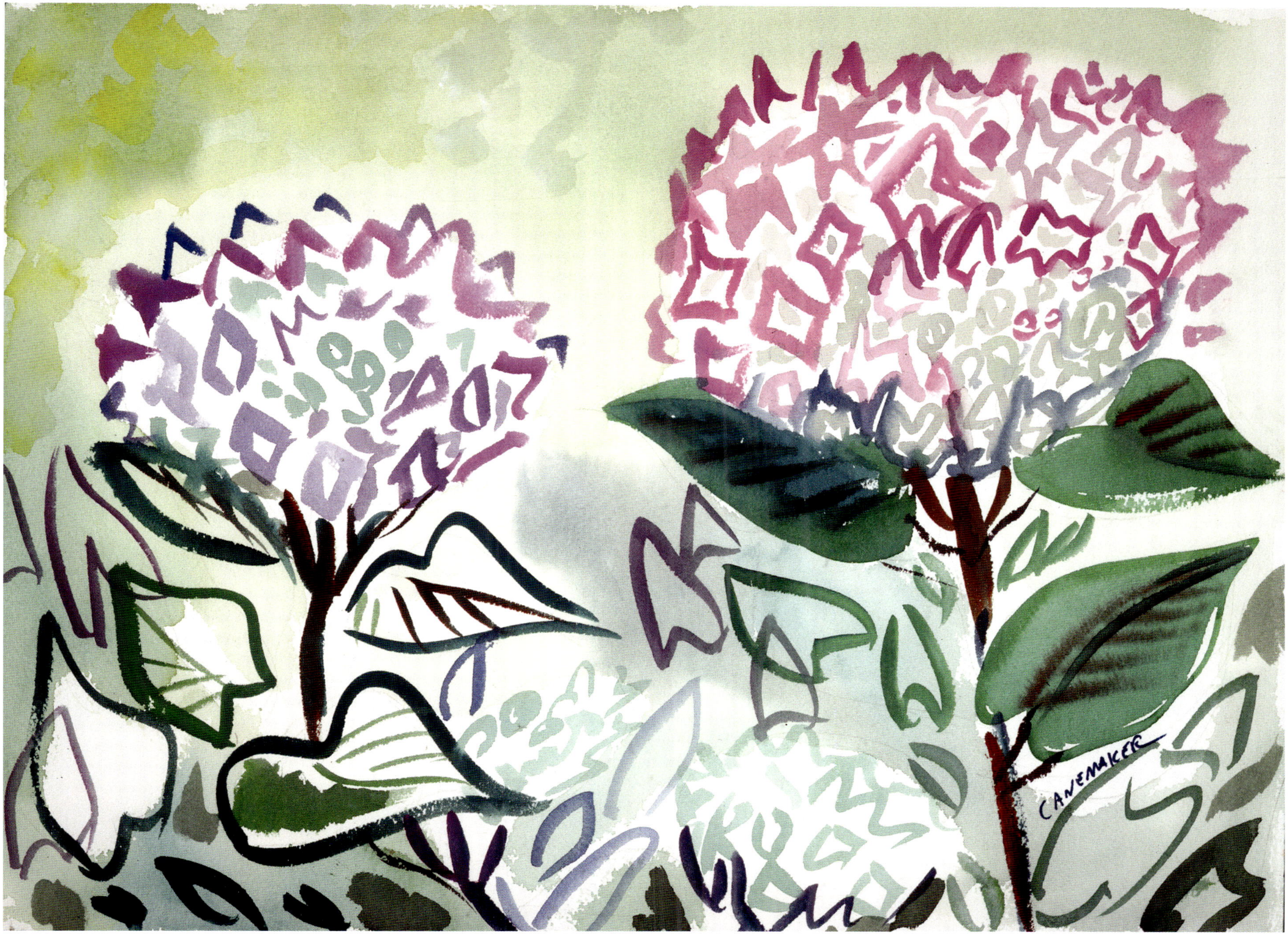
CANEMAKER

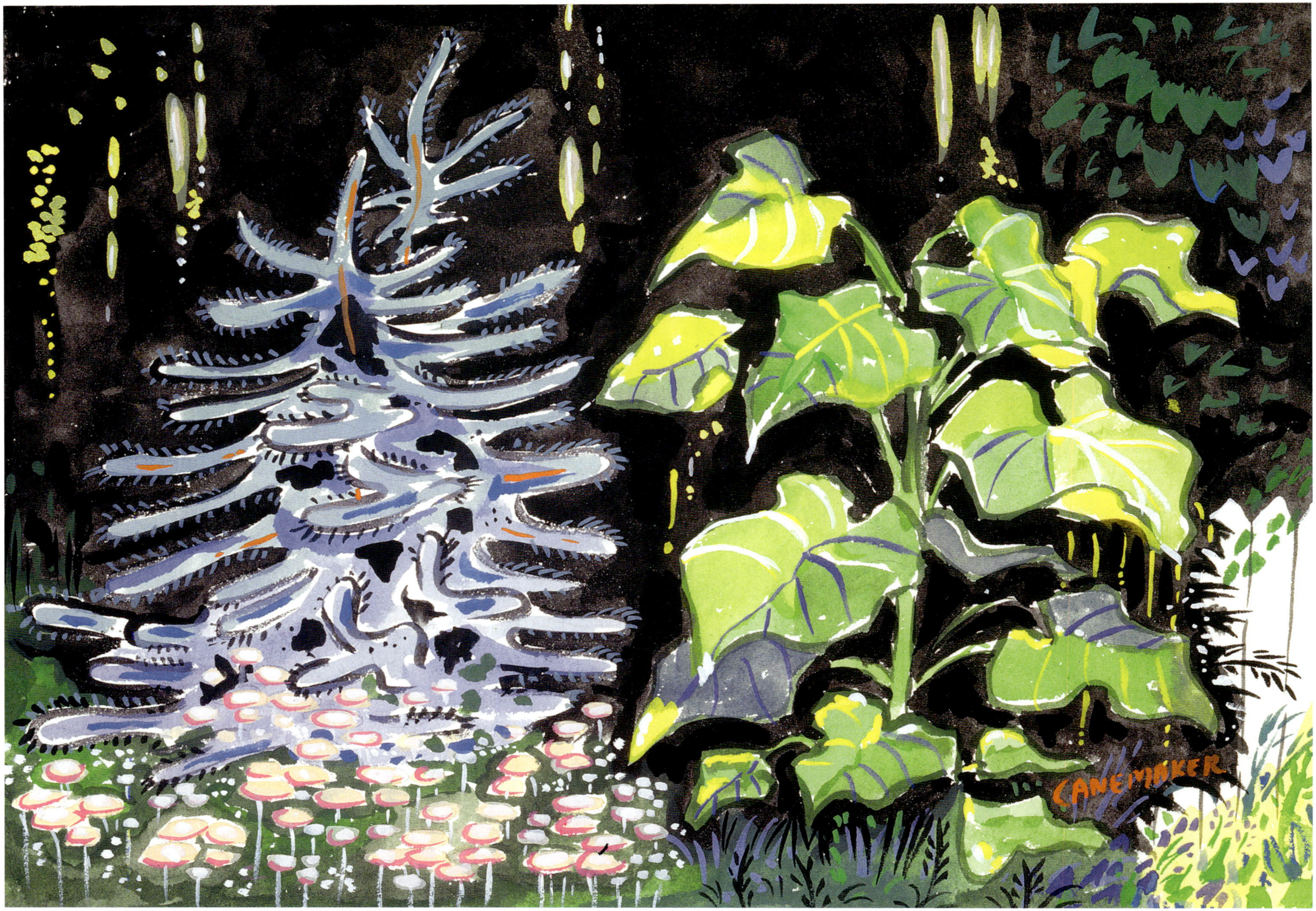
CANEMAKER

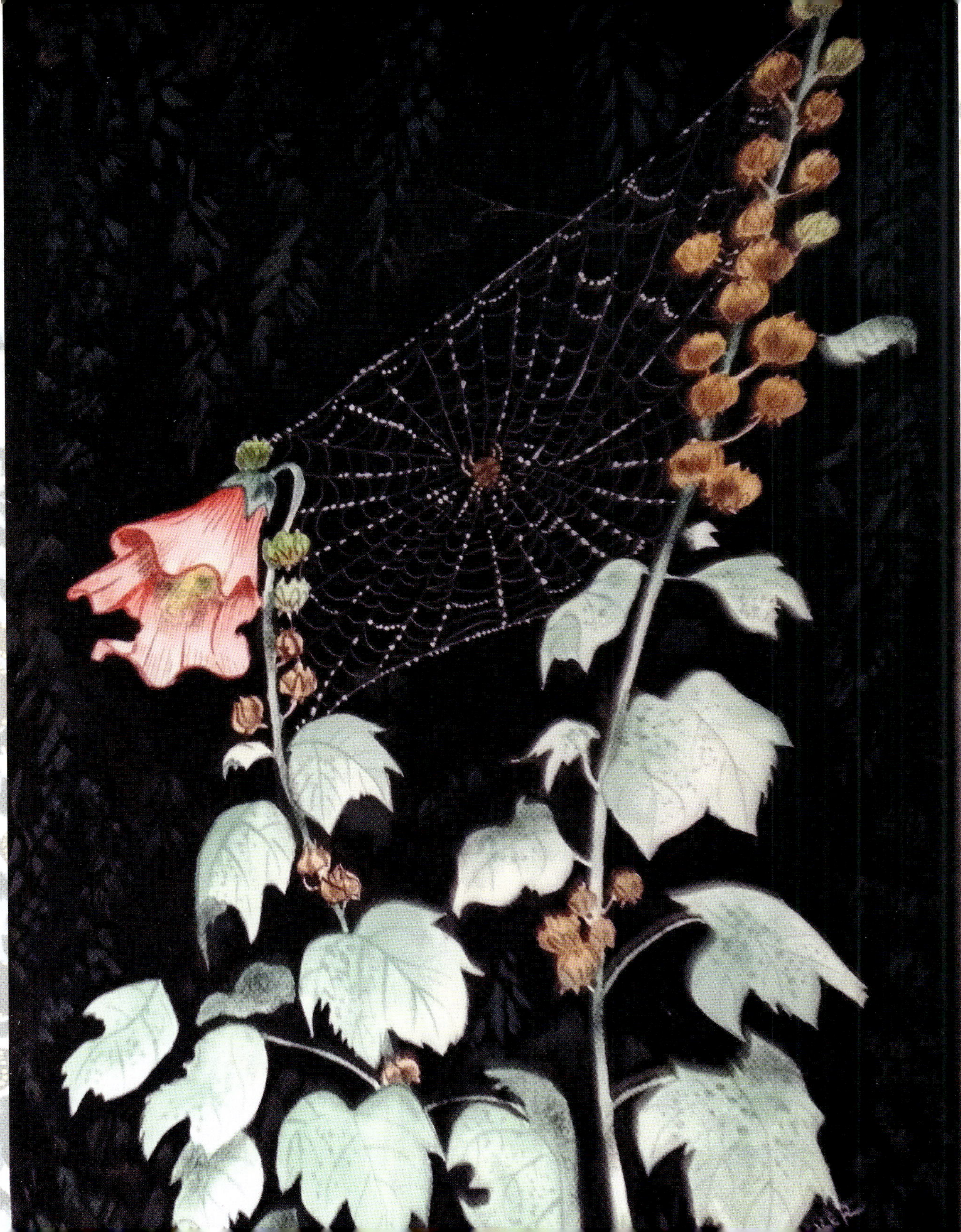

Far Left: SPRUCE & PAULOWNIA 10X14" gouache 2000

Left: SPIDER ON HOLLYHOCKS 12X16" gouache 2024

Following pages:
Page 78: OUR HOUSE 19X13" gouache 1992

Page 79: WHITE & RED ROSES 13 1/2x10" gouache 1991

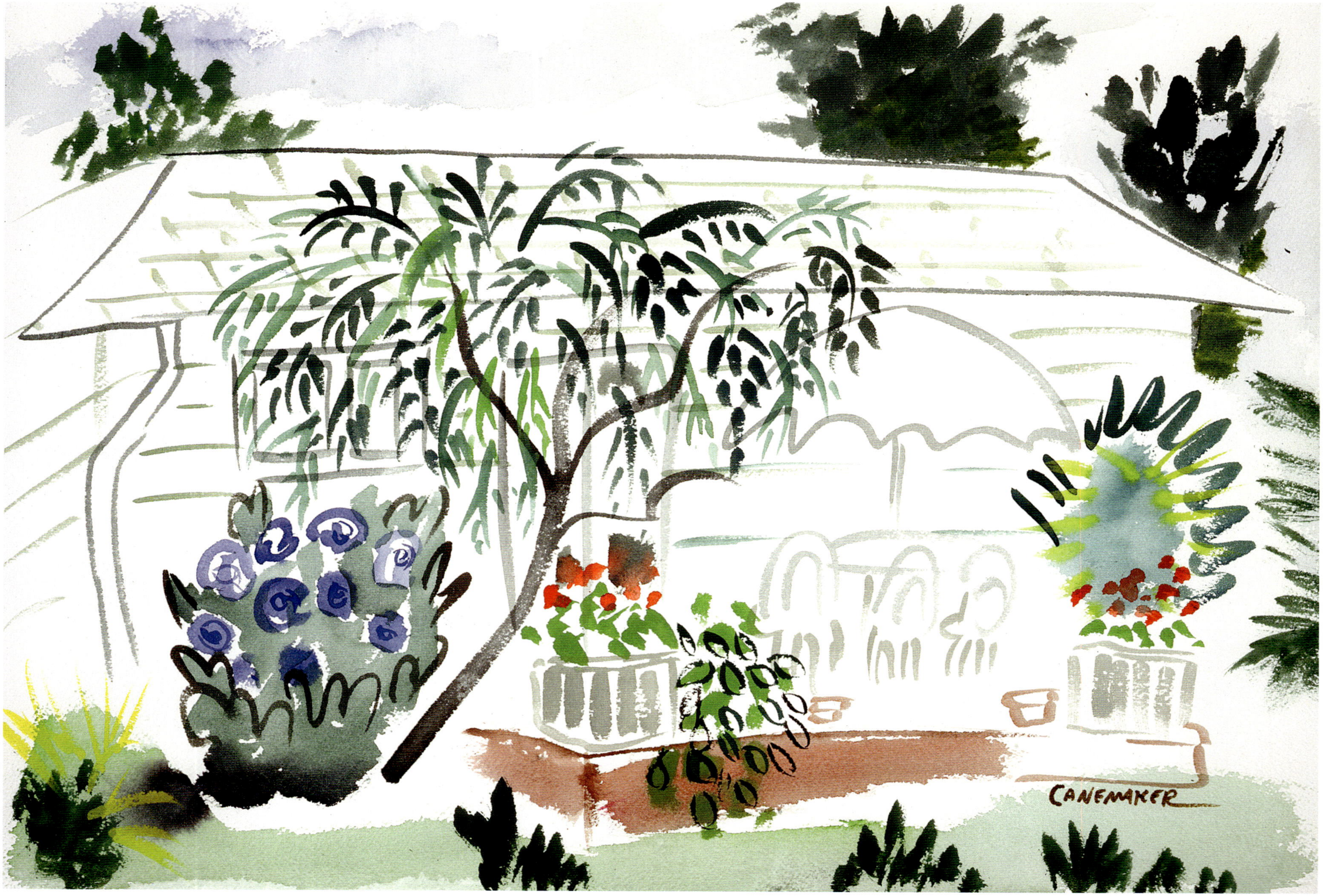
CANEMAKER

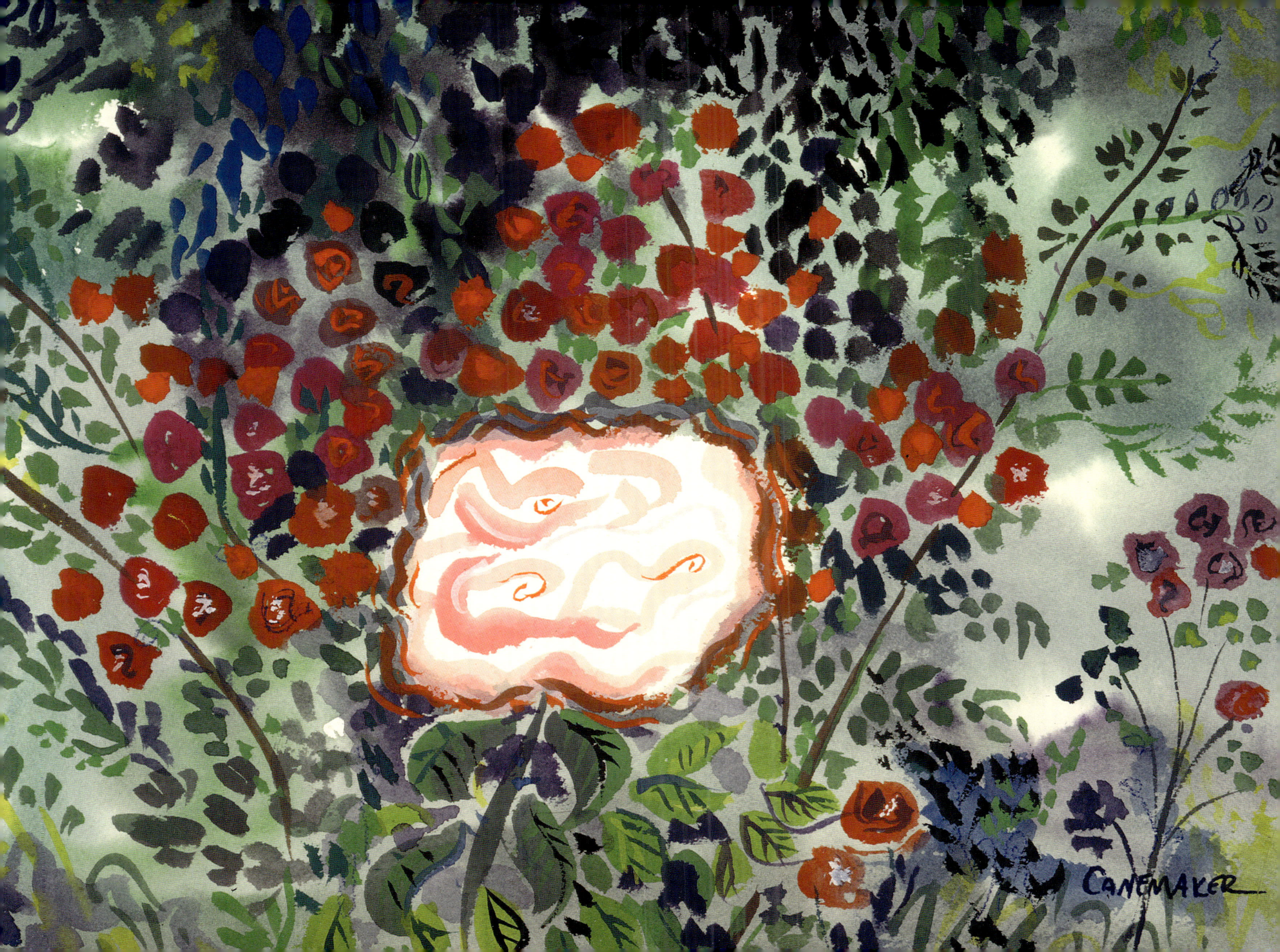
CANEMAKER

Right: NO PARKING 10x14″ goauche 2019

Far Right: EUPHORBIA 16X12 1/4″ gaouache 2021

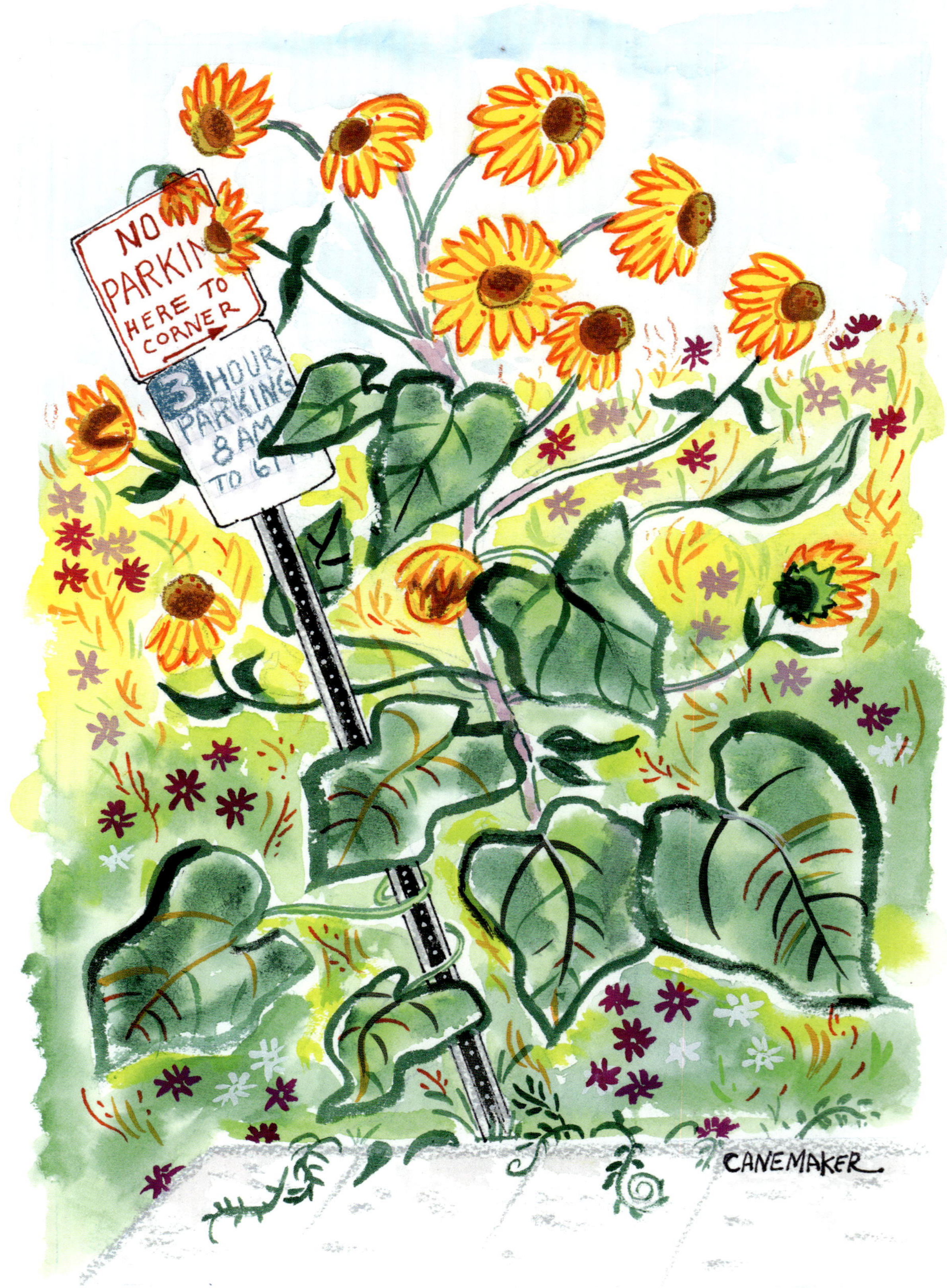

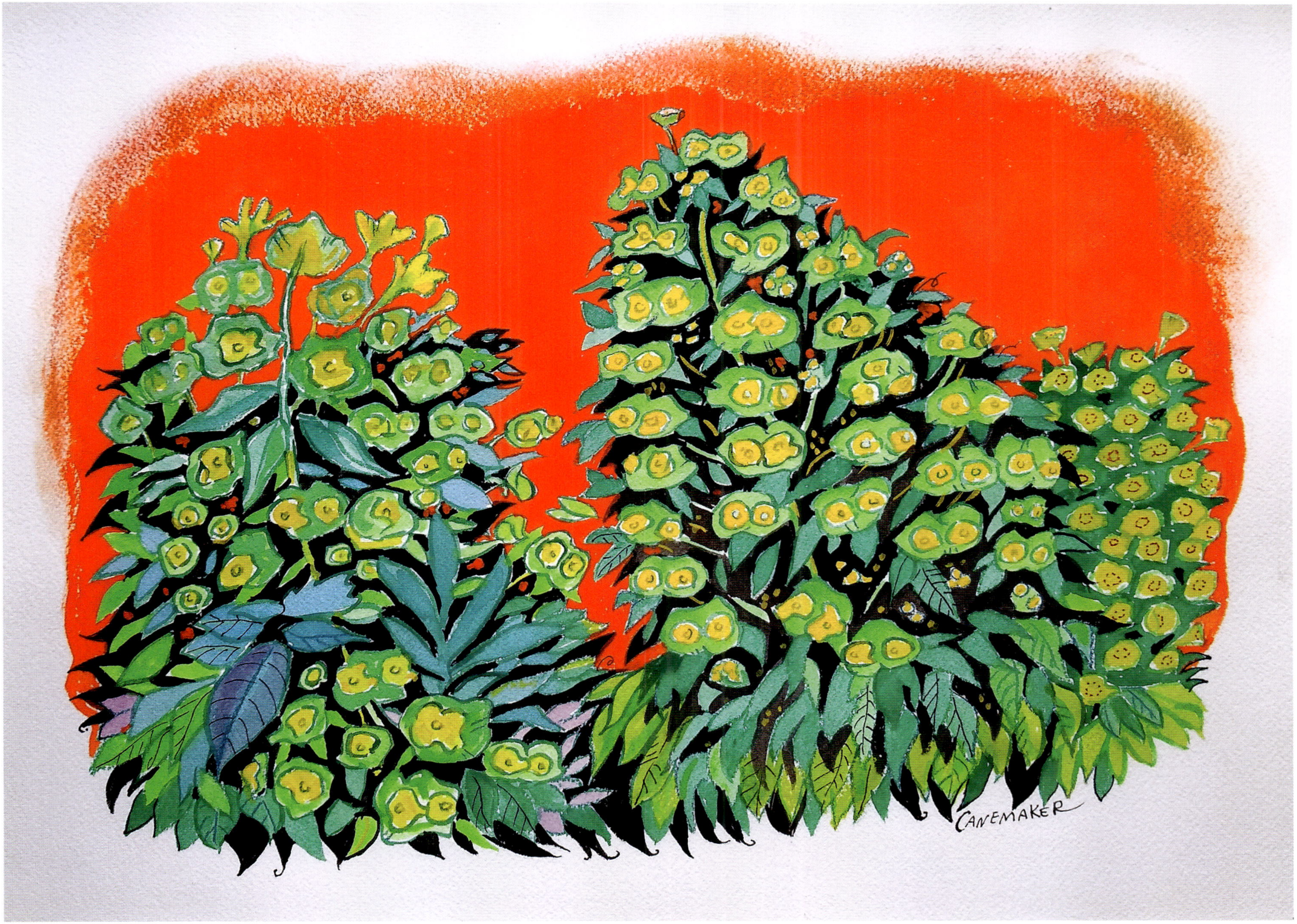
CANEMAKER

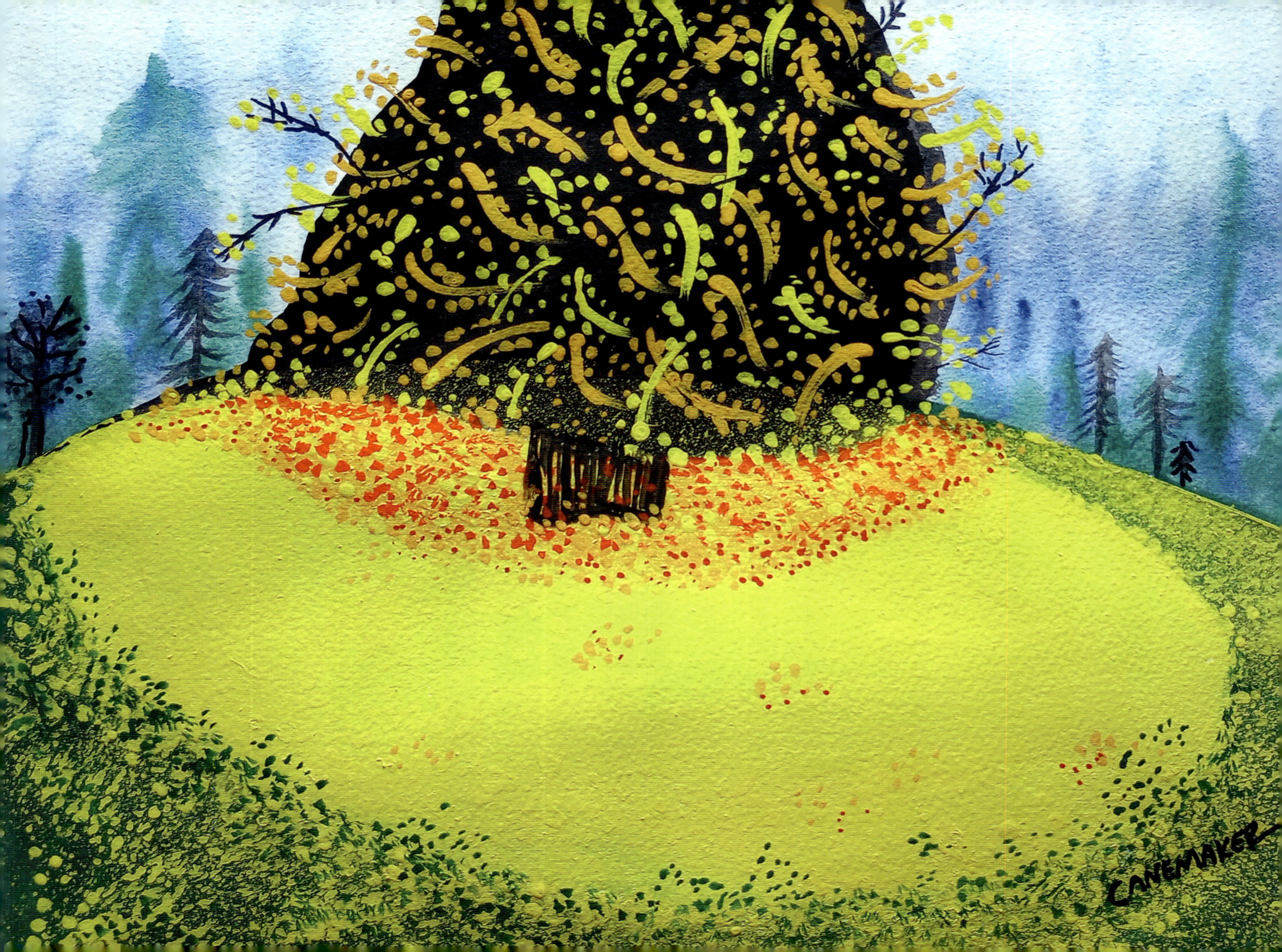
CANEMAKER

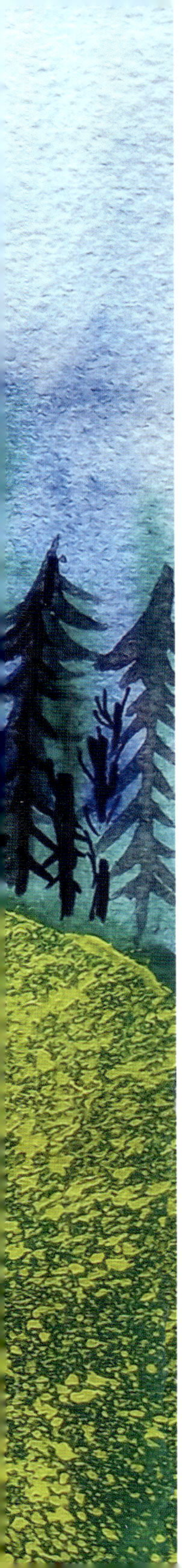

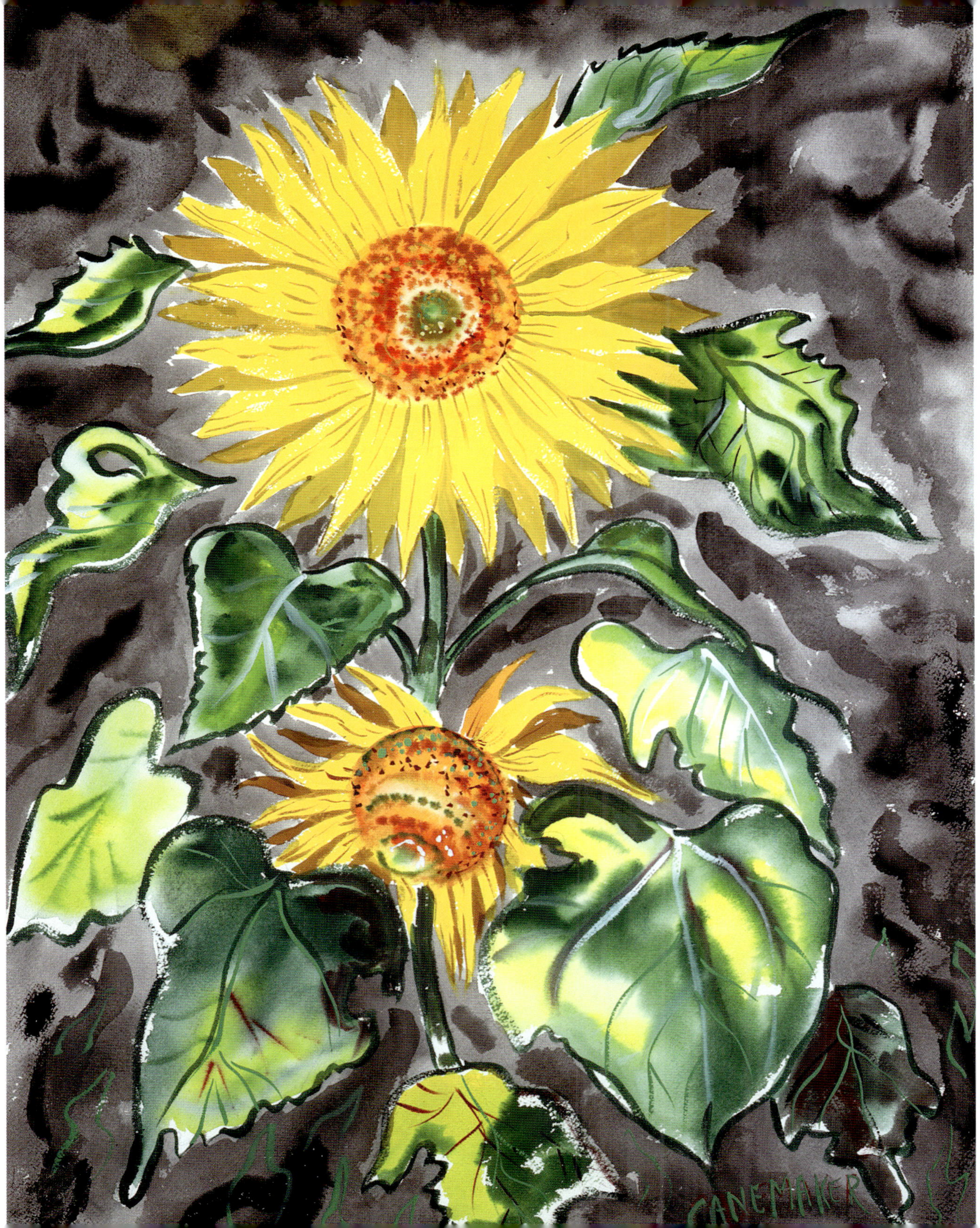

Far Left: GINGKO 14x10″ gouache 2023

Left: SUNFLOWERS 24X18″ gouache 1994

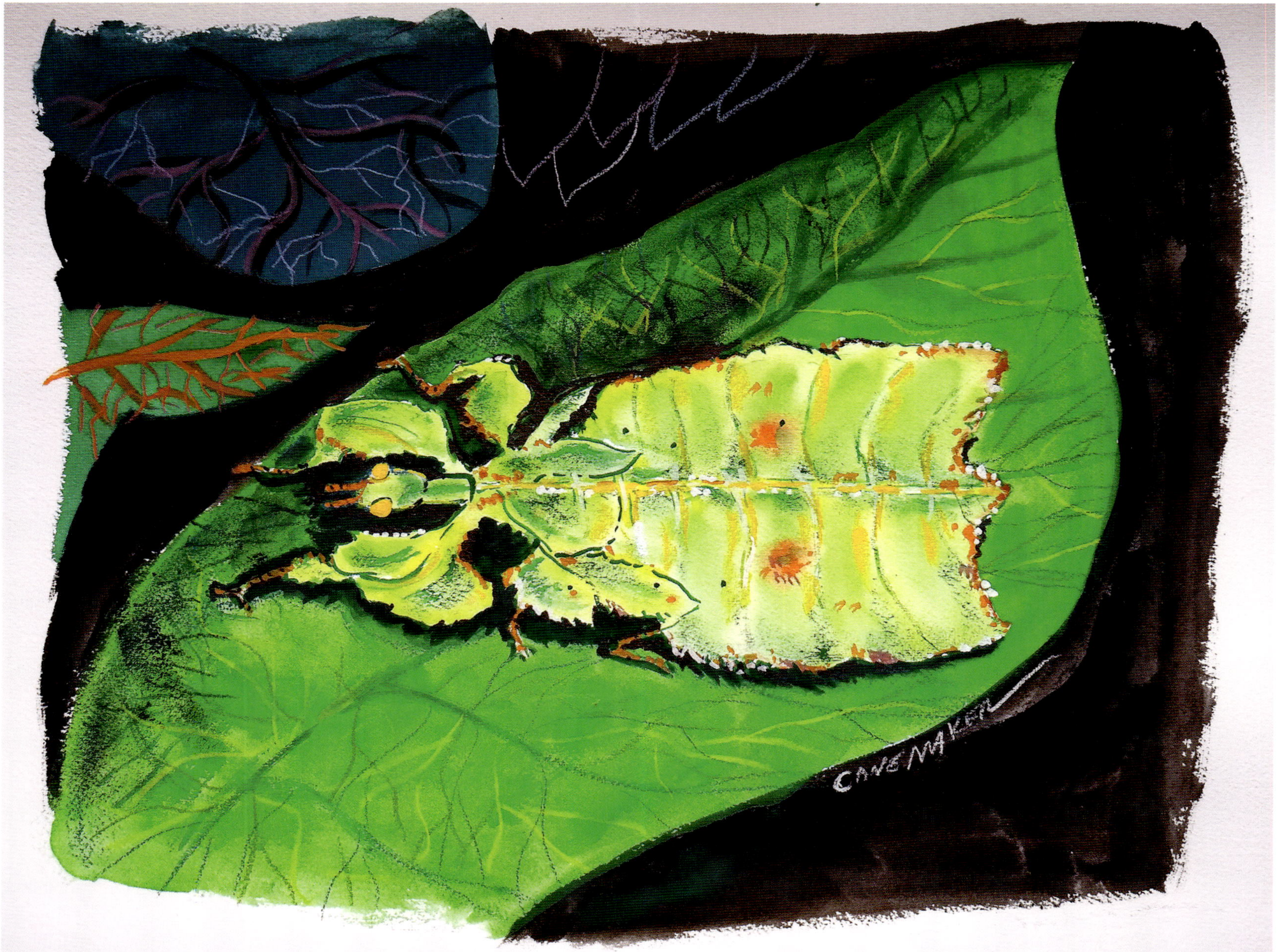

Left: PHYLLIUM ASEKIENSE
12x16" gouache 2021

Right: GOLDEN VALLEY 16x24"
gouache 2024

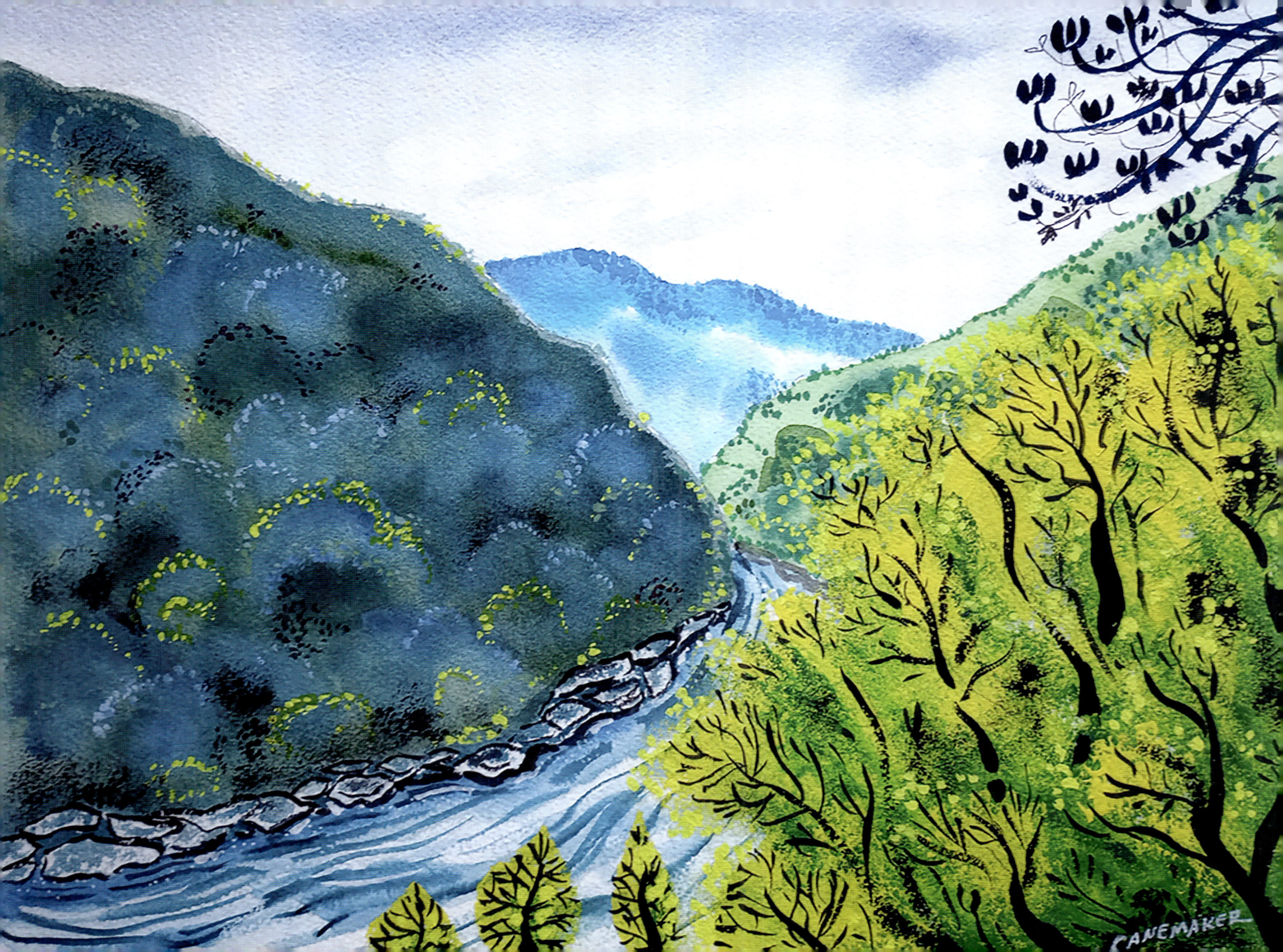
CANEMAKER

Winter

"If you will stay close to nature, to its simplicity, to the small things hardly noticeable, those things can unexpectedly become great and immeasurable."

\- Rainer Maria Rilke, *Letters to a Young Poet*

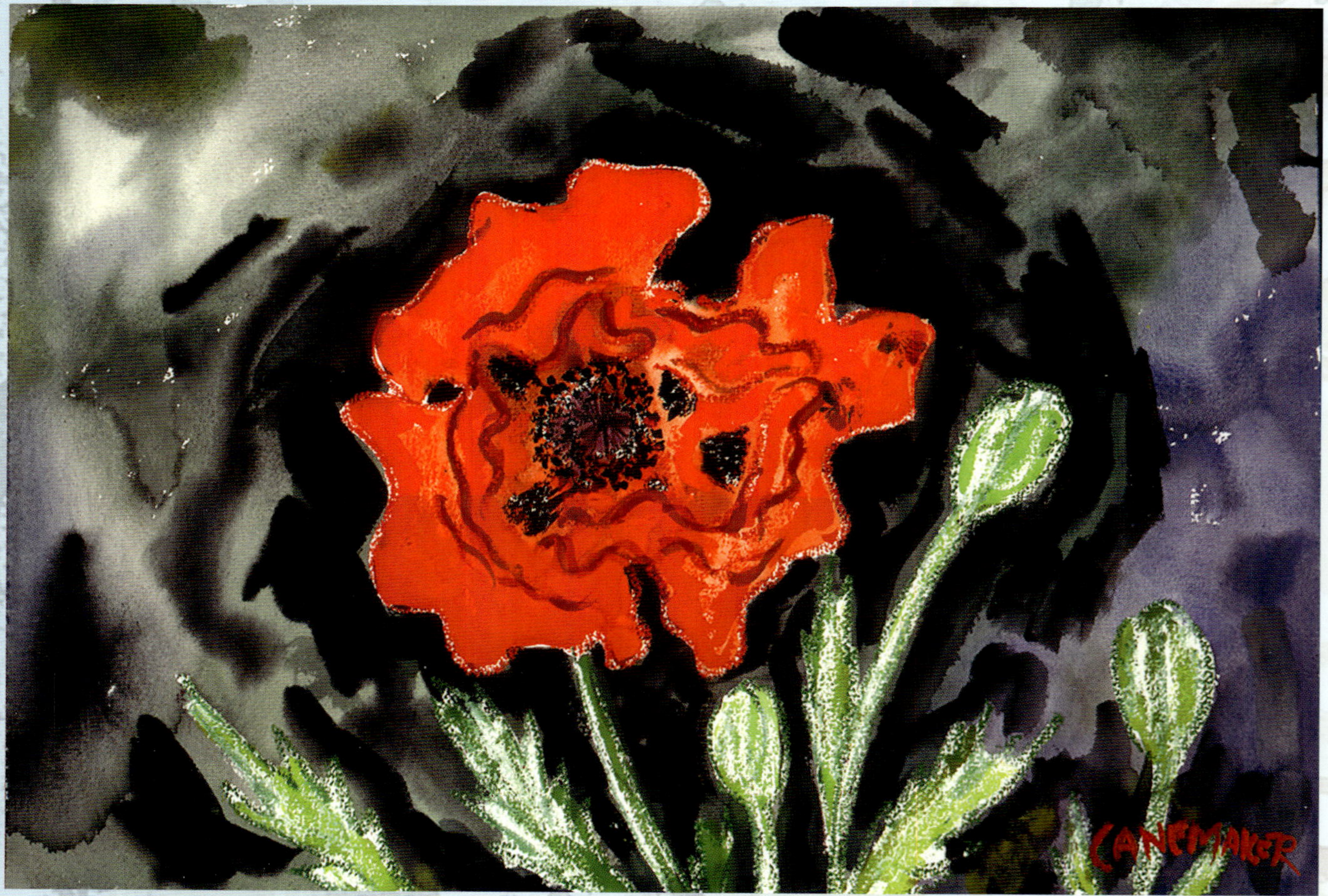

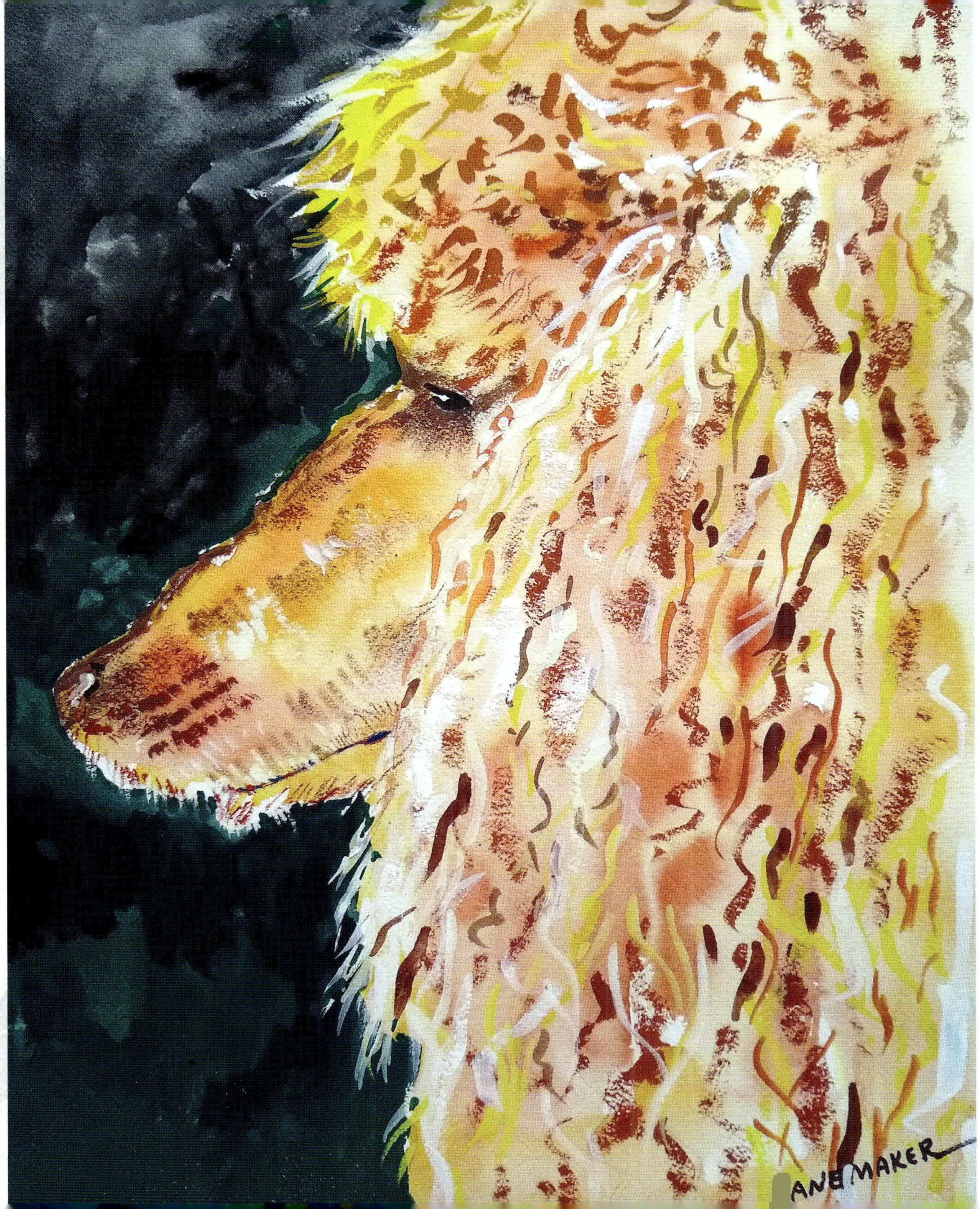

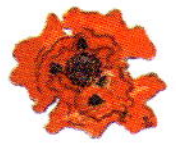

Far Left: CHRISTMAS POPPY 20X14"
gouache 1994

Left: CHARLIE DICKENS 16x12"
gouache 2021

Right: PADRAIG'S OWL 11X15" gouache 2021

Far Right: SILENT WOOD 16x12" gouache 2024

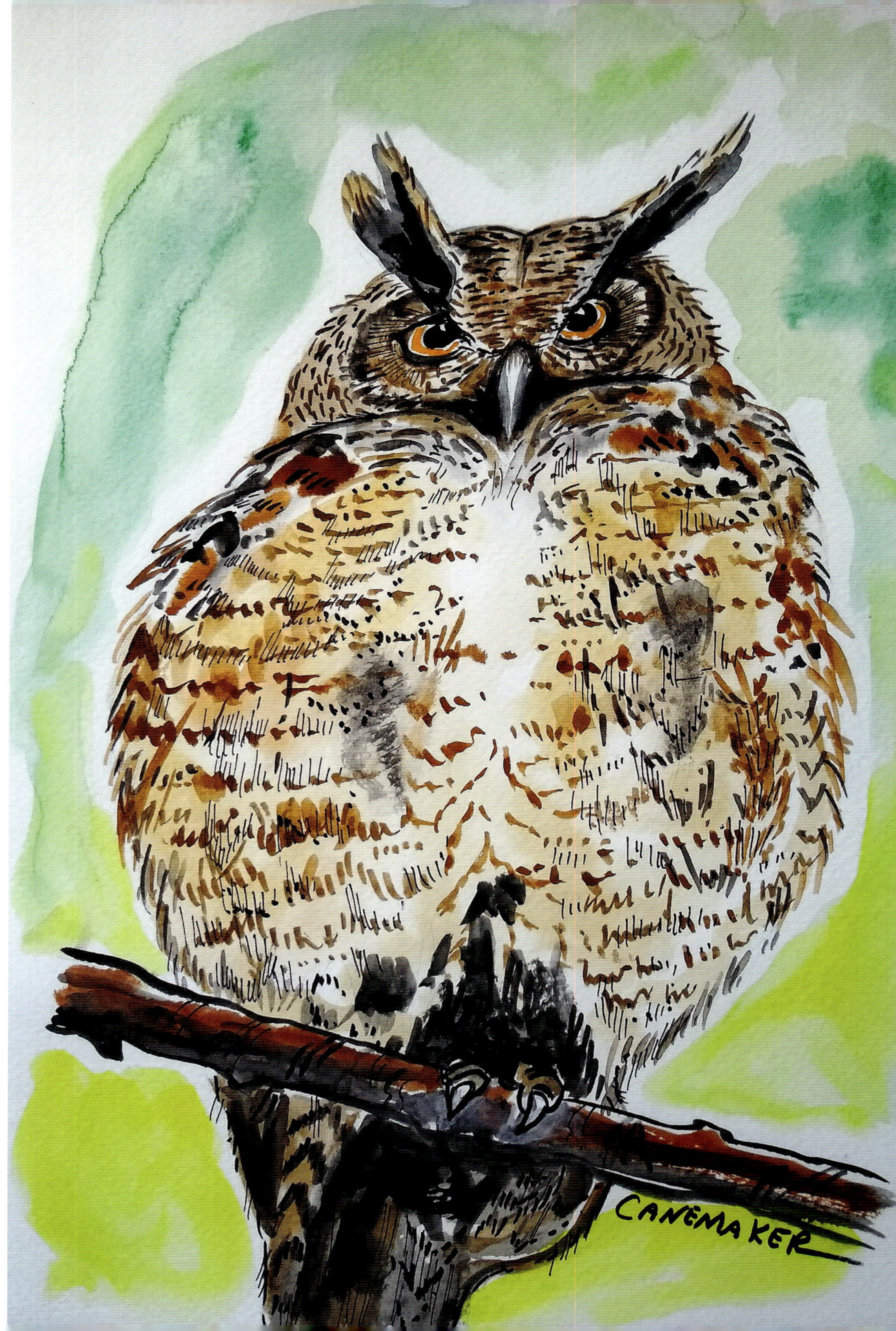

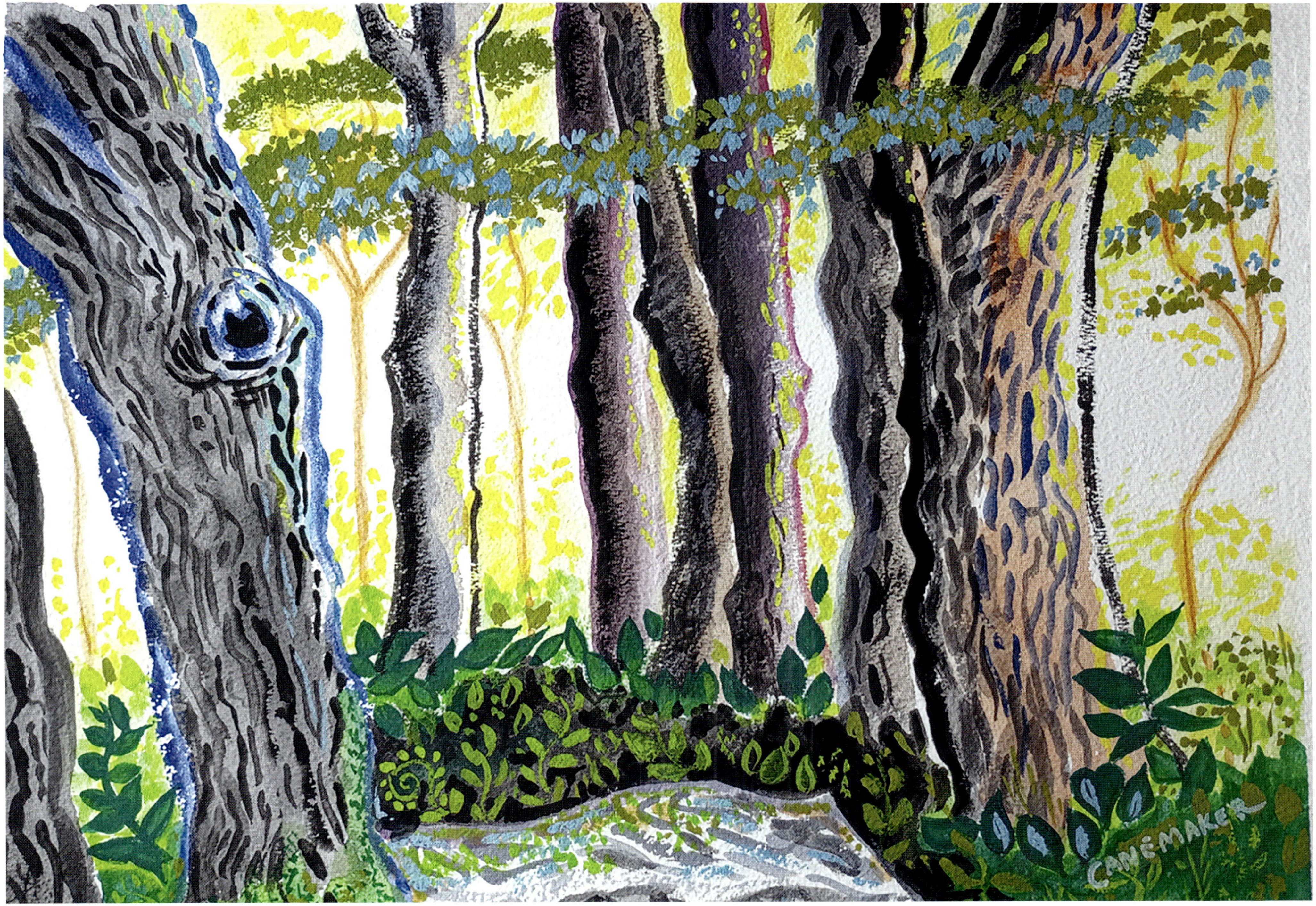
CANEMAKER

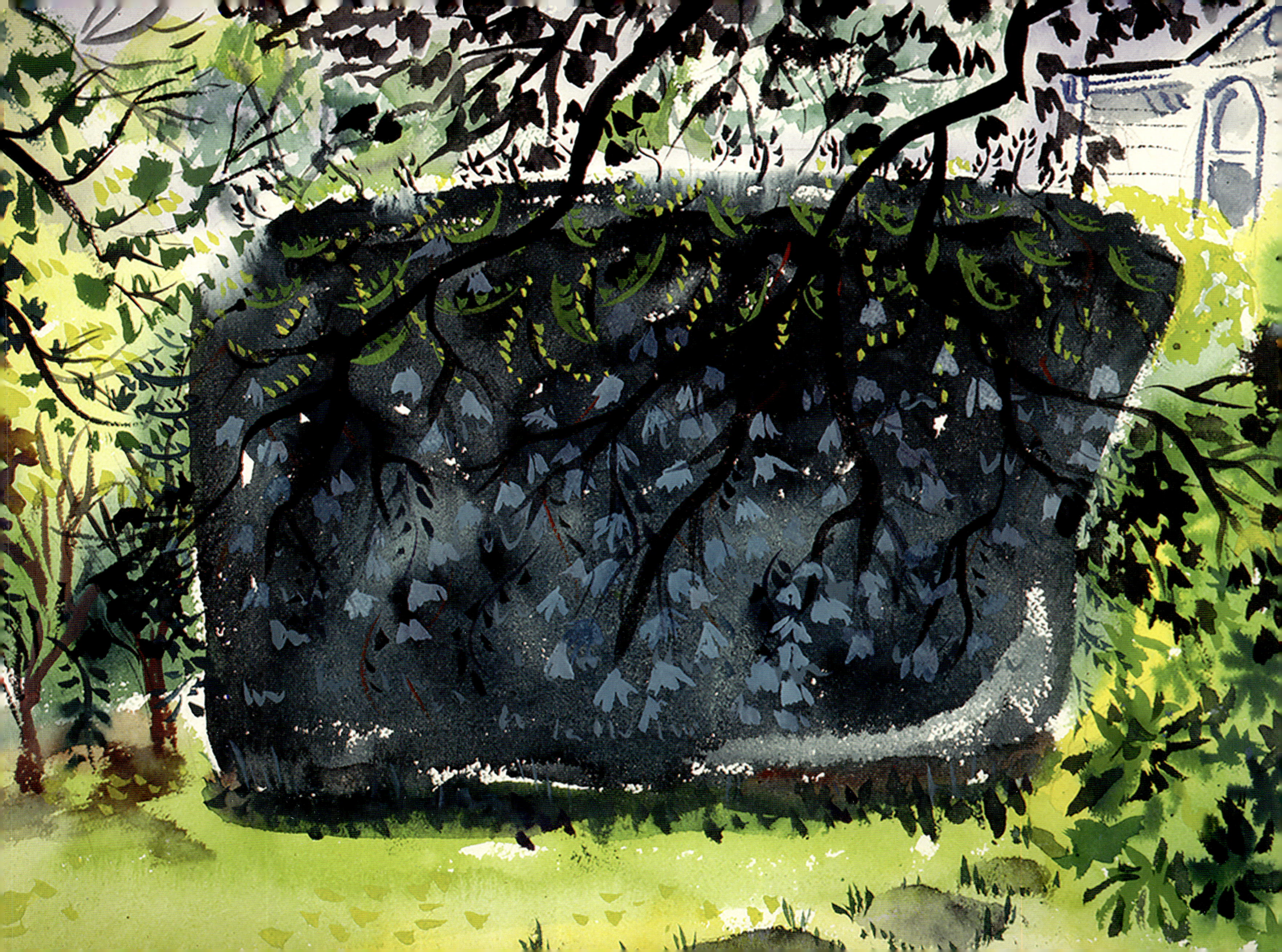

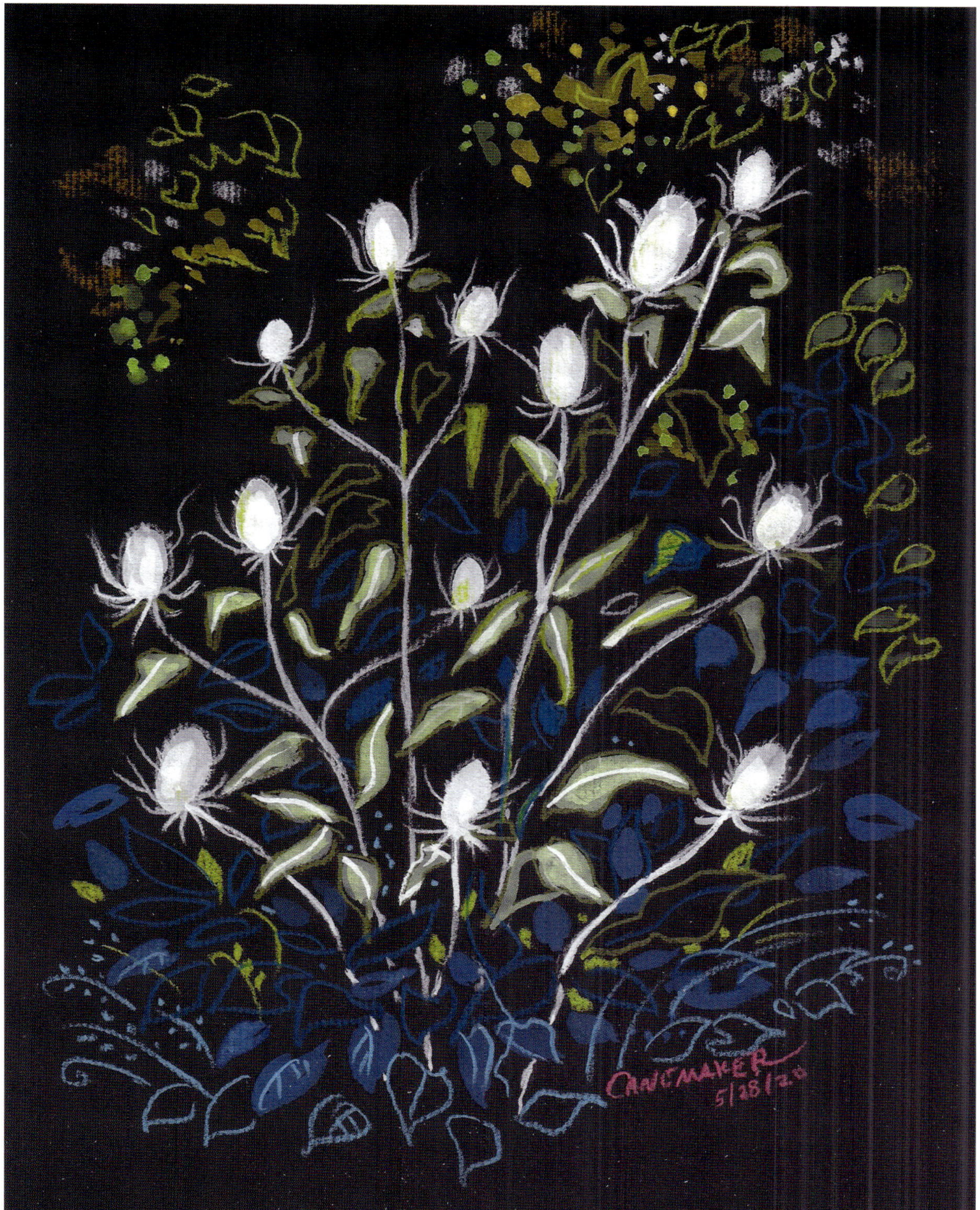

Far left: ARBOR VITAE HEDGE 16X12" gouache 1990

Left: NIGHT TEASELS 8 &1/2" x11" gouache 2020

Following pages:

Page 92: DEAD HYDRANGIA 13 &1/2"X10" gouache 1991

Page 93: THE ROAD LESS TRAVELED 24"X18&1/4 " gouache 1992

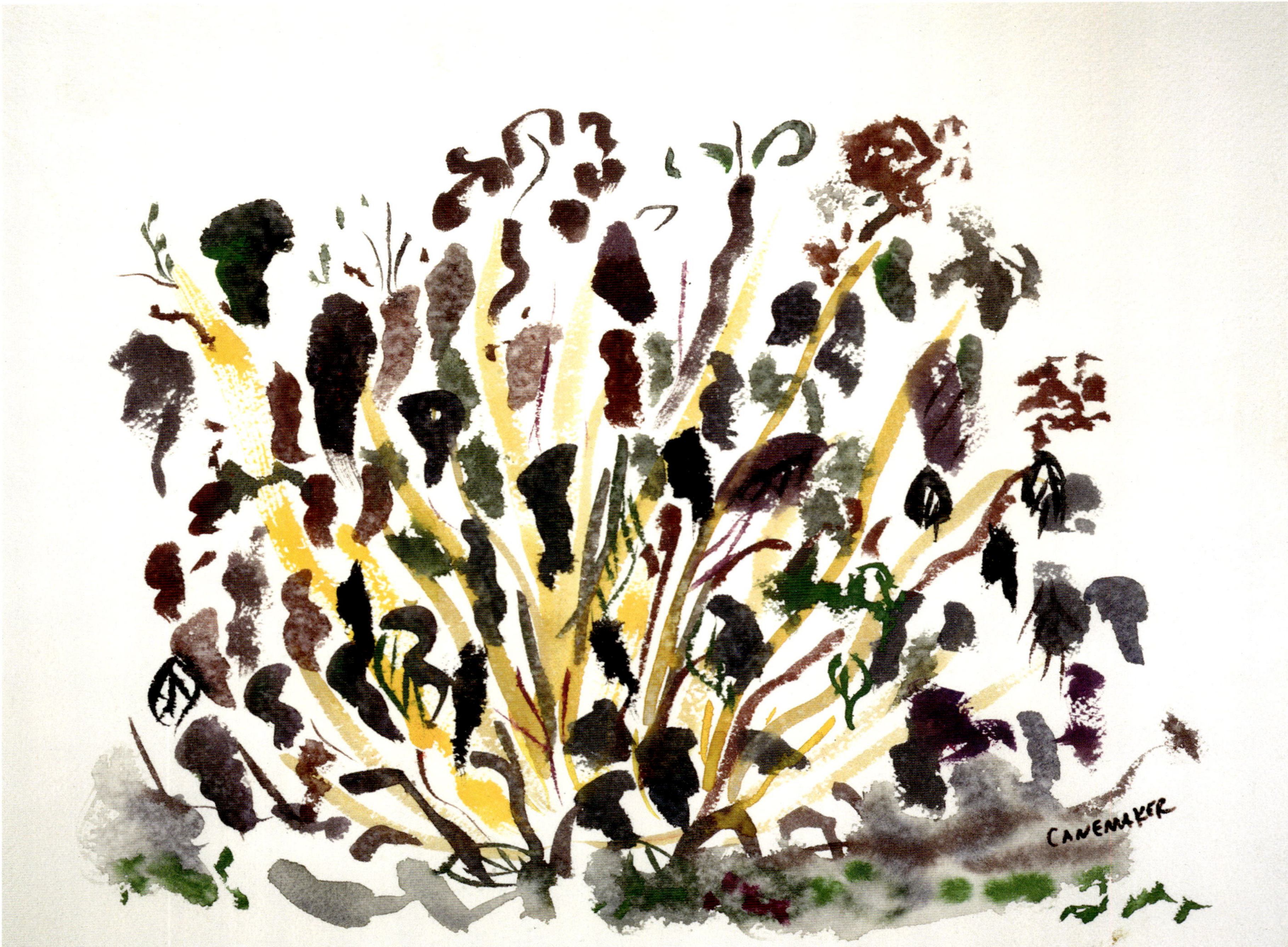
CANEMAKER

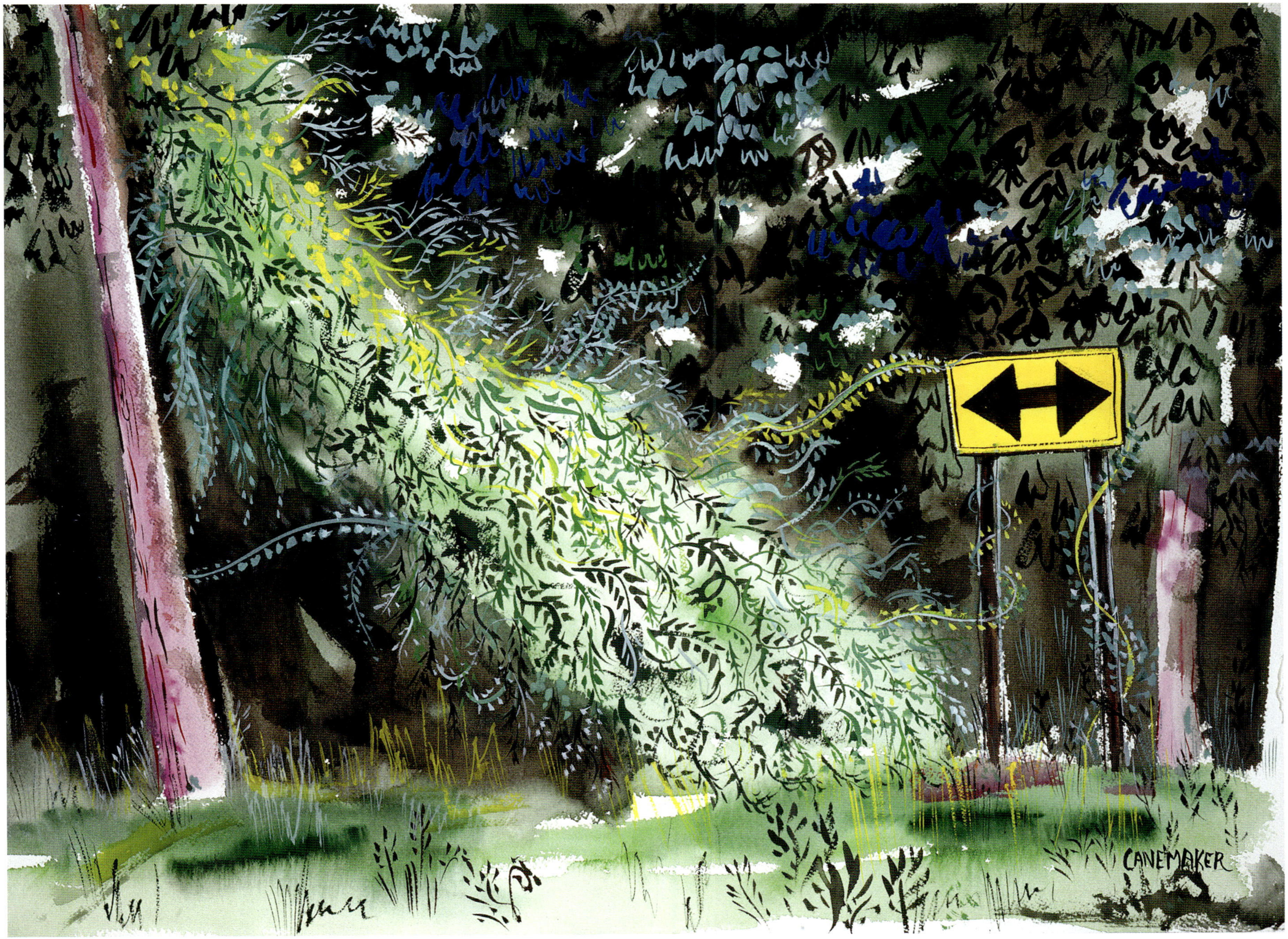
CANEMAKER

Right: FOUR THISTLES 15X11" gouache 2020

Far Right: DYING BEE 12x16" gouache 2019

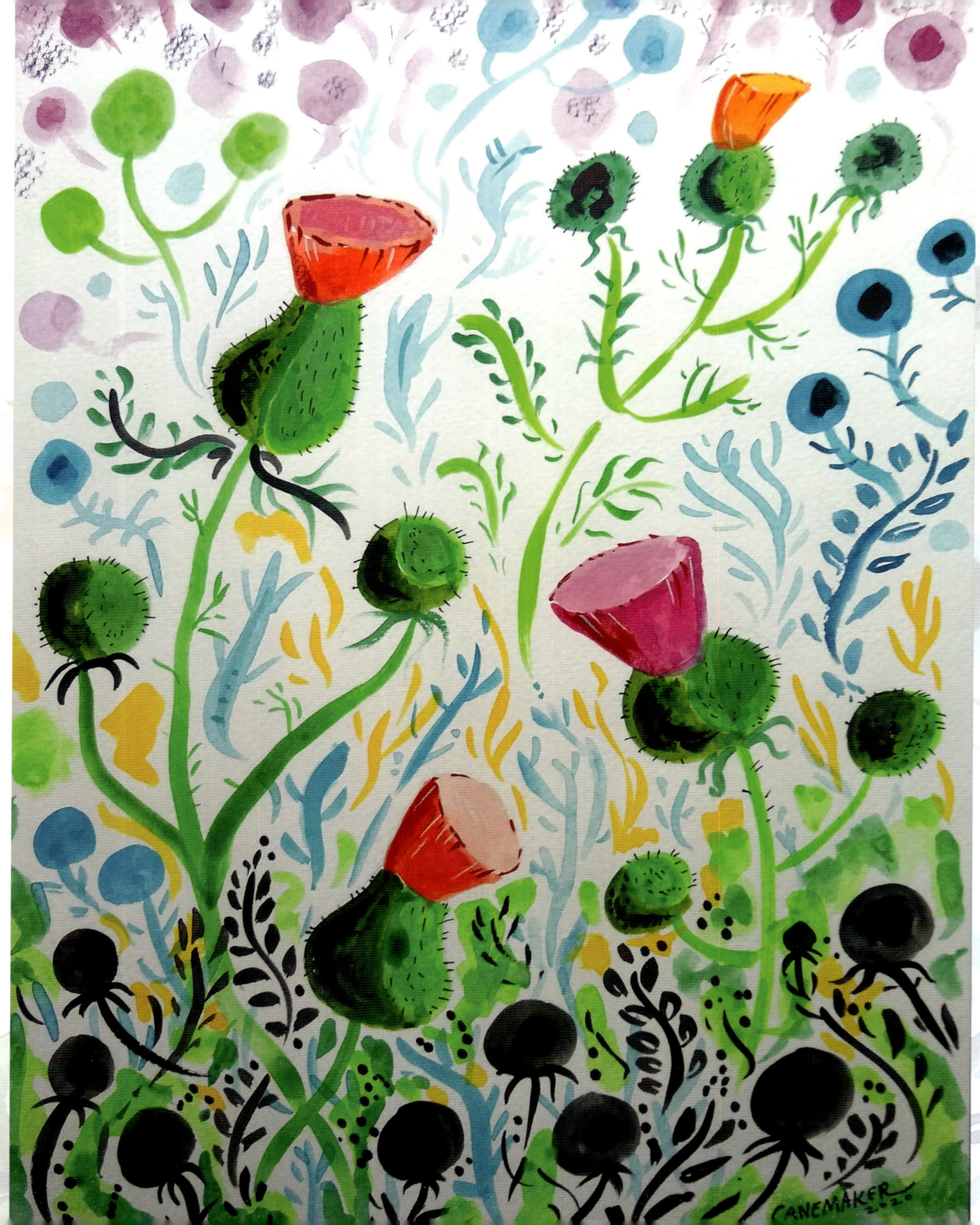

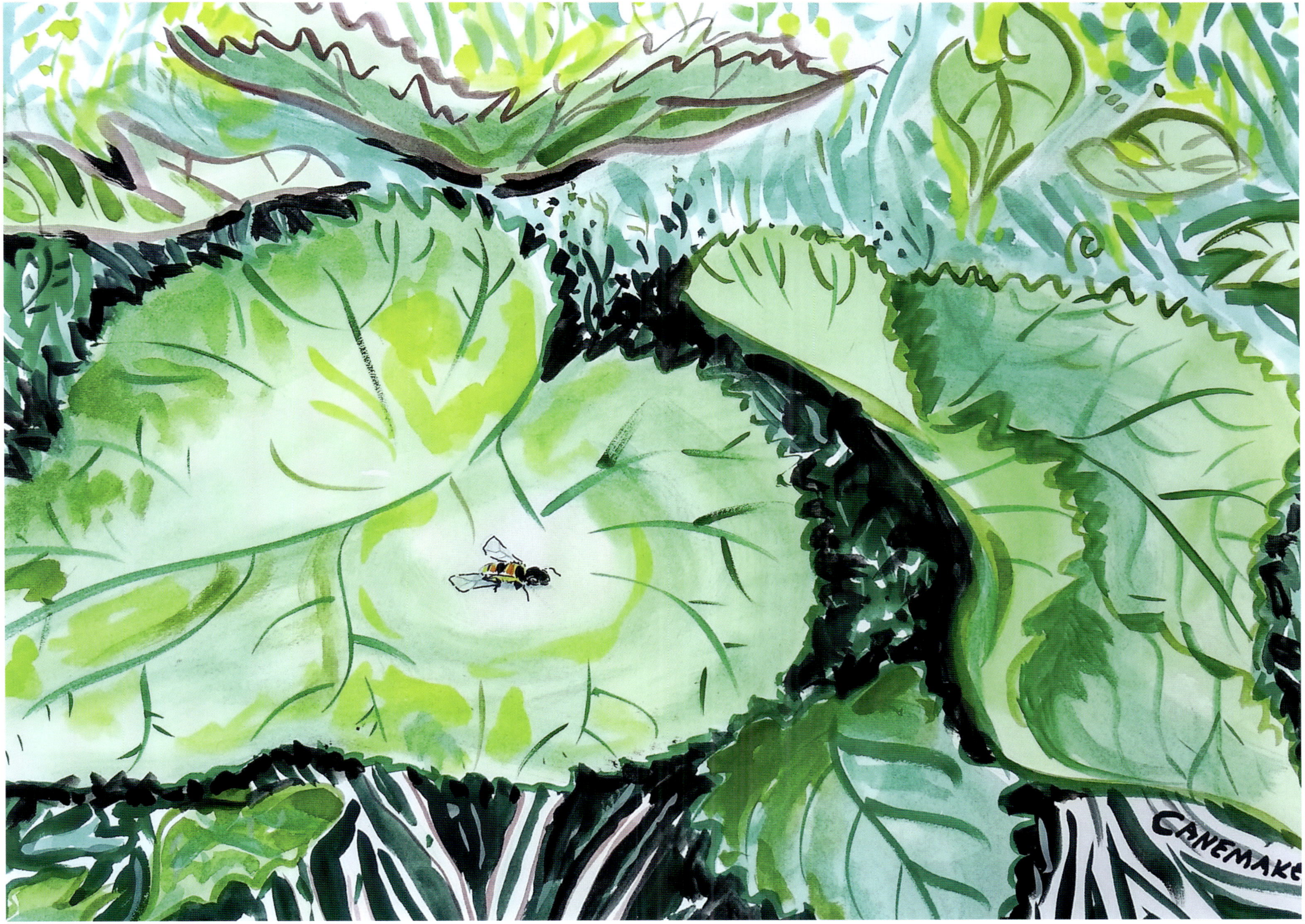
CANEMAKE

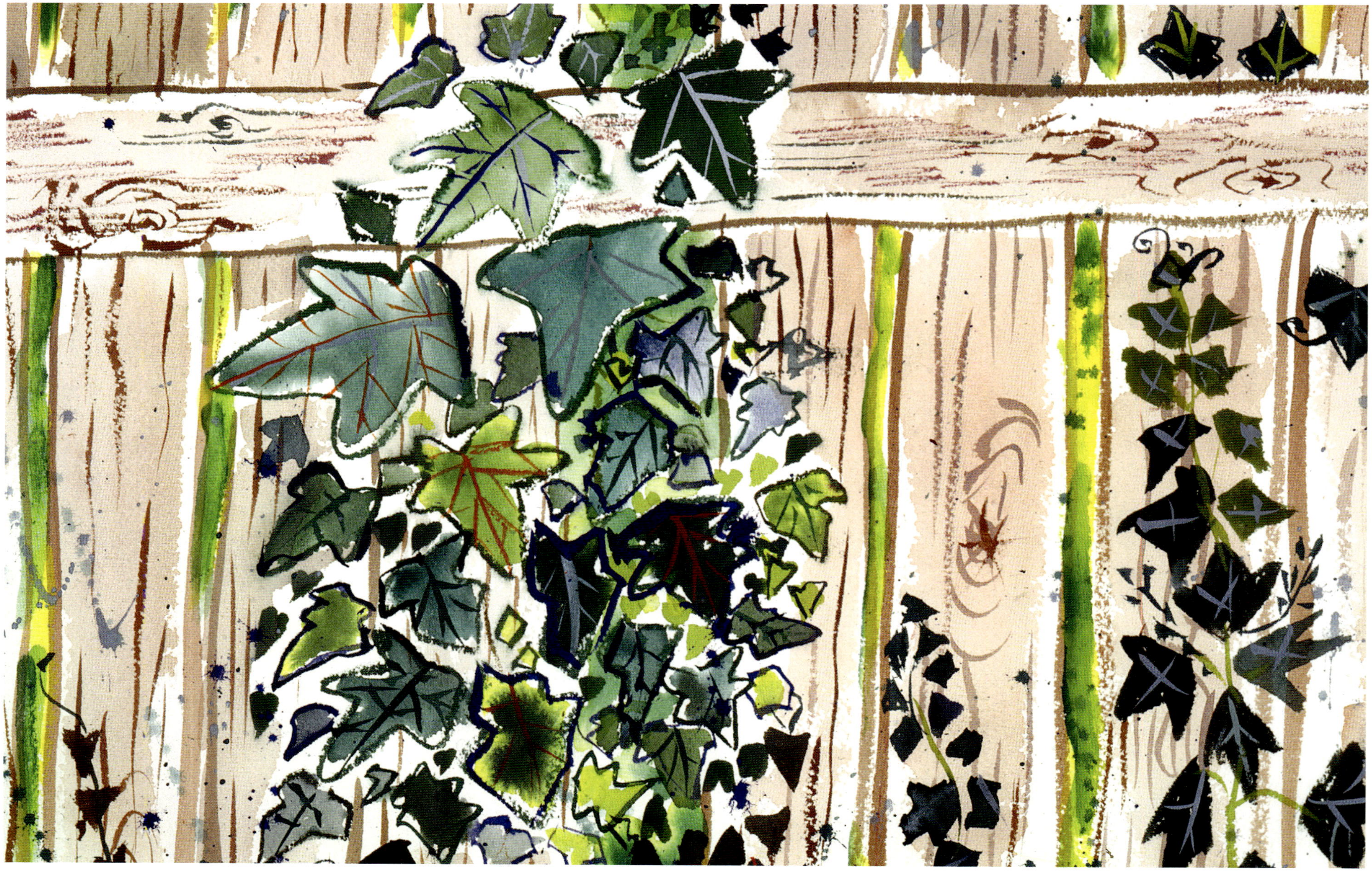

Left: IVY ON FENCE 15 x 11 &1/2" gouache 1991

Right: JOE"S KITCHEN ORCHID 14x17" gouache 2022

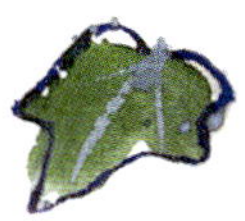

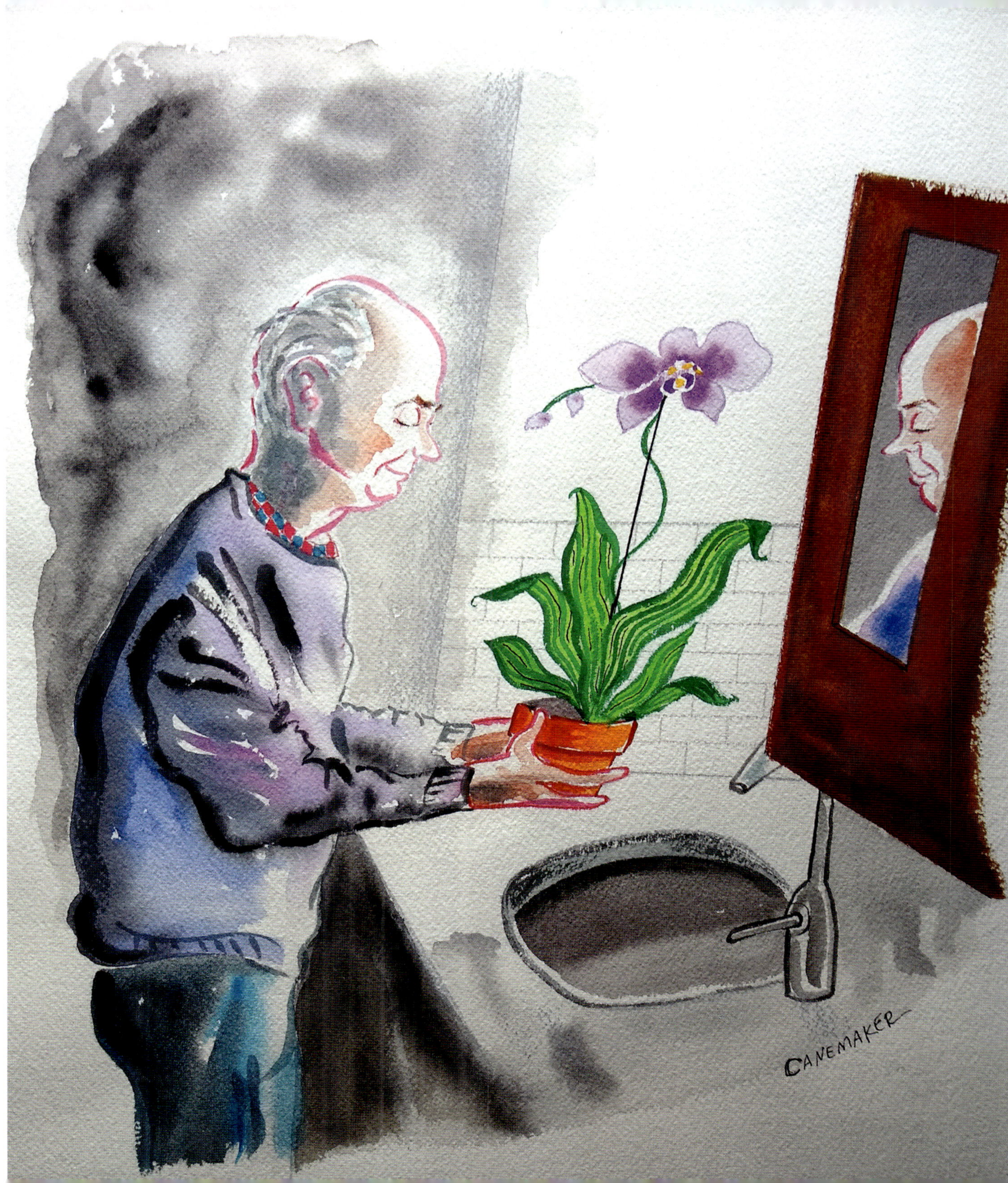

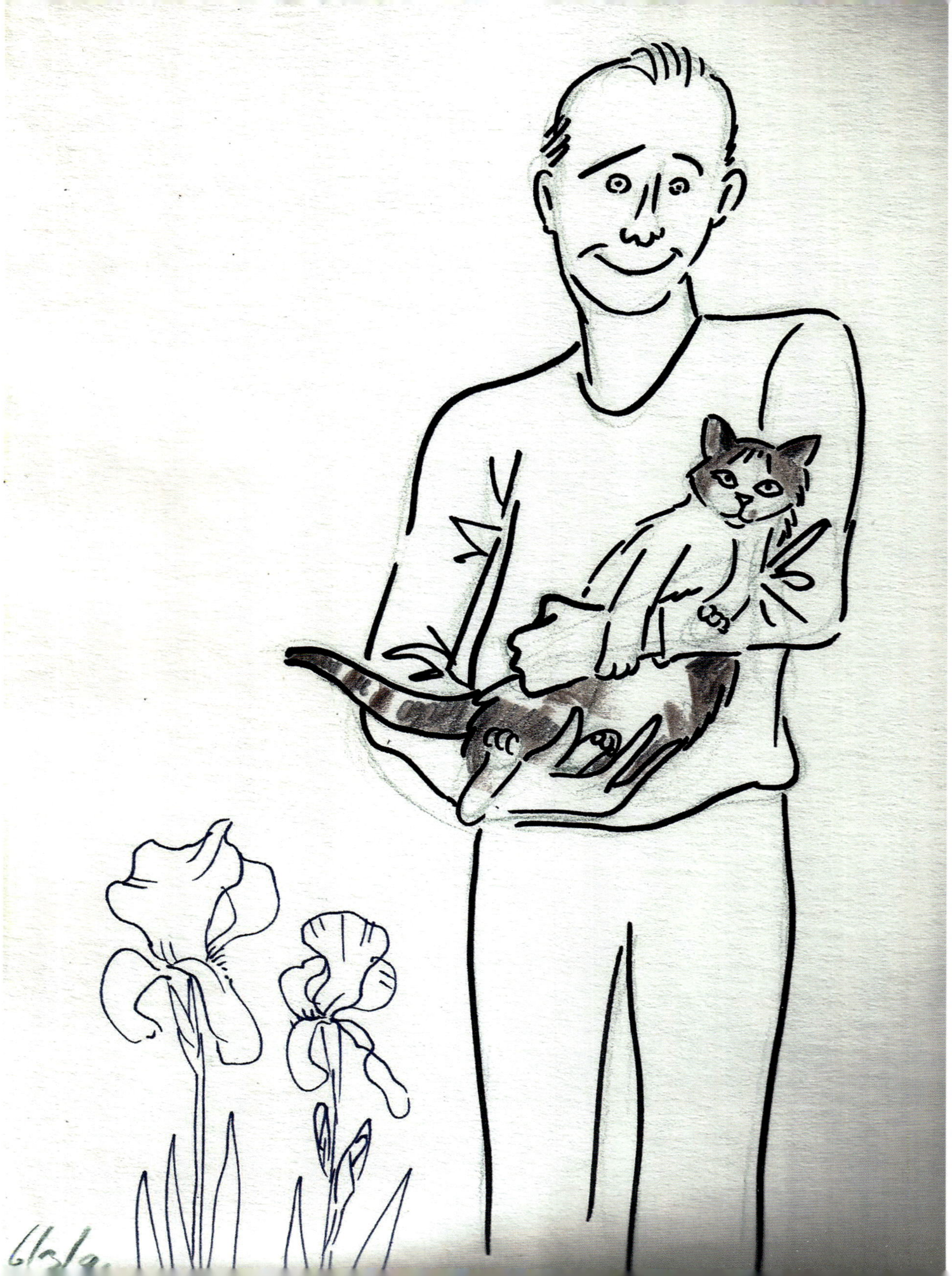

Left: *JOE & LUCY 1996*

Right: *LAST SUMMER HEIRLOOM TOMATOES 24x18" gouache 2010*

Following pages:

Page 100: LUCY IN REPOSE 12x16" gouache 1990

Page 101: LINDA'S SULLY 16X12" gouache 2021

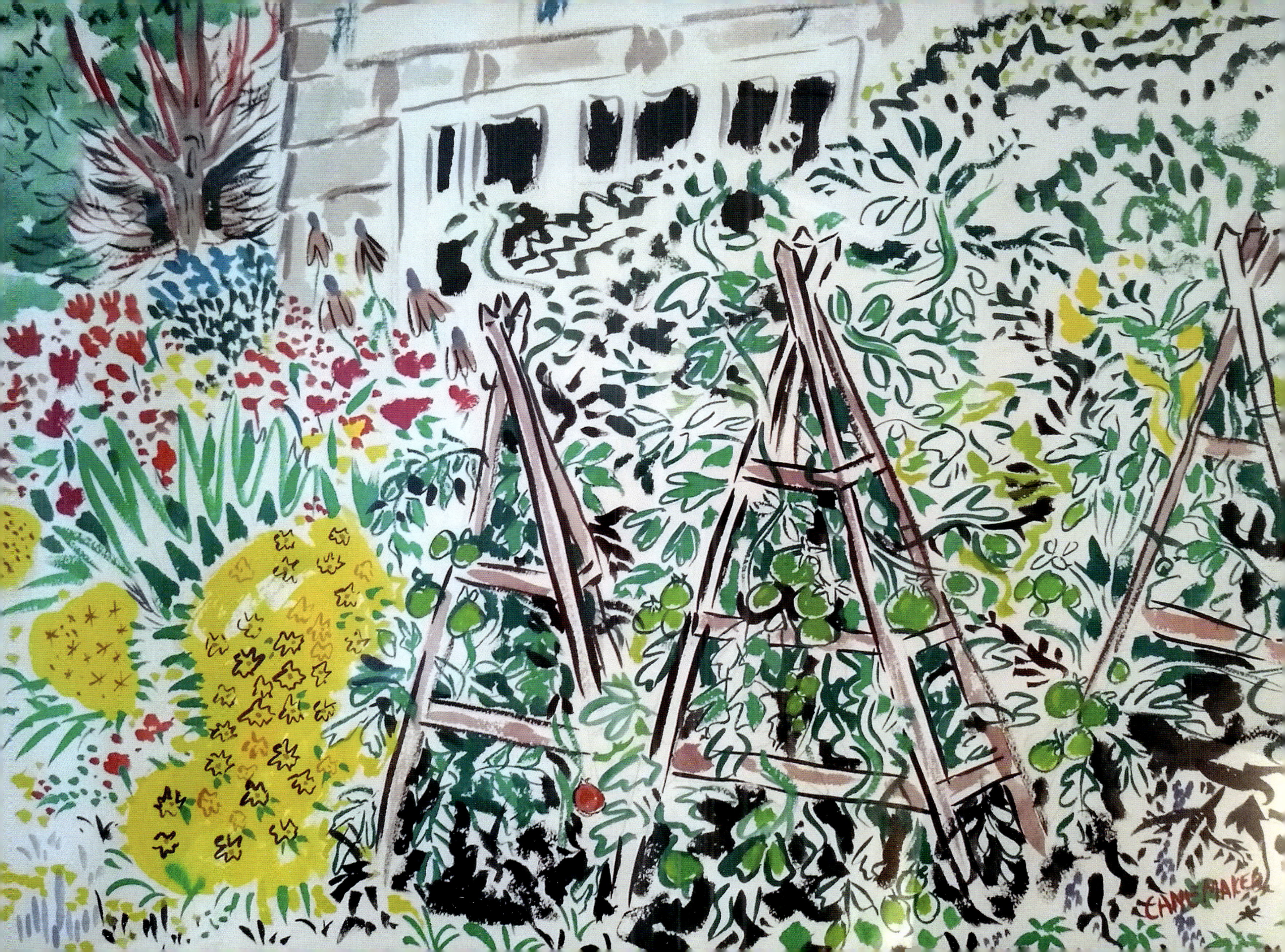

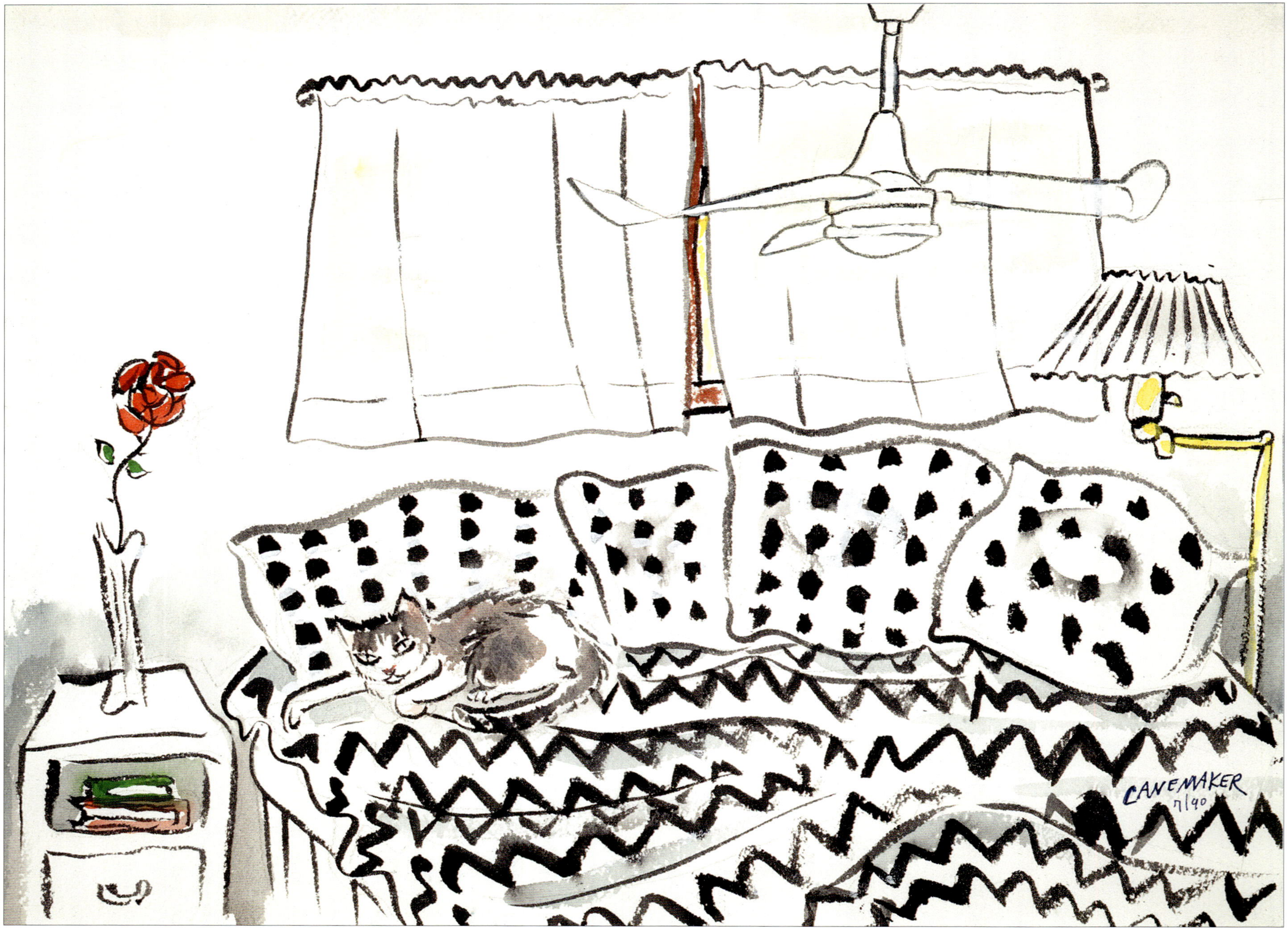
CANEMAKER
7/90

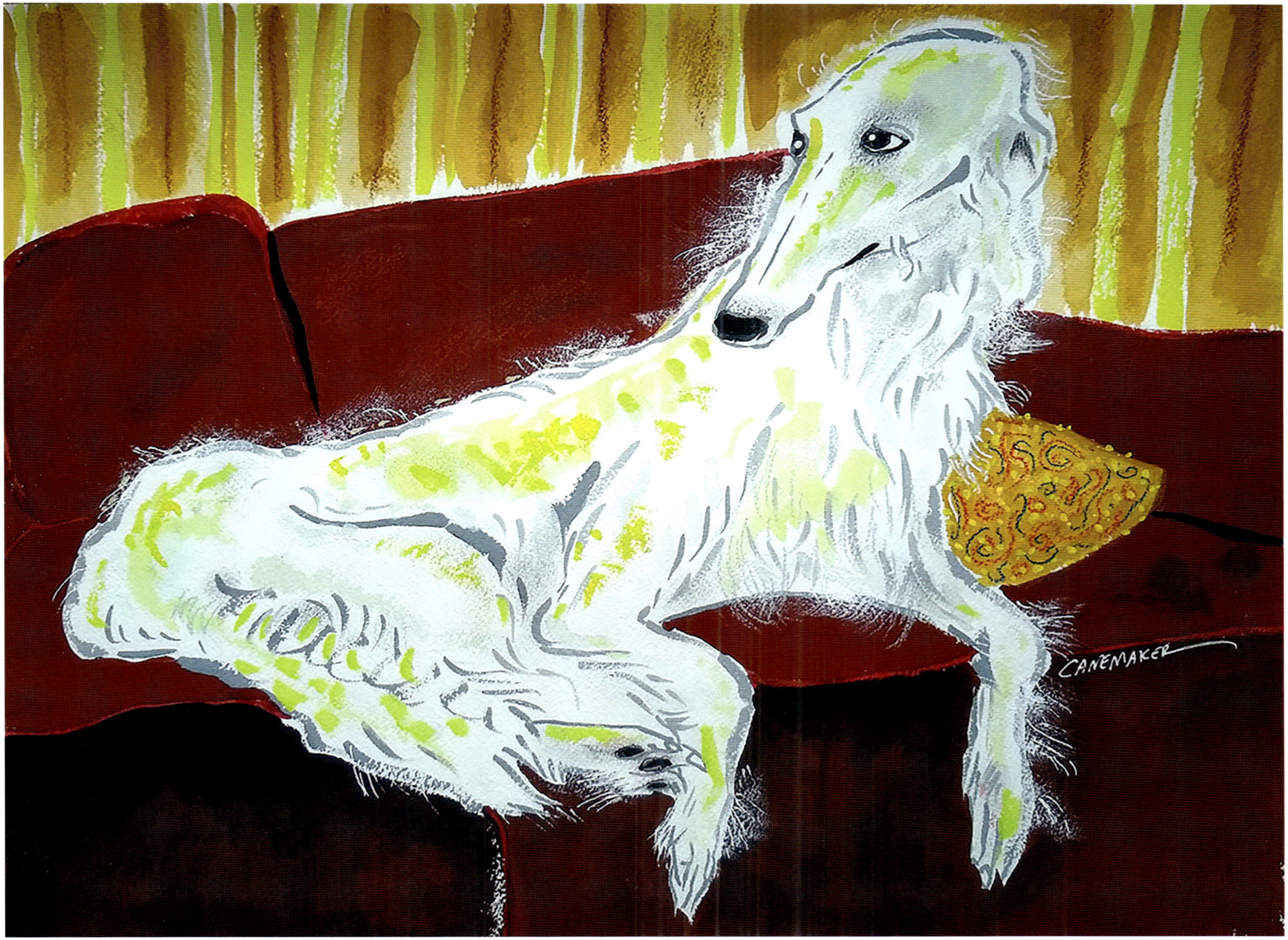
CANEMAKER

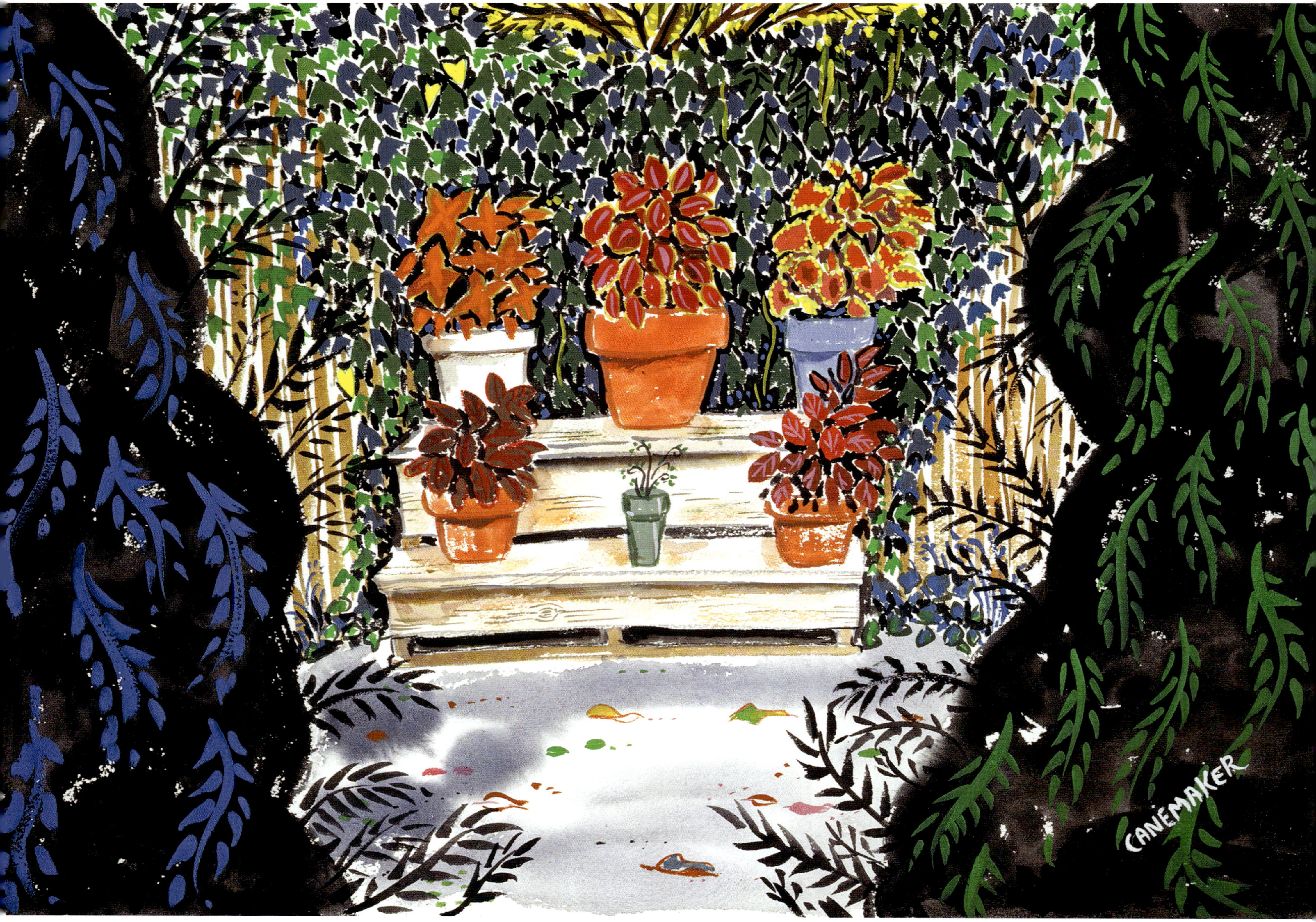
CANEMAKER

Left: THE SECRET GARDEN - POTTED PLANTS
20x14 &1/4" gouache 2000

Right:STAR OF PERSIA 24x18" gouache 2021

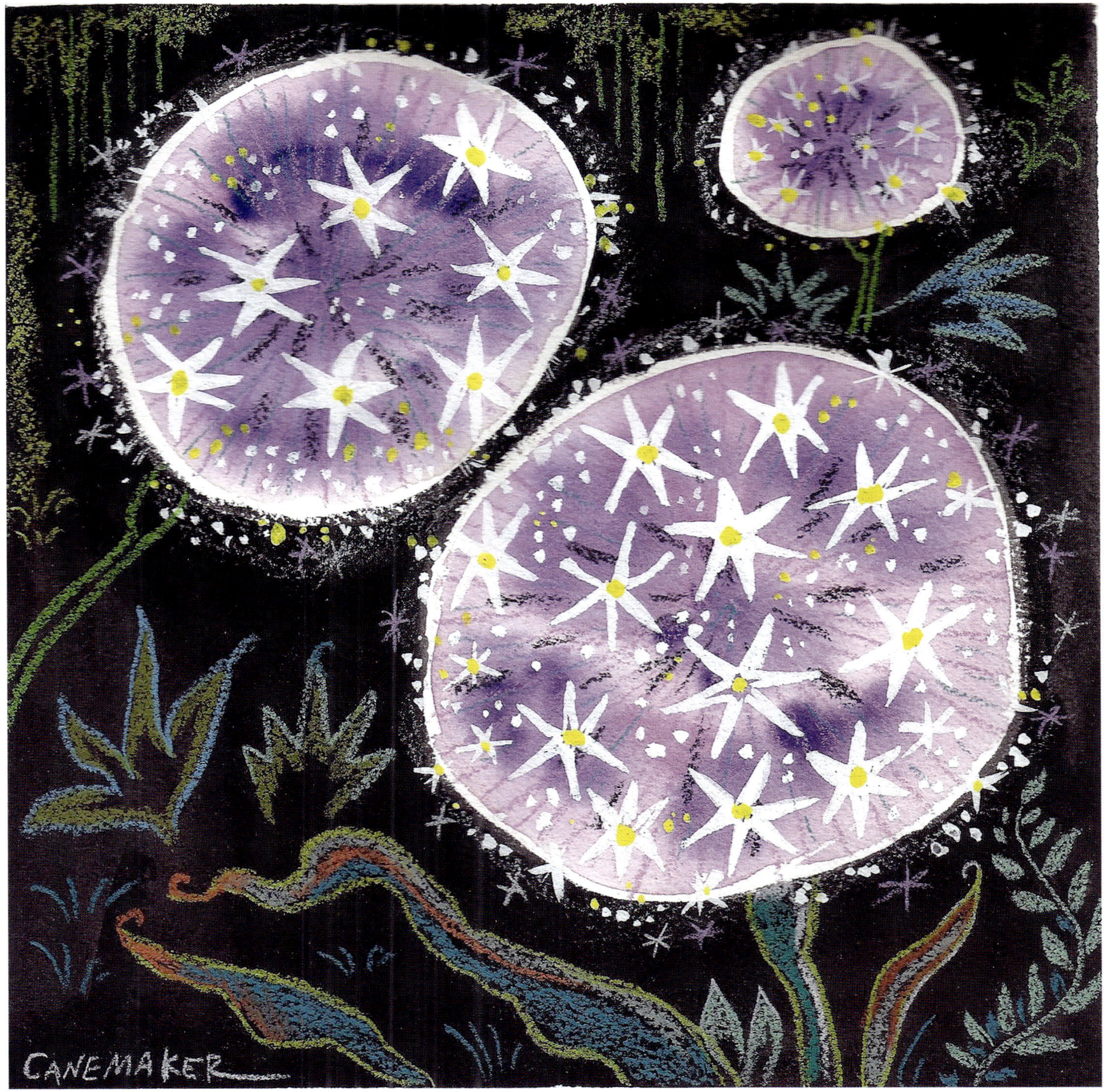

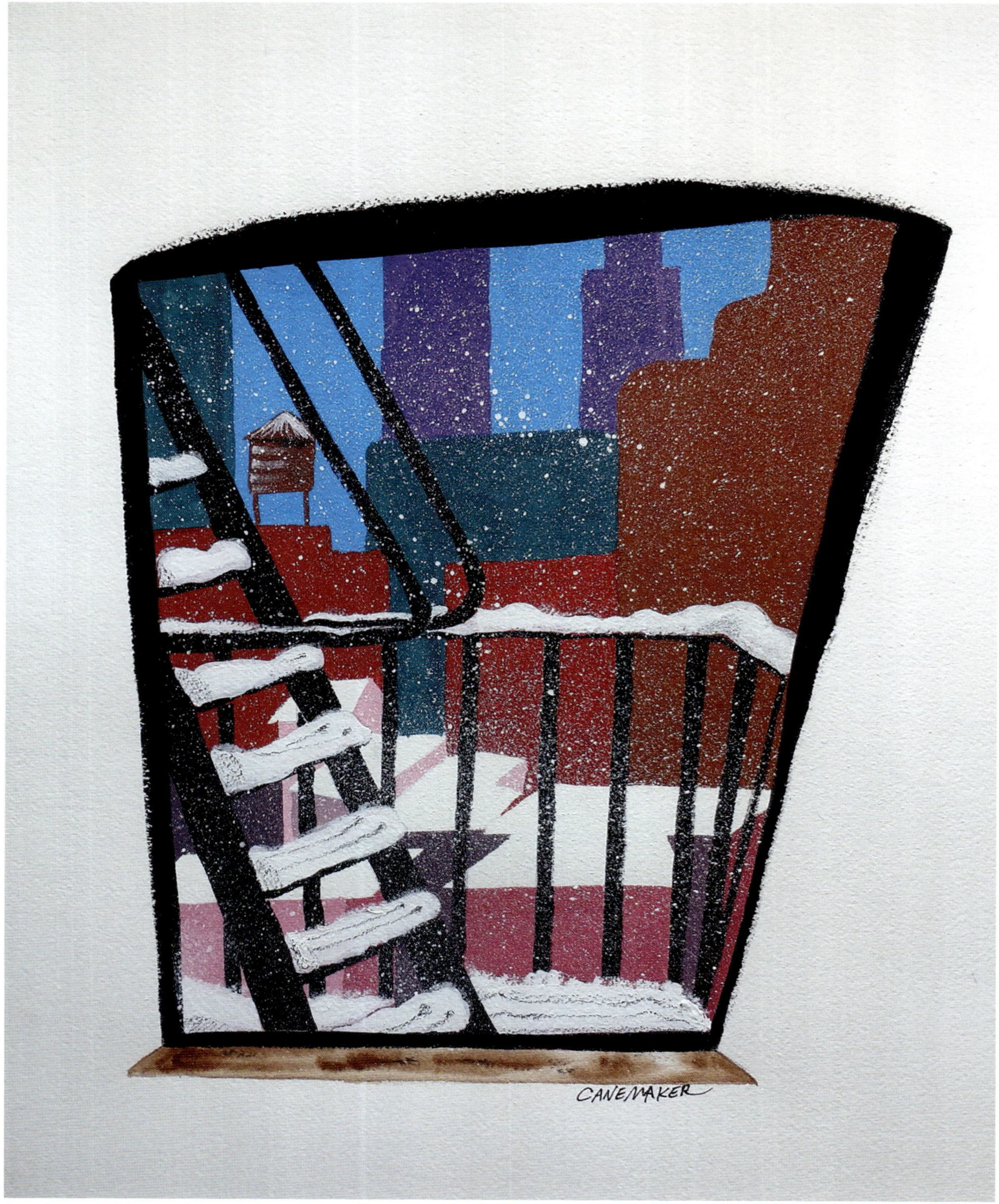
CANEMAKER

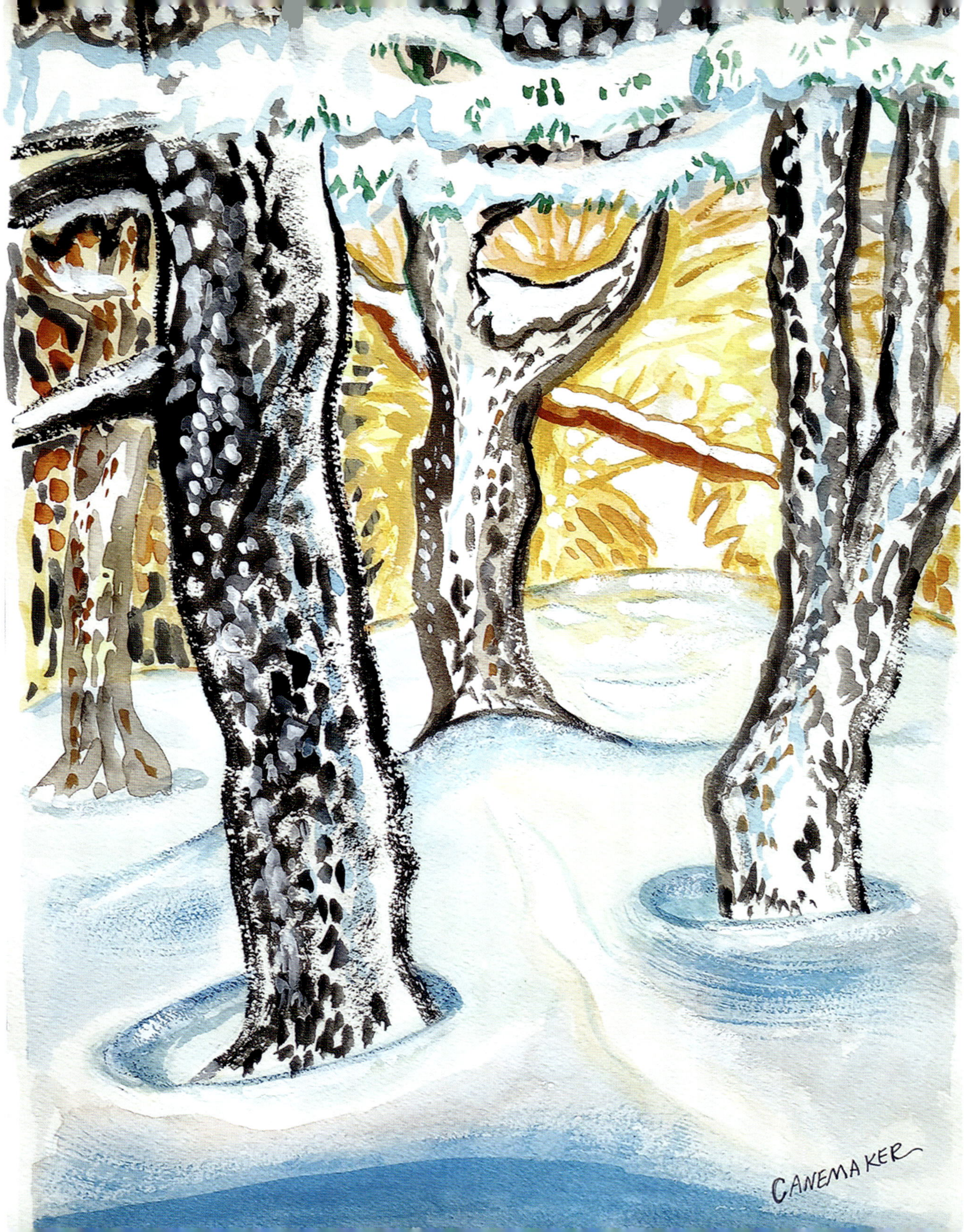

Far Left: SNOW TOWN 12x15" gouache 2021

Left: THROUGH THE WOODS 14 &1/4"x10 &1/4" gouache 2022

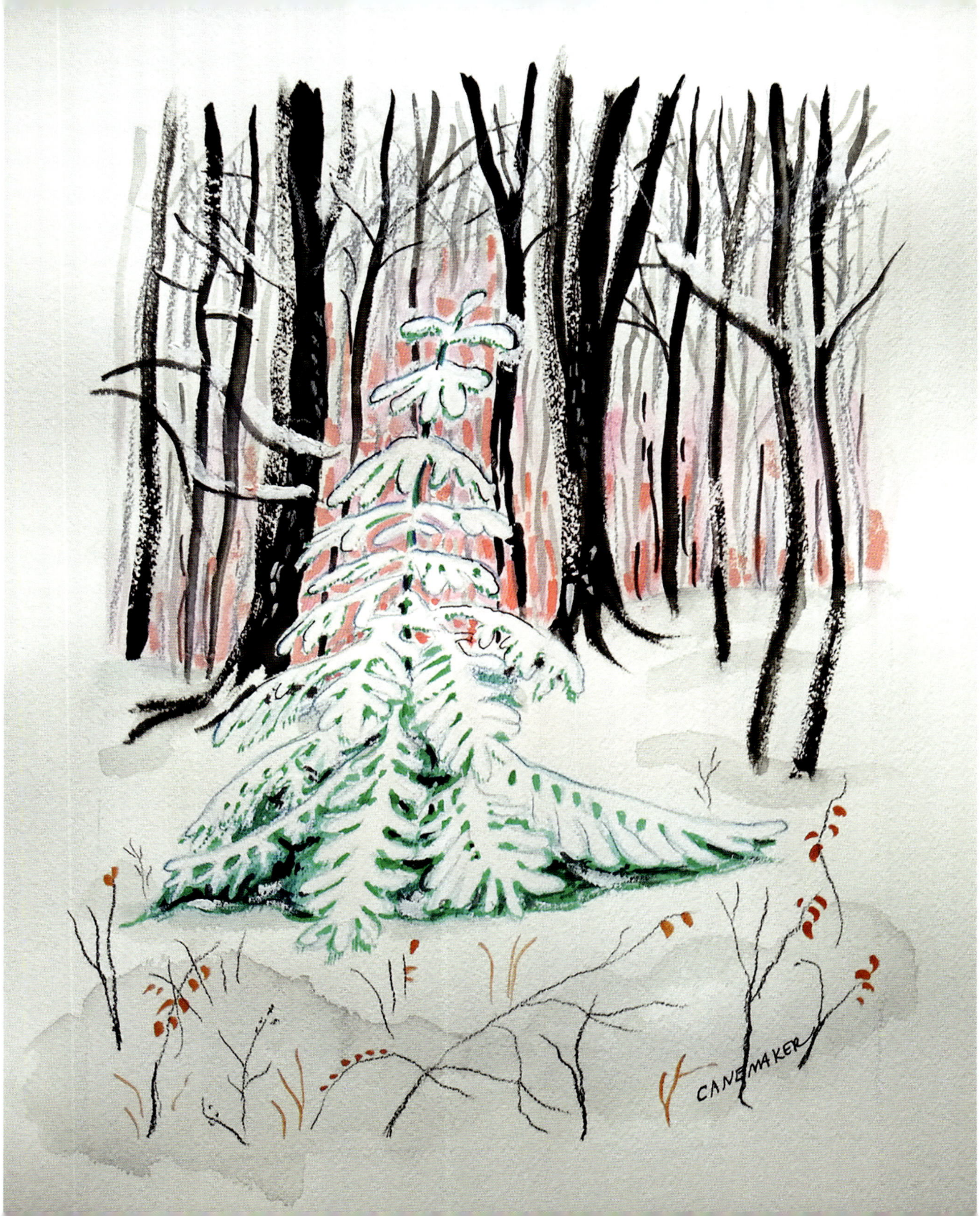

Left: WINTER PINE 12x16″ gouache 2021

Right: WINTER WONDERING 12x16″ gouache n.d

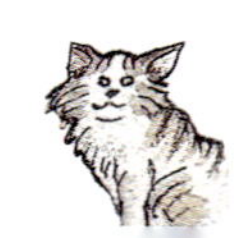

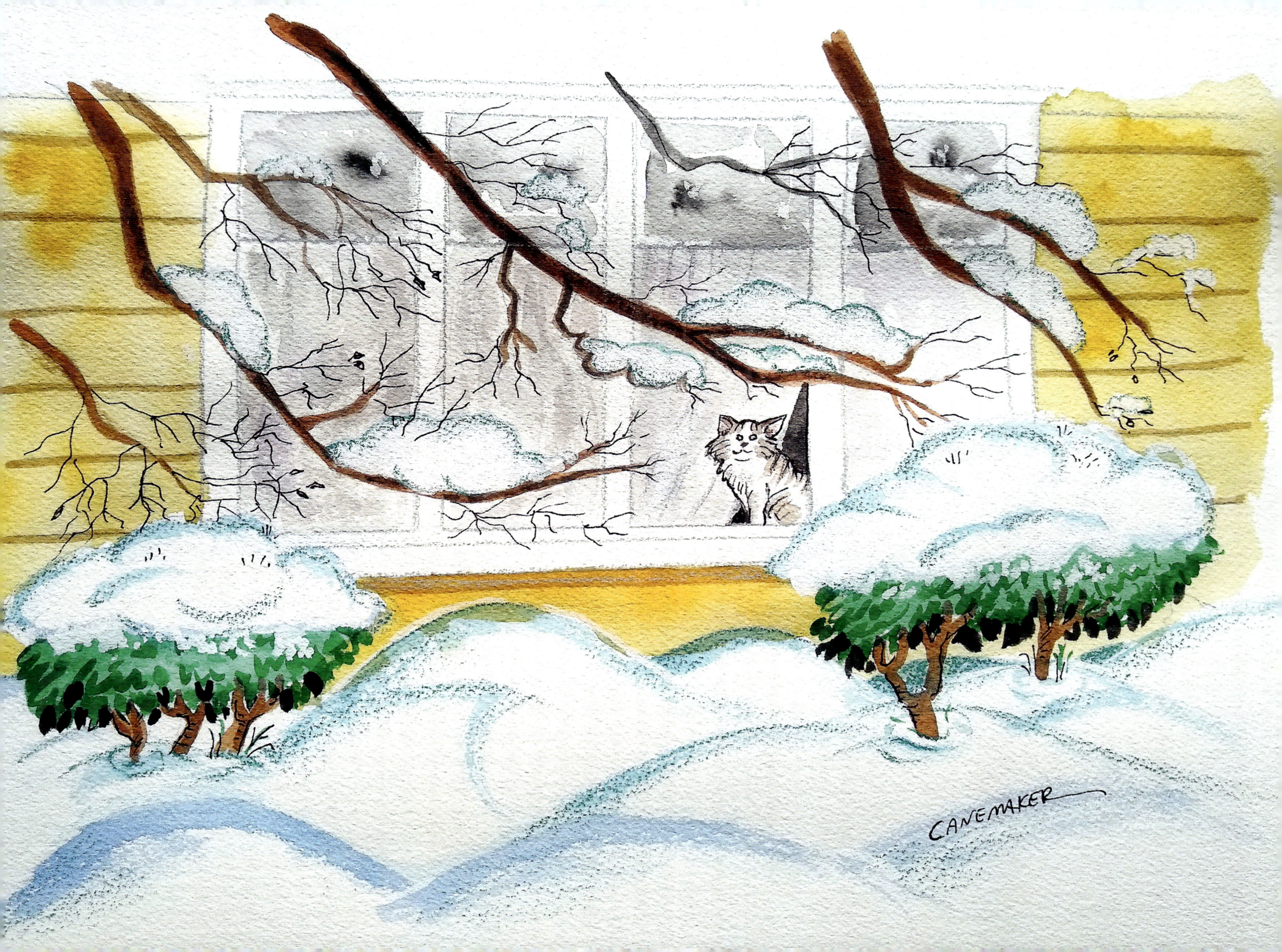
CANEMAKER

SPRING

"I know a bank where the wild thyme blows,
Where oxlips and the nodding violet grows,
Quite over-canopied with luscious woodbine,
With sweet musk-roses and with eglantine."

— Shakespeare, *A Midsummer Night's Dream*, Act 2, Scene 1

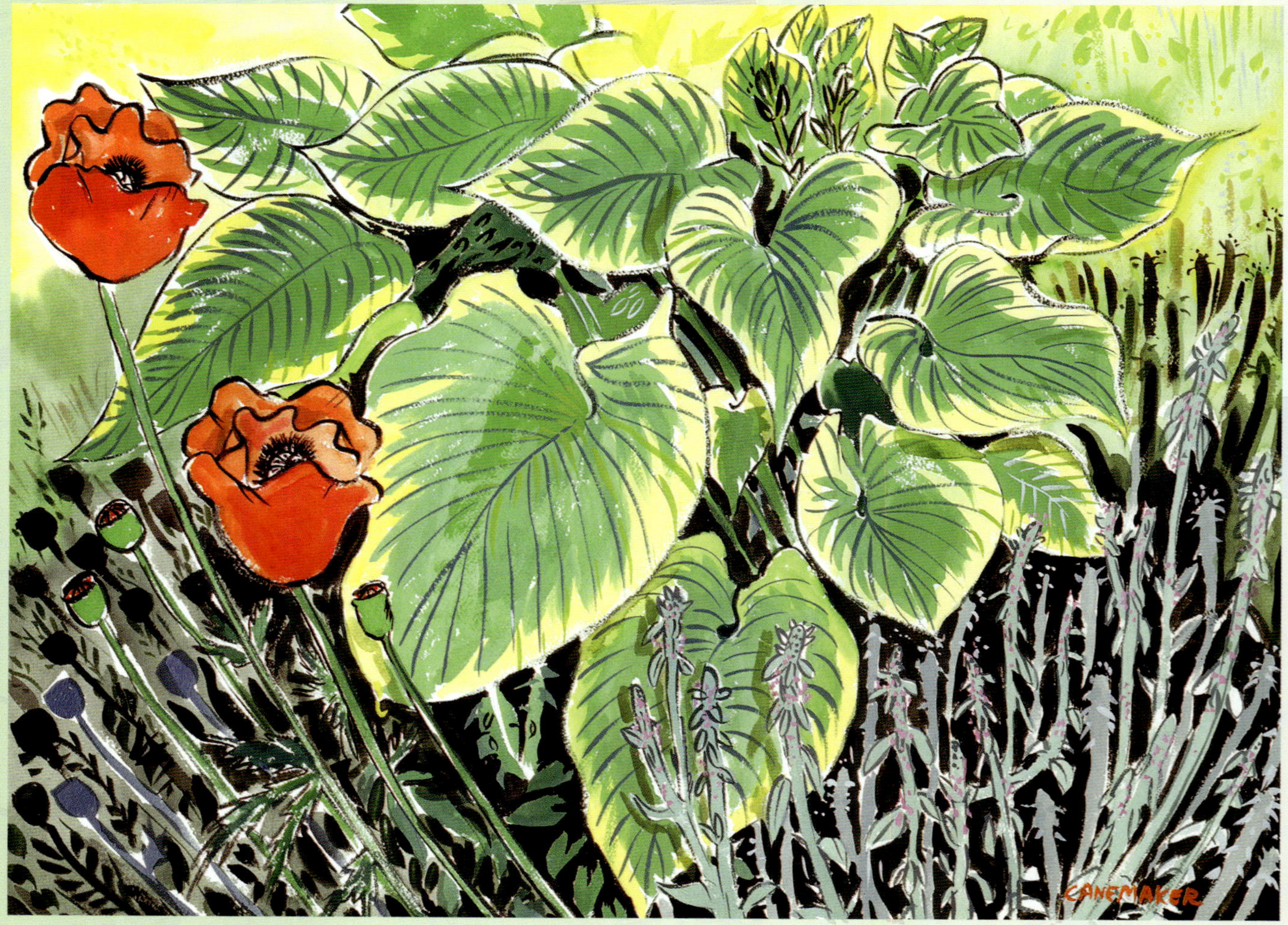

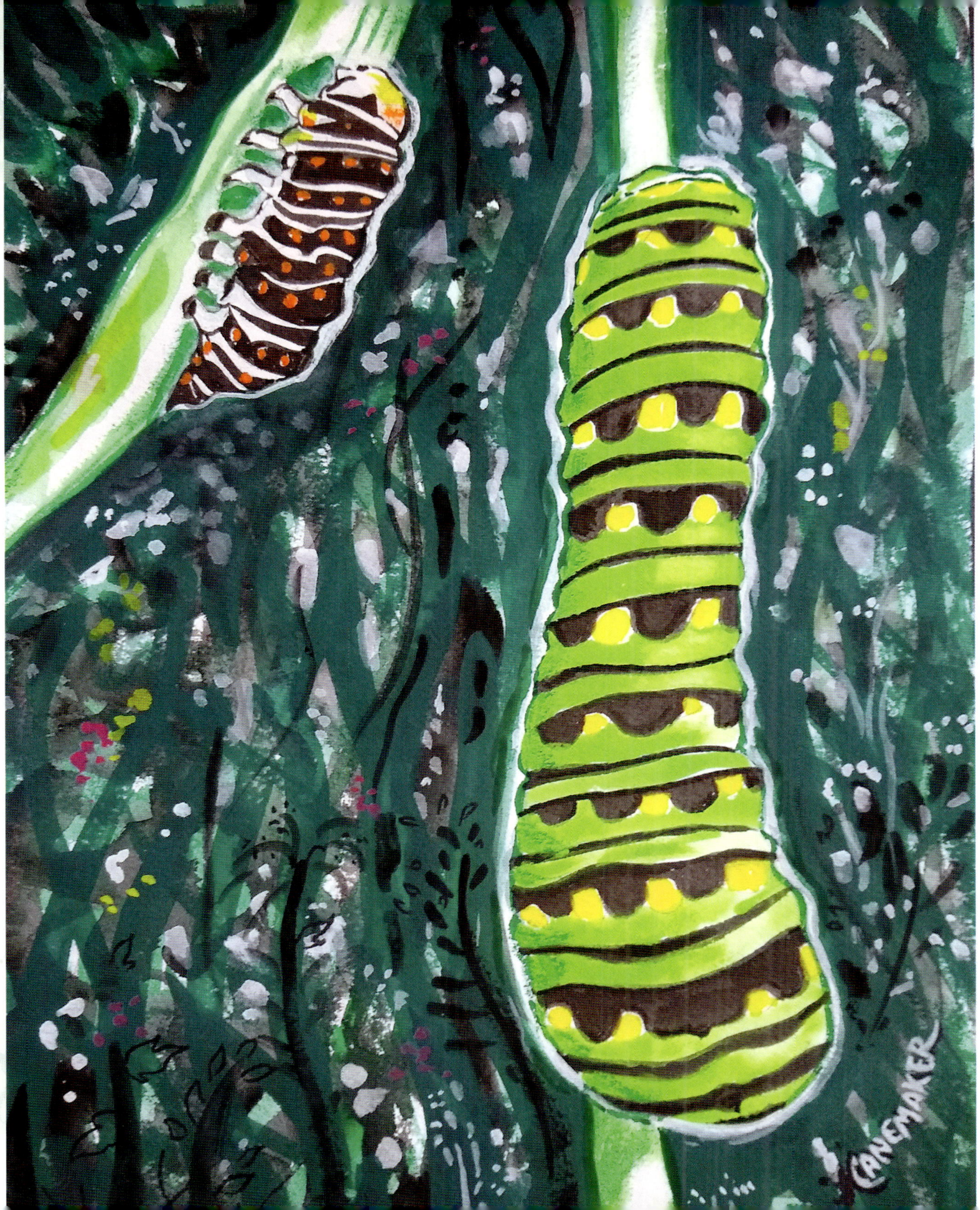

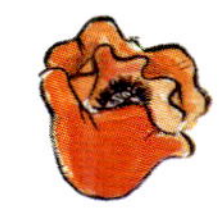

Far Left: HOSTA & POPPIES
24x18″ gouache 2000

Left: BLACK & ZEBRA SWALLOWTAIL CATERPILLARS
10x14″ gouache 2019

Right: GLADS 20x14″ gouache 1992

Far Right: GREEN POMPOMS 14x10″ gouache 2000

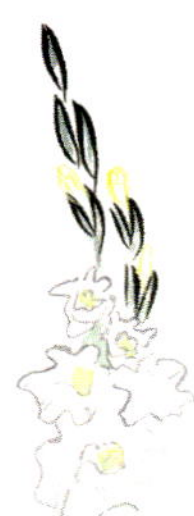

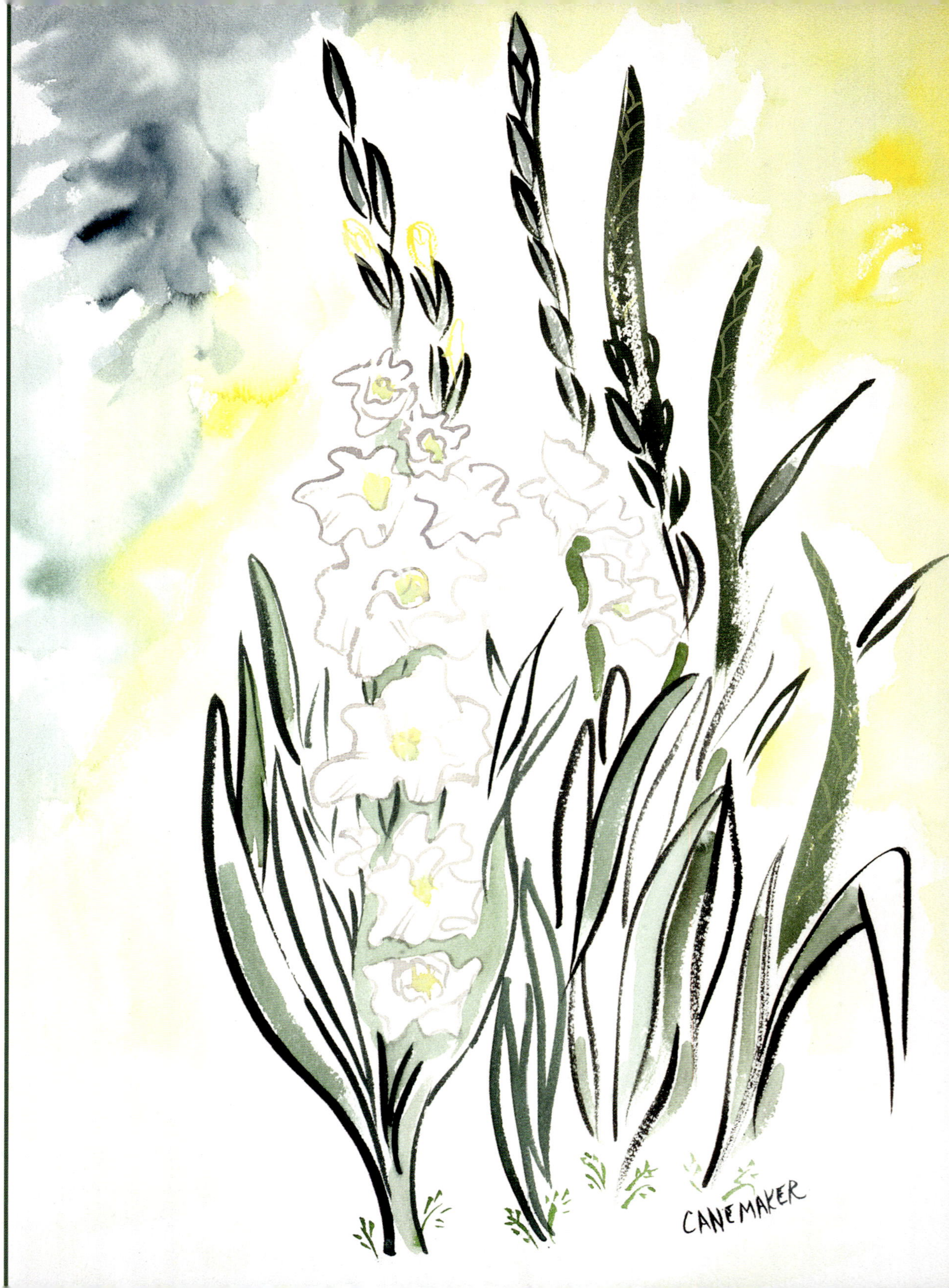

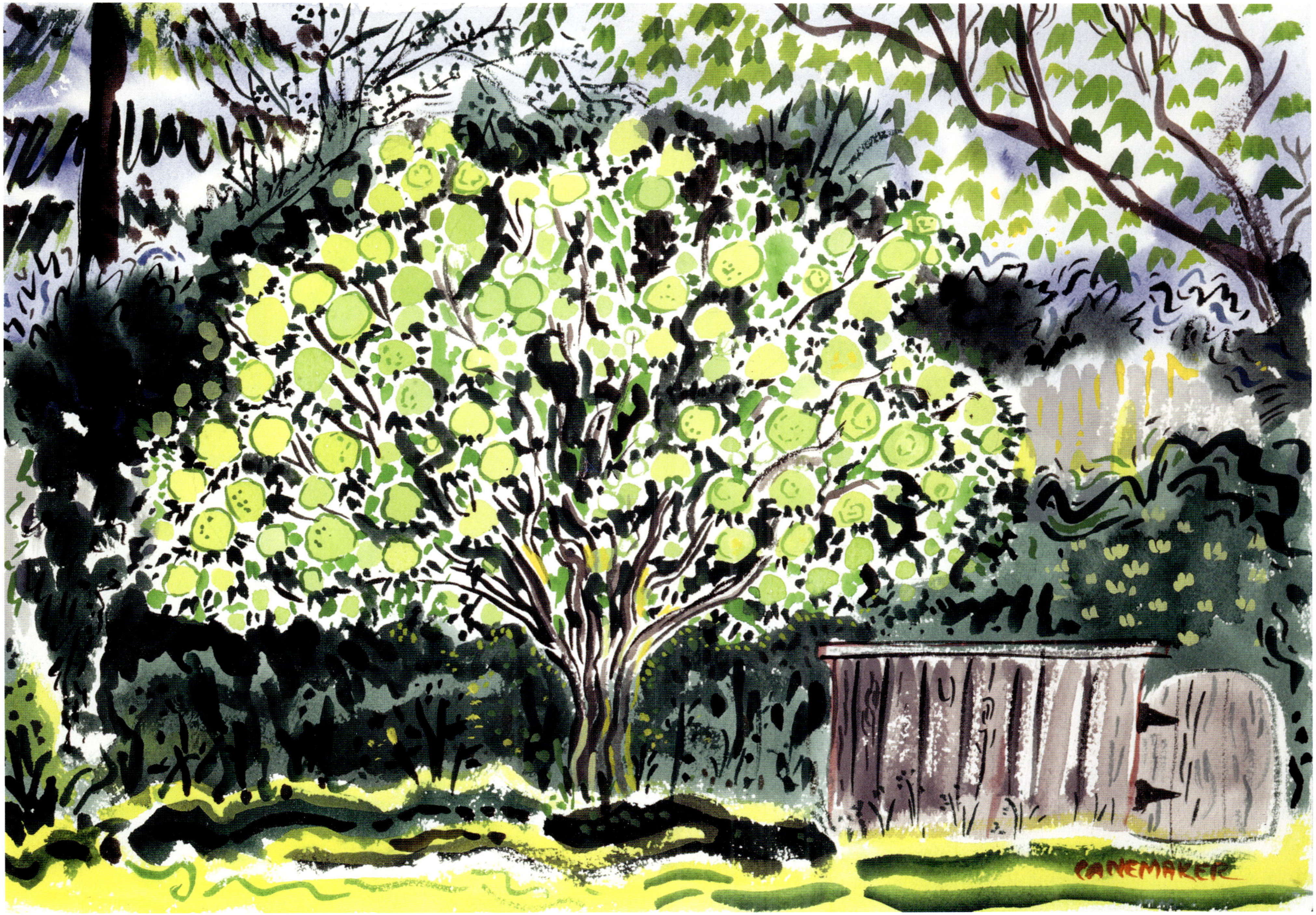
CANEMAKER

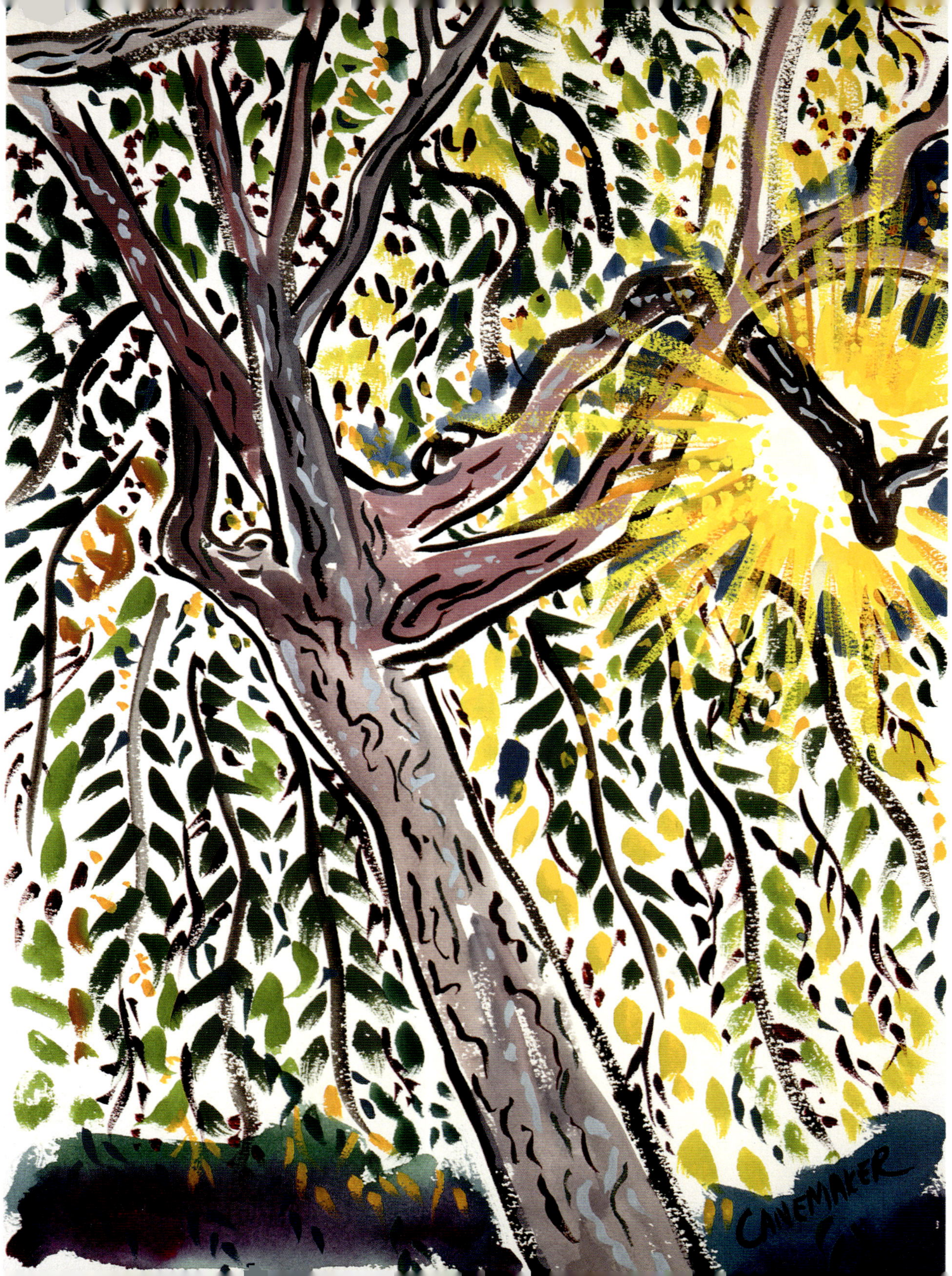

Left: CHERRY TREE AT DAWN 14 x 20"
gouache, 1994

Right: SHIMMERING VINES 14 x 17"
gouache, 1993

Following pages:

Page 114: SNOWBALL ROSES 13 1/2x9 1/2"
gouache 1991

Page 115: SPRING CHERRY TREES 12x16"
gouache 2021

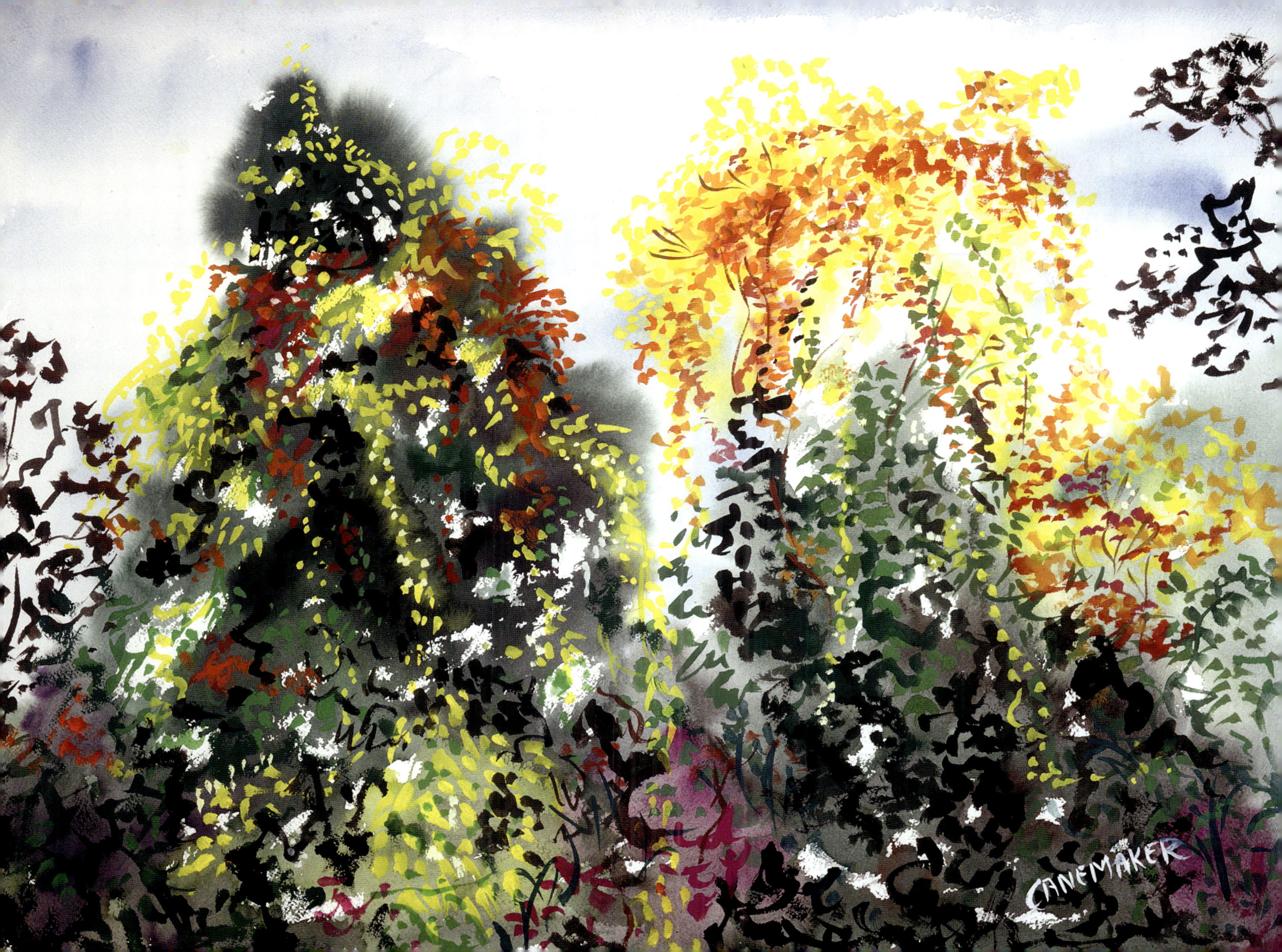
CANEMAKER

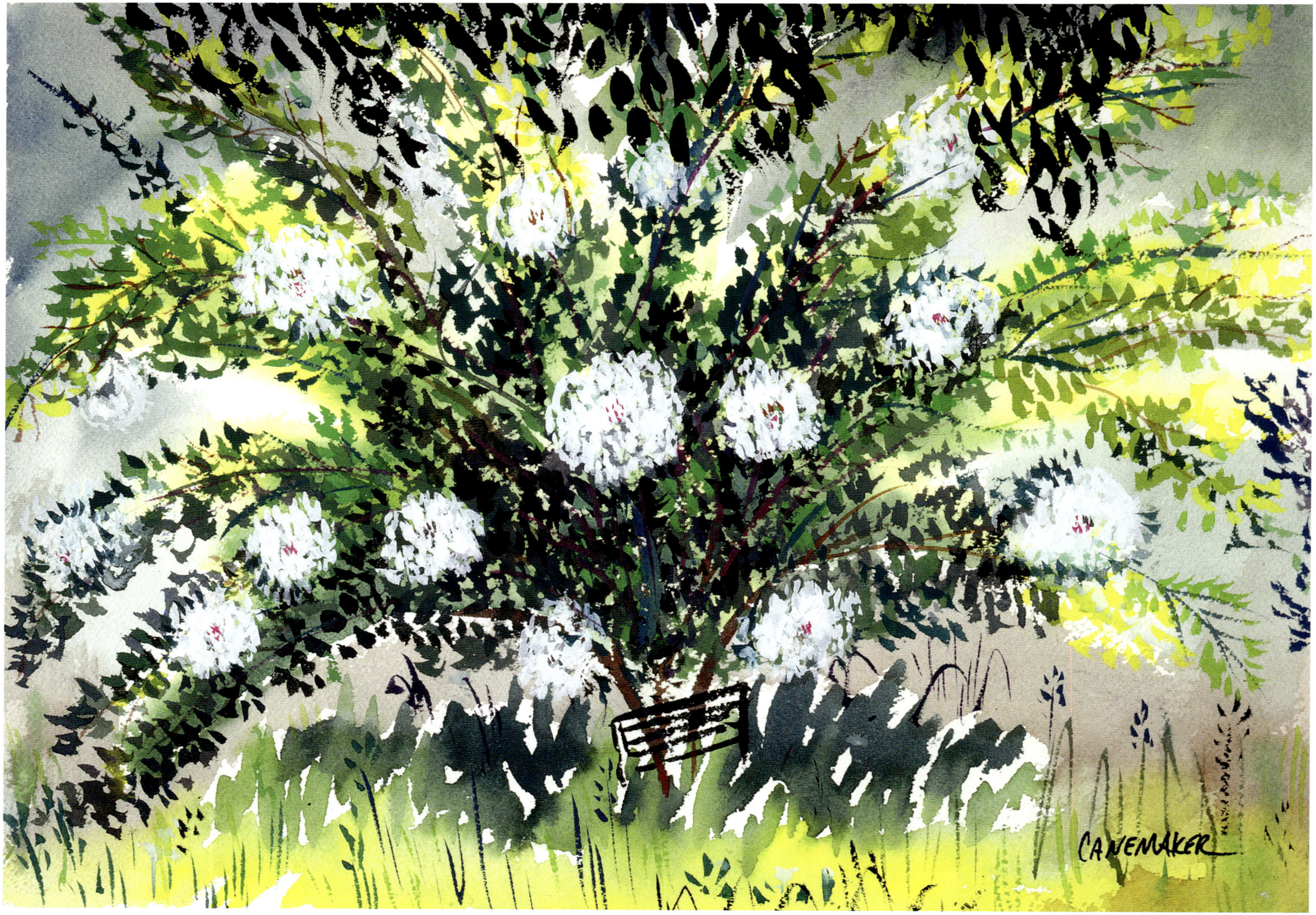
CANEMAKER

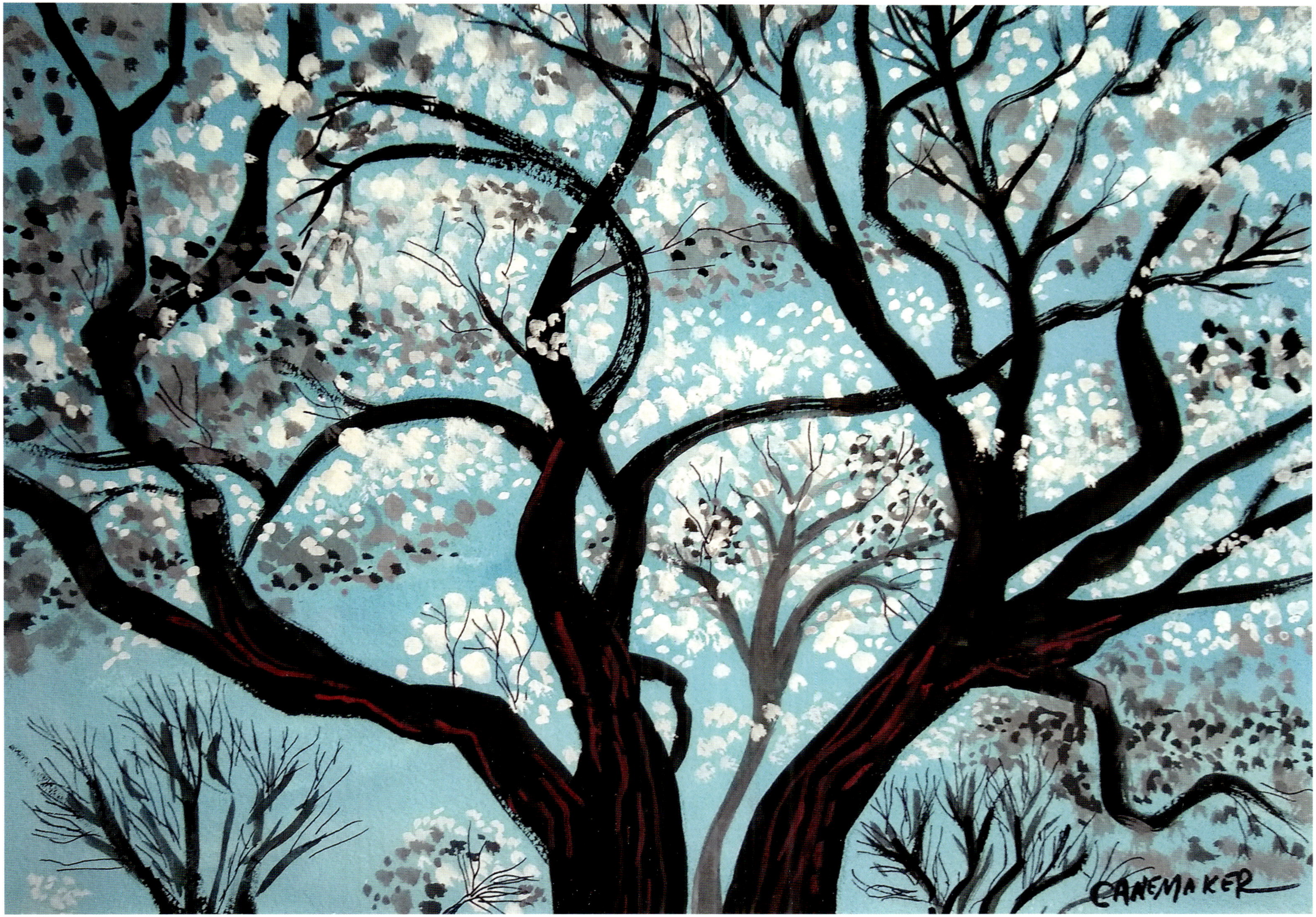
CANEMAKER

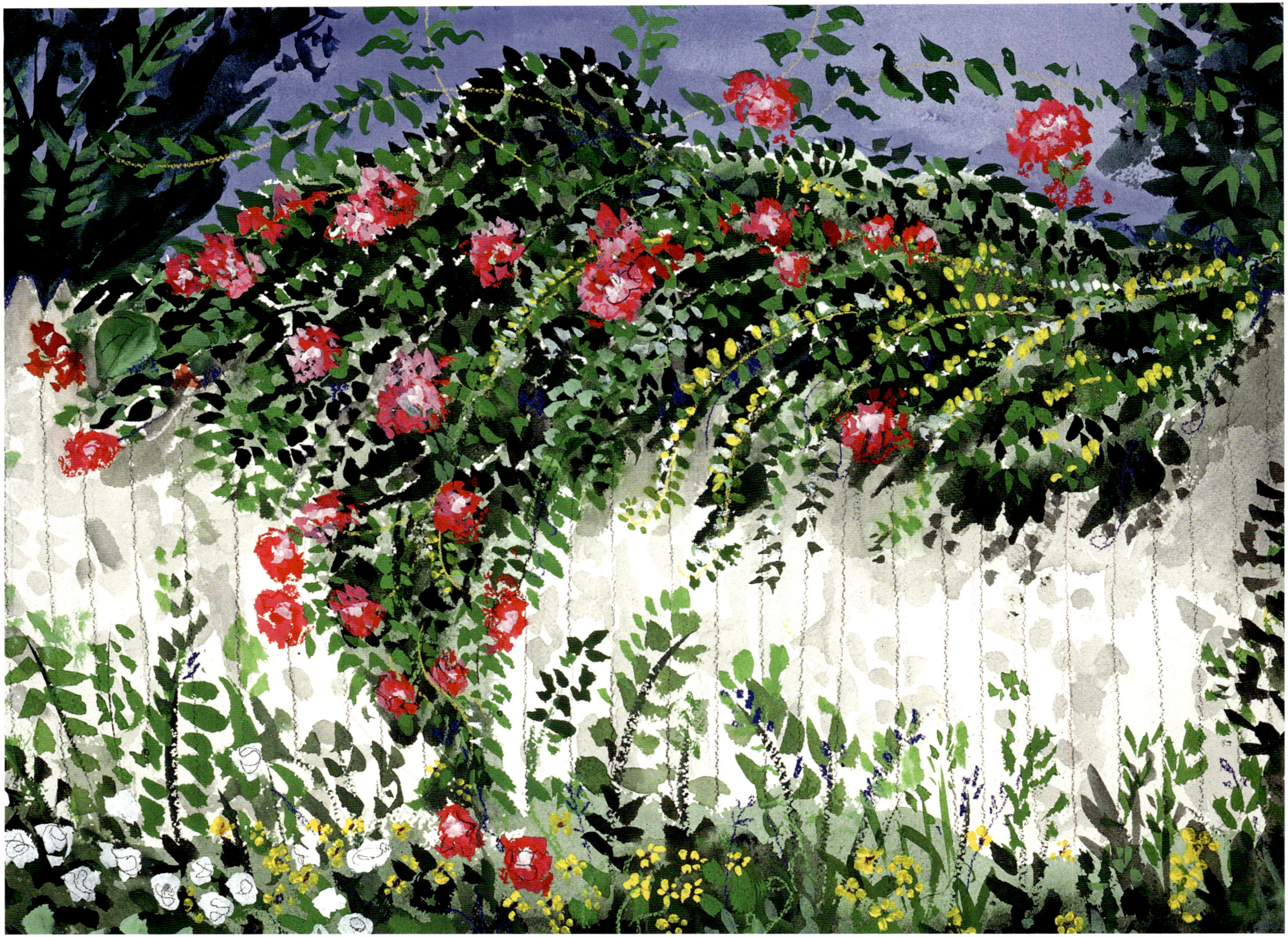

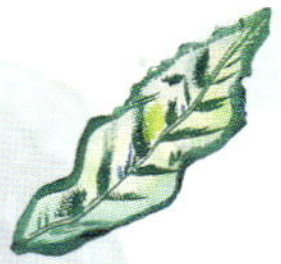

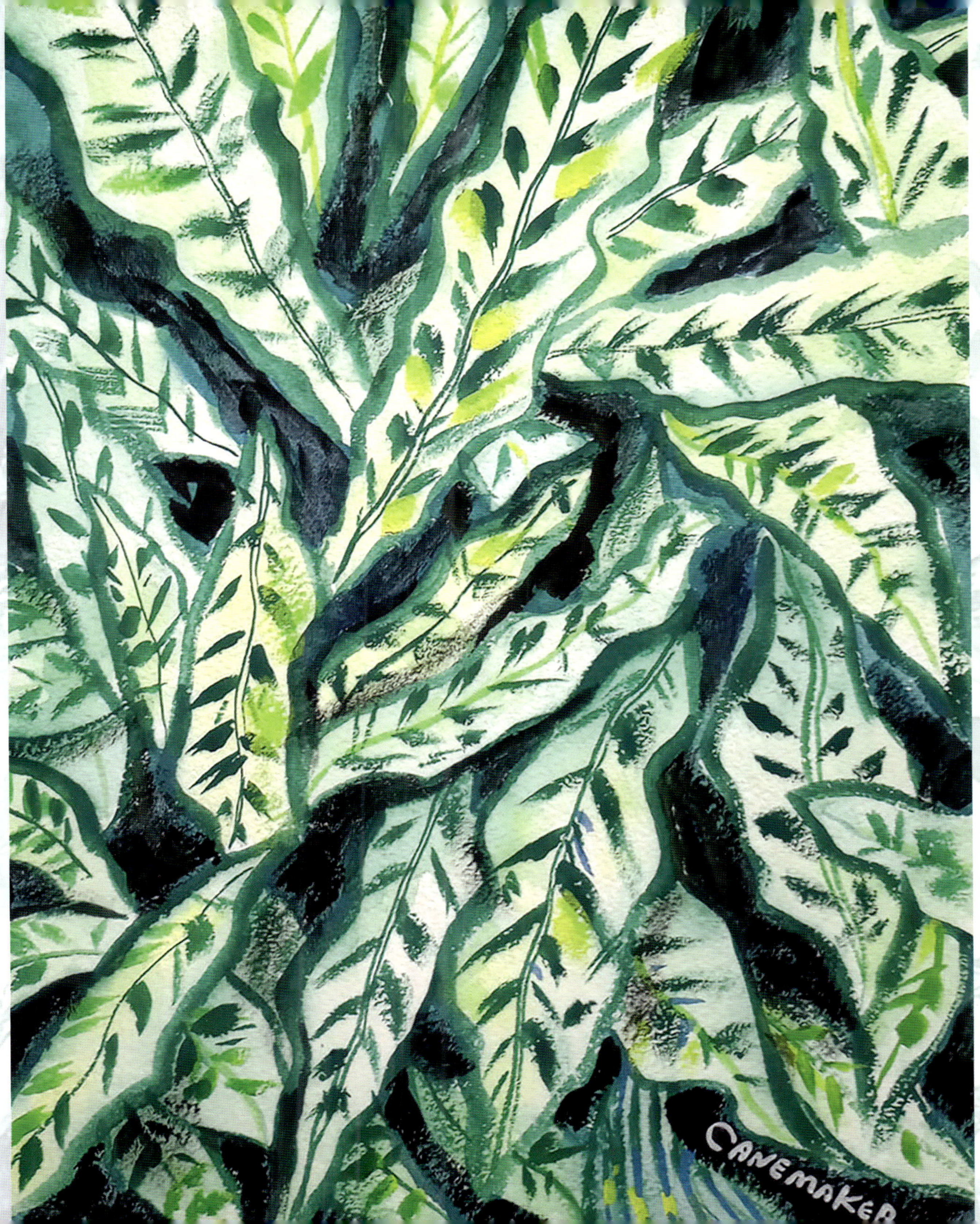

Left: SHIPWRECK ROSES 15x11 1/2″
gouache 1990

Right: COLD SPRING 9x12″
gouache 2024

Right: CLIMBERS 12x16″ gouache 1990

Far Right: BACKYARD 16x12″ gouache 1991

Following pages:

Page 120: JOE BUILDS STONE DECK 20x14″ gouache 2002

Page 121: PURPLE OSTEOSPERMUM 12x9″ gouache 2025

Page 122: FLEURS DE PRINTEMPS 12x9″ gouache 2024

Page 123: POLLINATOR BEES & RHODODENDRON 19x13 1/2″ gouache 1994

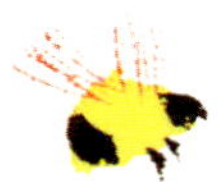

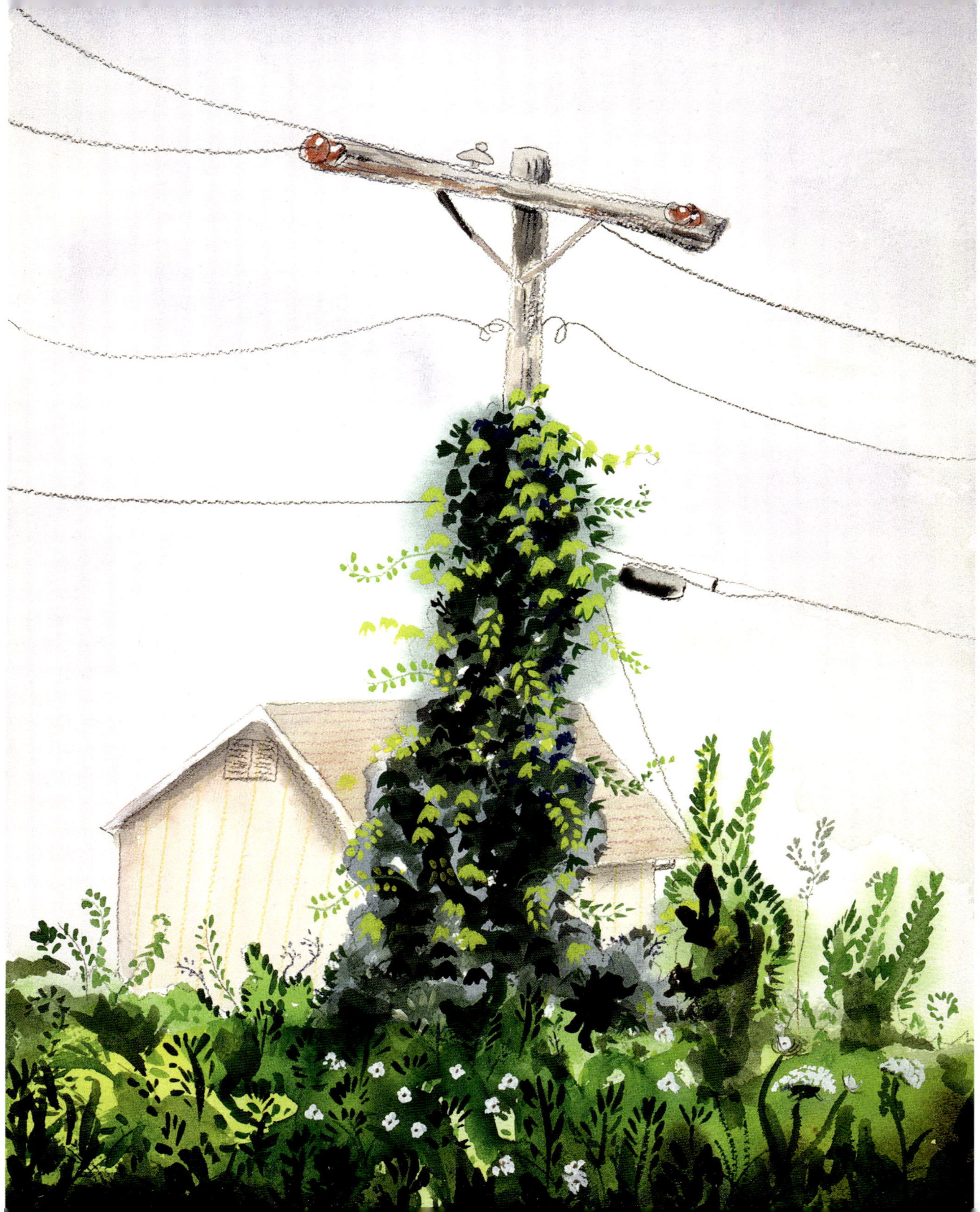

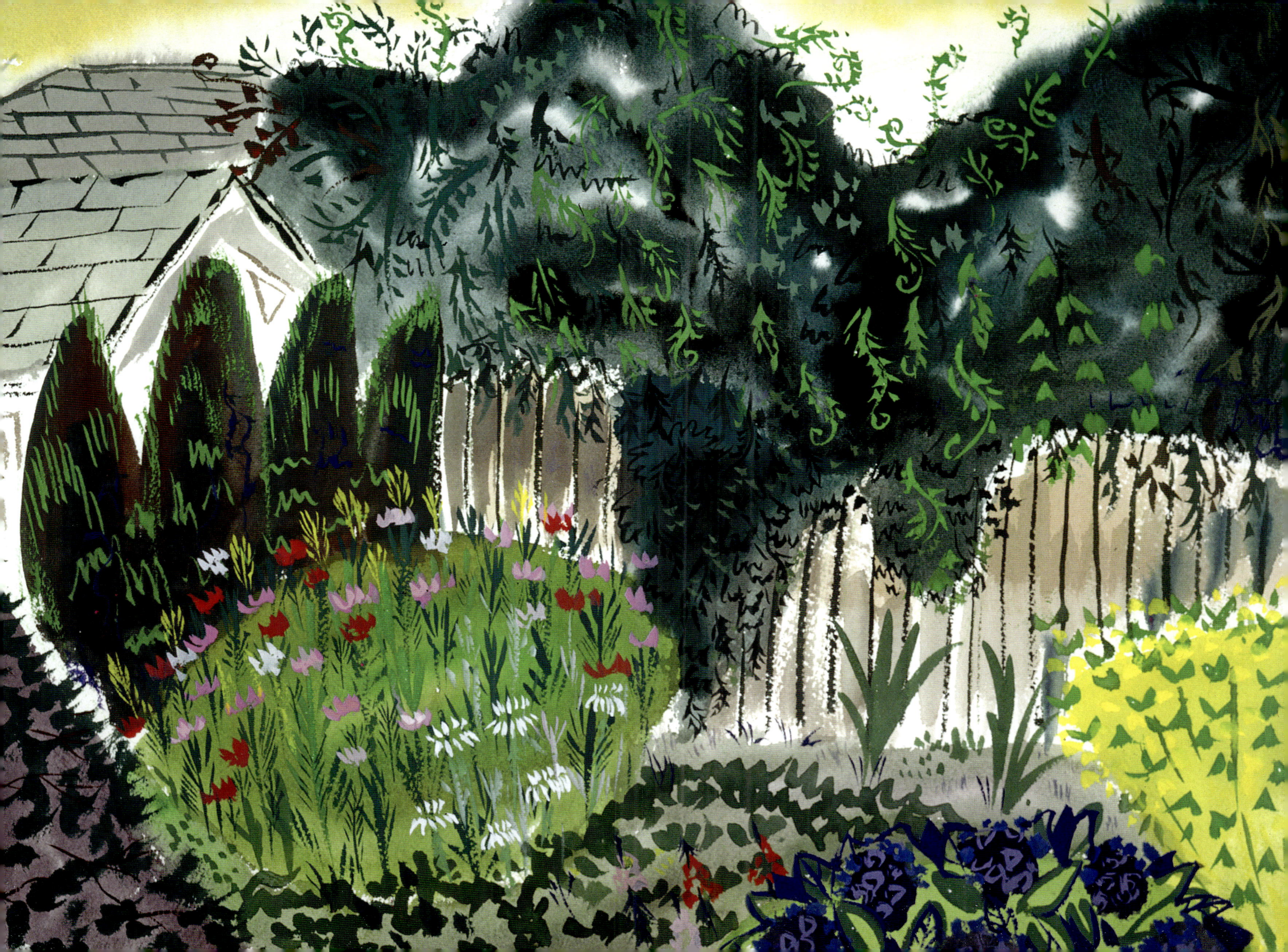

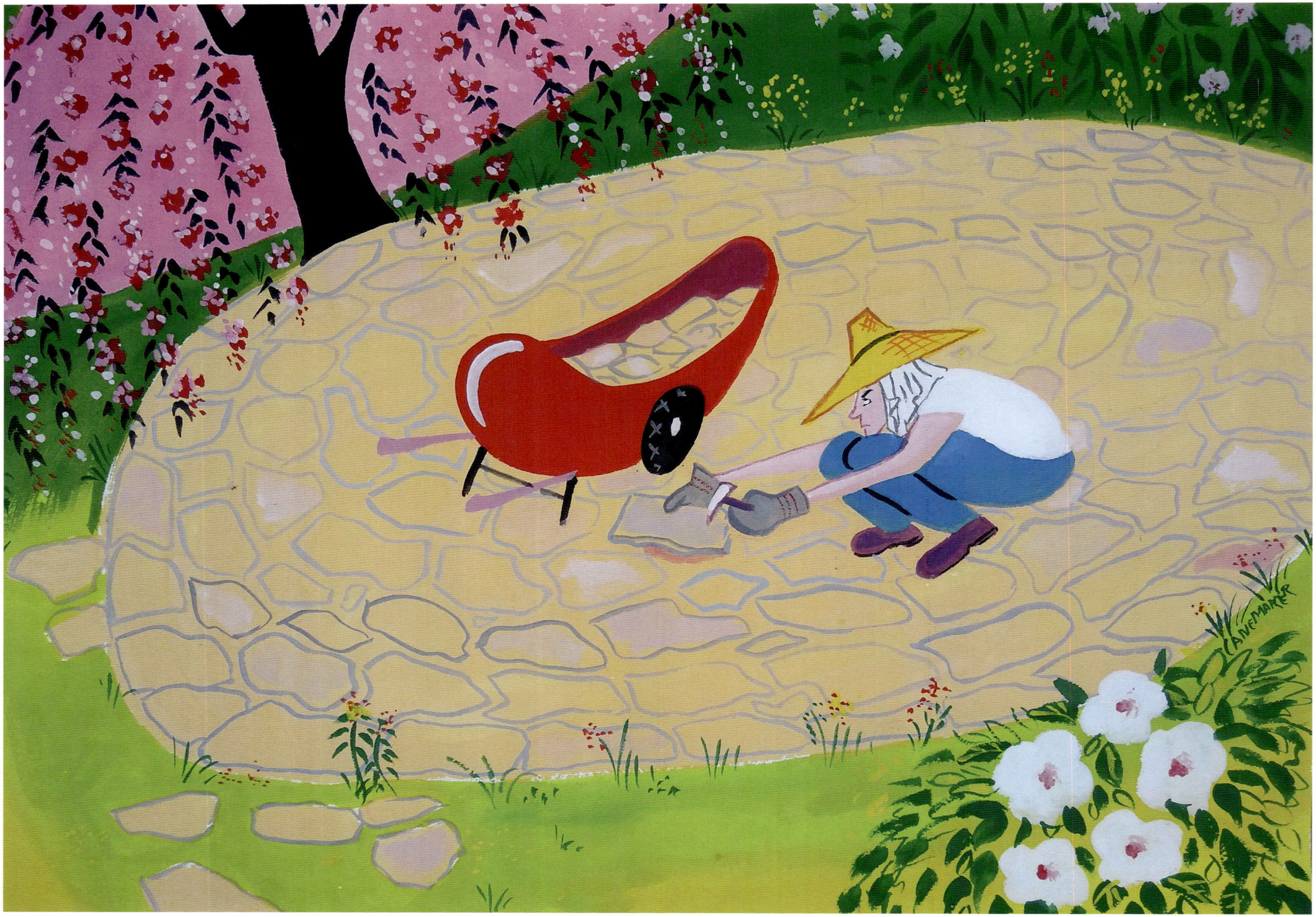
CANEMAKER

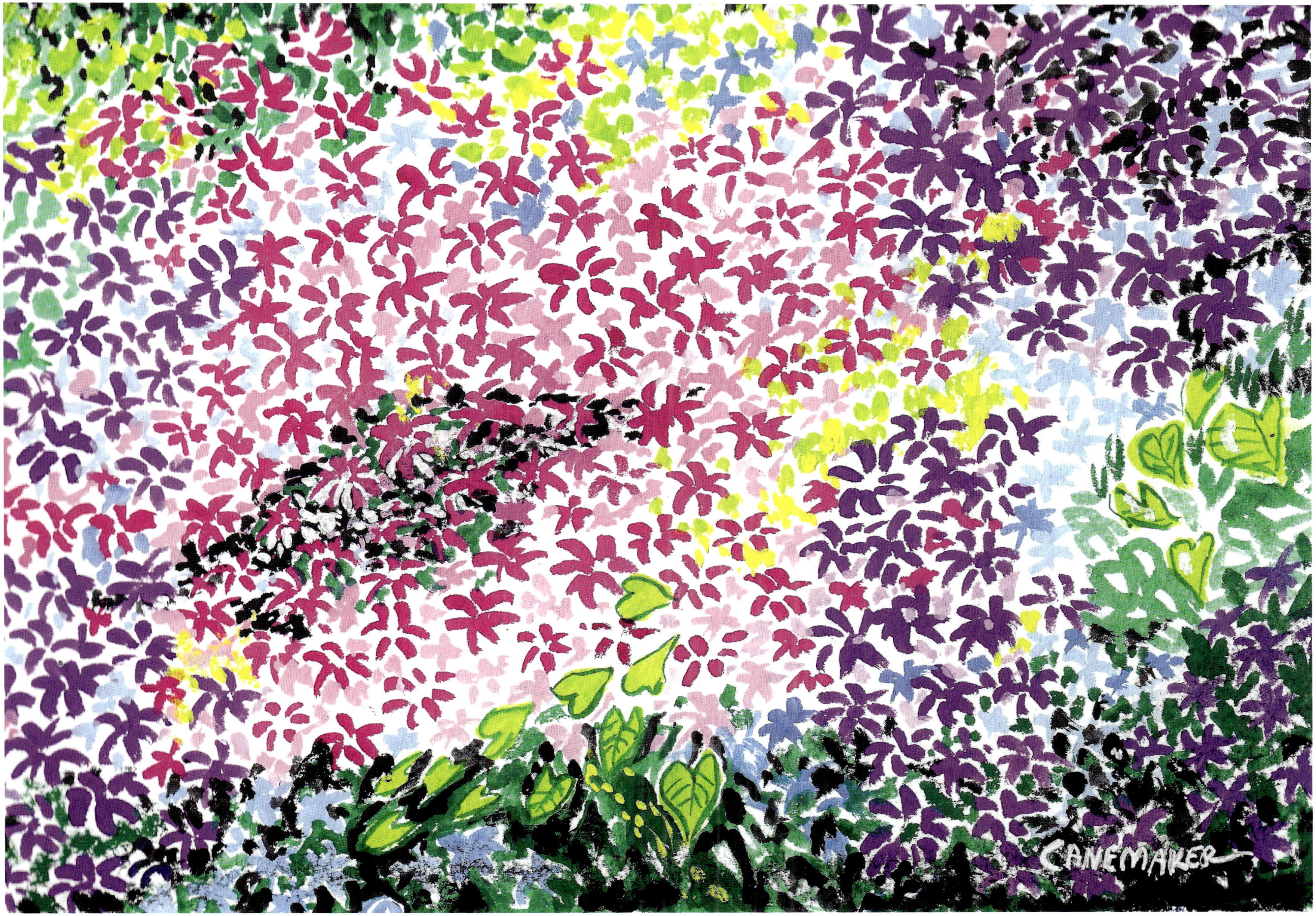
CANEMAKER

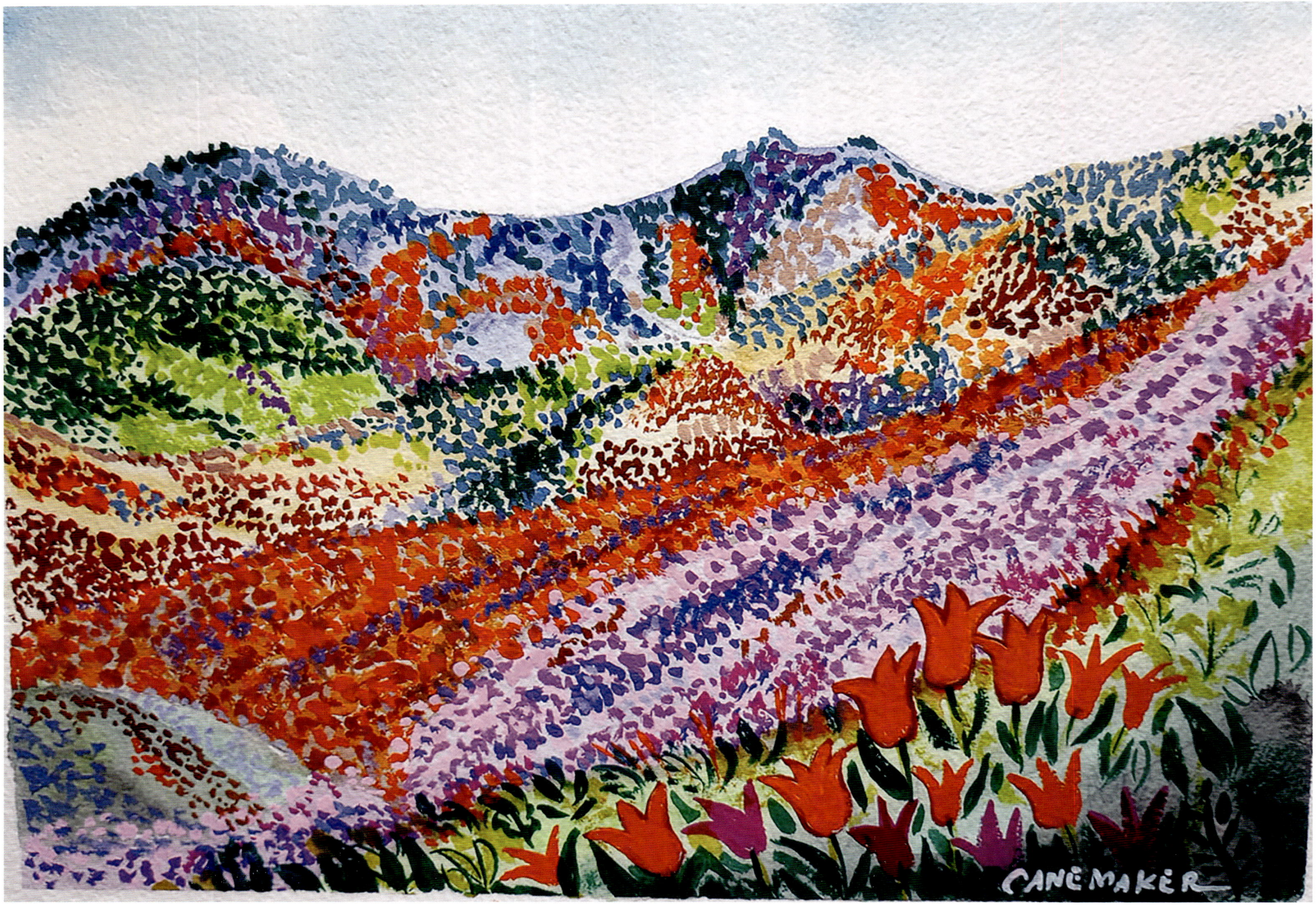
CANEMAKER

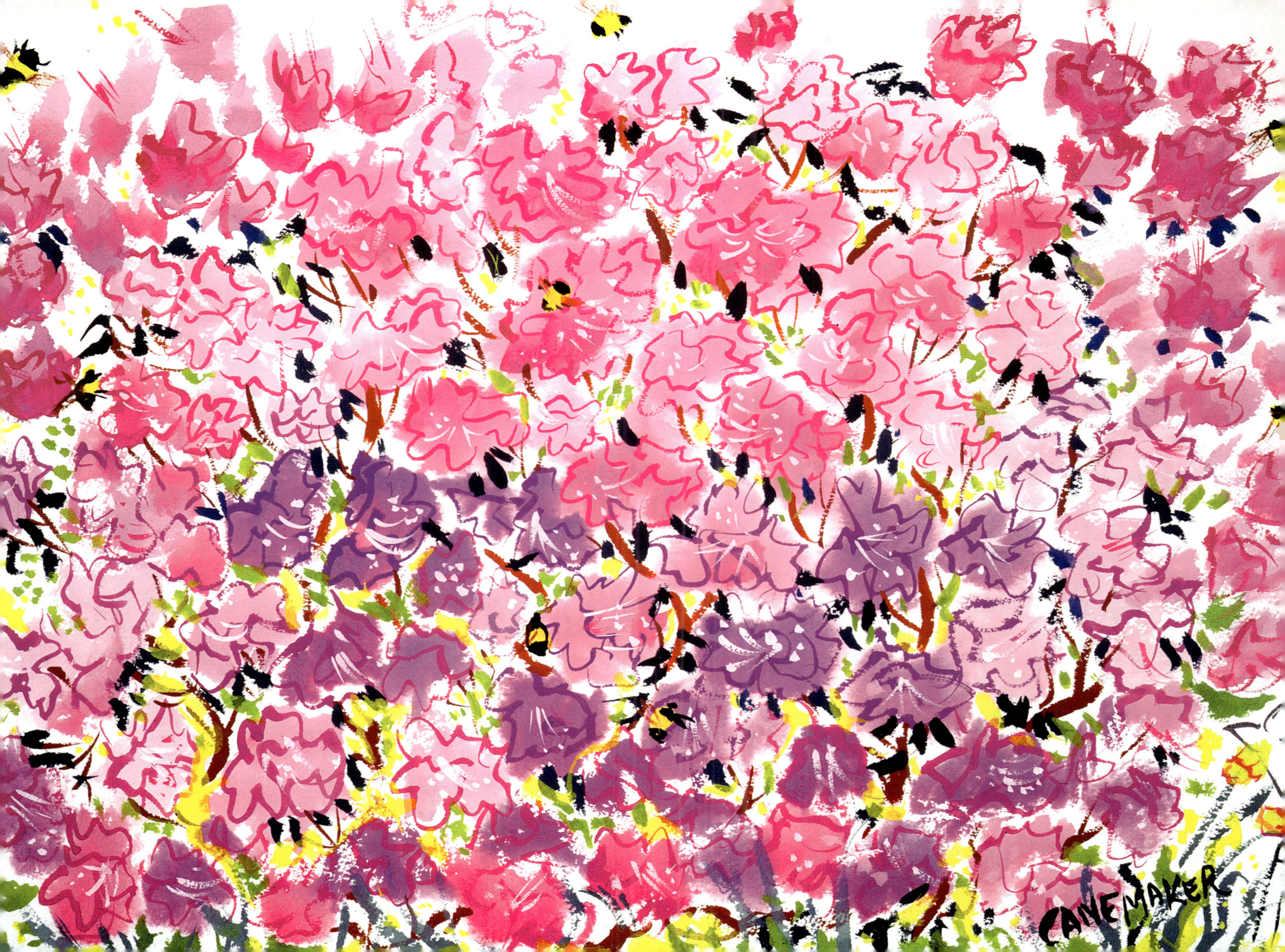
CANEMAKER

BRIDGEHAMPTON

THE MAKING OF AN ANIMATOR'S GARDEN...

ON FILM

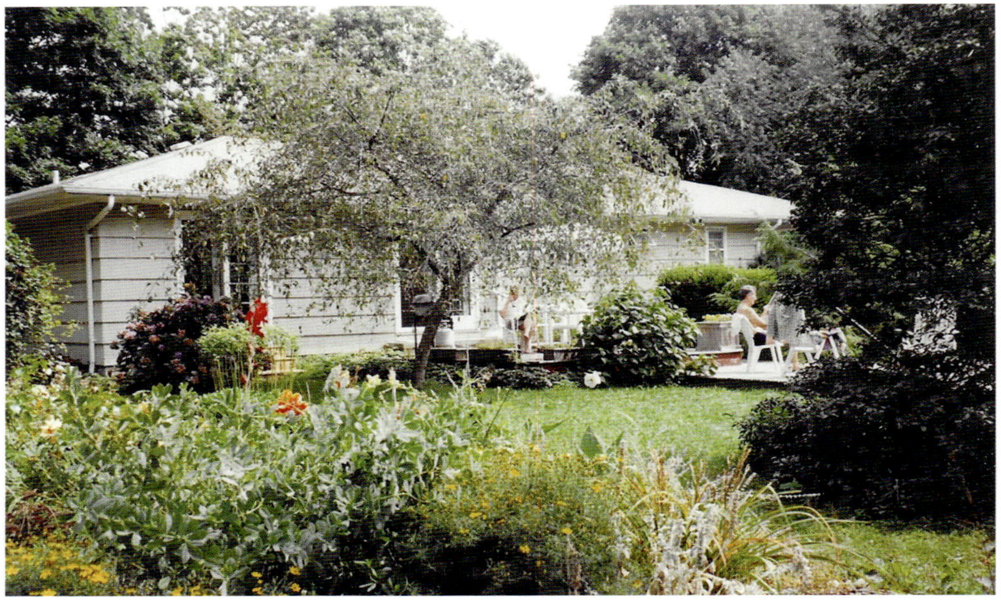

When we purchased a second home in the hamlet of Bridgehampton on eastern Long Island in 1988, it was a life changer. Country living was a complete mind-sweep. Our dormant appreciation of seasonal changes, and, in general, the presence of nature itself were reawakened. Phases of our lives became more upfront and distinct, as seasons changed. A slower, more contemplative pace took over.

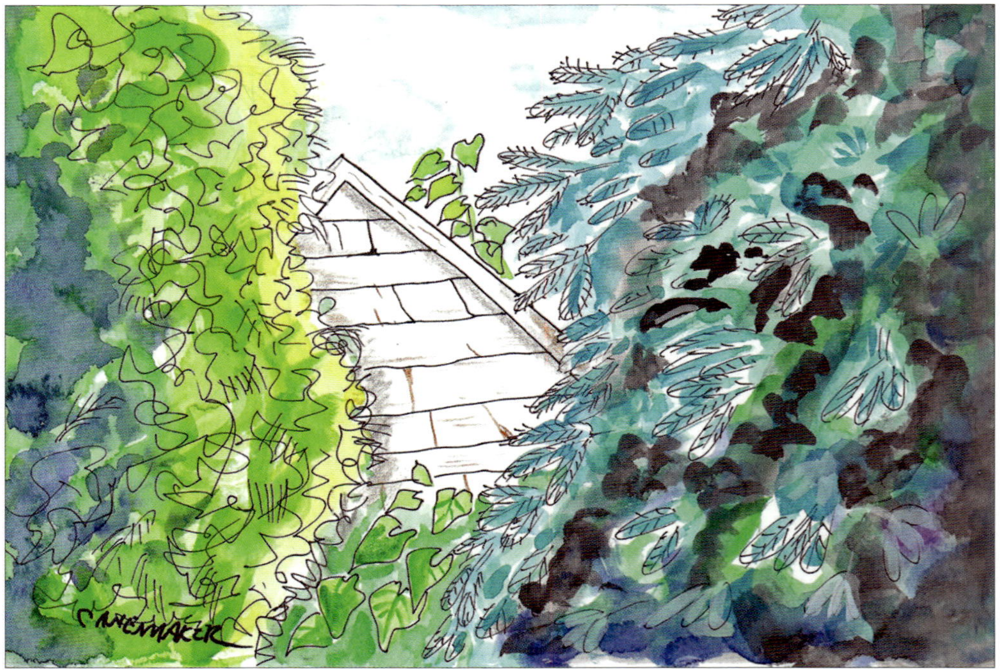

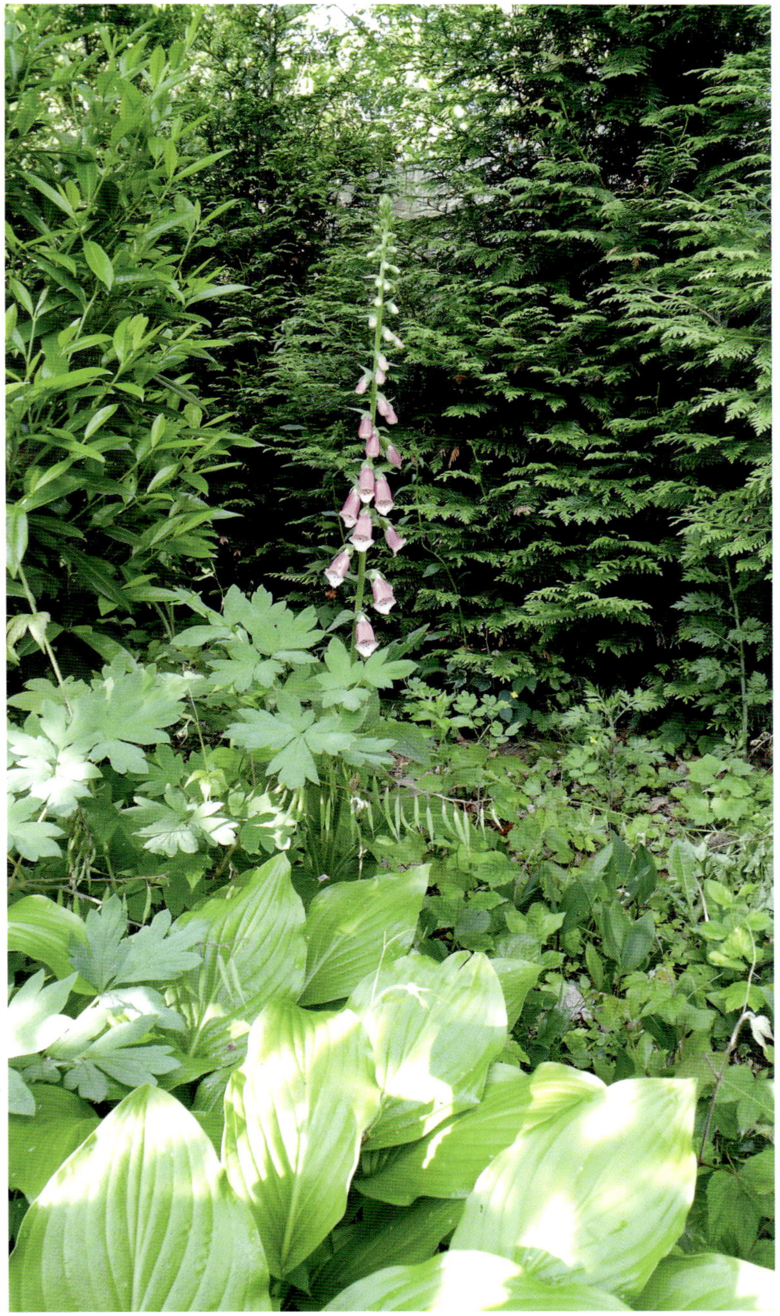

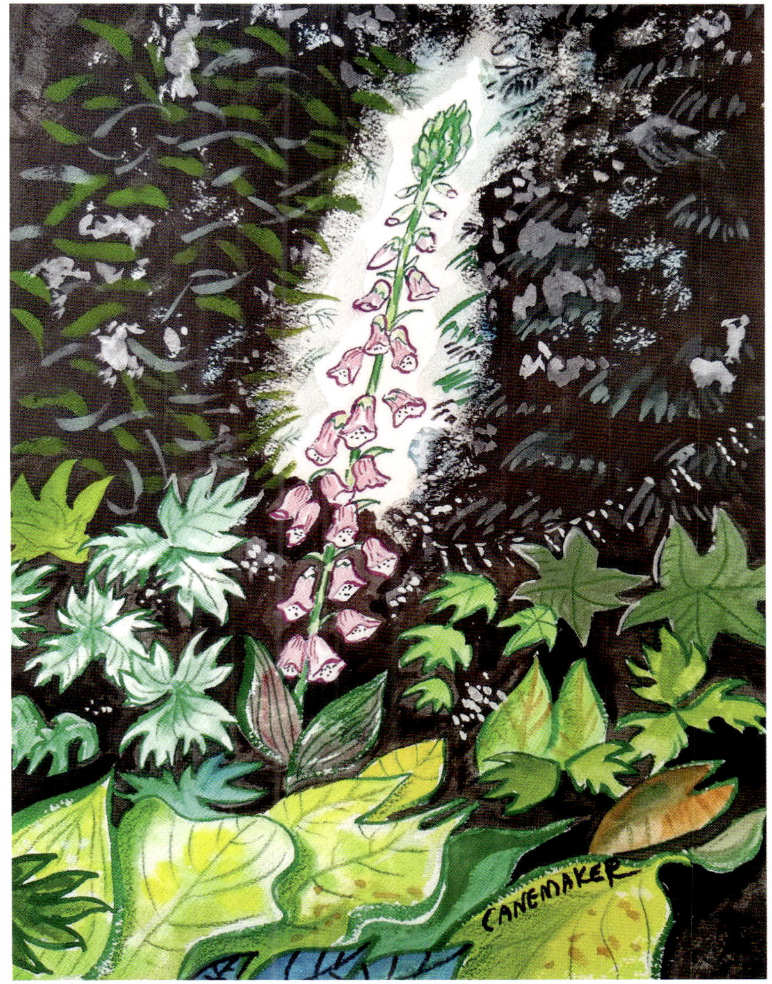

Page 124, top Left: The Garden and House at Bridgehampton

Bottom left: GABLE AND GARDEN 12X8" watercolor 2019

This page:
Photo of foxglove, alongside Canemaker's painting titled FOXGLOVE 14x20" gouache 2014

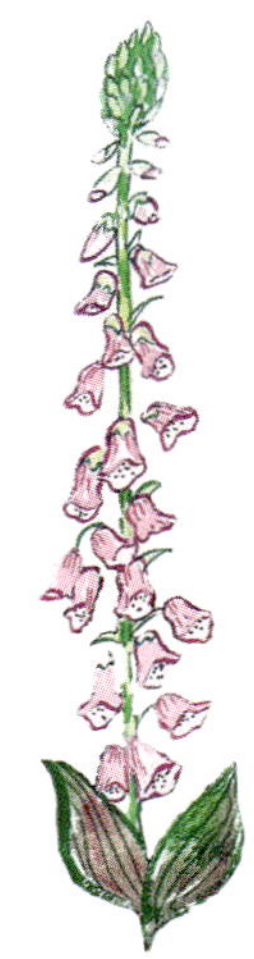

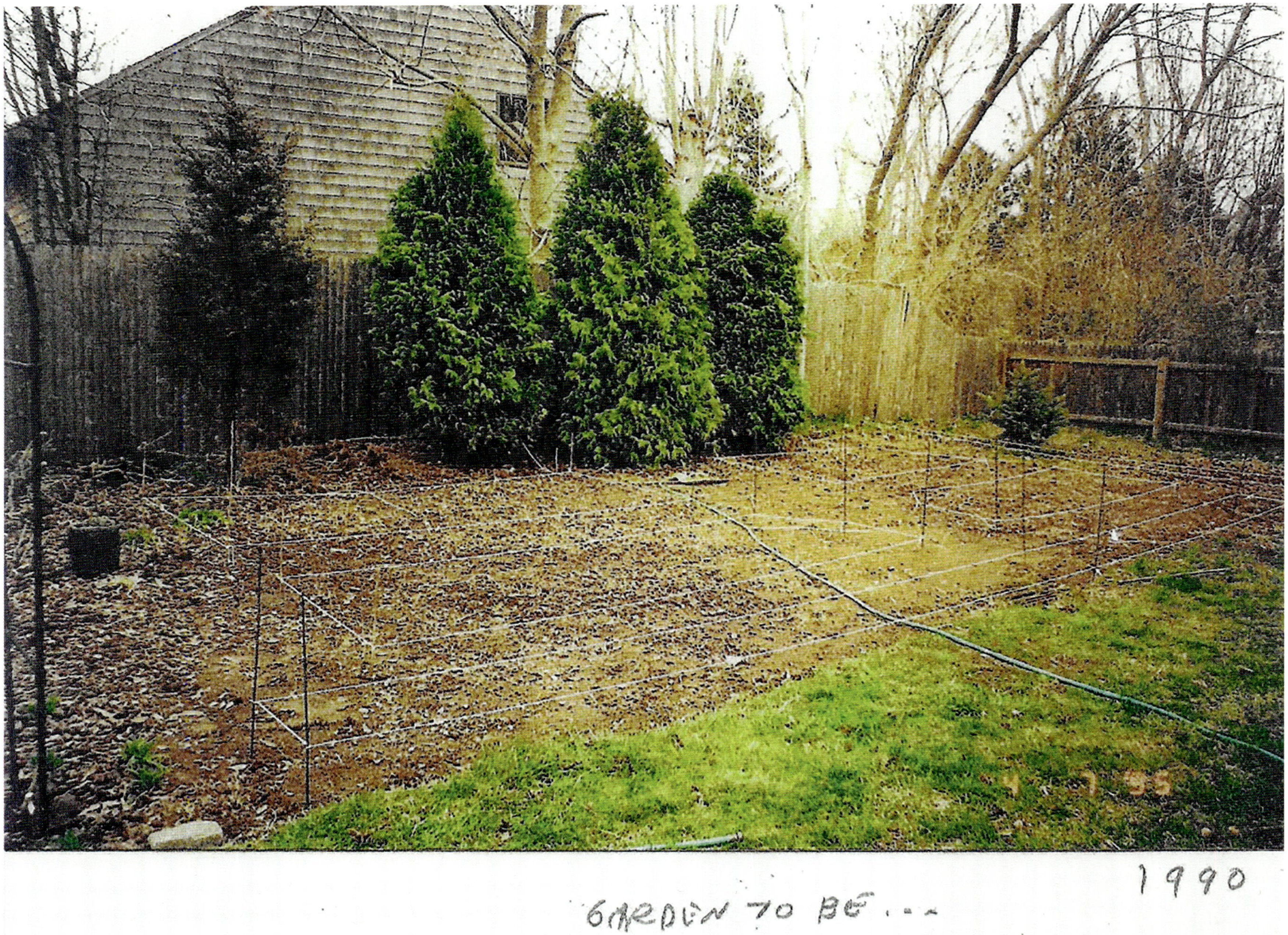

Barren ground in the backyard "soon to be garden"

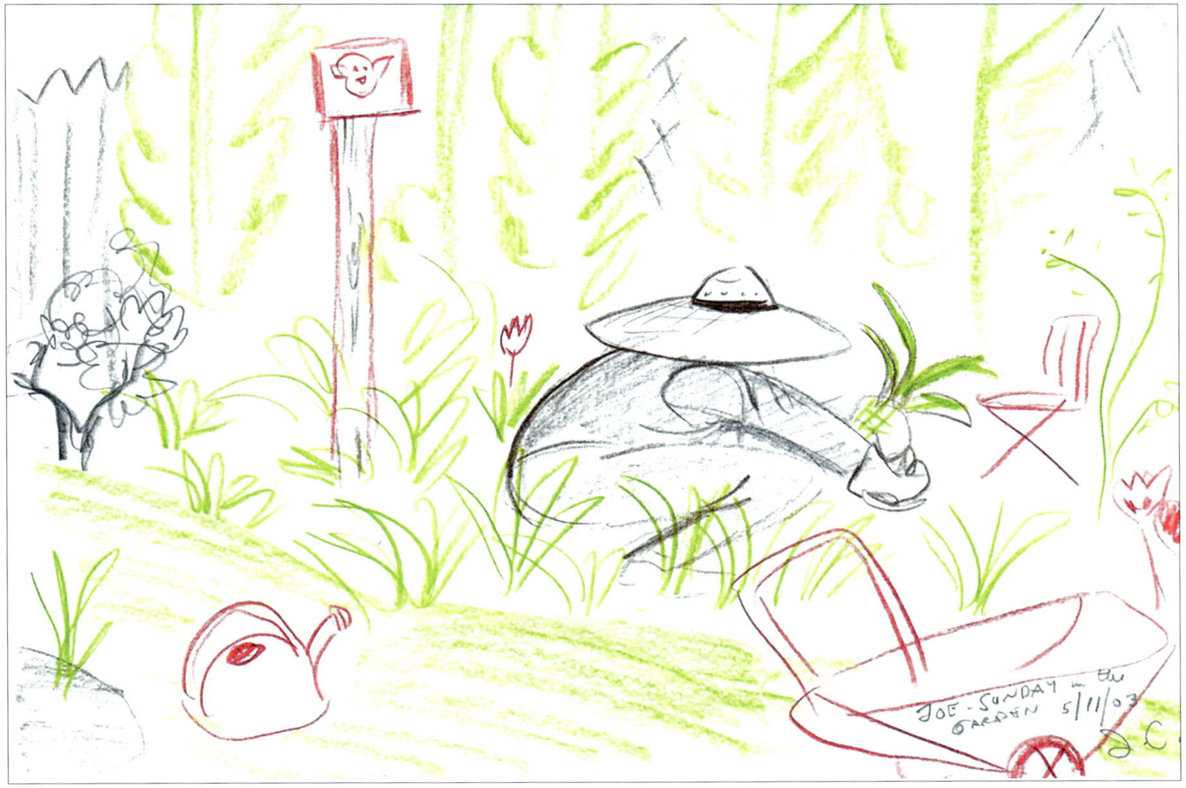

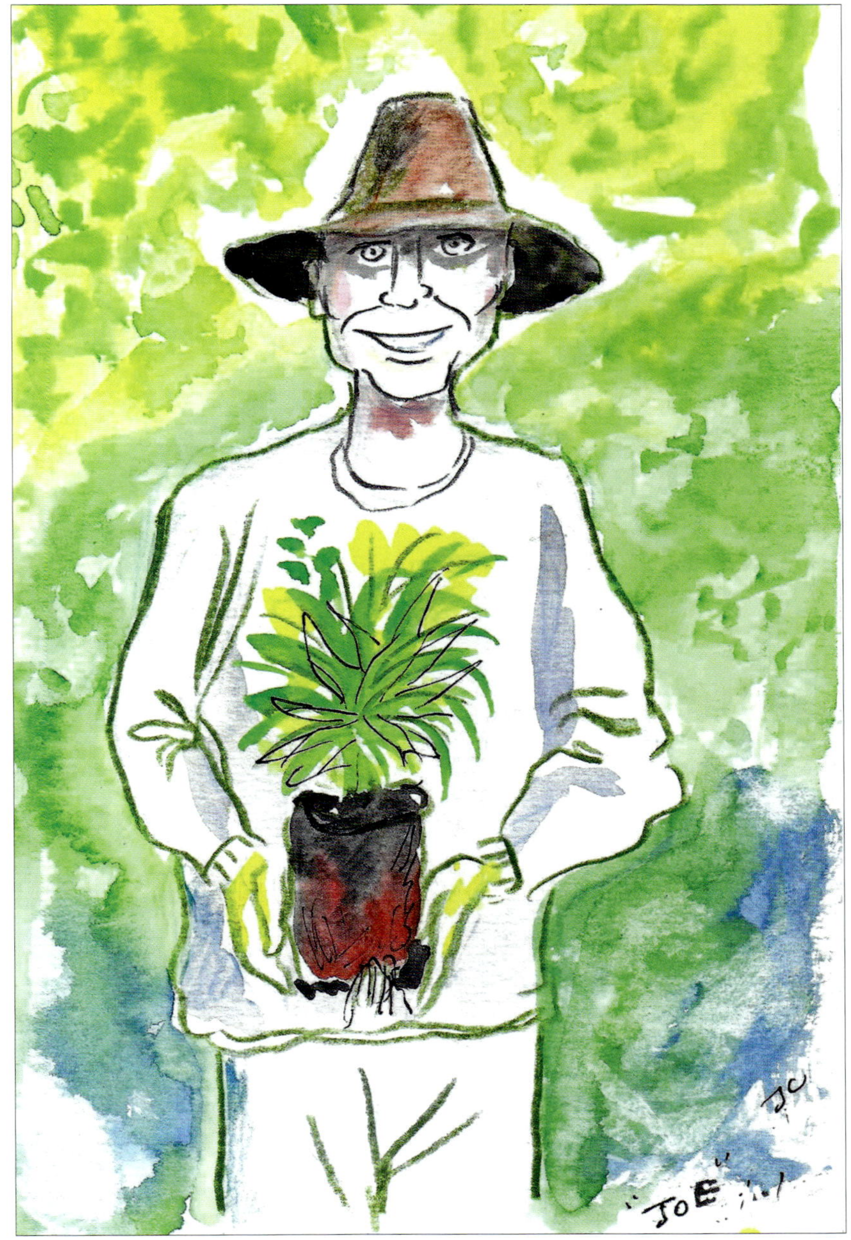

The garden-to-be was only in our minds, at the time. Mostly in Joe's optimistic imagination, for he planned the whole thing. At first, we faced a barren backyard after we mowed down a ton of weeds, leveled the ground and started marking off where flower beds and veggie plantings would go. Gradually, year after year, the garden grew, survived and thrived.

Above: Joe in a big hat bent over working on the garden, 2003

Right: Drawing of Joe the Gardener holding a bare root plant

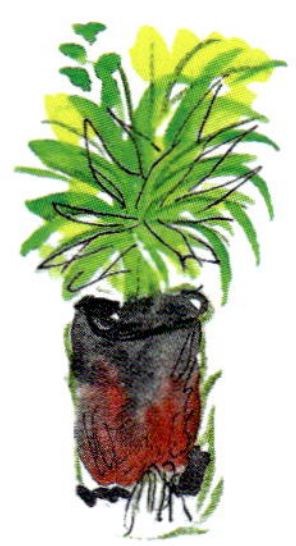

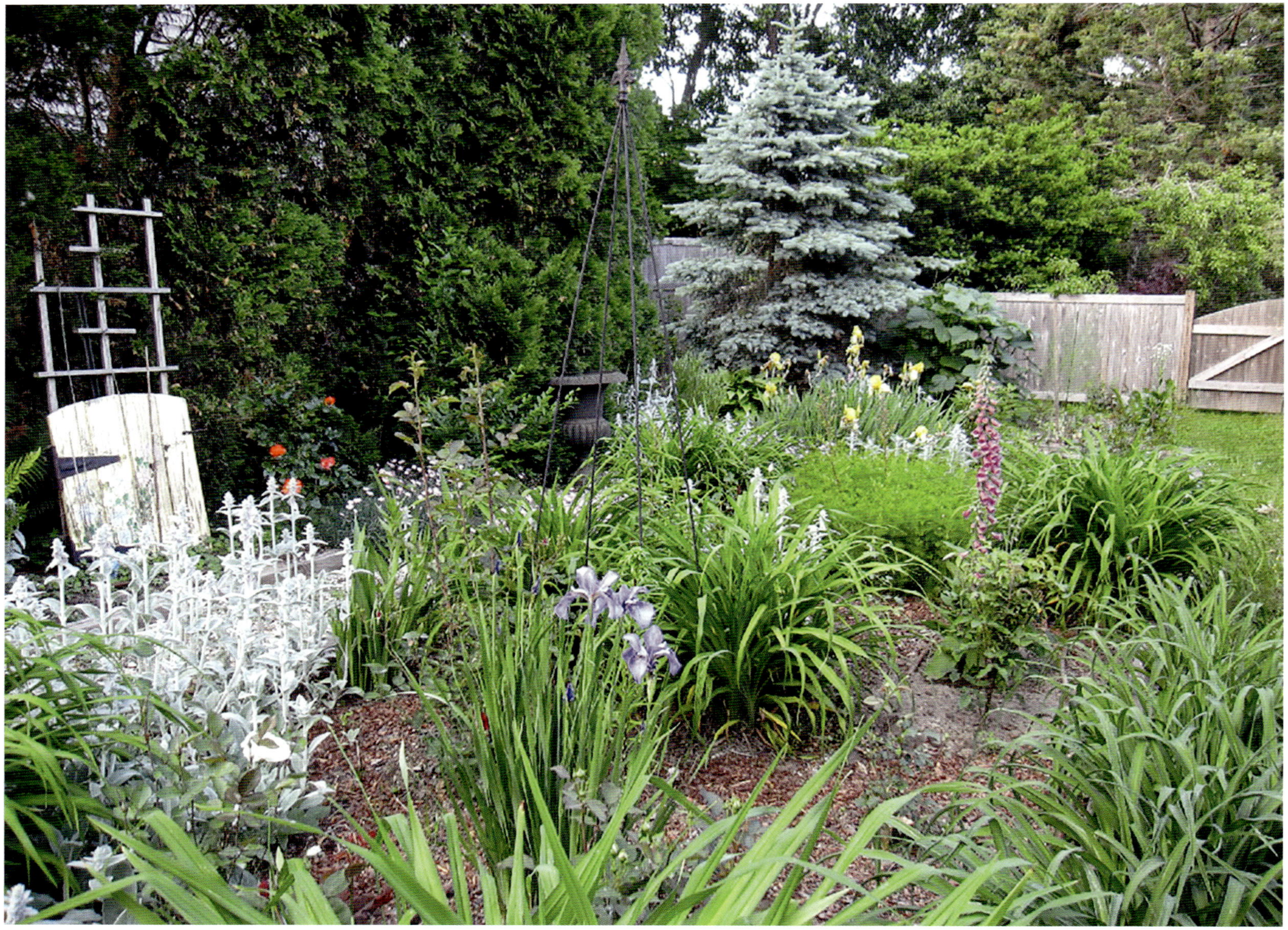

Left: Joe & John's Bridgehampton Garden

Right: SNOWBALL BUSH 12X9" gouache 2010

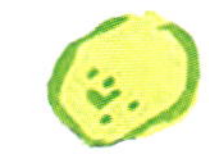

For more than three decades, we responded to seasonal rhythms: tilling soil by hand and hoe, dislodging weeds in spring, raking leaves in fall, protecting plants in winter. All required patience gloriously rewarded in summer -- the joy of seeing tiny plantings at last, blossom into fascinating organisms of great beauty. Joe's dream garden came true, spectacularly.

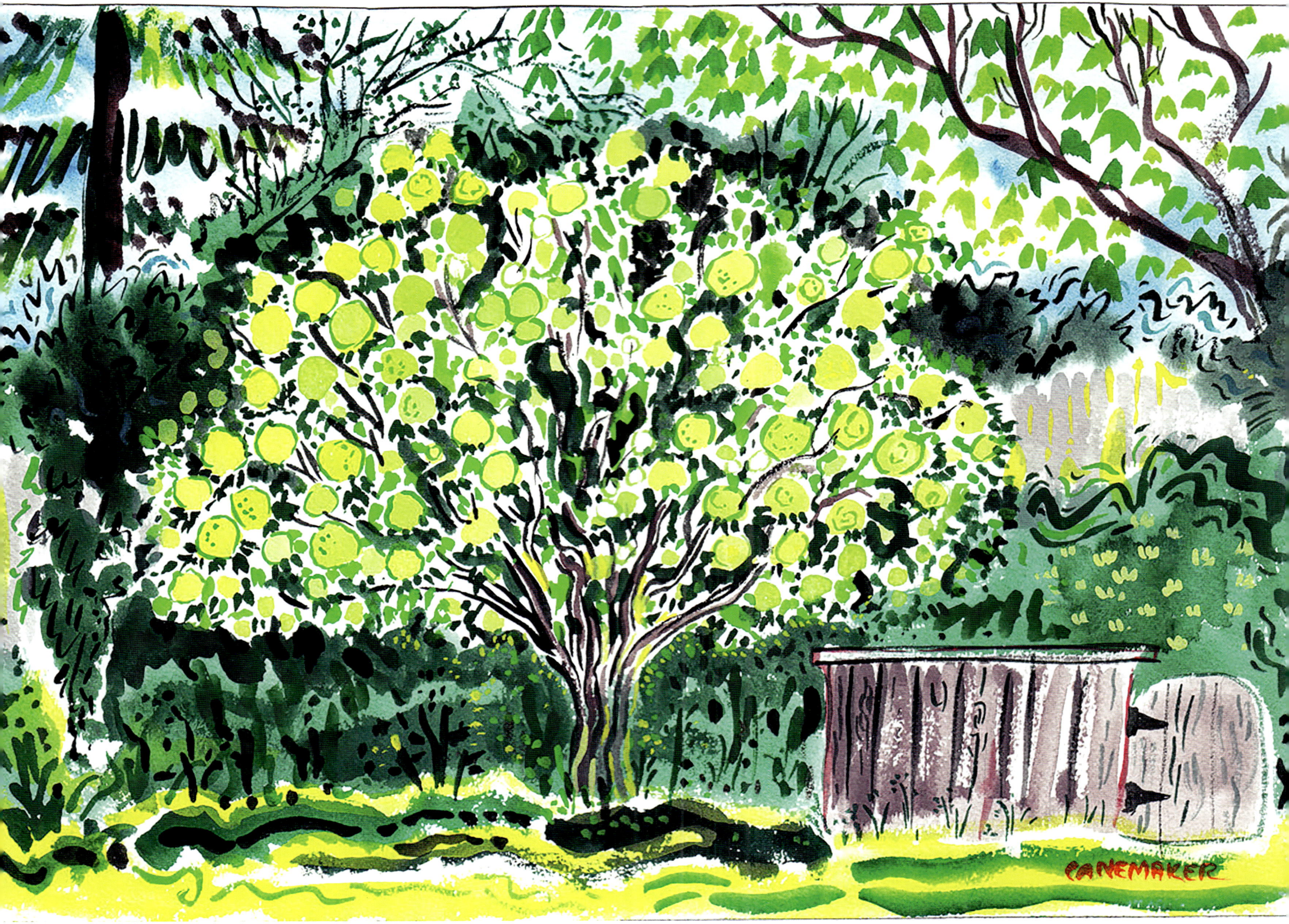
CANEMAKER

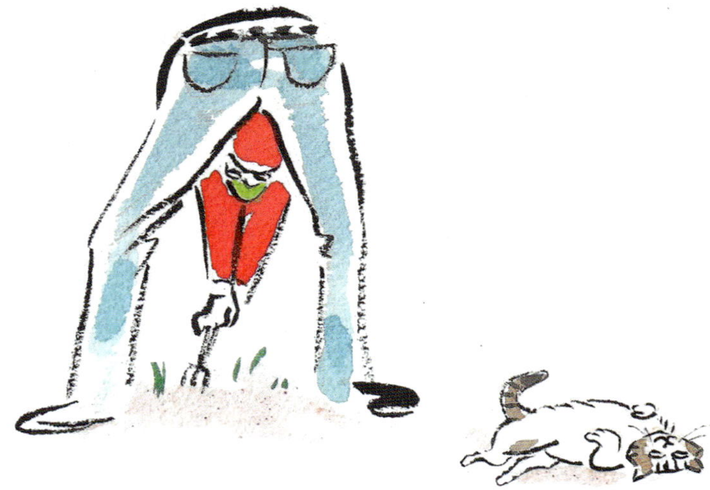

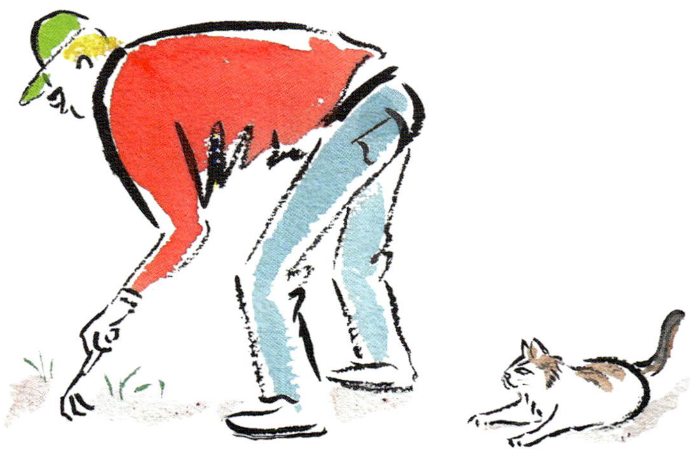

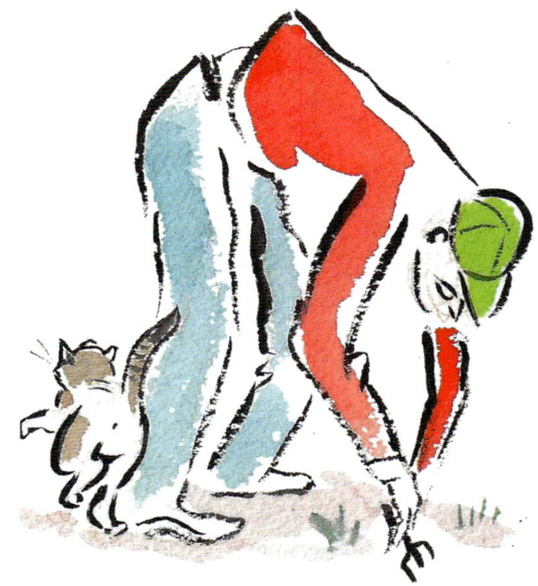

Nurturing a garden, I discovered, involves the same time-dissolving intensity every art form requires. From the start, nature's designs enticed me. I began making paintings of what I saw and felt in this ever-evolving, changeable botanical environment. Painting for its own sake was an area of my creative life I had not previously focused on in the city.

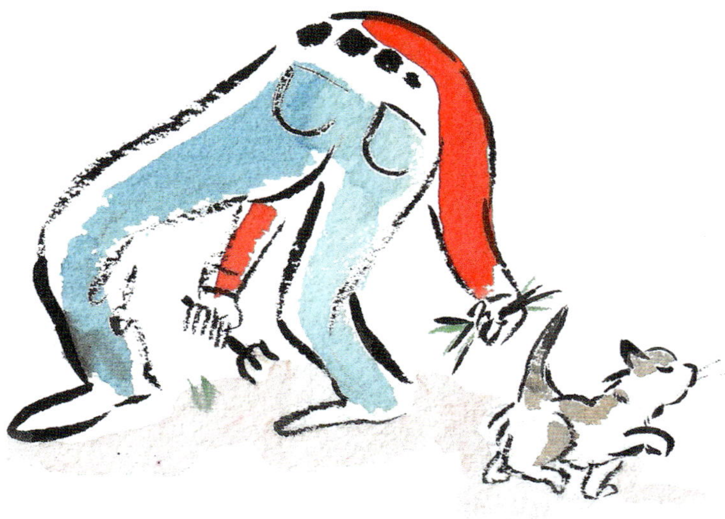

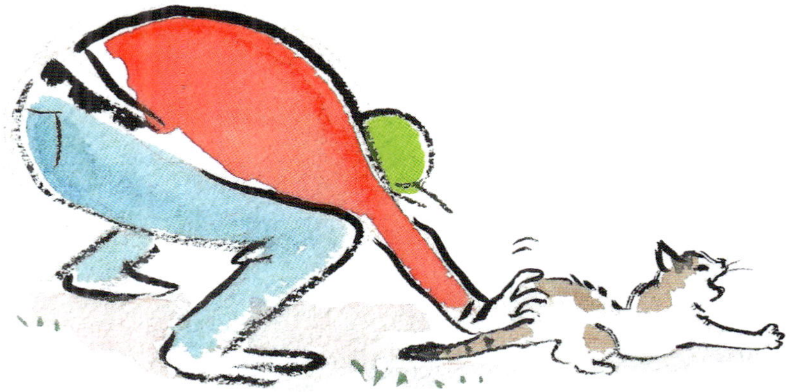

In our country garden and environs, I proceeded to draw and paint various flowers, trees, fungi, insects, birds, neighbor's dogs, feral cats, and our own cat, Lucy, who often assisted Joe with his gardening chores — in her own way.

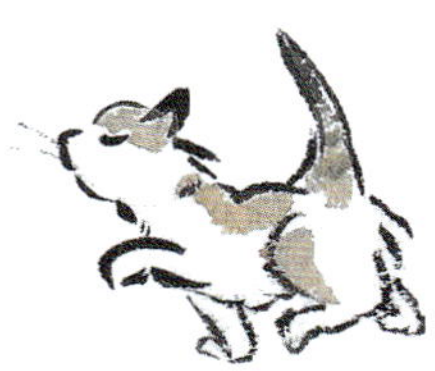

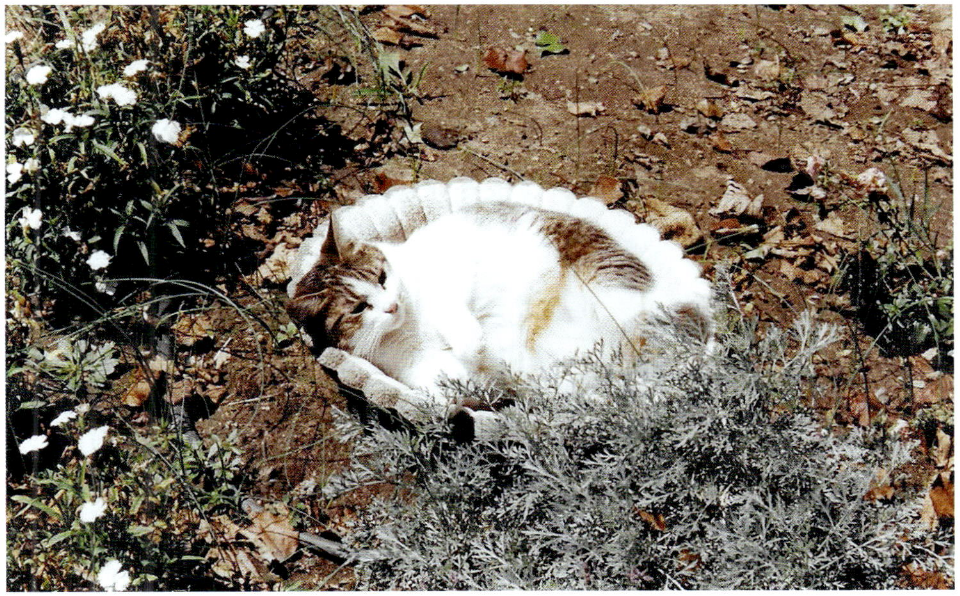

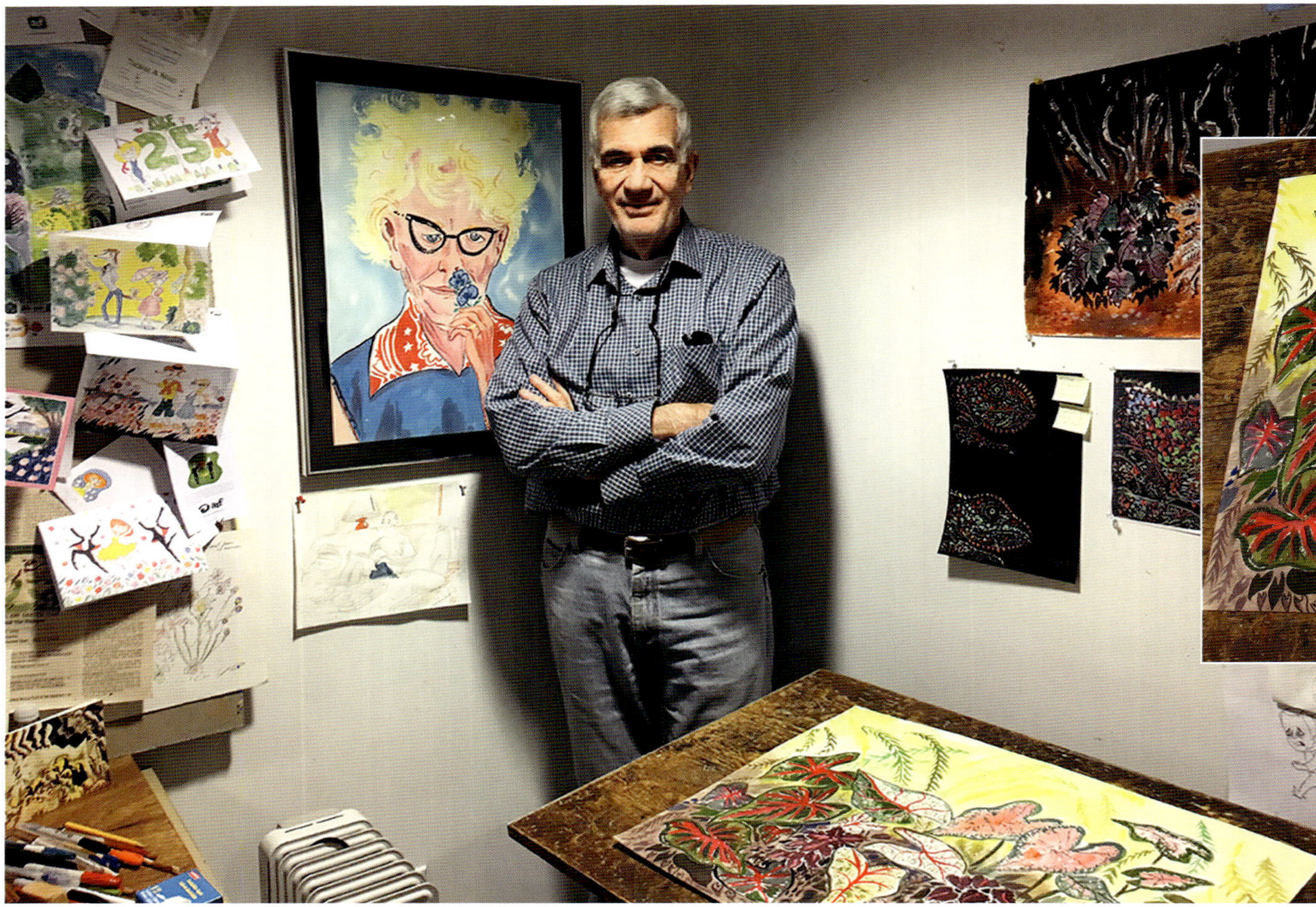

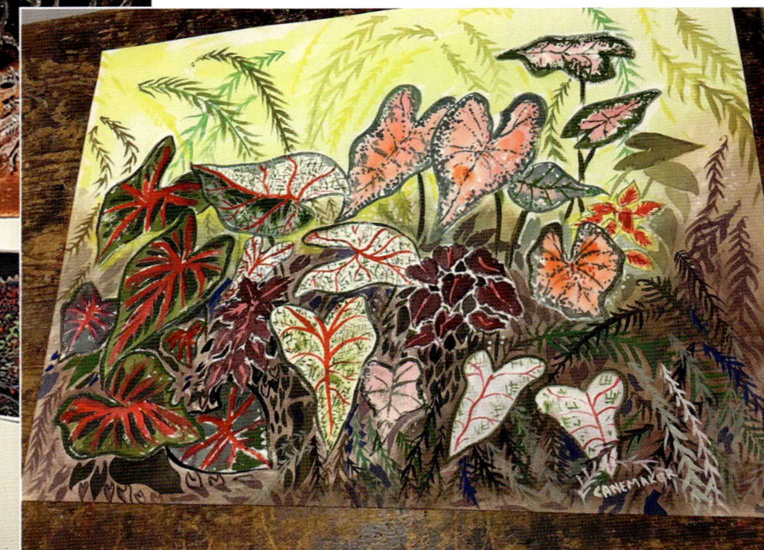

Left: A corner in John Canemaker's Bridgehampton studio; his mother's portrait; "Coral Bells, Fern and Bleeding Heart" painting on wall; "Coleus and Caladium" on easel. Photo by Zoya Baker.

Above: Garden shade plants on easel 2015
Photo: Zoya Baker

Right: COLEUS & CALADIUM
gouache, 24" X 18" 2015

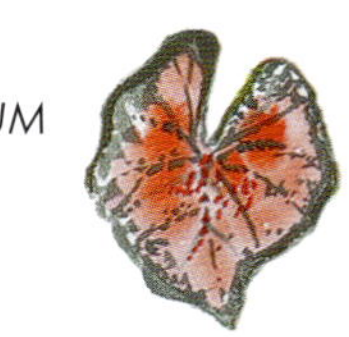

Eventually, I wanted to see my gouache and watercolor artworks come to life via the animation medium. In 1998, a celebration of our East End home and nature, appeared in a six-minute short I made titled "Bridgehampton." The film, which features an original piano score by the great jazz virtuoso Fred Hersch, found a wide audience in film festivals, and as part of "Jazz Score," a 2008 Museum of Modern Art retrospective of 50 films, celebrating "the best original jazz composed for film from the 1950s to the present." "Bridgehampton" was screened continuously in a MoMA gallery, accompanied by an exhibit of its art on paper.

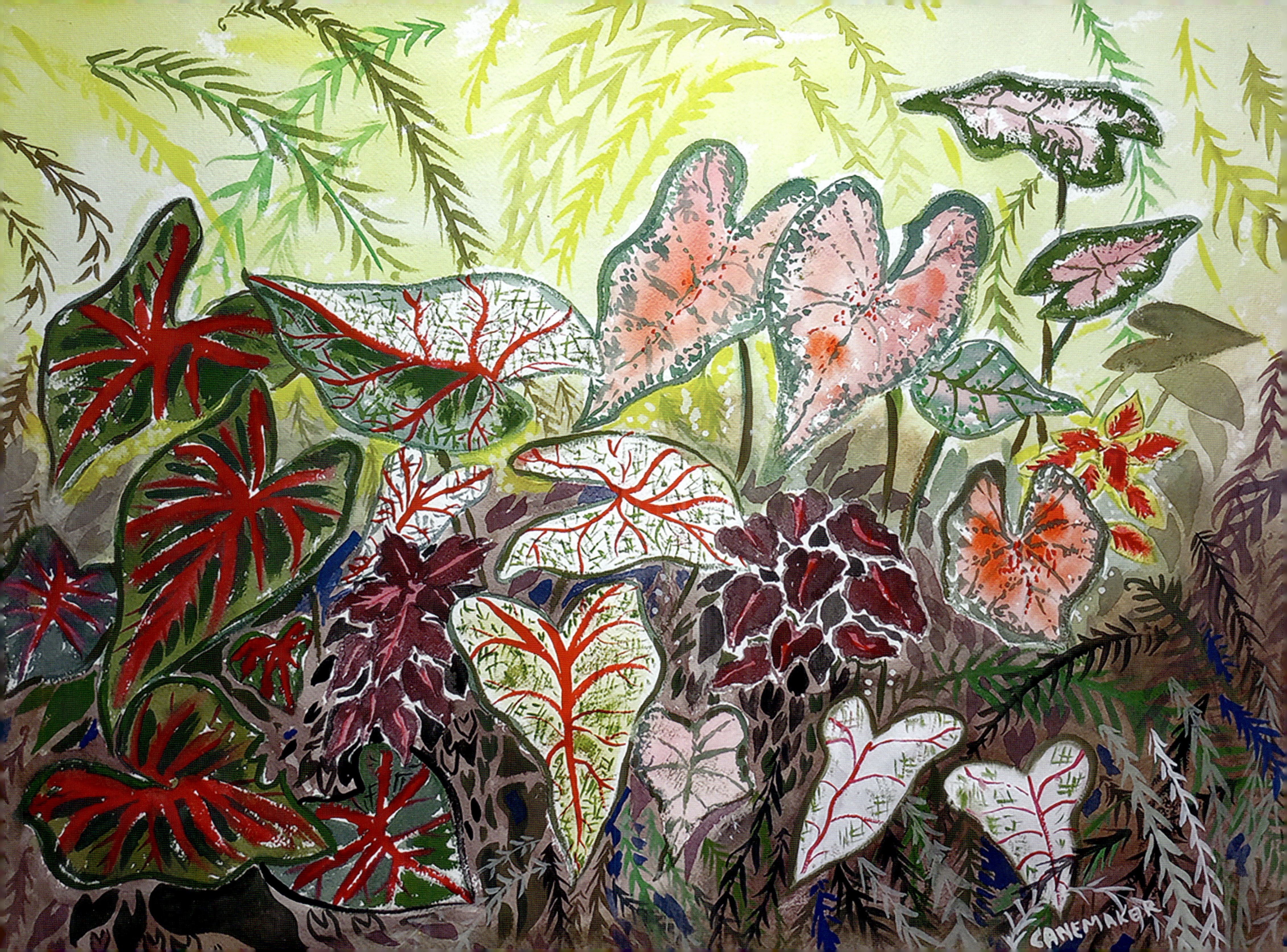
CANEMAKER

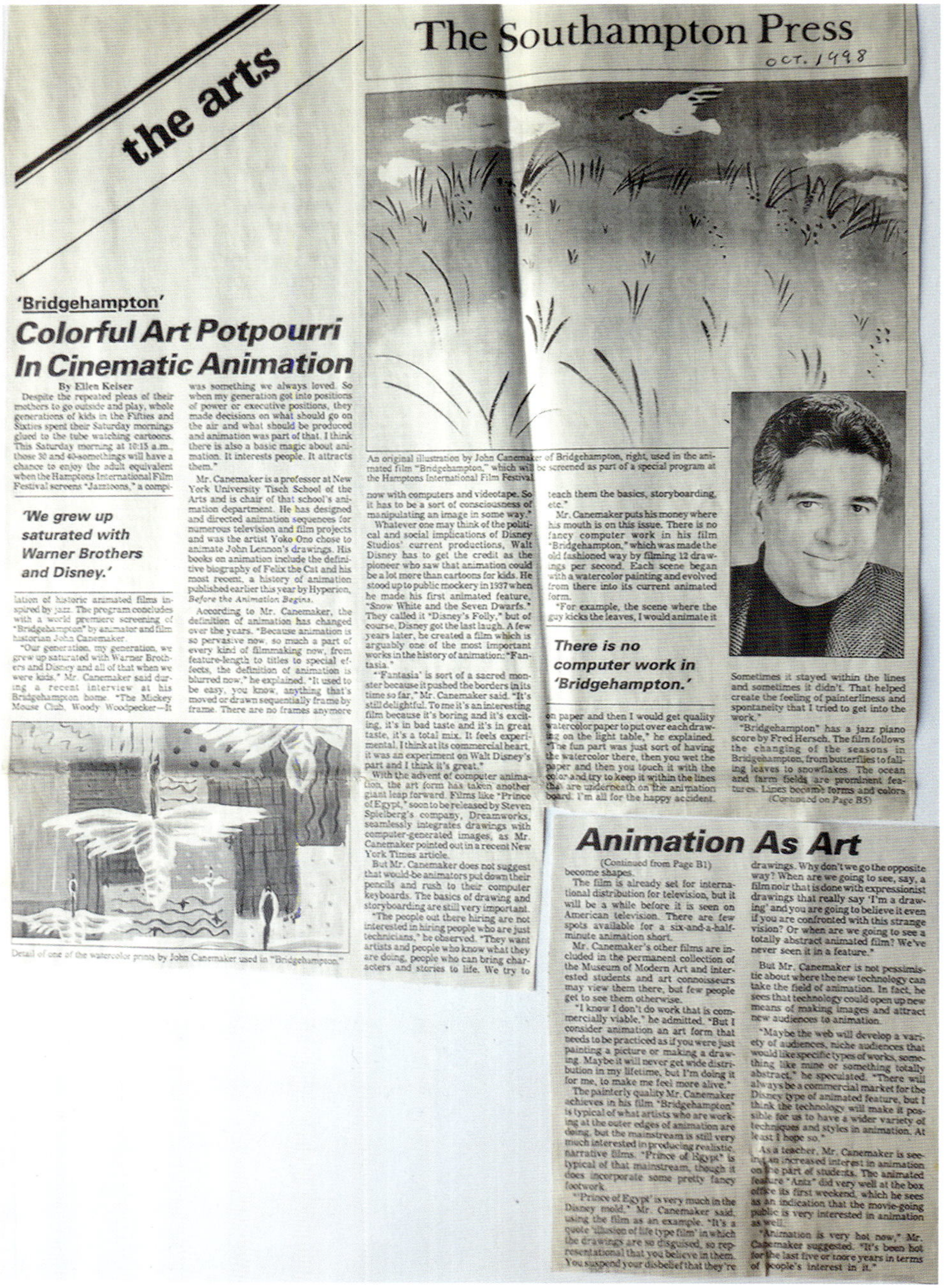

'Bridgehampton'

Colorful Art Potpourri In Cinematic Animation

By Ellen Keiser

Despite the repeated pleas of their mothers to go outside and play, whole generations of kids in the Fifties and Sixties spent their Saturday mornings glued to the tube watching cartoons. This Saturday morning at 10:15 a.m., those 30 and 40-somethings will have a chance to enjoy the adult equivalent when the Hamptons International Film Festival screens "Jamtoons," a compilation of historic animated films inspired by jazz. The program concludes with a world premiere screening of "Bridgehampton" by animator and film historian John Canemaker.

'We grew up saturated with Warner Brothers and Disney.'

"Our generation, my generation, we grew up saturated with Warner Brothers and Disney and all of that when we were kids," Mr. Canemaker said during a recent interview at his Bridgehampton home. "The Mickey Mouse Club, Woody Woodpecker—It was something we always loved. So when my generation got into positions of power or executive positions, they made decisions on what should go on the air and what should be produced and animation was part of that. I think there is also a basic magic about animation. It interests people. It attracts them."

Mr. Canemaker is a professor at New York University Tisch School of the Arts and is chair of that school's animation department. He has designed and directed animation sequences for numerous television and film projects and was the artist Yoko Ono chose to animate John Lennon's drawings. His books on animation include the definitive biography of Felix the Cat and his most recent, a history of animation published earlier this year by Hyperion, *Before the Animation Begins.*

According to Mr. Canemaker, the definition of animation has changed over the years. "Because animation is so pervasive now, so much a part of every kind of filmmaking now, from feature-length to titles to special effects, the definition of animation is blurred now," he explained. "It used to be easy, you know, anything that's moved or drawn sequentially frame by frame. There are no frames anymore now with computers and videotape. So it has to be a sort of consciousness of manipulating an image in some way."

An original illustration by John Canemaker of Bridgehampton, right, used in the animated film "Bridgehampton," which will be screened as part of a special program at the Hamptons International Film Festival

Whatever one may think of the political and social implications of Disney Studios' current productions, Walt Disney has to get the credit as the pioneer who saw that animation could be a lot more than cartoons for kids. He stood up to public mockery in 1937 when he made his first animated feature, "Snow White and the Seven Dwarfs." They called it "Disney's Folly," but of course, Disney got the last laugh. A few years later, he created a film which is arguably one of the most important works in the history of animation: "Fantasia."

"'Fantasia' is sort of a sacred monster because it pushed the borders in its time so far," Mr. Canemaker said. "It's still delightful. To me it's an interesting film because it's boring and it's exciting, it's in bad taste and it's in great taste, it's a total mix. It feels experimental. I think at its commercial heart, it was an experiment on Walt Disney's part and I think it's great."

With the advent of computer animation, the art form has taken another giant leap forward. Films like "Prince of Egypt," soon to be released by Steven Spielberg's company, Dreamworks, seamlessly integrates drawings with computer-generated images, as Mr. Canemaker pointed out in a recent New York Times article.

But Mr. Canemaker does not suggest that would-be animators put down their pencils and rush to their computer keyboards. The basics of drawing and storyboarding are still very important.

"The people out there hiring are not interested in hiring people who are just technicians," he observed. "They want artists and people who know what they are doing, people who can bring characters and stories to life. We try to teach them the basics, storyboarding, etc."

Mr. Canemaker puts his money where his mouth is on this issue. There is no fancy computer work in his film "Bridgehampton," which was made the old fashioned way by filming 12 drawings per second. Each scene began with a watercolor painting and evolved from there into its current animated form.

"For example, the scene where the guy kicks the leaves, I would animate it

There is no computer work in 'Bridgehampton.'

on paper and then I would get quality watercolor paper to put over each drawing on the light table," he explained. "The fun part was just sort of having the watercolor there, then you wet the paper and then you touch it with the color and try to keep it within the lines that are underneath on the animation board. I'm all for the happy accident. Sometimes it stayed within the lines and sometimes it didn't. That helped create the feeling of painterliness and spontaneity that I tried to get into the work."

"Bridgehampton" has a jazz piano score by Fred Hersch. The film follows the changing of the seasons in Bridgehampton, from butterflies to falling leaves to snowflakes. The ocean and farm fields are prominent features. Lines become forms and colors

(Continued on Page B5)

Detail of one of the watercolor prints by John Canemaker used in "Bridgehampton."

Animation As Art

(Continued from Page B1)

become shapes.

The film is already set for international distribution for television, but it will be a while before it is seen on American television. There are few spots available for a six-and-a-half-minute animation short.

Mr. Canemaker's other films are included in the permanent collection of the Museum of Modern Art and interested students and art connoisseurs may view them there, but few people get to see them otherwise.

"I know I don't do work that is commercially viable," he admitted. "But I consider animation an art form that needs to be practiced as if you were just painting a picture or making a drawing. Maybe it will never get wide distribution in my lifetime, but I'm doing it for me, to make me feel more alive."

The painterly quality Mr. Canemaker achieves in his film "Bridgehampton" is typical of what artists who are working at the outer edges of animation are doing, but the mainstream is still very much interested in producing realistic narrative films. "Prince of Egypt" is typical of that mainstream, though it does incorporate some pretty fancy footwork.

"'Prince of Egypt' is very much in the Disney mold," Mr. Canemaker said, using the film as an example. "It's a quote 'illusion of life type film' in which the drawings are so disguised, so representational that you believe in them. You suspend your disbelief that they're drawings. Why don't we go the opposite way? When are we going to see, say, a film noir that is done with expressionist drawings that really say 'I'm a drawing' and you are going to believe it even if you are confronted with this strange vision? Or when are we going to see a totally abstract animated film? We've never seen it in a feature."

But Mr. Canemaker is not pessimistic about where the new technology can take the field of animation. In fact, he sees that technology could open up new means of making images and attract new audiences to animation.

"Maybe the web will develop a variety of audiences, niche audiences that would like specific types of works, something like mine or something totally abstract," he speculated. "There will always be a commercial market for the Disney type of animated feature, but I think the technology will make it possible for us to have a wider variety of techniques and styles in animation. At least I hope so."

As a teacher, Mr. Canemaker is seeing an increased interest in animation on the part of students. The animated feature "Antz" did very well at the box office its first weekend, which he sees as an indication that the movie-going public is very interested in animation as well.

"Animation is very hot now," Mr. Canemaker suggested. "It's been hot for the last five or more years in terms of people's interest in it."

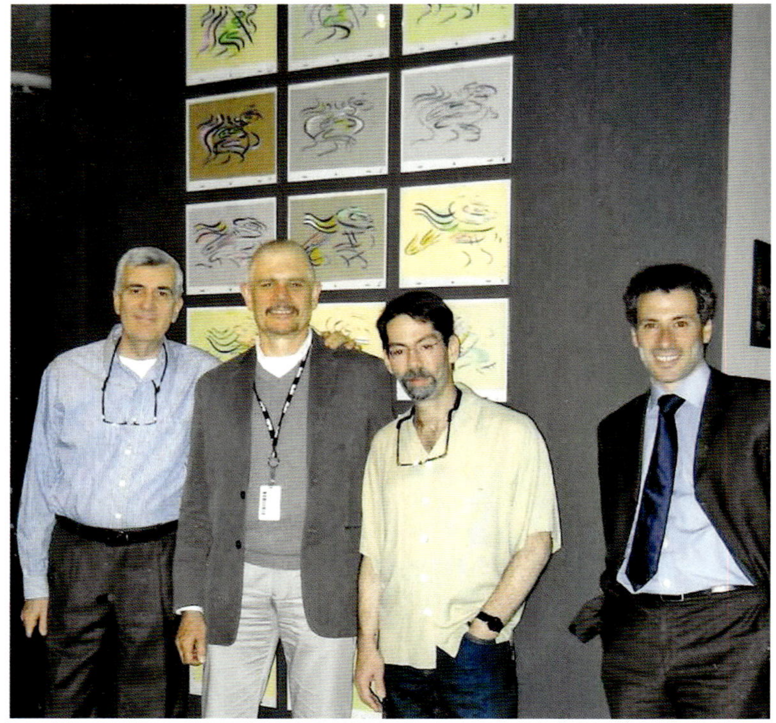

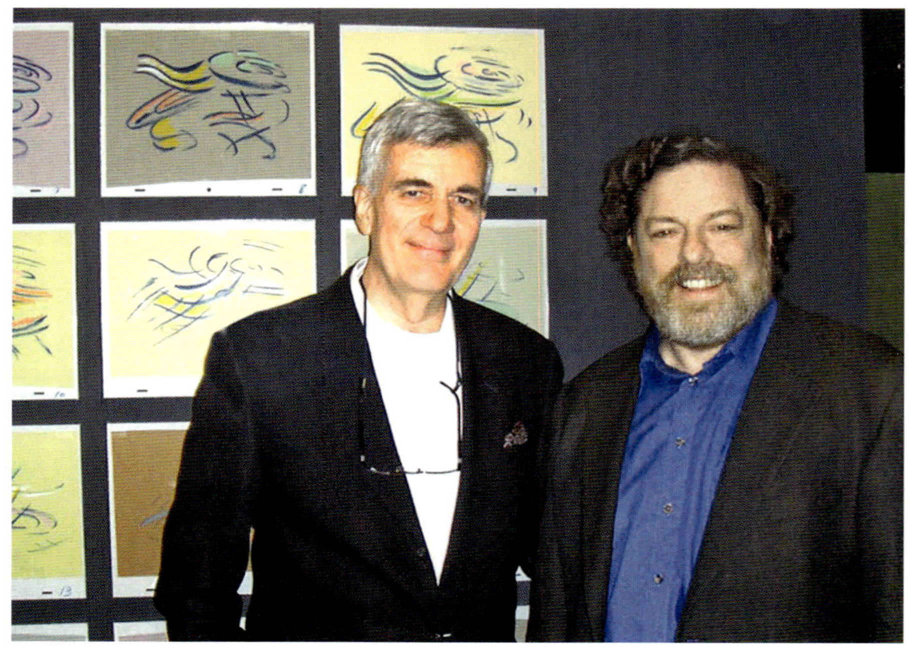

Far left: Southampton Press, L.I. newspaper article October 1998, "Colorful Art Potpourri in Cinematic Animation."

Left: Photo at "Jazz Score," a 2008 MoMA exhibition of "Bridgehampton" artwork (l - r) John Canemaker, MoMA film exhibition curator Ron Magliozzi, composer/pianist Fred Hersch, and Josh Siegel, MoMA film curator. May 14, 2008.

Below: At MoMA exhibition, John Canemaker and animator Michael Sporn stand before original "Bridgehampton" animation drawings.

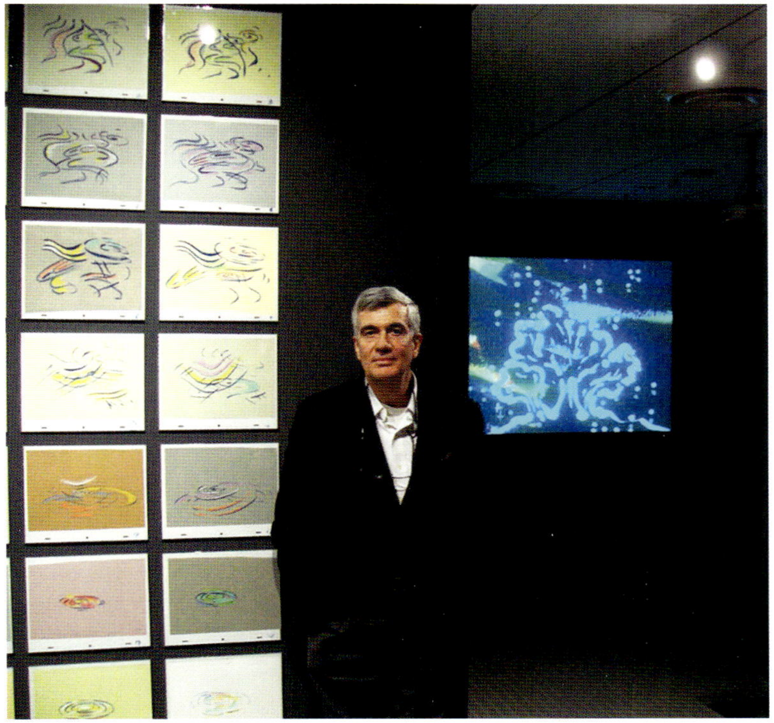

John Canemaker at Museum of Modern Art, NYC in 2008 with a display of his BRIDGEHAMPTON animation drawings and film.

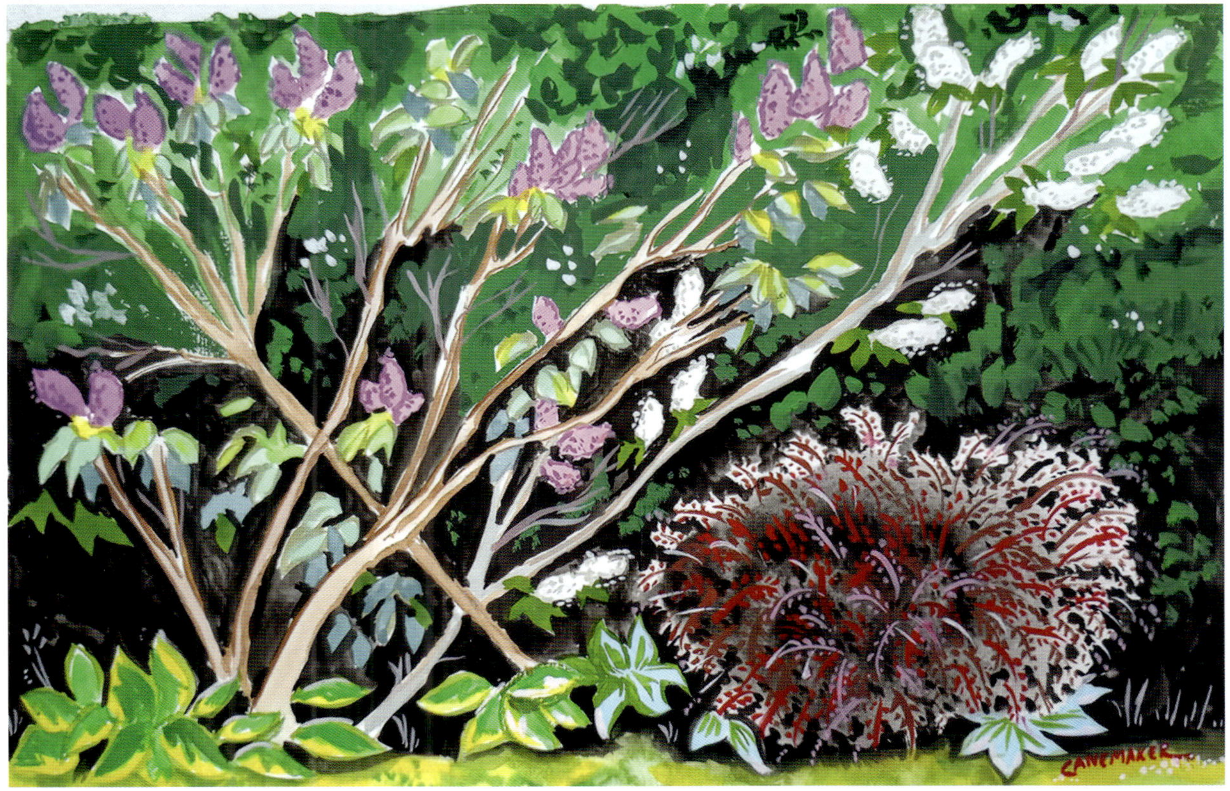

LILAC AND BARBERRY 15X10" gouache 2014

VISUALIZING

All creative endeavors, such as making a film or a garden, share similar processes. The following illustrations and captions describe some of the main stages in the animation process for the film, "Bridgehampton."

Many films begin with the written word, perhaps from a novel or a play. Characters and stories often start an animation artist to imagine and draw early ideas for character designs and important moments in the narrative. A top Disney story artist (Vance Gerry) once told me that merely the title of a story can inspire him; for example, "Beauty and the Beast." Two characters, two personalities to discover and bring to life. Exploration of the period in which the story takes place can also lead to early inspirational sketches, as concept drawings were called at the Disney Studio.

For me, nature was my story, my inspiration. I drew idea sketches, or color conceptual paintings, which is arguably the earliest, most creative phase of a project. It is a time for dreaming. And thinking, researching, and exploring the many visual possibilities.

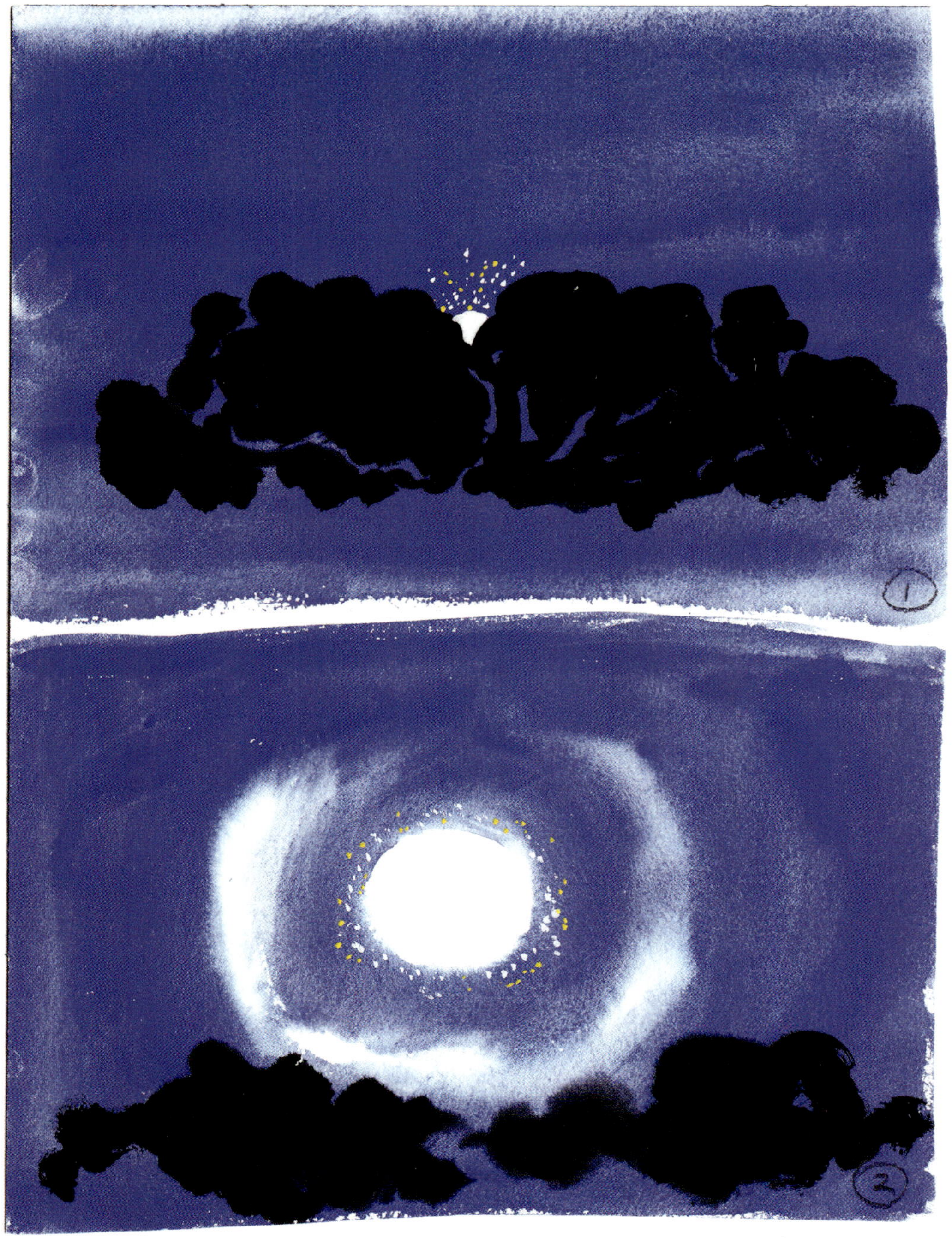

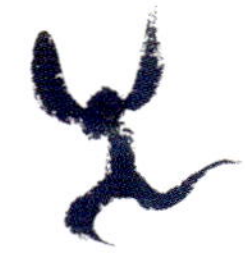

Left: Moon and cloud concept.

Below: Seagull over sand dune.

Right: Flying figures concept.

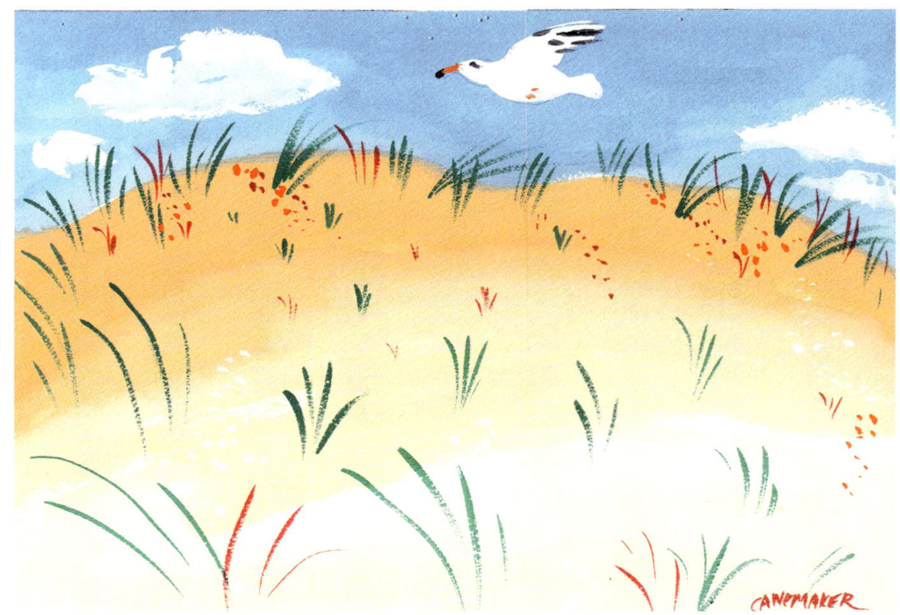

For the film I hoped to make, I sought ways to bring botanical shapes and colors in movement to tell a "story" about the seasons. Many paintings I made through the years suggested mood and color possibilities.

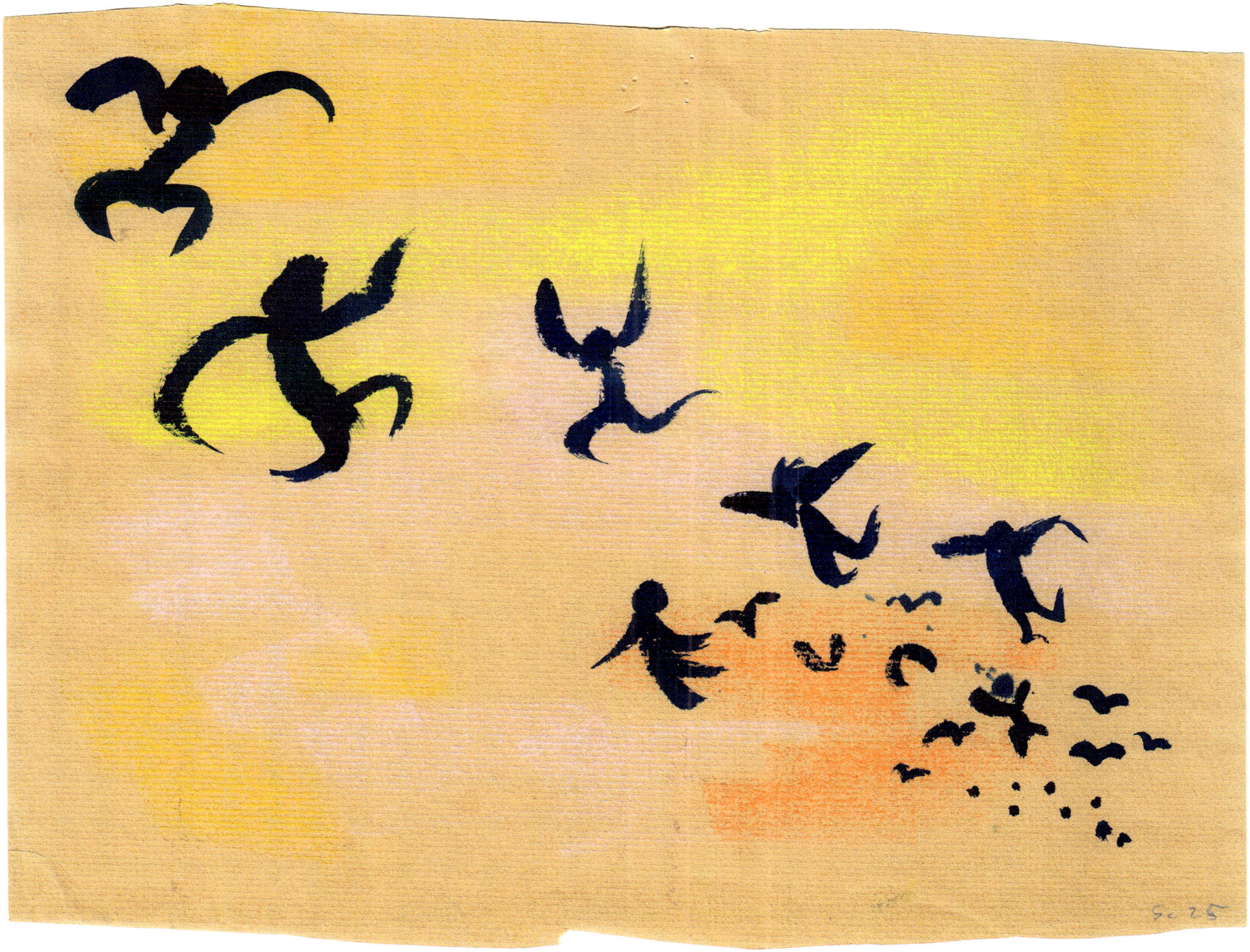
Sc 25

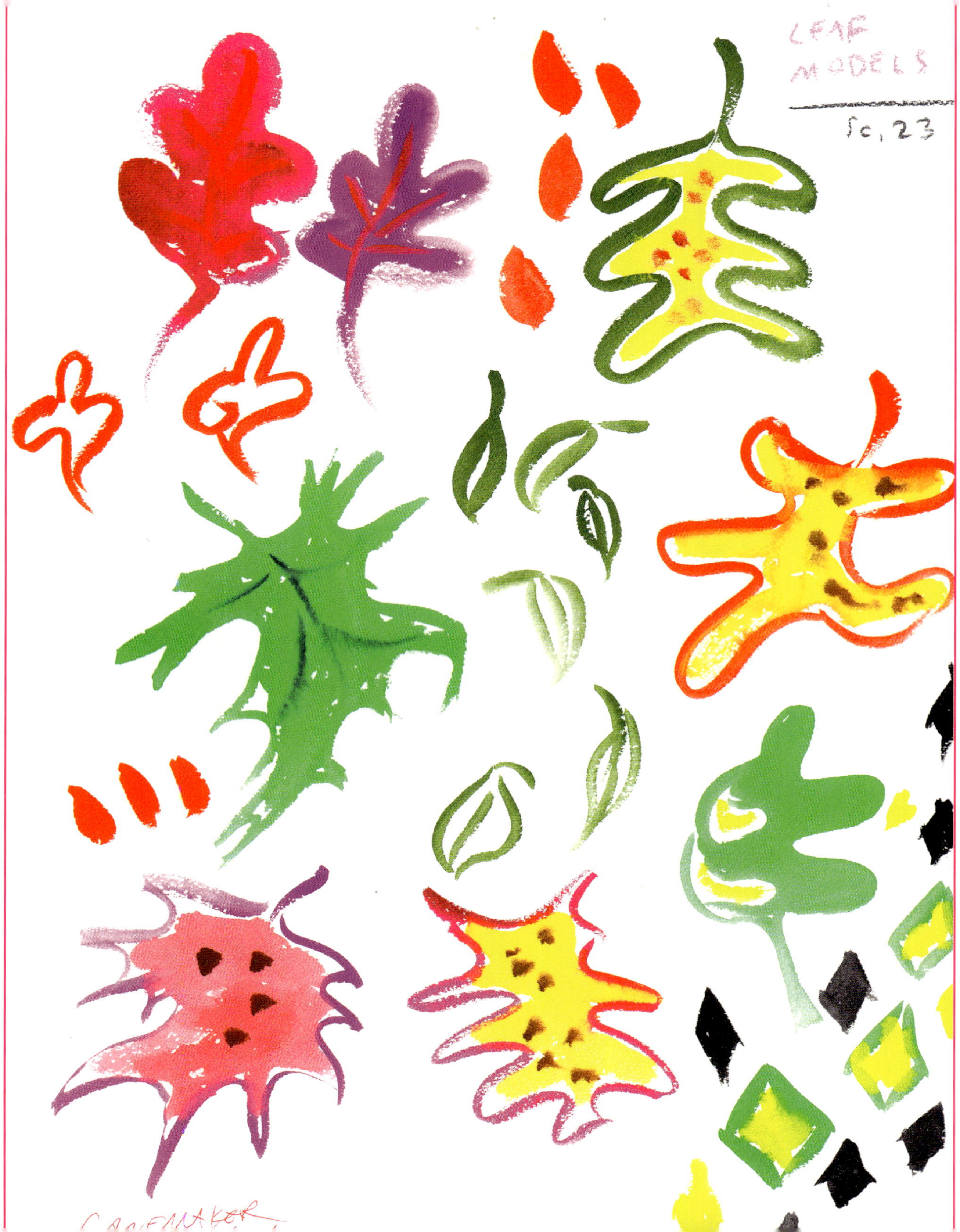

Left: Dancing leaves, 1995.

Page 139
Top left: Bridgehampton concept drawing

Bottom left: Bridgehampton pear tree

Right: Bridgehampton cherry tree

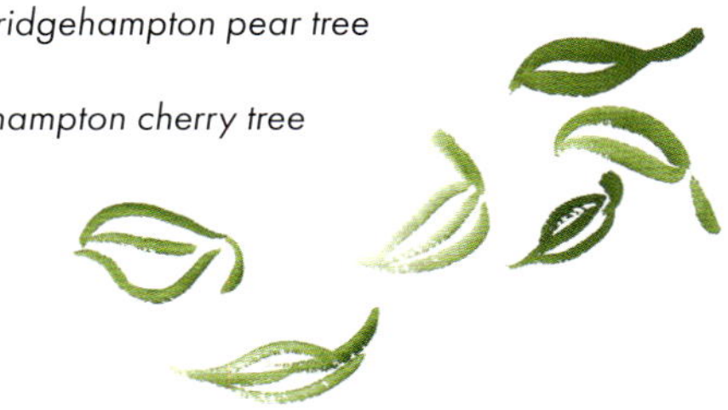

An early sketch depicted ideas for anthropomorphic flora or leaves dancing on the wind;

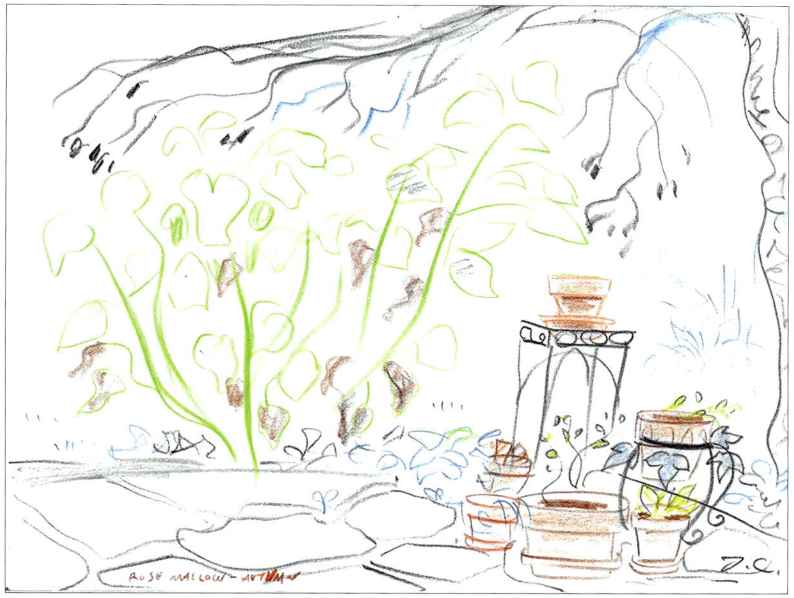
ROSE MALLOW - AUTUMN
Z.C.

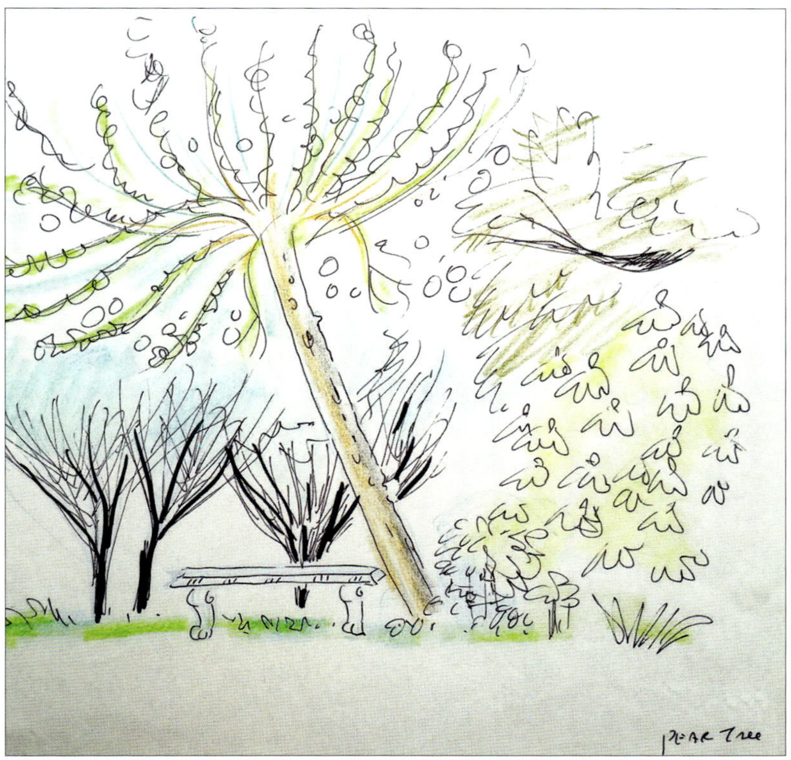
PEAR Tree

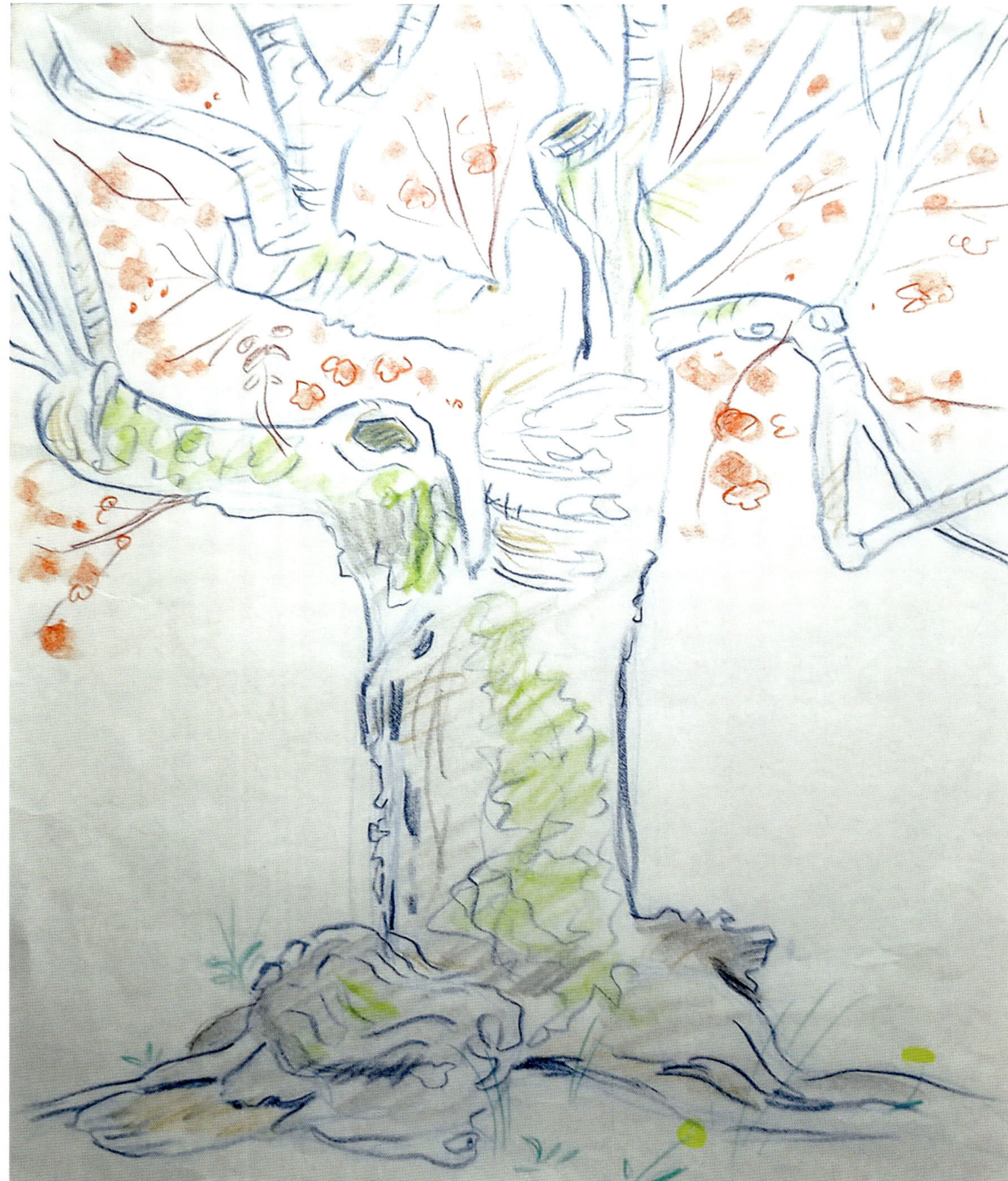

Some veered into abstractions of musical forms and symbols.

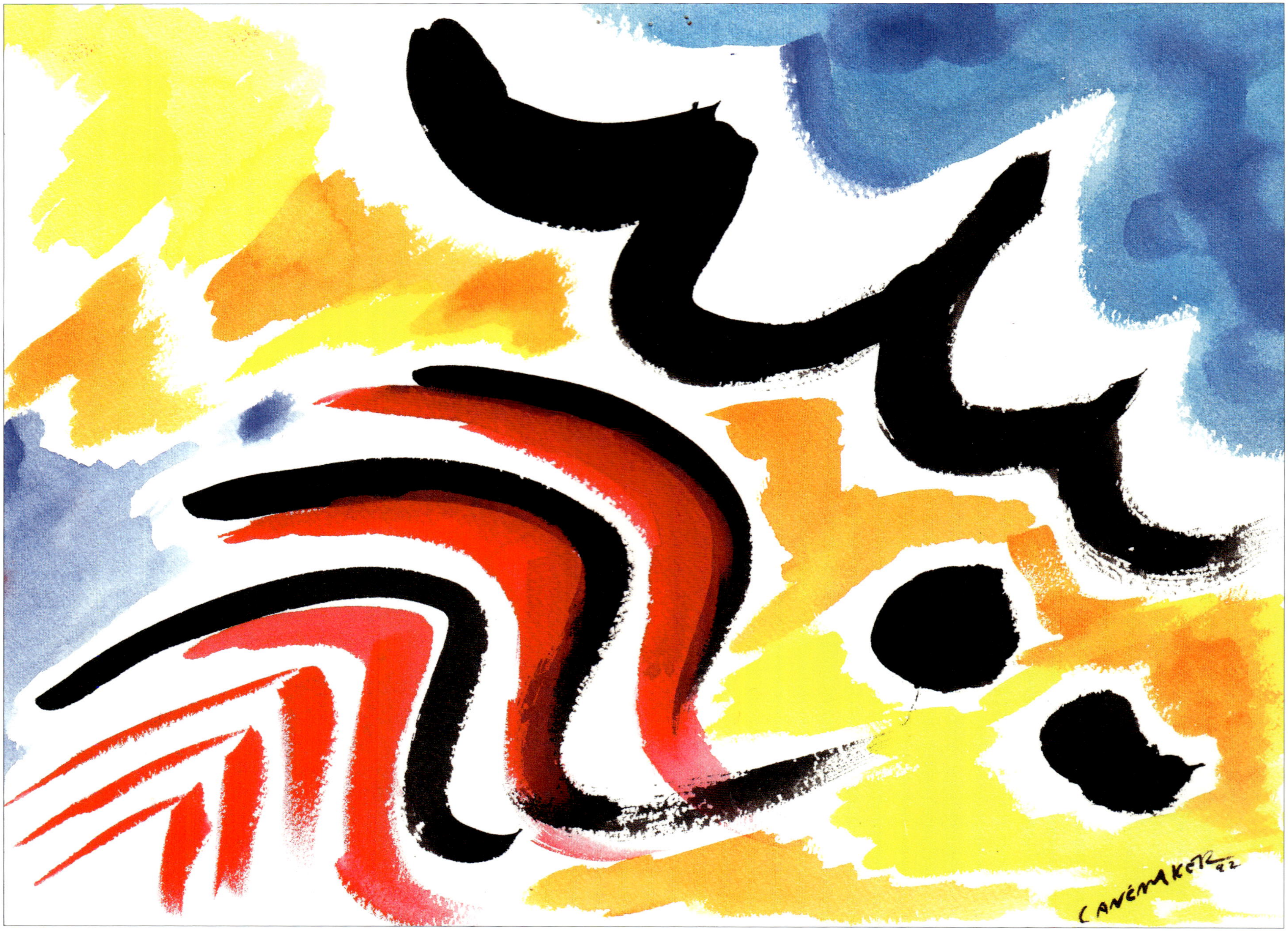

Left and Right: Color abstract concepts.

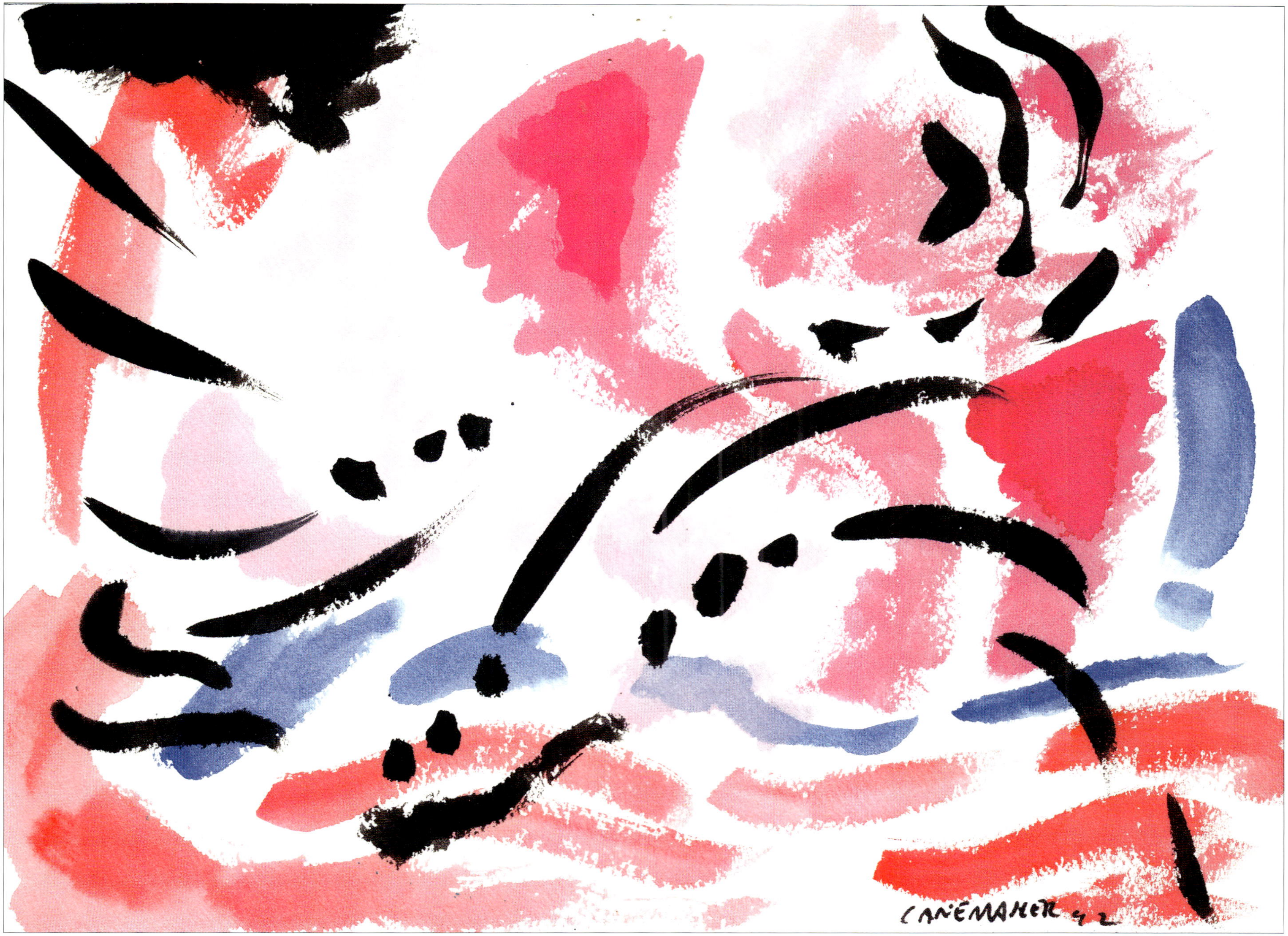

This page top right: JAZZ FLOWERS #1 12 1/2x9 1/4" collage 1981

Bottom right: JAZZ FLOWERS #2 12 1/2x9 1/4" collage 1981

Page 143: JAZZ FLOWERS #3 12 1/2X9 1/4" collage 1981

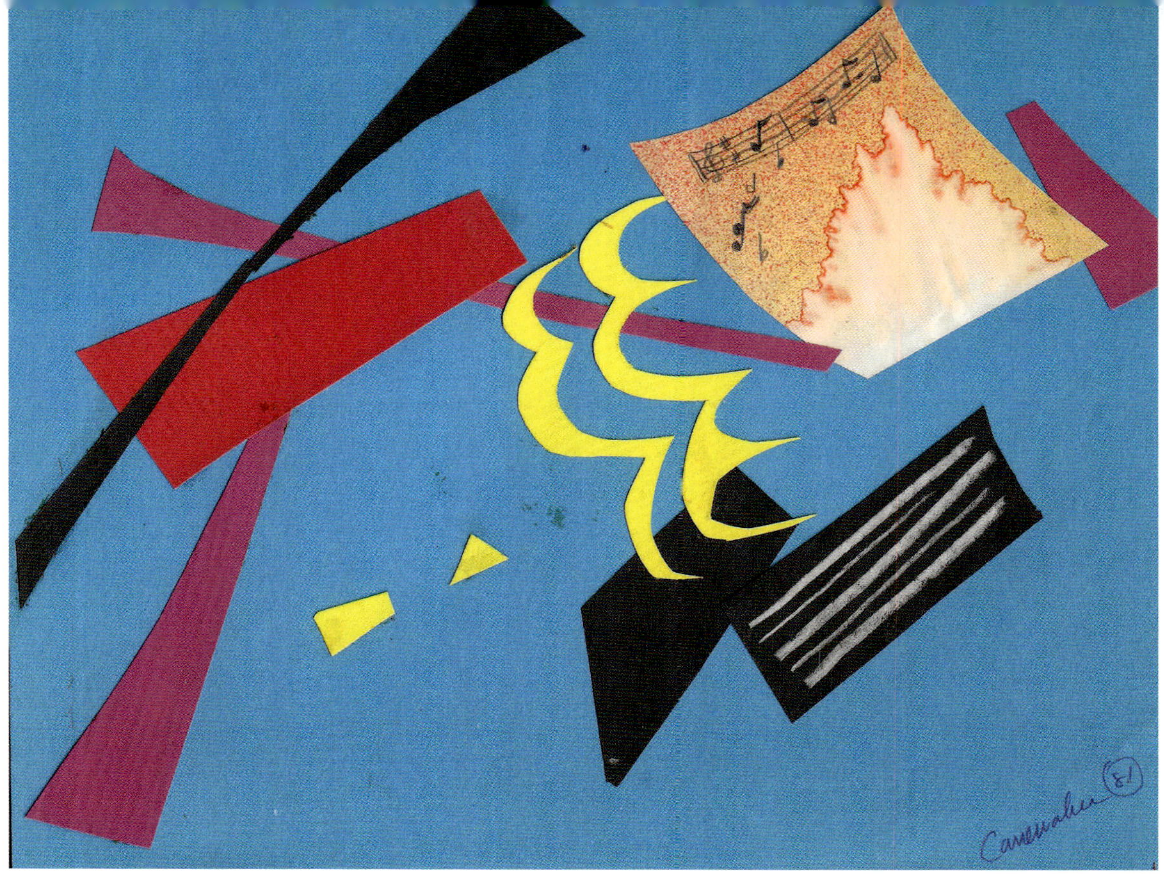

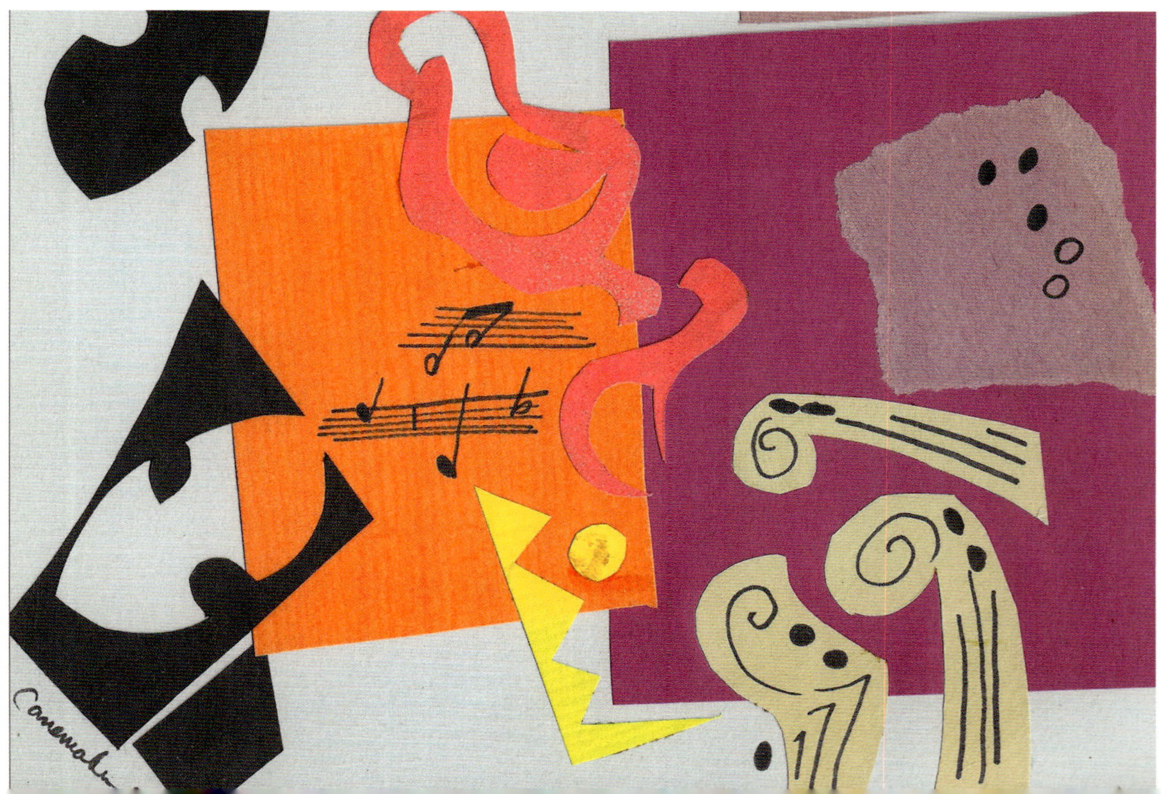

The animation medium adds the element of time and music to graphics, making sequential choreography an essential compositional element.

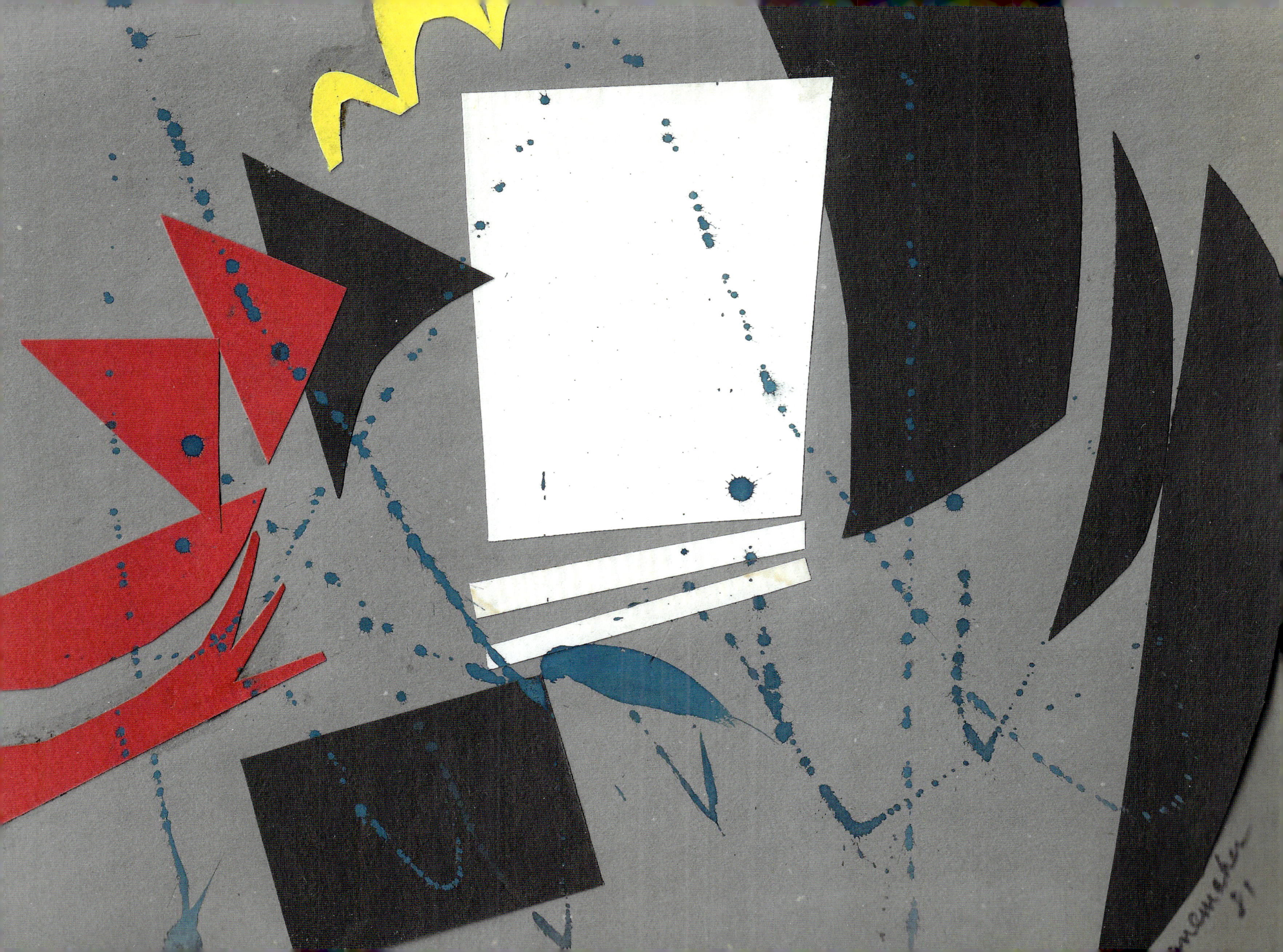

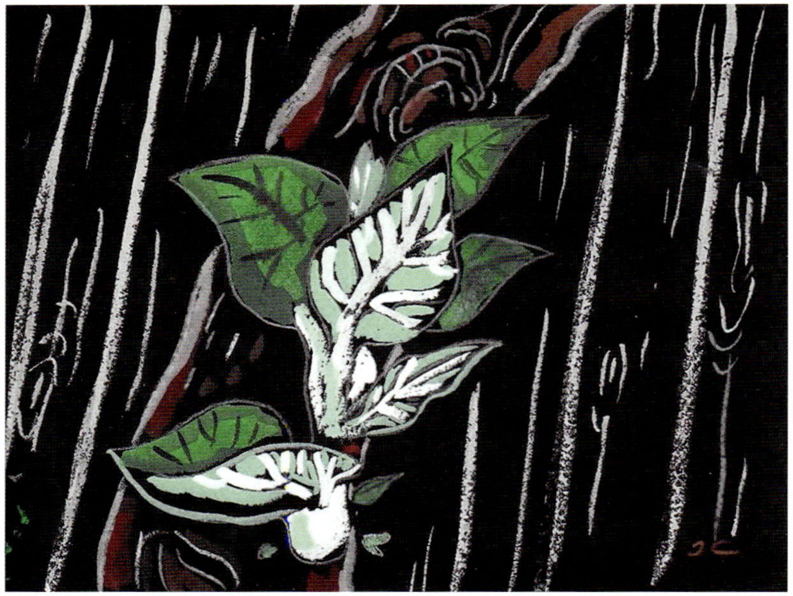

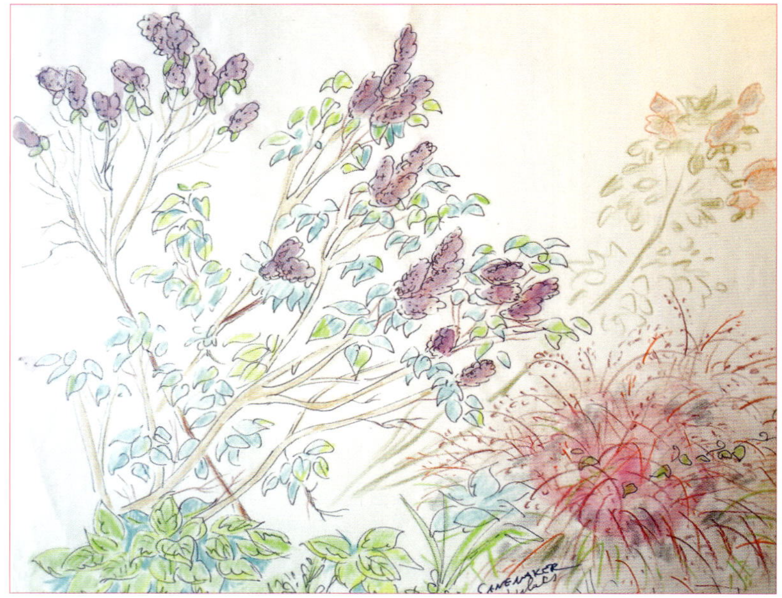

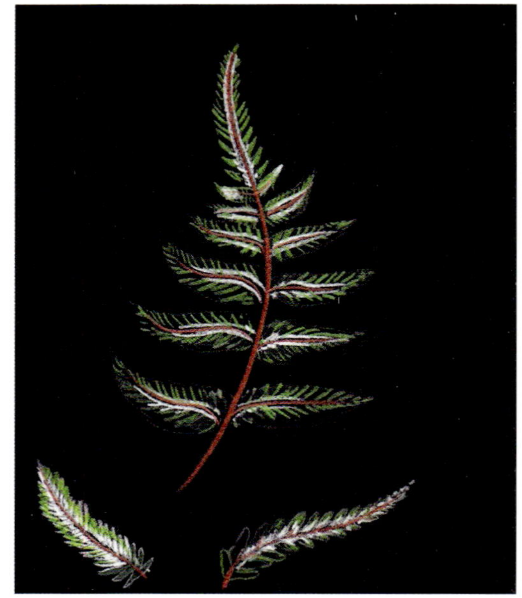

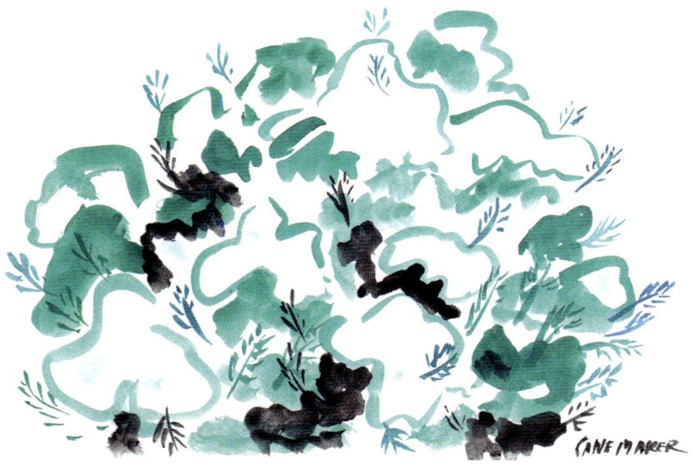

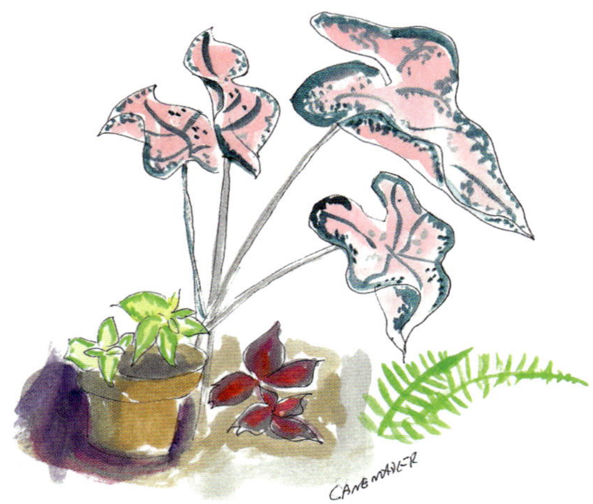

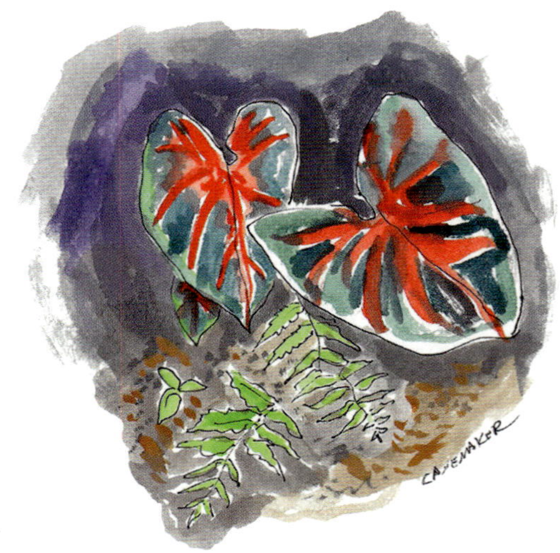

A few of many concept drawings for Bridgehampton.

Upper Left: Bridgehampton concept drawing: Leaf

Upper middle: Bridgehampton concept drawing: May Lilac

Upper Right: Bridgehampton concept drawing: Fern

Lower Left: Bridgehampton concept drawing: Winter

Lower middle: Bridgehampton concept drawing: Caladium

Lower right: Bridgehampton concept drawing: Two Caladium

Storyboarding

Many animated tilms begin with a written script. For Bridgehampton, the conceptual artwork were considered first and weeded out before moving on to the next major phase in animation filmmaking: Storyboards, a visual presentation in the form of sequential sketches of the ideas and pictorial continuity.

The storyboards you see here were actually created after the full color concepts were shown and thoroughly discussed with composer/pianist Fred Hersch. Following the seasonal narrative suggested in the sketches, he then improvised the film's beautiful solo piano soundtrack. I based these *Bridgehampton* story continuity boards, drawn in a rough calligraphic shorthand, on Hersch's jazz score. His music tempos and their changes guided me in making final decisions regarding scene placements, camera moves, color and movement contrasts, editing and animation of the imagery. https://www.moma.org/multimedia/audio/50/992

Bridgehampton is a "beautiful, subdued lyrical work," wrote Chris Robinson, director of the Ottawa International Animation Festival, in his 2010 book, *Animators Unearthed: A Guide to the Best of Contemporary Animation*. "Fred Hersch's gentle Vince Guaraldi-like piano piece is a gentle breeze, a quiet passionate travel mate guiding us through the lush landscapes."

The film was screened at the 2007 Tribeca Film Festival in a special retrospective program, *The Animated World of John Canemaker*. The next year *Bridgehampton* was continuously screened along with a selection of original artwork from the film at MoMA as part of *Jazz Score* (April 16 - September 17, 2008), an exhibit about the confluence of jazz and film artists in the movies.

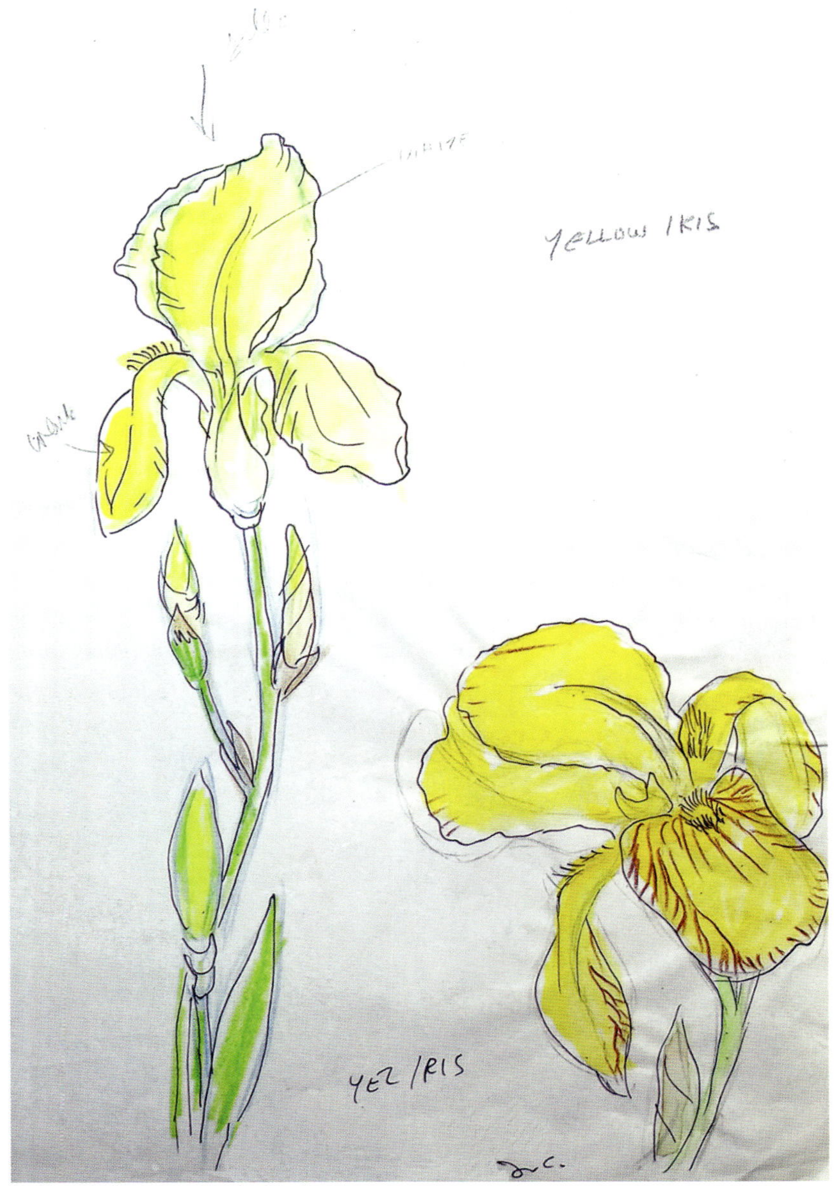

Bridgehampton concept drawing: Yellow Iris.

The following 8 pages, 146-153, contain storyboards for the film BRIDGEHAMPTON.

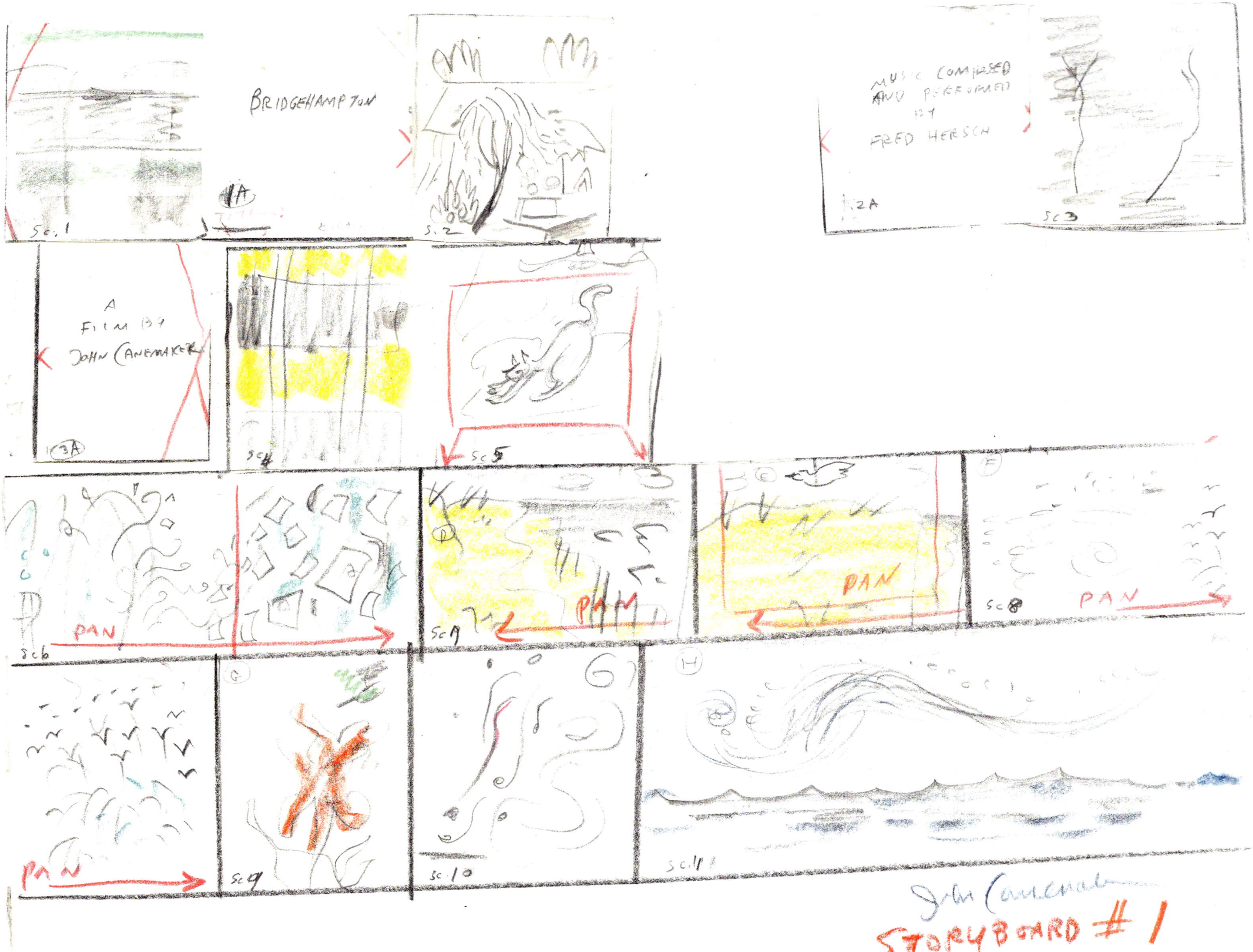
BRIDGEHAMPTON
MUSIC COMPOSED AND PERFORMED BY FRED HERSCH
A FILM BY JOHN CANEMAKER
PAN
PAN
PAN
PAN
PAN
STORYBOARD #1

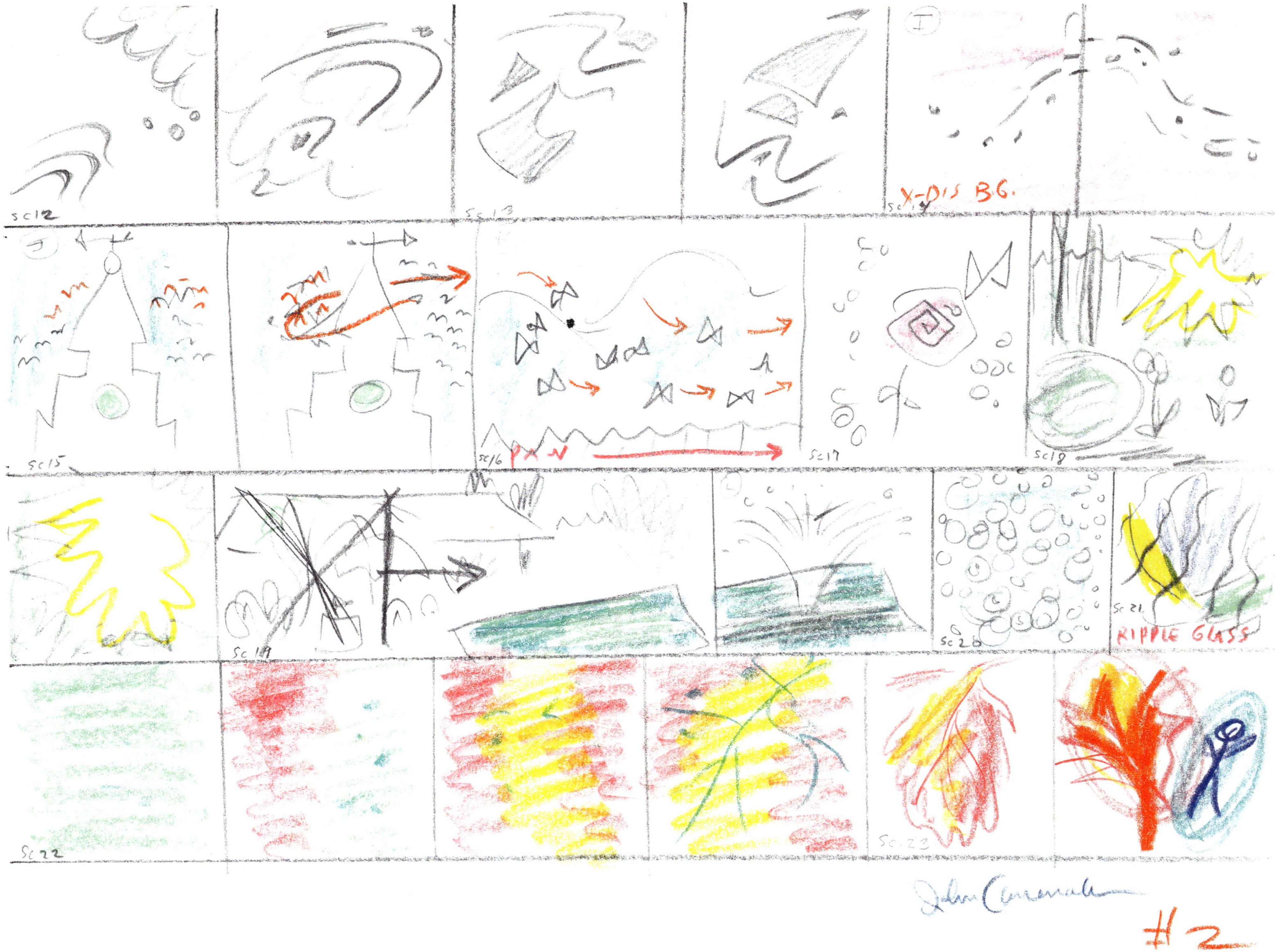
Sc12
Sc13
X-DIS B.G.
Sc15
Sc16
PAN
Sc17
Sc18
Sc19
Sc20
Sc21
RIPPLE GLASS
Sc22
Sc23
#2

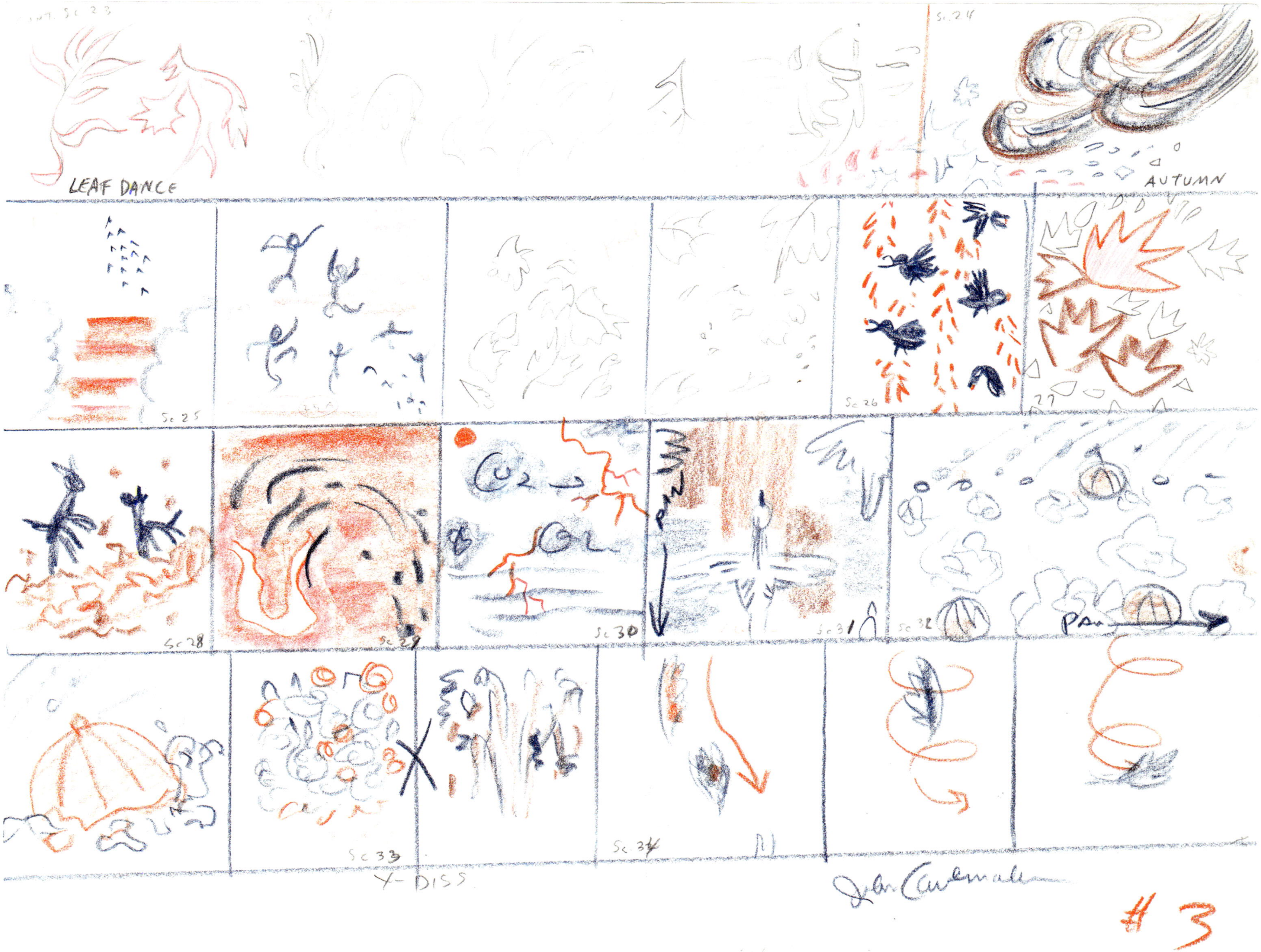
LEAF DANCE
AUTUMN
Sc 25
Sc 26
27
Sc 28
Sc 30
Sc 31
Sc 32
PAN
Sc 33
X-DISS
#3

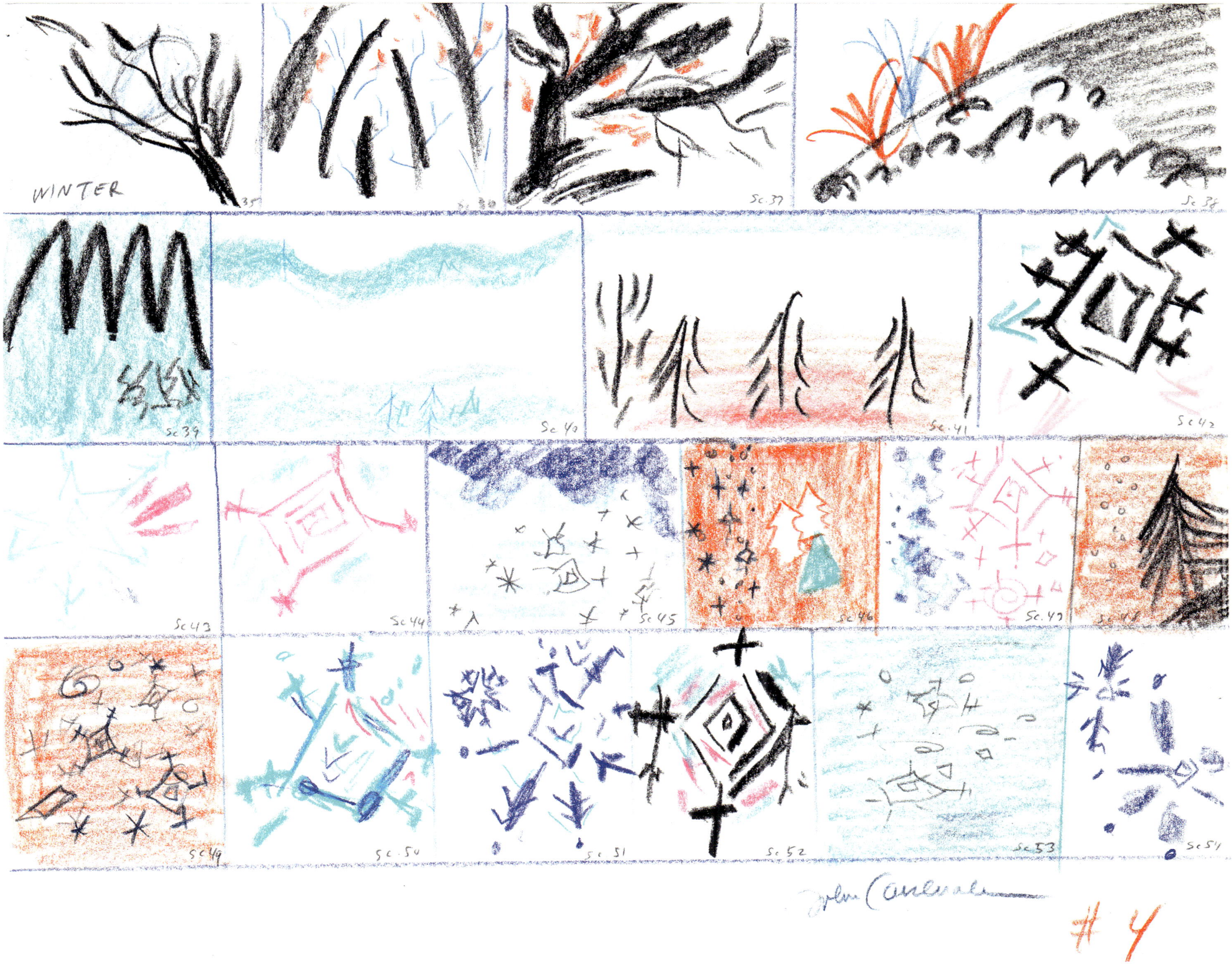
WINTER
Sc 37
Sc 38
Sc 39
Sc 40
Sc 41
Sc 42
Sc 43
Sc 44
Sc 45
Sc 46
Sc 47
Sc 49
Sc 50
Sc 51
Sc 52
Sc 53
Sc 54
4

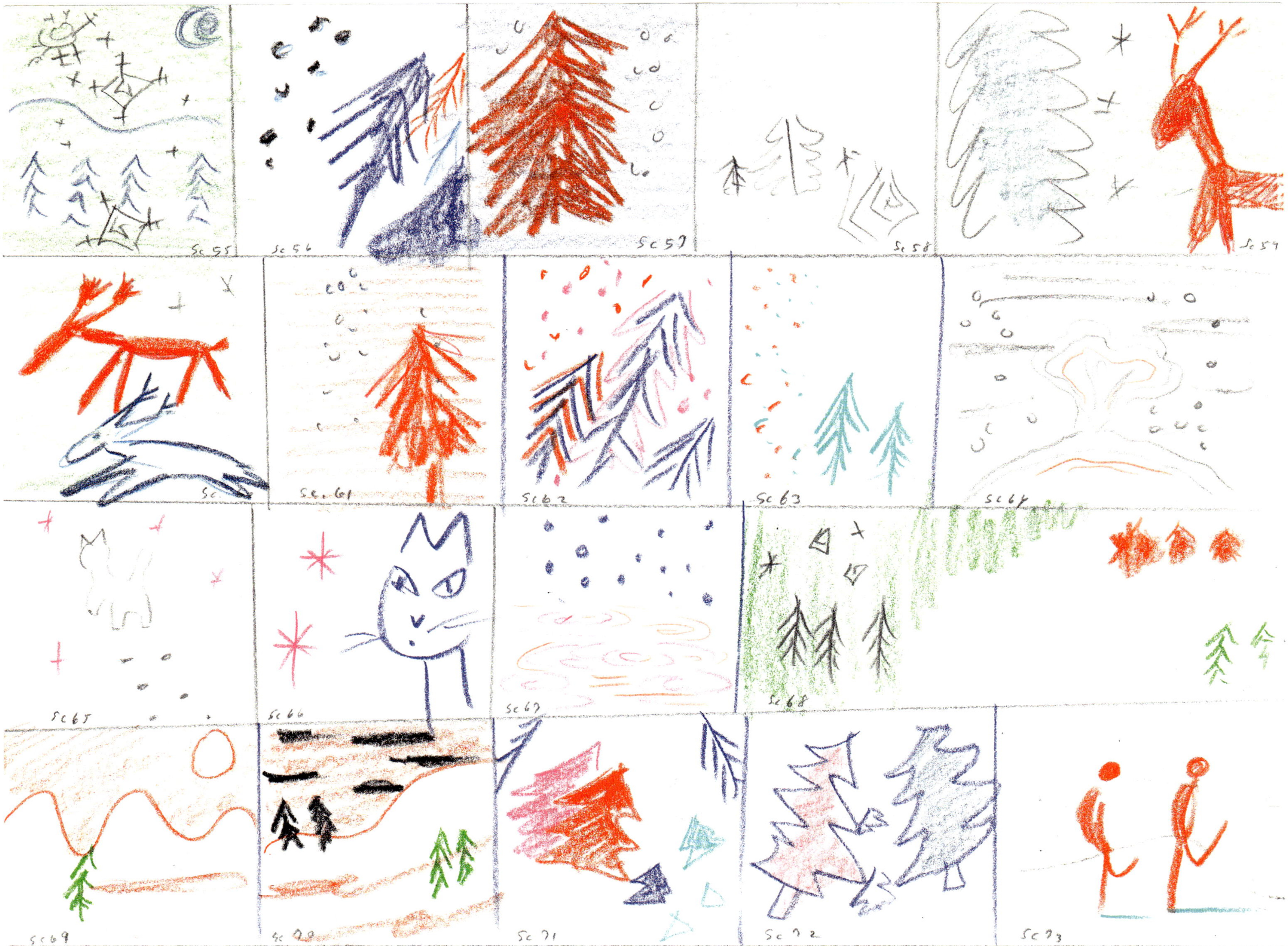
Sc 55
Sc 56
Sc 57
Sc 58
Sc 59
Sc
Sc 61
Sc 62
Sc 63
Sc 64
Sc 65
Sc 66
Sc 67
Sc 68
Sc 69
Sc 71
Sc 72
Sc 73
#5

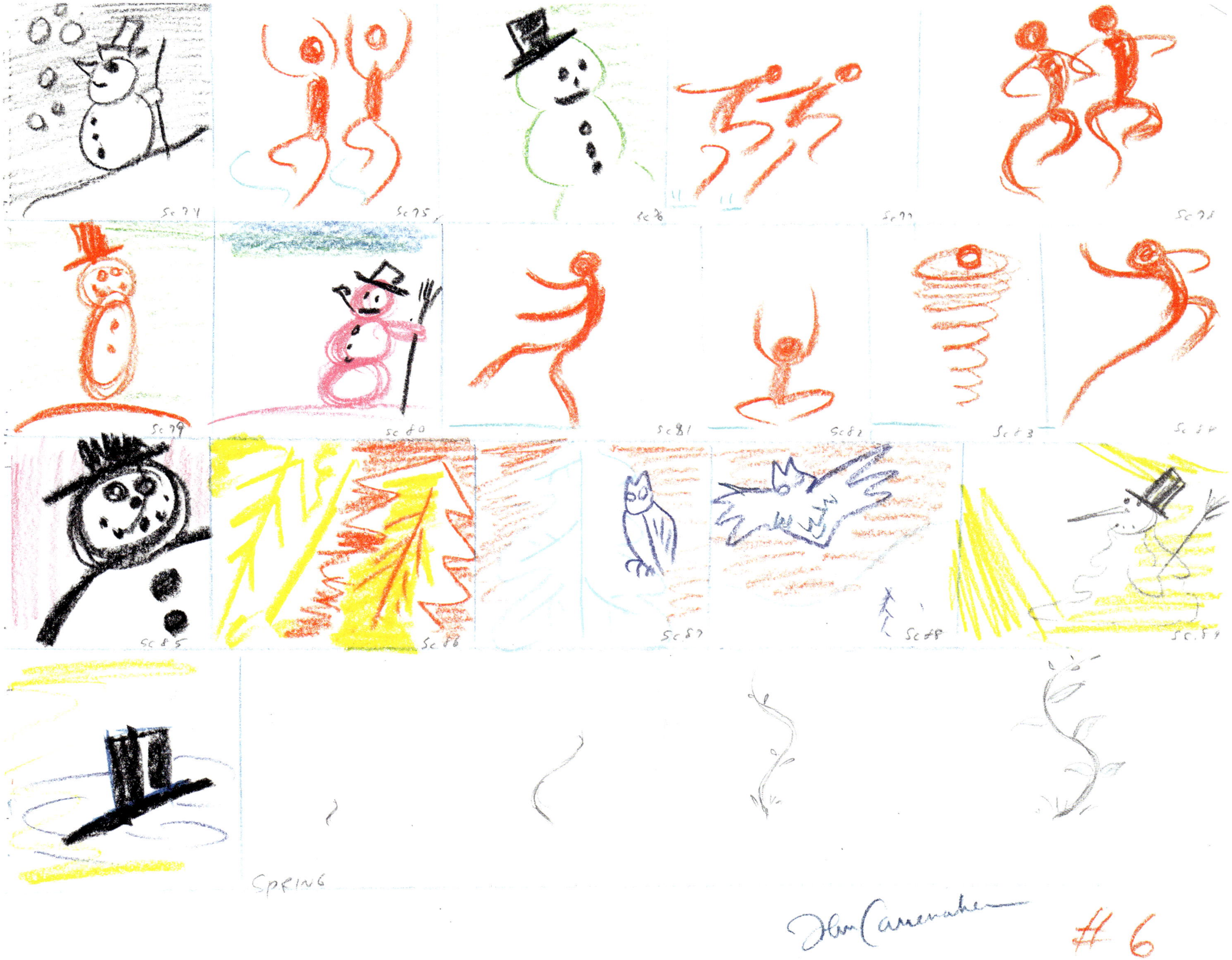
SPRING
#6

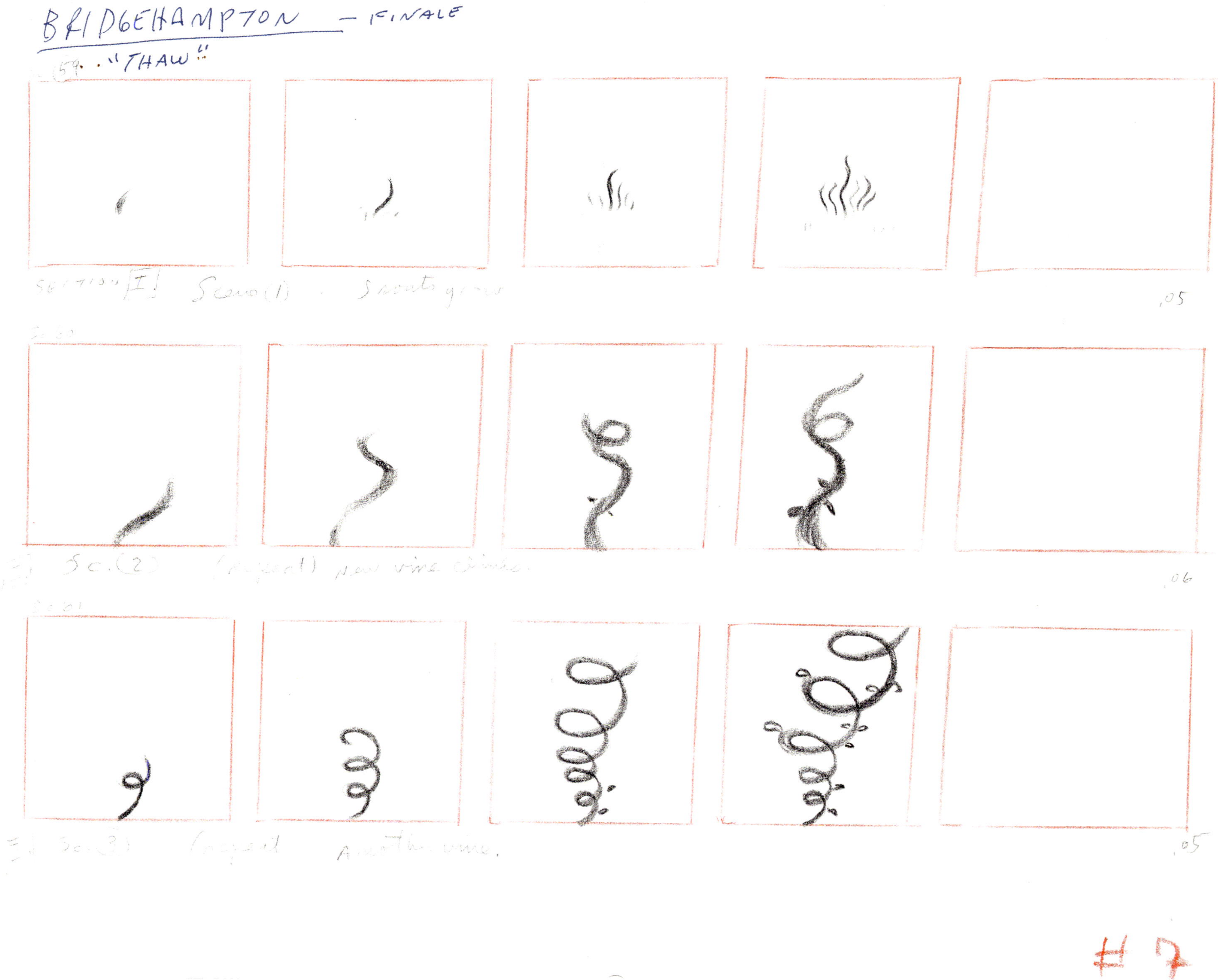
BRIDGEHAMPTON — FINALE
"THAW"
.05
.06
.05
#7

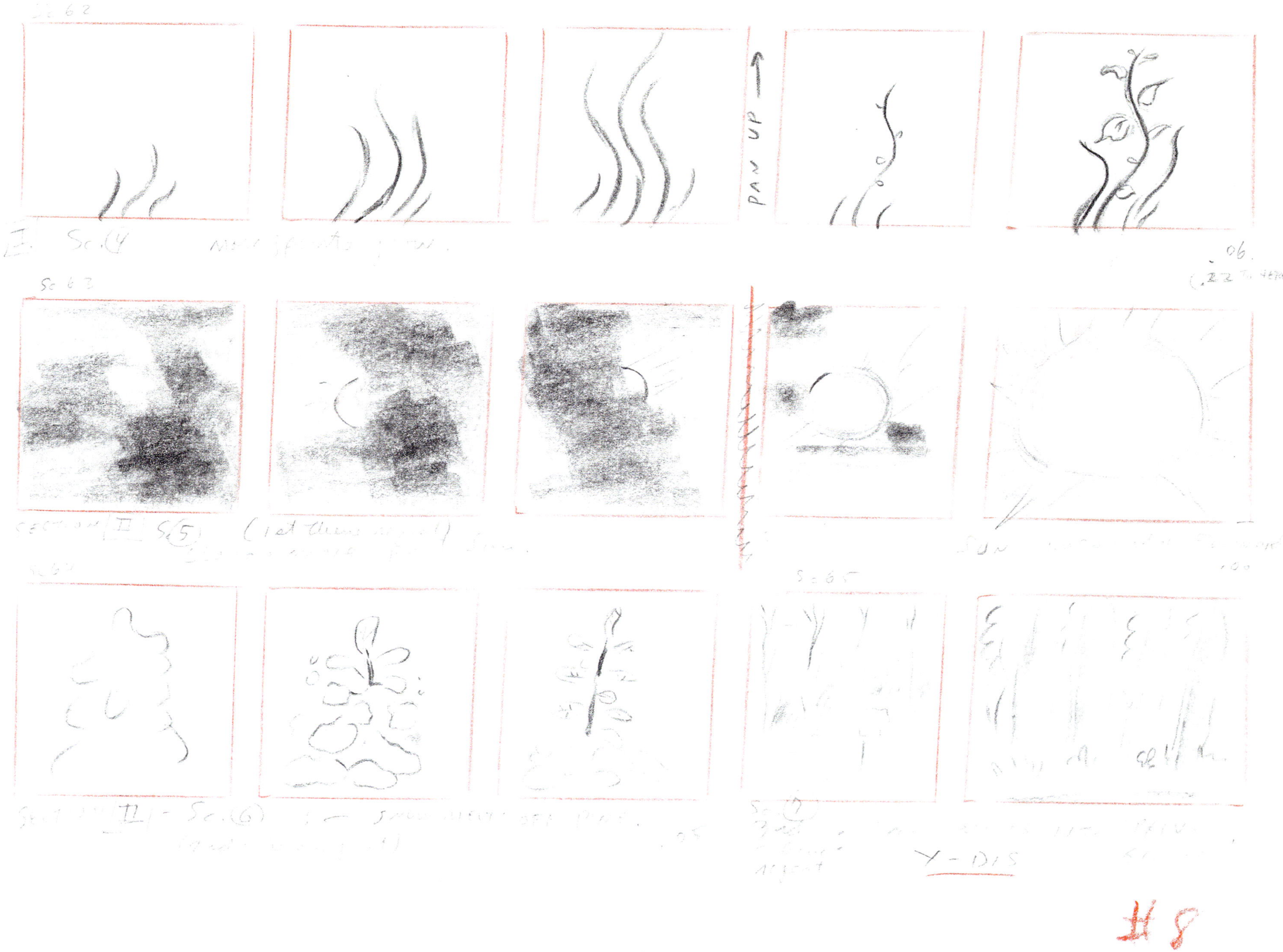
PAN UP

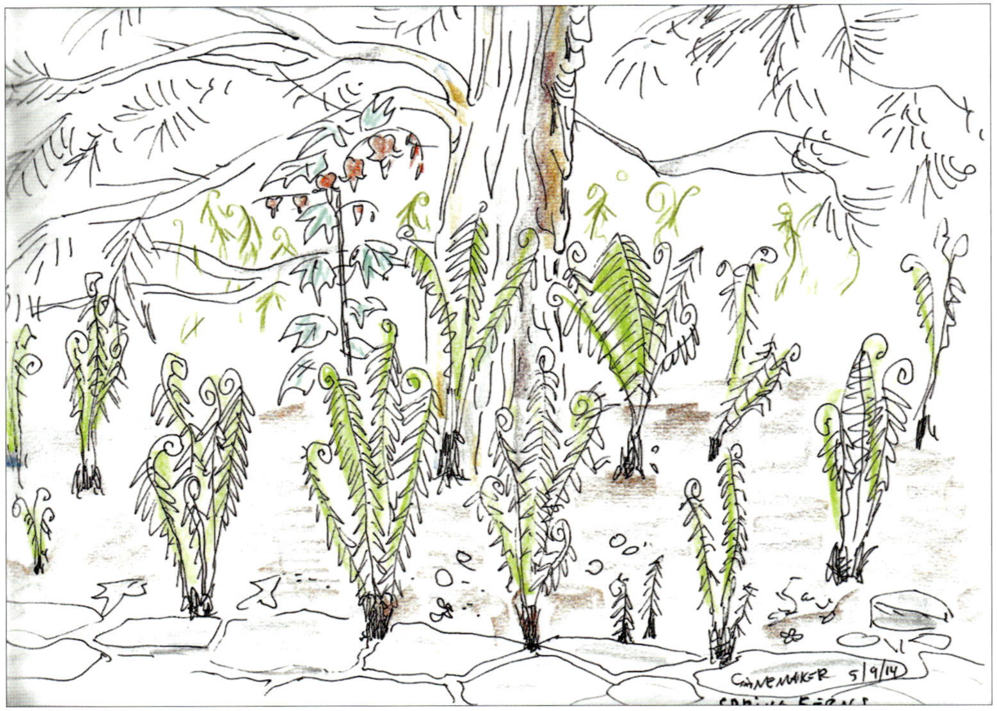

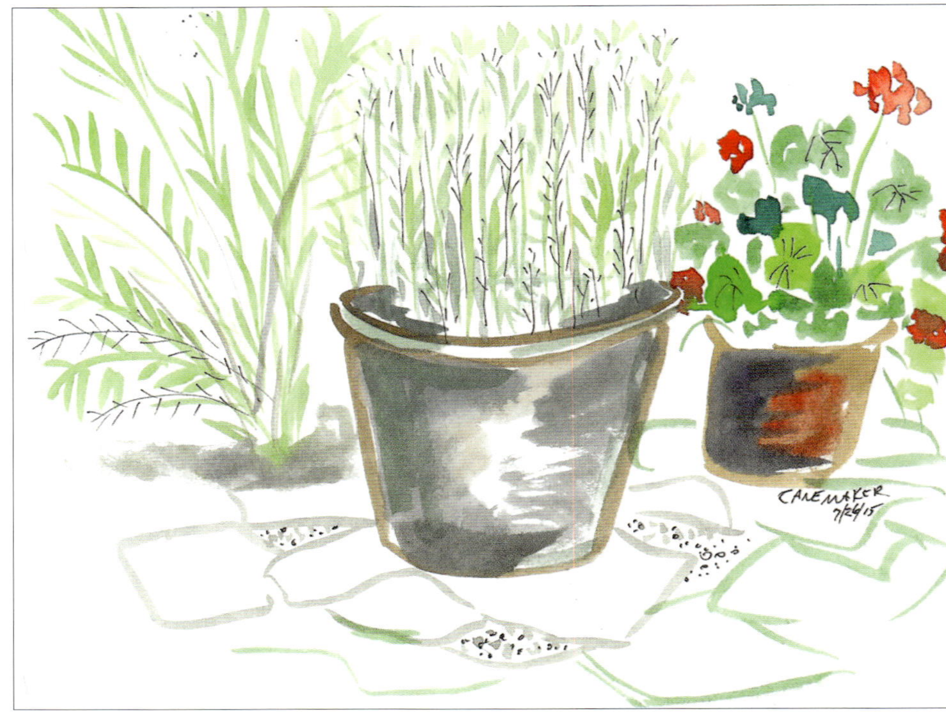

Upper left: Ferns in spring 2014

Upper right: Two Pots 2015

Lower left: Christmas Plant 2010

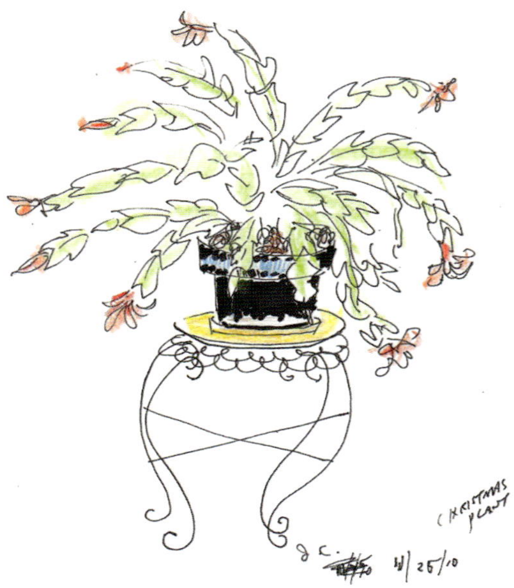

LAYOUTS, CELS & BACKGROUNDS

Layout drawings are the stage on which my characters play. Cels are transparent plastic sheets which are painted on and placed over opaque backgrounds for single frame photography. Modern digital technology has changed all that, but I remain committed to hand-drawn animation.

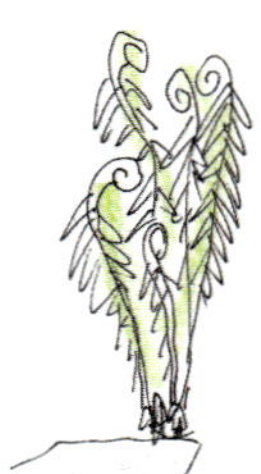

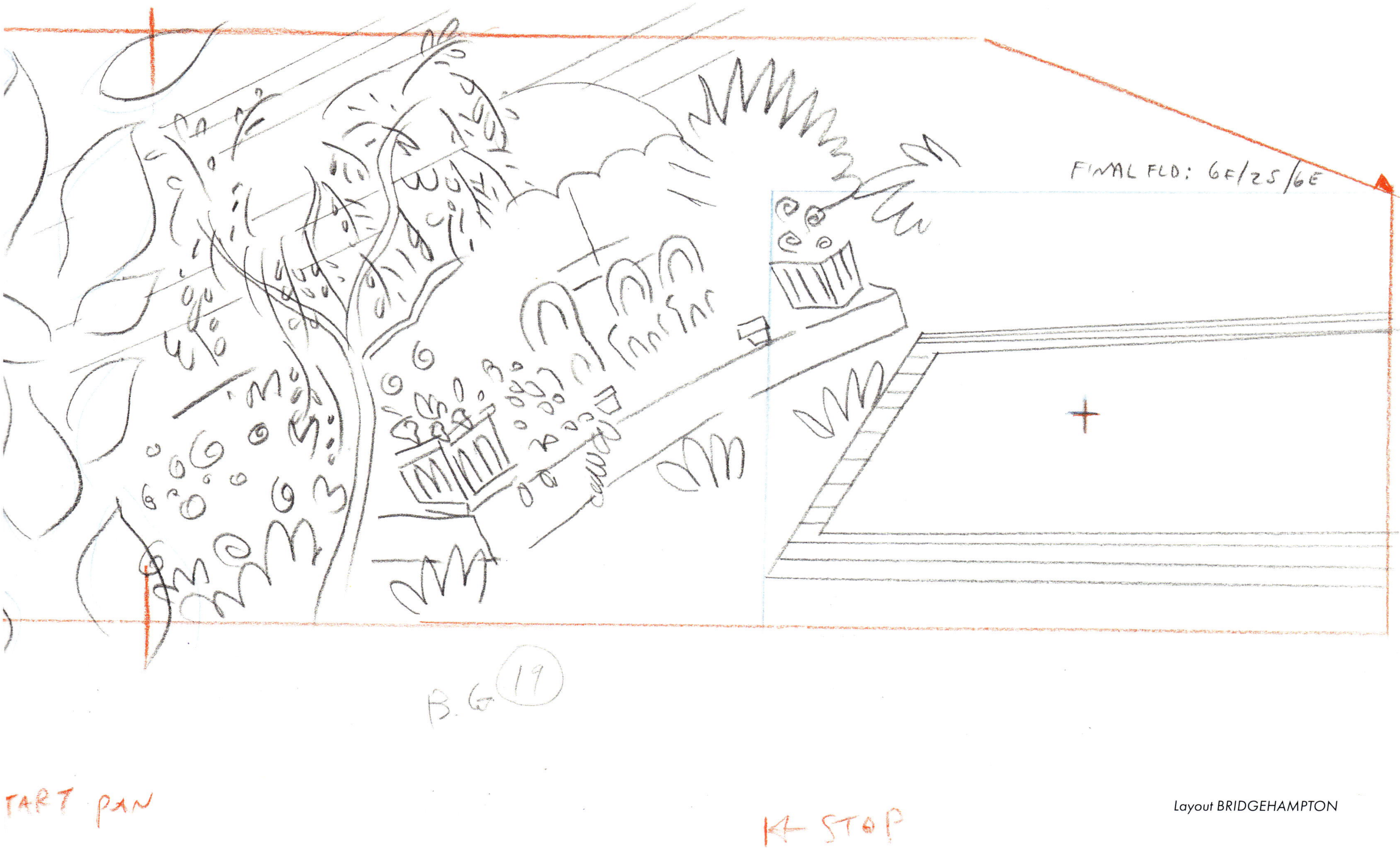

Layout BRIDGEHAMPTON

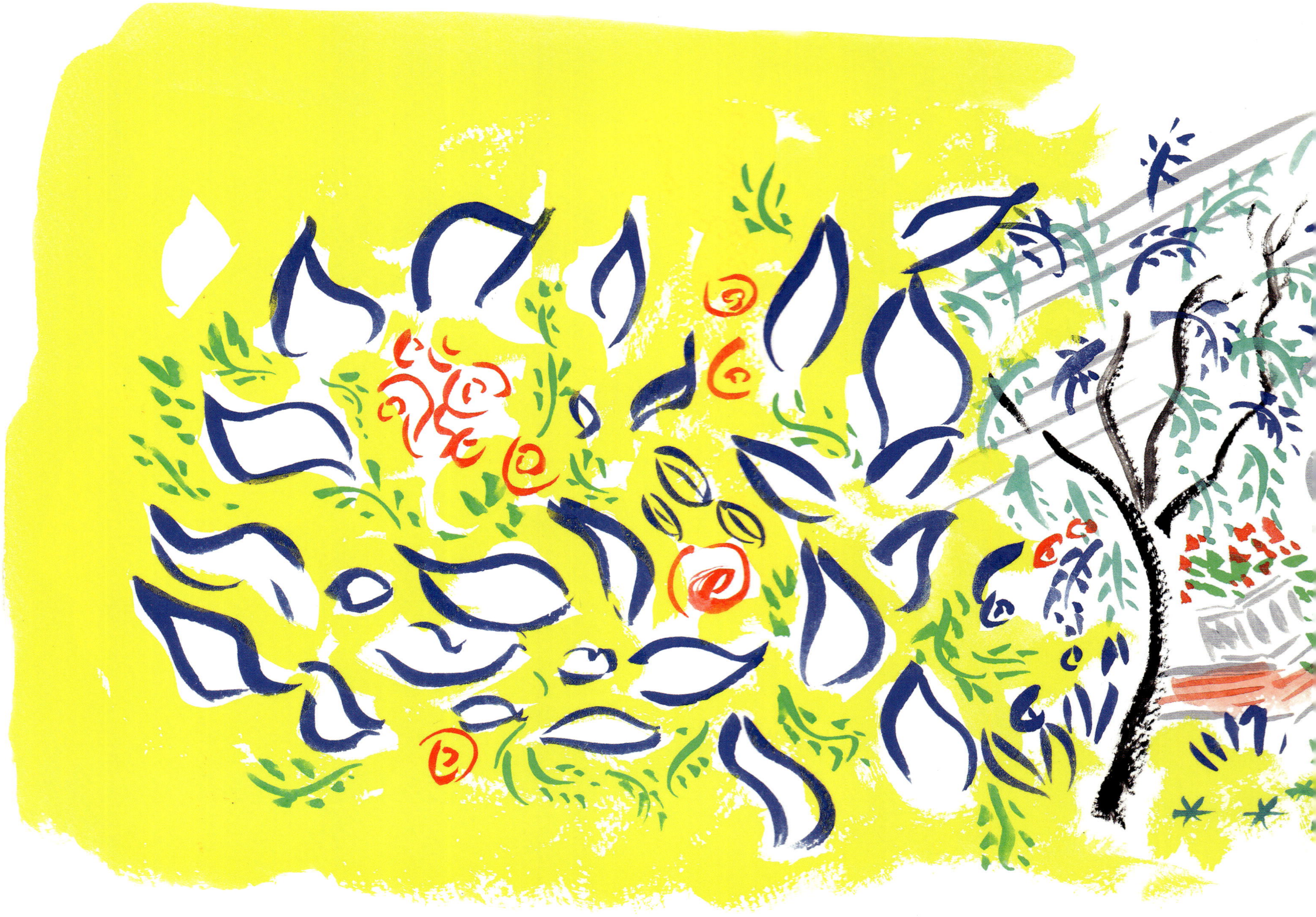

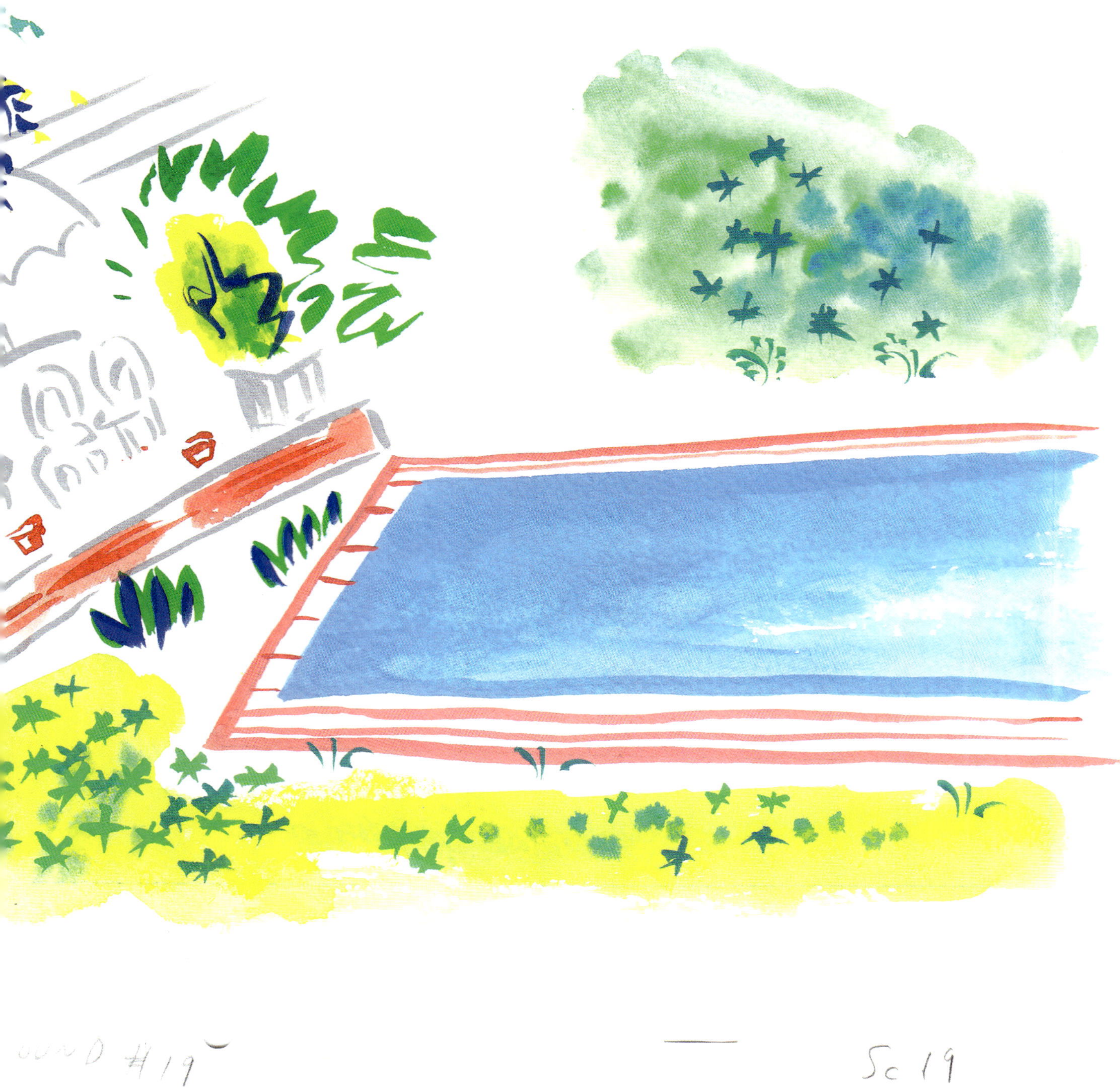

Background 2
BRIDGEHAMPTON

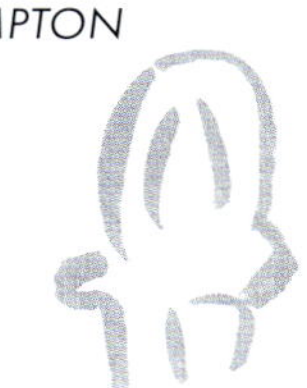

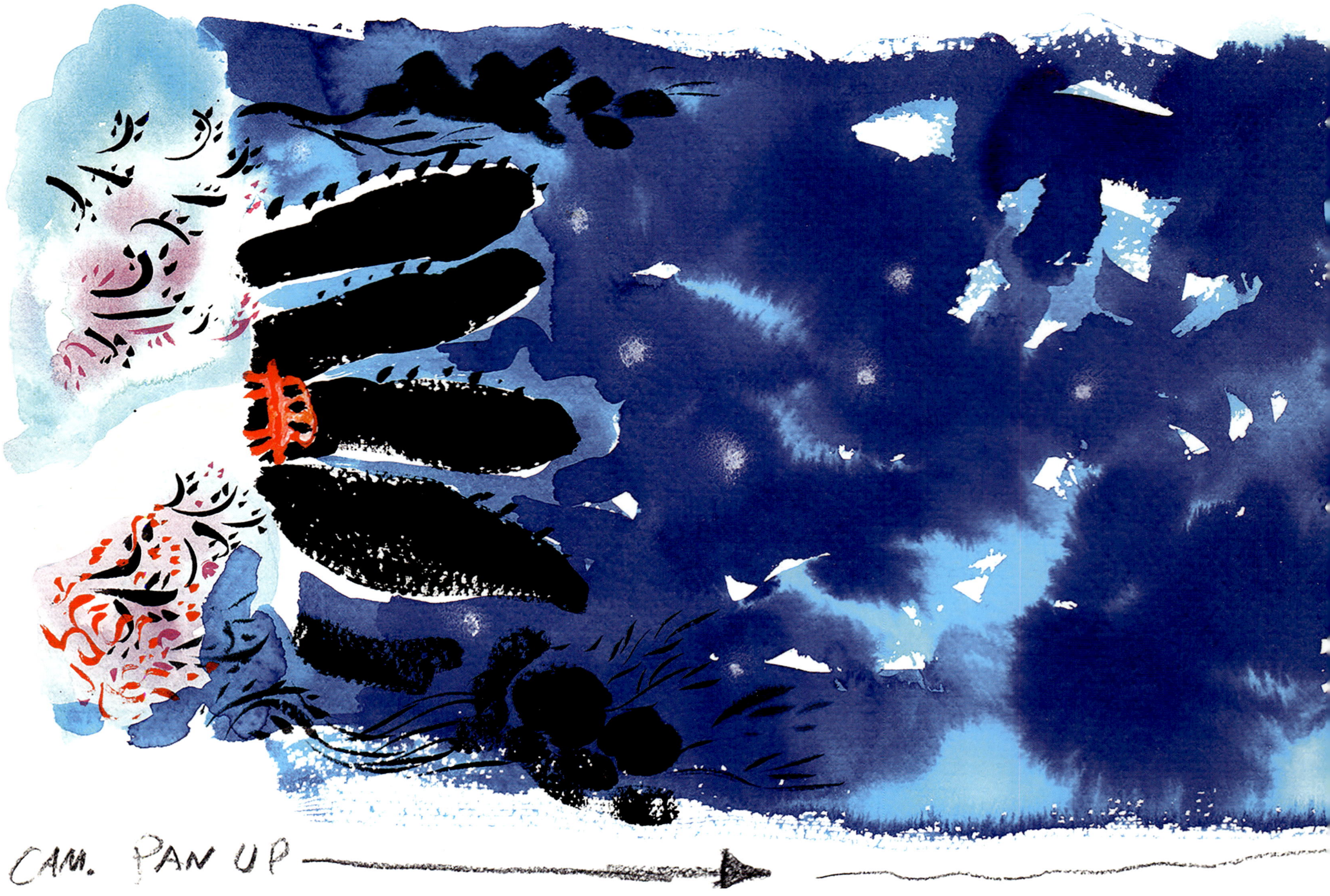
CAM. PAN UP

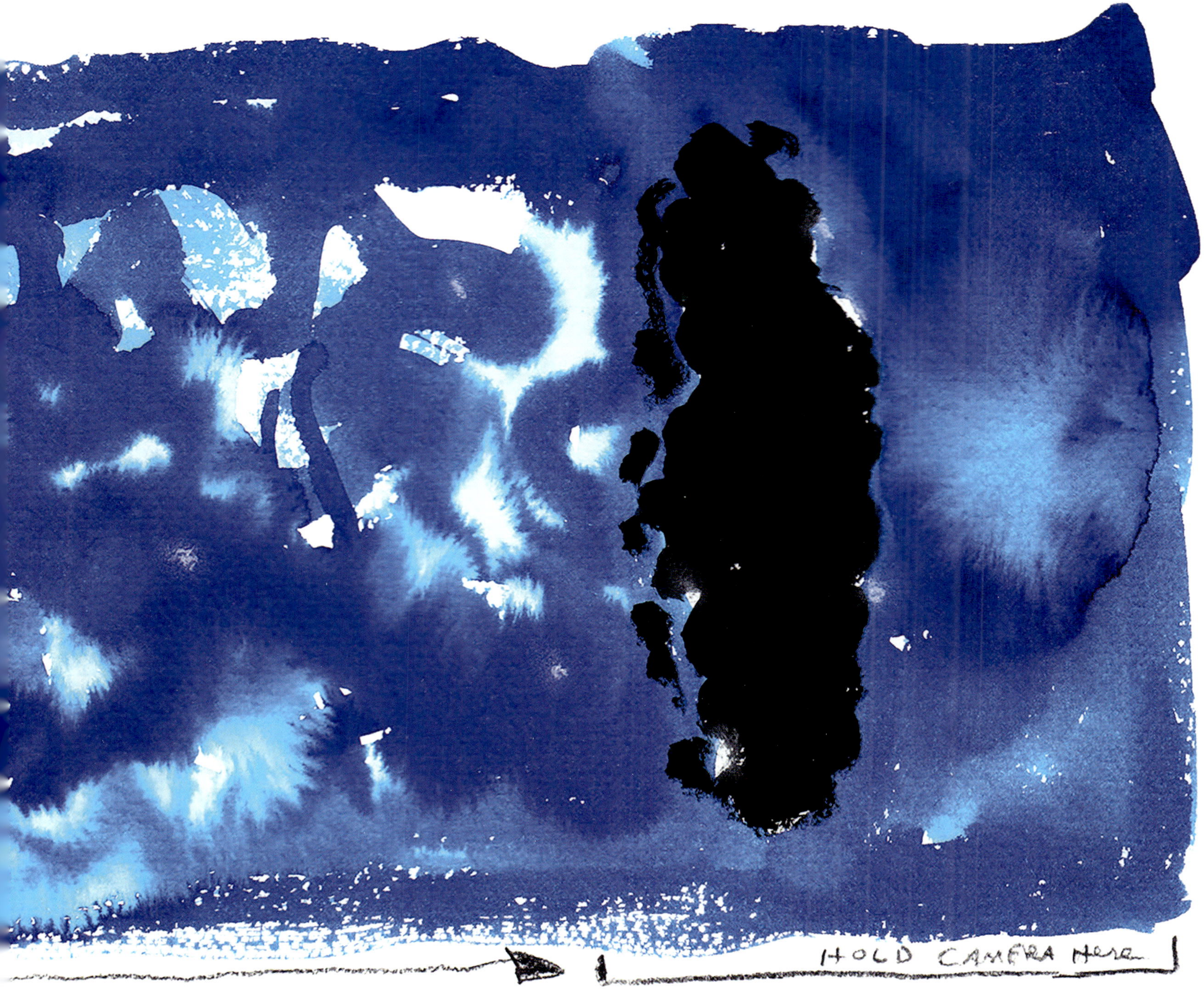

Vertical Pan Background
BRIDGEHAMPTON

Turn the book verically to see the illustration and get the impact of the pan.

Background 1
BRIDGEHAMPTON

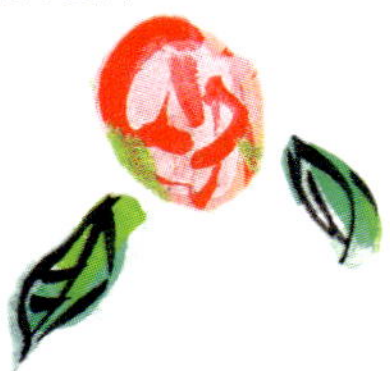

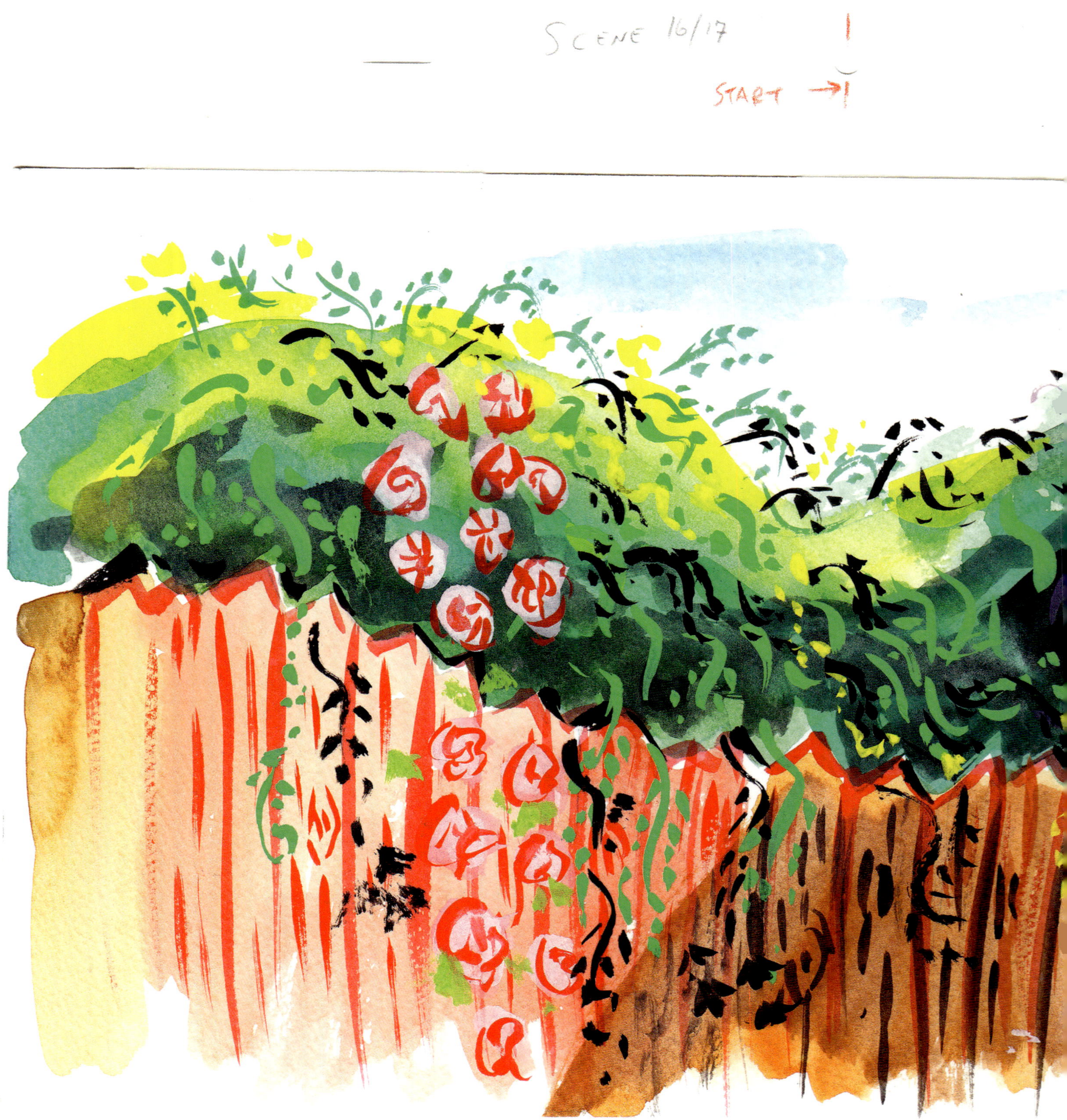

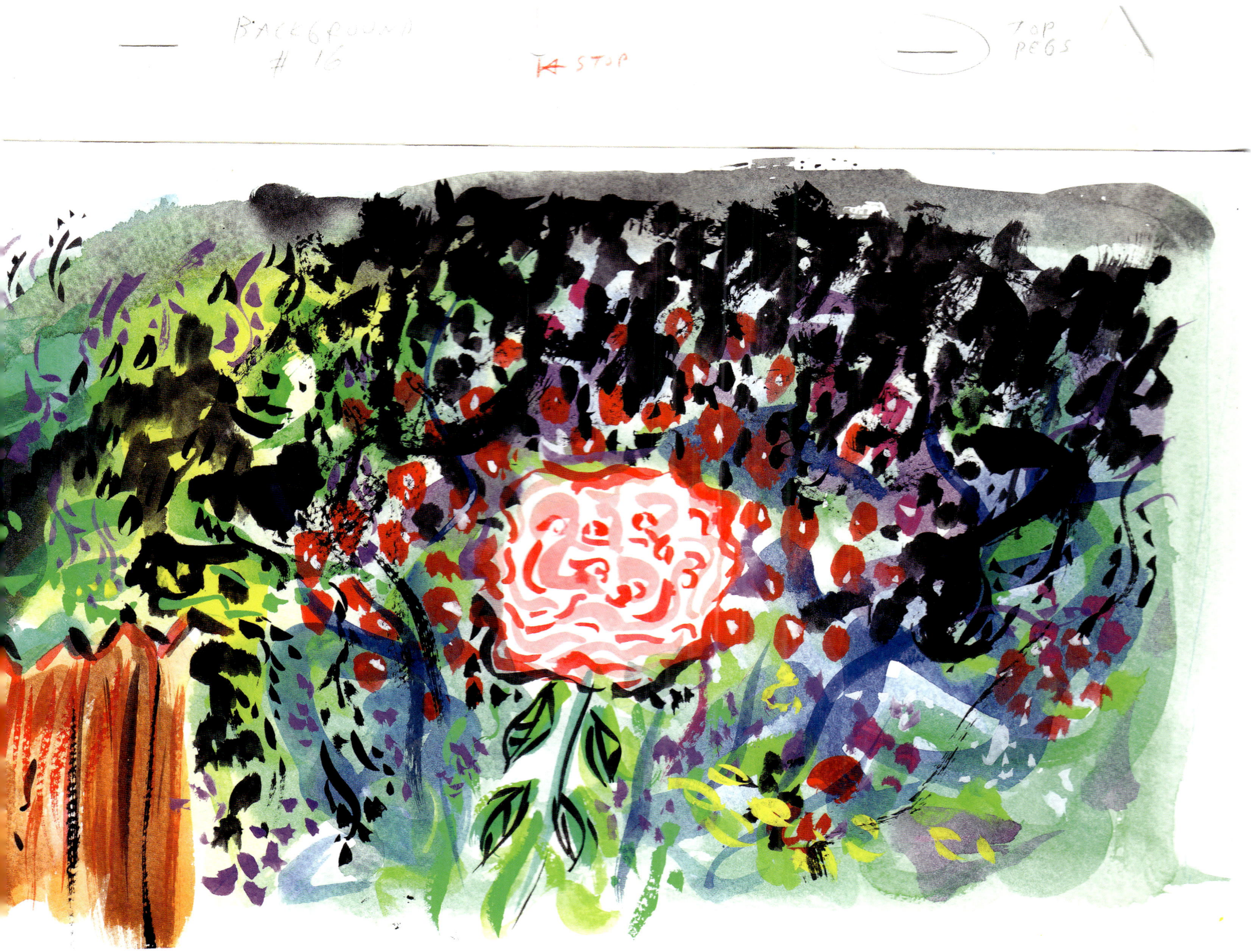
BACKGROUND
16
STOP
TOP
PEGS

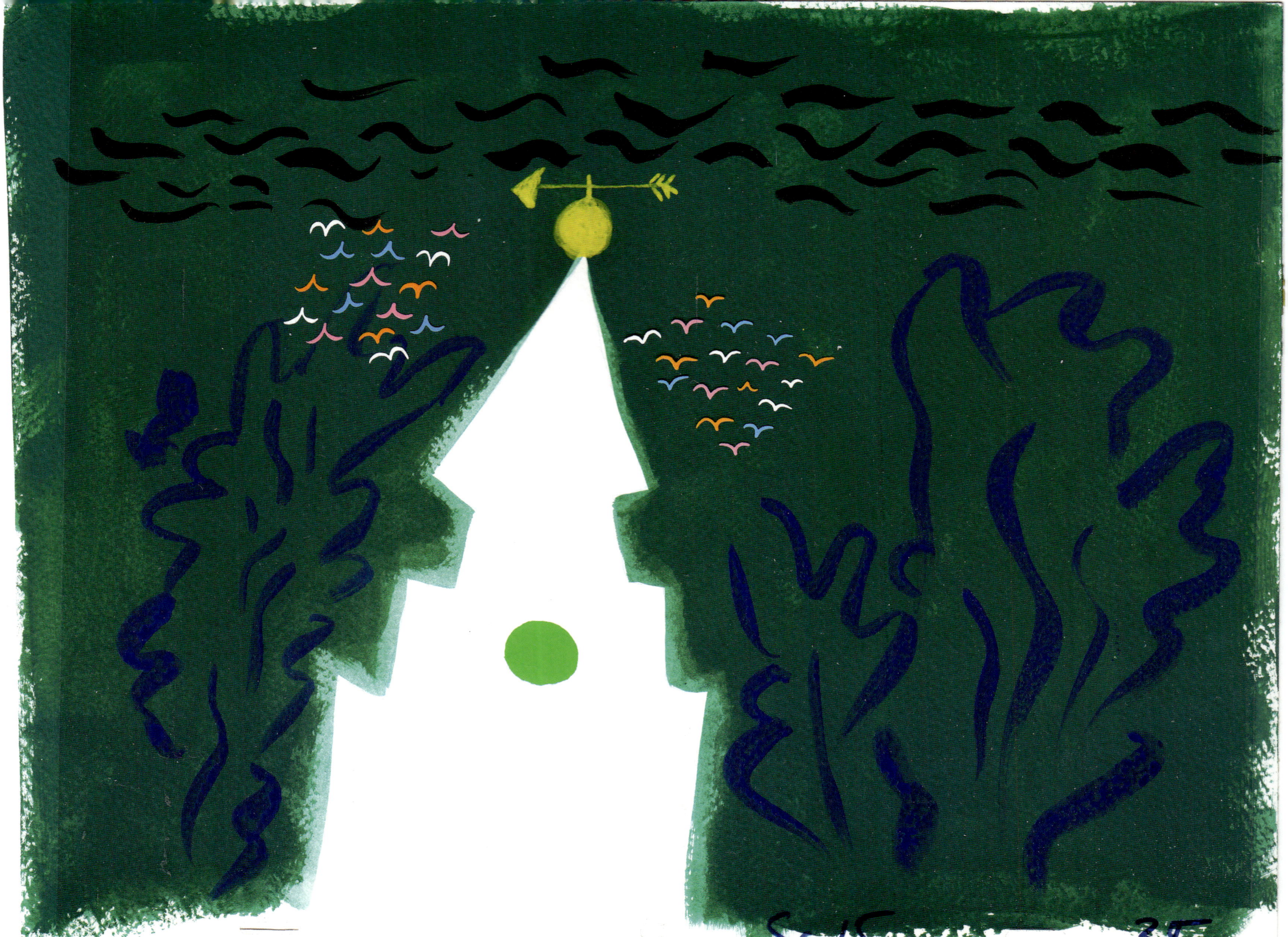

"BRIDGEHAMPTON" SC 15 35

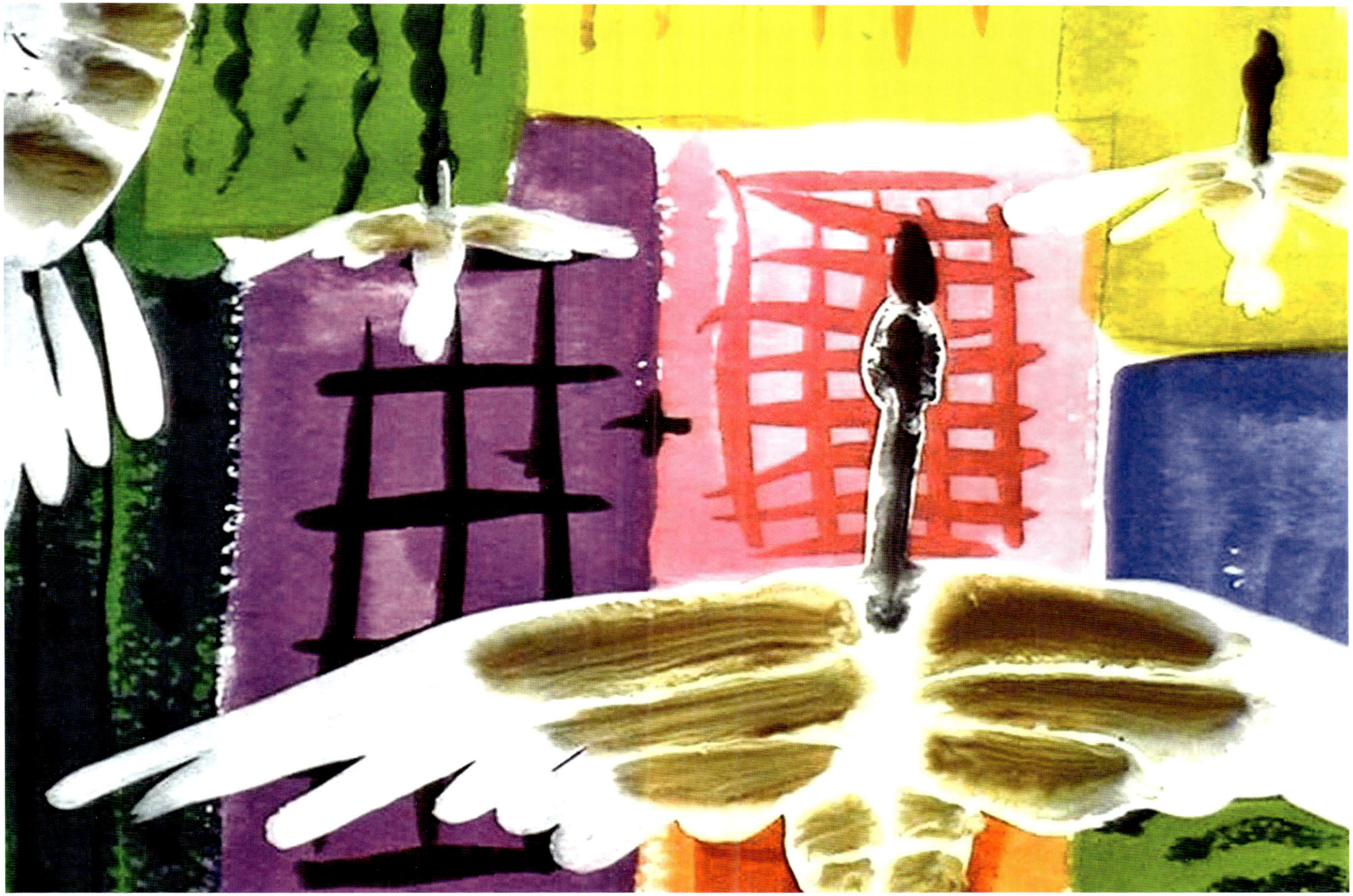

Left: Animation Cel & Background - BRIDGEHAMPTON

Right: Flying geese cel and background -- a frame capture from the film.

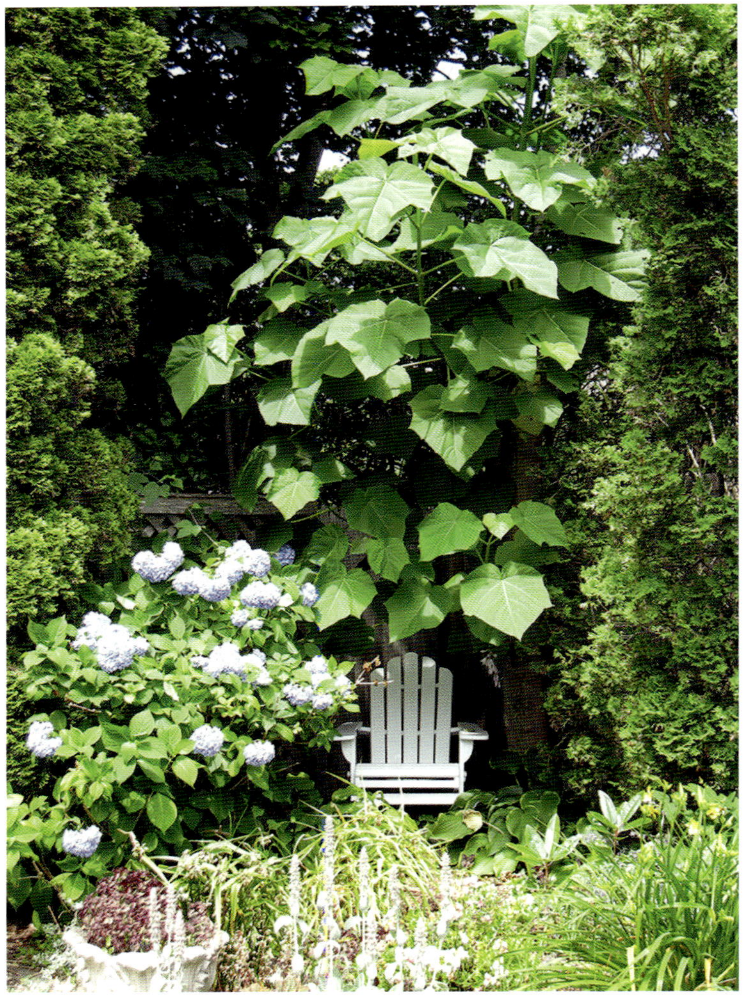

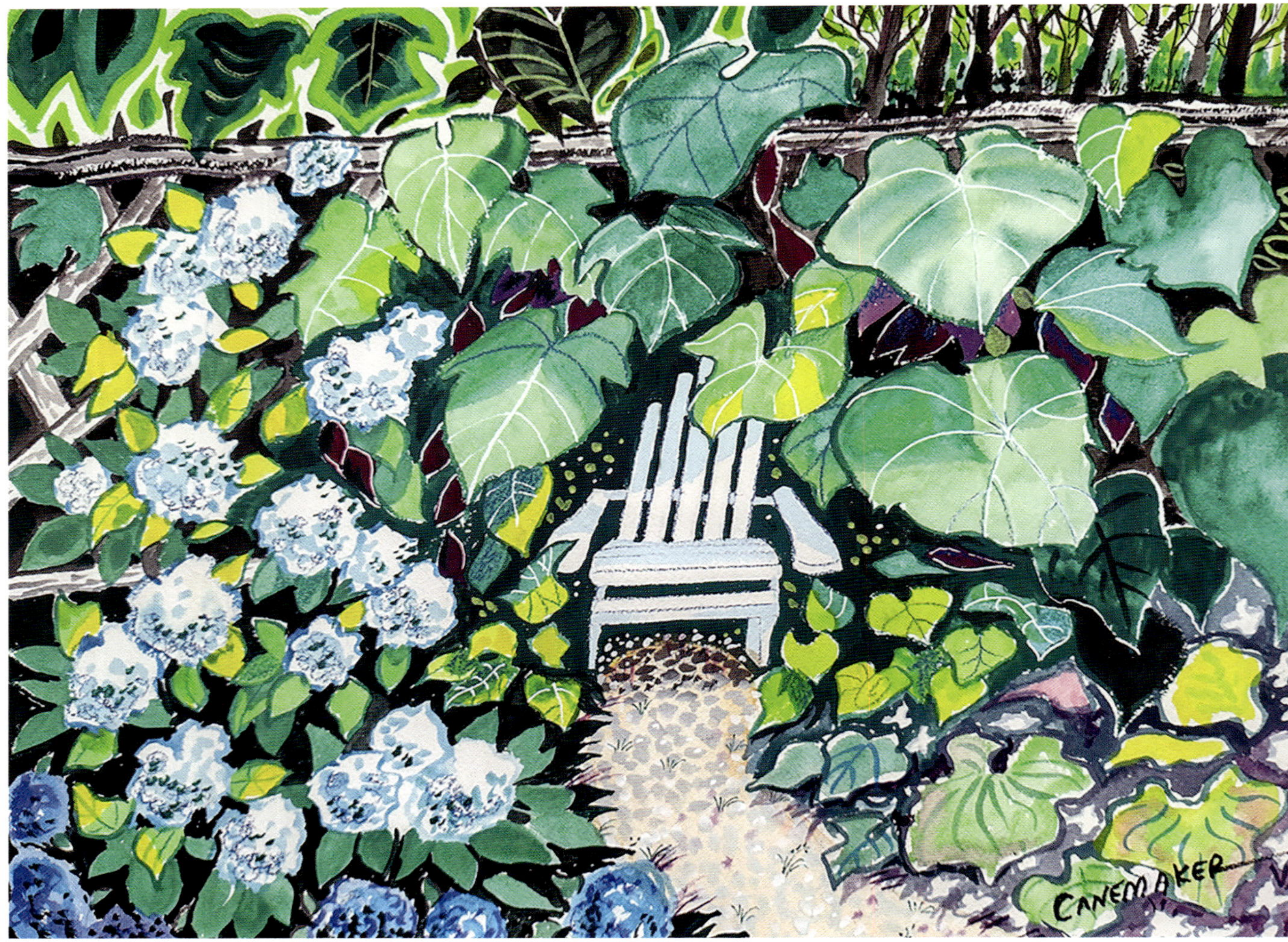

Above left: The Artist's Corner

Above right: THE ARTIST'S CORNER gouache

Page 165
Top left: The view from the Artist's Corner

Bottom Left: Bleeding Heart gouache 2021

Right: Concept art Winter 3 Bridgehampton

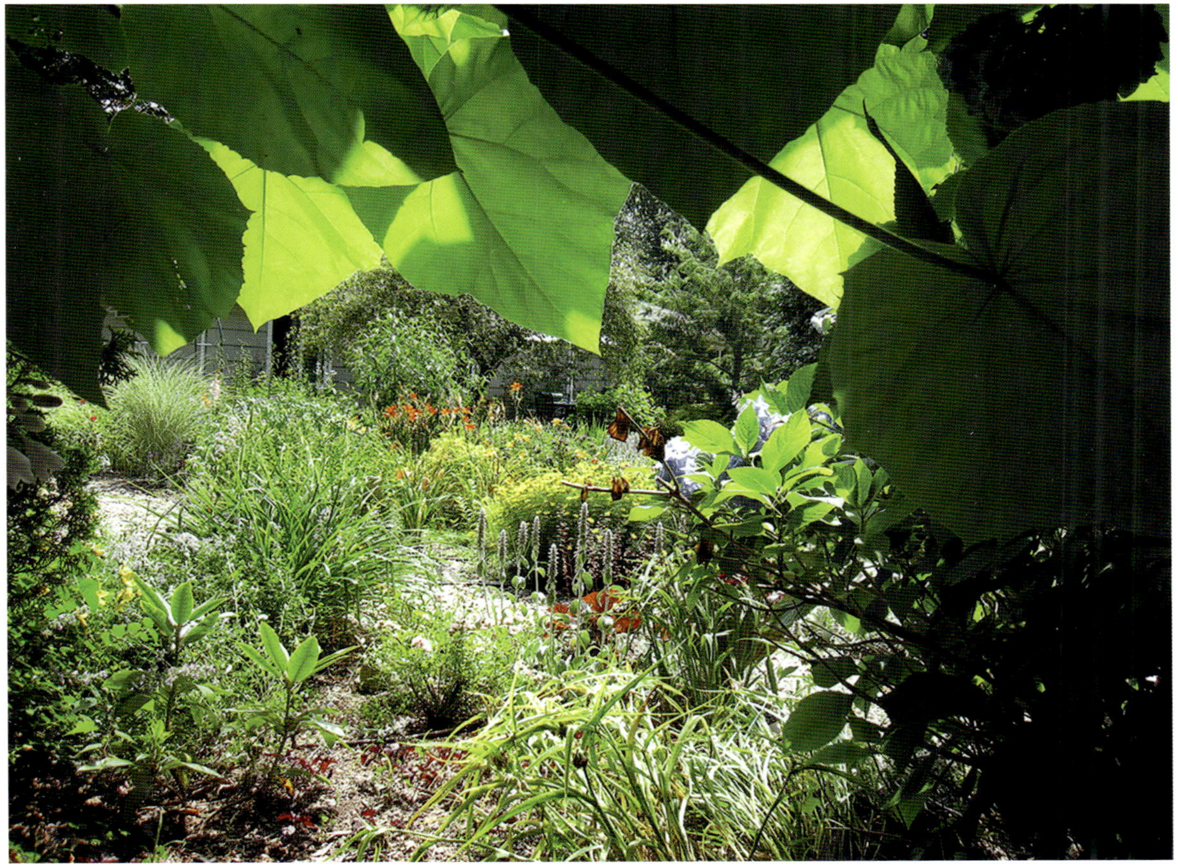

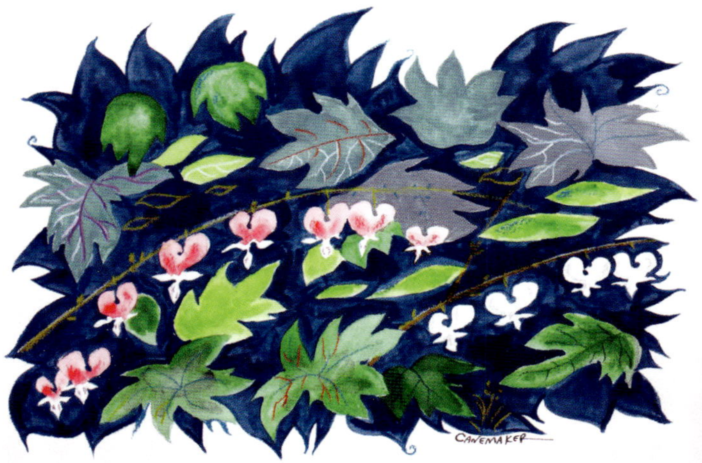
CANEMAKER

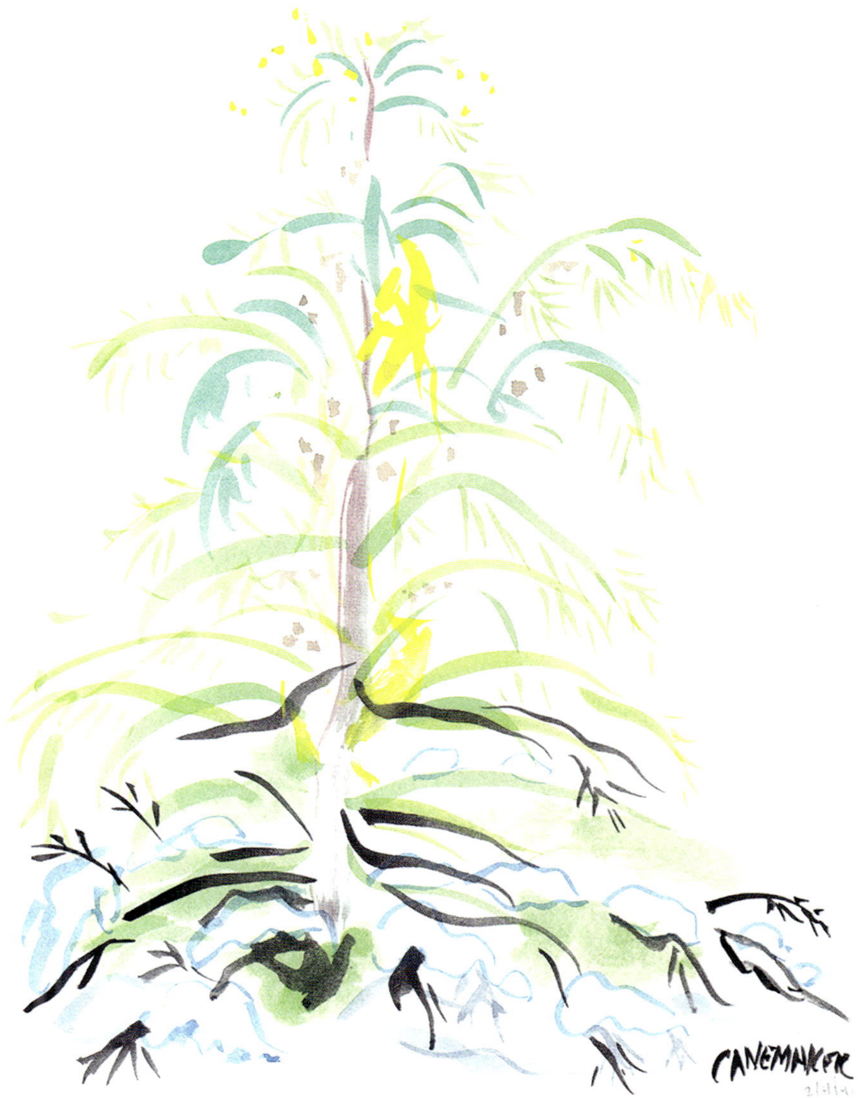
CANEMAKER

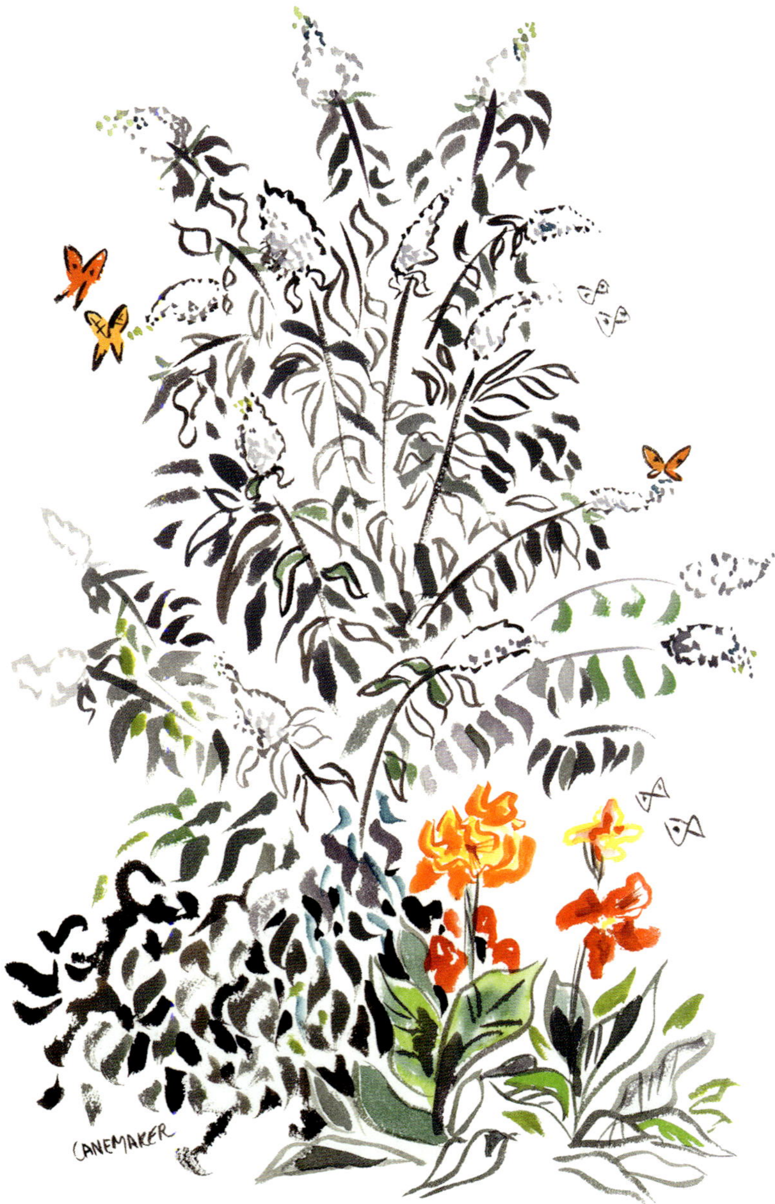

A garden is a labor of love, an inspiration, a celebration and, above all, a dream of what might be. After 32 years of joyfully "toiling in the field," Joe and I sold our Bridgehampton property in 2020.

The new owners had a very different vision and removed all the plantings seen in this book.

And so, our dream lives on in memory – and in the images here. We hope your enjoyment of them will keep the memory alive forever.

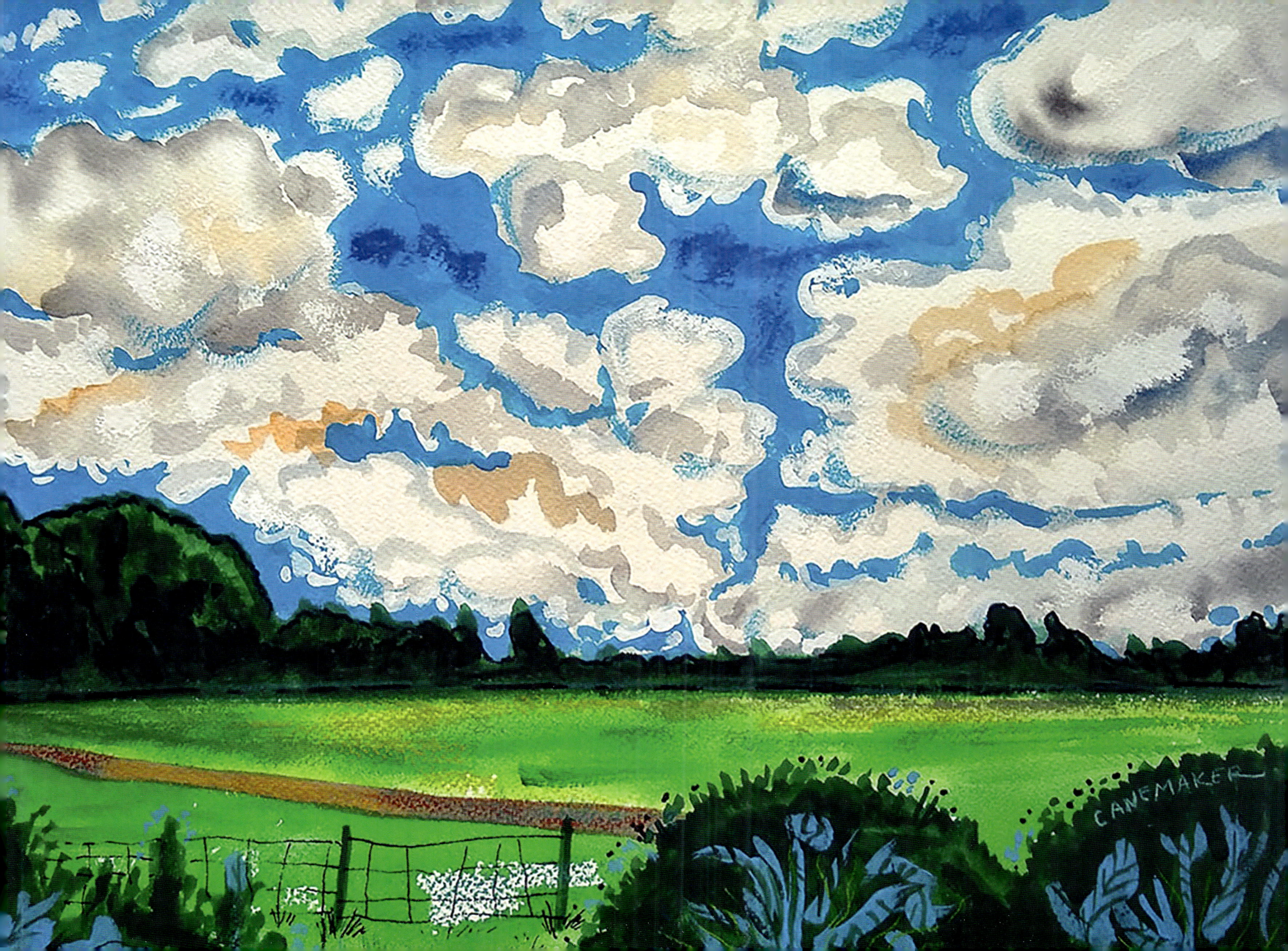
CANEMAKER

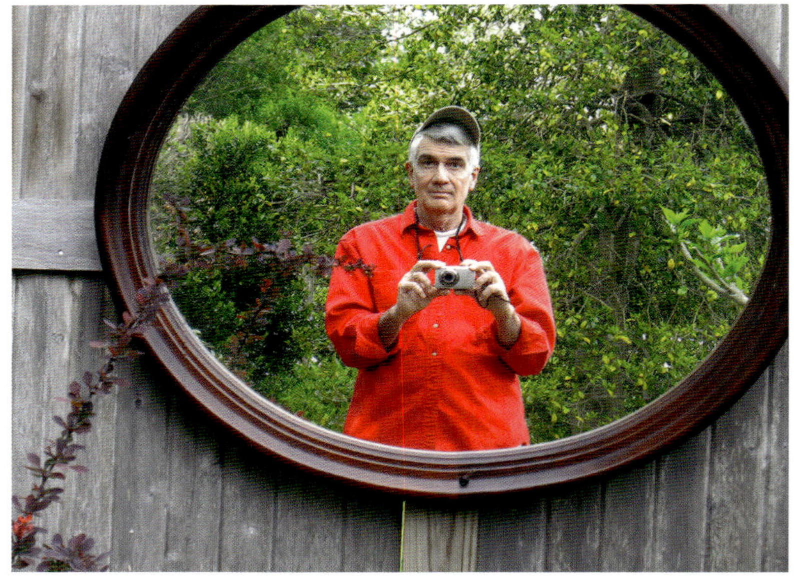

Acknowledgements

First and foremost, I extend my deepest thanks to David and Nancy Bossert and the entire team at The Old Mill Press for their invaluable expertise in bringing this book to life. It has been a true pleasure working with these two gifted and enthusiastic artists—both wise wizards of the book-making world. Nancy's brilliant design sense and Dave's publishing savvy brought me immense joy. They are, without a doubt, a class act. And a special thanks to editor Victor Wartman, copyeditor Diane Hodges, and cover designer John Beach who contributed to the flowering of this book.

I am especially grateful to Josh Siegel, Film Curator at MoMA, for his elegant Foreword. In 2008, he and fellow MoMA Film Curator Ron Magliozzi graciously screened my animated film *Bridgehampton* as part of the exhibition *Jazz Score*, accompanied by an installation of its original animation art.

Fred Hersch, one of the world's finest jazz pianists, composed the evocative score for *Bridgehampton*. His music not only enhanced the film but also shaped the very way I imagined my painted imagery could—and should—move.

I am fortunate to count Dennis Doros and Amy Heller among my close friends. Through their exceptional company, Milestone Film & Video, they have made my films—including *Bridgehampton*—available to the public.

My thanks to Zoya Baker for permission to include her outstanding photographs in this book. Early on, she and Jules Koetsch offered insightful encouragement about the idea of publishing a collection of my paintings.

To my esteemed literary agent and dear friend of nearly forty years, Robert Cornfield: thank you, once again, for your wise counsel and steadfast support.

I'm also grateful to all the friends and followers on social media who have seen my paintings over the years and urged me—often and with great enthusiasm—to make a book of them. Well, here it is!

And finally, to Joe Kennedy—my husband and muse—who created the original garden we shared: your brilliant mind, unwavering support, and deep love have been at the heart of my life and work for more than half a century. I am endlessly grateful.

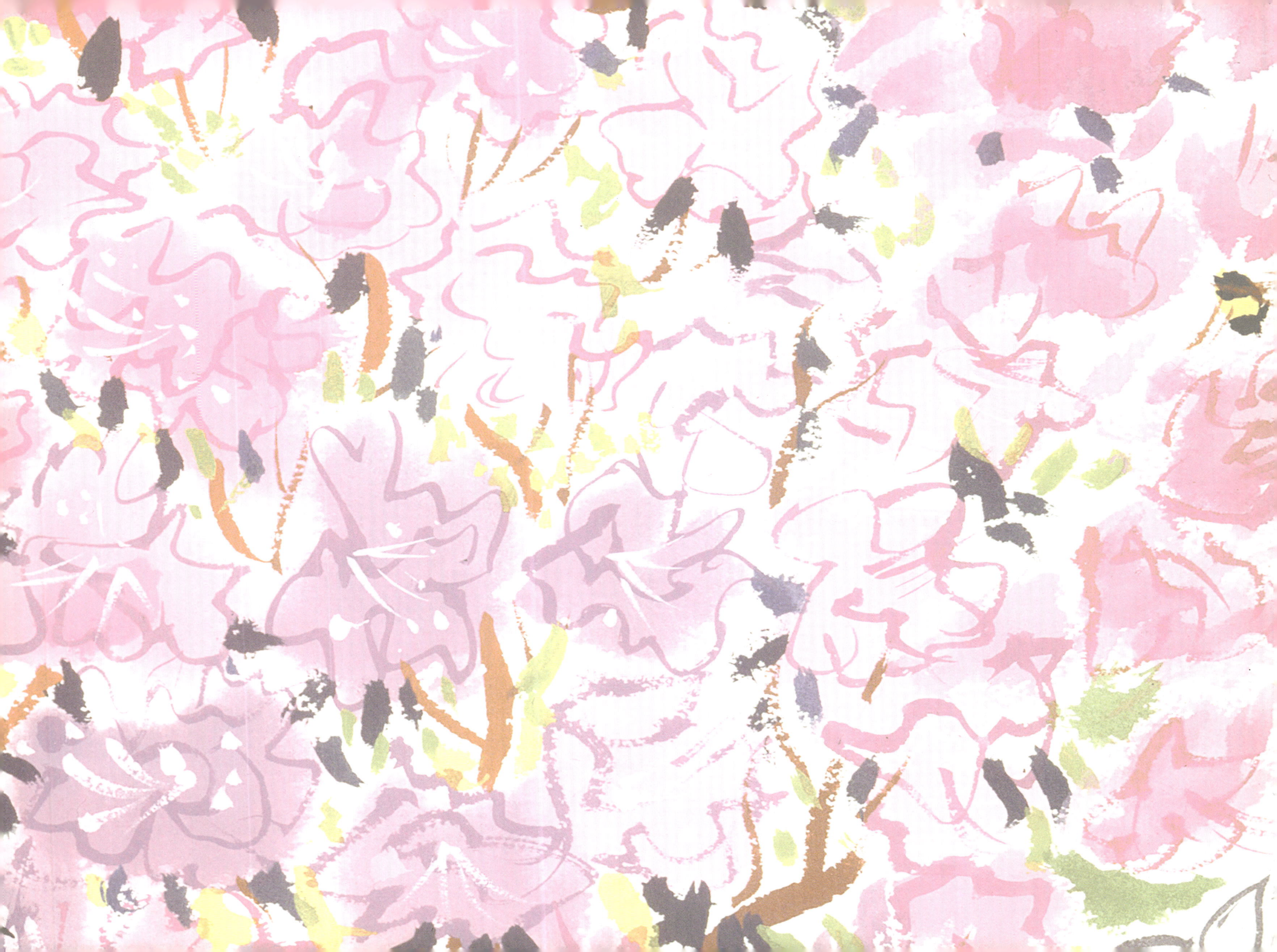